Allegory and Philosophy in Avicenna (Ibn Sînâ)

University of Pennsylvania Press
MIDDLE AGES SERIES
Edited by Edward Peters
Henry Charles Lea Professor
of Medieval History
University of Pennsylvania

A listing of the available books in this series
appears at the back of this volume

Allegory and Philosophy in Avicenna (Ibn Sînâ)

With a Translation of the Book of the Prophet Muḥammad's Ascent to Heaven

Peter Heath

University of Pennsylvania Press
Philadelphia

Printed in the United States of America

Library of Congress Cataloging-in-Publication Data
Heath, Peter, 1949–
Allegory and philosophy in Avicenna (Ibn Sînâ) : with a translation of the Book of the Prophet Muhammad's ascent to heaven / Peter Heath.
p. cm. — (Middle Ages series)
Includes bibliographical references and index.
ISBN 0-8122-3151-1
1. Avicenna, 980–1037—Symbolism. 2. Allegory. 3. Philosophy, Islamic. 4. Avicenna, 980–1037. Mi'rāj'nāmah. I. Avicenna, 980-1037. Mi'rāj'nāmah. English. 1992. II. Title. III. Series. B751.Z7H43 1992
181'.5—dc20 92-10961
CIP

For
S. Roy Heath, Jr., my Father
and
Martin S. Dickson, my Teacher
In Memoriam

Contents

Note on Transliteration and Dates

In this book I generally follow the transliteration system of the *International Journal of Middle East Studies* (*IJMES*) for Arabic and Persian words. I use the circumflex rather than the macron to represent long vowels, however, and I make two minor modifications in the transcription of the Arabic definite article (*al-*) for purposes of phonetic verisimilitude. First, I show the assimilation of the *lâm* of the definite article by the Sun letters (*t, th, d, dh, r, z, s, sh, ṣ, ḍ, ṭ, ẓ, l, m*), as in, for example, *Fî ta'bîr ar-ru'yâ*. Second, I indicate elision of the definite article with a preceding vowel (*hamzat al-waṣl*), as in *Mabḥath 'an al-quwa n-nafsâniyya*. (Note how the long *â* of *quwâ* becomes short in such constructions.)

In regard to dates, I follow the standard practice of providing first the *hijrî* date according to the Muslim lunar calender (which began in C.E. 622) followed by a backslash and the Common Era equivalent.

List of Abbreviations

JOURNALS AND REFERENCE WORKS

EI^1	*The Encyclopedia of Islam*, 1st ed., 4 vols. Leiden and Leipzig: E. J. Brill, 1913–34
EI^2	*The Encyclopedia of Islam*, new ed., vol. 1–, Leiden: E. J. Brill, 1954–
BSOAS	*Bulletin of the School of Oriental and African Studies,* University of London
GAL	Brockelmann, Carl. *Geschichte der arabischen Litteratur.* 2 vols. 2nd ed. Leiden: E. J. Brill, 1943–49. (Citations refer to 2nd ed. page numbers.)
GAL S.	Brockelmann, Carl. *Geschichte der arabischen Litteratur: Den Supplementbänden angepasste Auflage*. 3 vols. Leiden: E. J. Brill, 1937–42
JAL	*Journal of Arabic Literature*
JAOS	*Journal of the American Oriental Society*
ZDMG	*Zeitschrift der Deutschen Morgenländischen Gesellschaft*

TITLES OF WORKS BY AVICENNA

al-Aḍḥawiyya	*al-Aḍḥawiyya (fi l-ma'âd)*
Aḥwâl an-nafs	*Aḥwâl an-nafs: Risâla fi n-nafs wa-baqâ'ihâ wa-ma'âdihâ*
al-'Arshiyya	*al-'Arshiyya fî ḥaqâ'iq at-tauḥîd wa-ithbât an-nubuwwa*
Fî aqsâm al-'ulûm	*Fî aqsâm al-'ulûm al-'aqliyya*
Al-Firdaus	*al-Firdaus fî mâhiyyat al-insân*
Fî ta'bîr ar-ru'yâ	*On the Interpretation of Dreams* [Arabic text]. "A Unique Treatise on the Interpretation of Dreams"
Mabḥath	*Mabḥath 'an al-quwa n-nafsâniyya*

Preface

This book explores the interaction among allegory, allegoresis, and philosophy in the thought of the premodern Muslim philosopher Avicenna (Ibn Sînâ, 370/980–428/1037). This is a question of some complexity, and each of the four parts of this study tackles it from a slightly different perspective.

Part One focuses on historical issues. Chapter One offers a preliminary sketch of how Avicenna's writings fit into the context of the general history of Islamic allegory, on the one hand, and the study of the interaction between philosophy and allegory, on the other. Chapter Two introduces Avicenna as a historical figure.

The three chapters of Part Two turn to details of doctrine and their respective modes of representation by examining the degree to which Avicenna's cosmological, psychological, and epistemological theories find parallel, if diverse, expression in the different formats of philosophical exposition and allegorical narration. Experts on Avicenna's philosophy will find some material in these chapters familiar (as in Chapter Two), but I consider it important to provide this overview for audiences less well-versed in premodern Islamic philosophy. Avicenna's psychology and noetics receive especially full attention because of the degree to which they influenced strains of theological, mystical, and literary thought in subsequent Islamic cultural history.

Part Three illustrates the philosopher's allegorical practice by offering a translation of the *Miʿrâj Nâma* (The Book of the Prophet Muḥammad's Ascent to Heaven), a short treatise in Persian generally attributed to Avicenna. A discussion concerning the authenticity of this text may be found in Appendix B, where I argue in support of this attribution. I recognize that a final decision on this question is probably premature at this stage of our philological recovery of Avicenna's texts, but whatever its origin the *Miʿrâj Nâma* indisputably reflects Avicenna's philosophical views and offers a good example of principles and techniques typical of his hermeneutic approach. From this perspective, the issue of the authenticity of the treatise is less relevant here than its usefulness in providing a representative sample of methods of allegoresis characteristic of the philosopher.

Parts Two and Three thus introduce the reader to pertinent features of the philosopher's theories and styles of exposition, as well as providing an idea of how they function within a specific sample text. This, in turn, paves the way for the two chapters that constitute Part Four. The first of these explores the function of Avicenna's allegories within the framework of both his theory and his practice of allegory. The second examines modes of description and the metaphorical structure of his narratives with a view toward placing them, again, within a general context of the history of Islamic allegory.

Attached to the monograph are four appendices. Appendix A offers a theoretical overview of allegory; Appendix B surveys the question of the authenticity of the *Miʿrâj Nâma*; Appendix C lists its known manuscripts; and Appendix D provides the text of Avicenna's version of the *miʿrâj* narrative divested of the philosopher's own commentary.

There are many who deserve thanks for helping me complete this project. Sari Nusseibeh, then of Birzeit University, first introduced me to Avicenna's allegories, while Birzeit University provided an initial stipend for summer research that enabled me to consult manuscripts and texts of the *Miʿrâj Nâma* and other works by Avicenna.

In the course of this project I had the pleasure of using the British Library in London, the Statsbibliothek in Berlin, and the libraries of the Hebrew University in Jerusalem, the American University in Cairo, Harvard University, Princeton University, the University of Chicago, and Saint Louis University. I am grateful to the staffs of all of these libraries for their friendly treatment of a visiting scholar. Special thanks goes to the staff of Olin Library at Washington University for their ongoing help and support.

My research was generously funded by a summer research grant from the National Endowment for the Humanities in 1987. Washington University also granted me summer research support in 1988, 1989, and 1990 and has been throughout extremely supportive of my research activities. My appreciation goes to both of these institutions.

Finally, I wish to thank the many friends and colleagues who read and commented on parts or all of this study, in particular, Cornell Fleischer, Ahmet Karamustafa, and the late Steven S. Schwarzschild, all of Washington University, Everett Rowson of the University of Pennsylvania, and Wolfhart Heinrichs of Harvard University. My deep appreciation goes as well to Fatemeh Keshavarz-Karamustafa, of Washington University, for meticulously checking my translation of the *Miʿrâj Nâma*, and to Beata

Grant, also of Washington University, for smoothing the style of a large portion of my text. I am especially grateful to Professor Hermann Landolt, of McGill University, who was kind enough to send an unknown scholar a copy of Heravî's new edition of the *Mi'râj Nâma* and who took time to read my manuscript very carefully and to offer many useful comments. Finally, I wish to thank the editors of the University of Pennsylvania Press for their diligence and support. All the above have made valuable contributions to my project and have saved me from numerous errors; I owe them a large debt of gratitude. The views espoused in this work or any errors of detail are, of course, my own responsibility.

Part I

Introduction

1 Avicenna and Islamic Allegory

Islamic allegory represents a vast body of literature. It encompasses diverse genres—romance, "visionary recital," exegesis, debate (*munâẓara*), and fable. And its encoded "messages" stem from such varied disciplines as philosophy, mysticism, theology, political theory, and social and political satire. Despite this diversity in form and content, Islamic allegory is the product of a cohesive literary tradition. Writers of allegories belonged to a cosmopolitan class of Muslim elites who shared a common, often multilingual, educational background in the religious, intellectual, and literary sciences. One has only to note the frequency and ease with which individual scholars or writers moved throughout the Islamic world, as testified to by the peripatetic lives of such figures as Muḥyi d-Dîn ibn 'Arabî (d. 638/1240) or Jalâl ad-Dîn Rûmî (d. 672/1273), or to consider the significant degree of cultural interaction in which, for example, the Ottoman, Safavid, and Mogul elites engaged, to appreciate the extent of the cultural homogeneity that reigned throughout the 800-year period (from the 4th/10th to the 12th/18th centuries) in which Islamic allegory flourished.[1]

Composers of allegories were eminently aware that they participated in a unified literary tradition. They were intimately versed in the major contributions of their predecessors and frequently were influenced by, reacted against, or interacted with earlier works. As a result, the tradition as a whole displays a high measure of literary and intellectual self-consciousness and intertextual reference.[2]

Few figures contributed as significantly to this tradition of allegory as the prominent Muslim philosopher, Abû 'Ali l-Ḥusain ibn Sînâ (Avicenna, 370/980–428/1037). He stands close to its historical starting point, and he exerted an enormous influence on its later development, both as the creator of an authoritative philosophical system and as an important practitioner of the genre. Indeed, his literary activities encompassed all aspects of allegory. He composed several prominent narratives (*Ḥayy ibn Yaqẓân, Risâlat aṭ-ṭair, Salâmân and Absâl*) that are significant in themselves and exerted a profound influence on later proponents of the genre.[3] He wrote interpretive allegory or allegoresis, including the *Mi'râj Nâma* and short commentaries on selected verses or chapters of the Qur'ân.[4] Finally, Avicenna's allegories were themselves the subject of exegesis, receiving frequent attention from later philosophers, theologians, and mystics.[5]

The Study of Premodern Islamic Allegory

Despite the existence of a coherent tradition of allegory from relatively early times, there has been a profound lack of modern scholarly study of Islamic allegory. No general historical survey exists, even in the form of a straightforward bibliographical description, that endeavors to chart the linguistic, temporal, and geographical parameters of the field. General literary historians, such as E. G. Browne and Jan Rypka for Persian literature or E. J. W. Gibb for Ottoman poetry, note the allegorical nature of individual works and at times provide interpretive decoding of allegories, but they do not address the concomitant historical or theoretical issues in any direct fashion. Even such recent contributions as the volume edited by Ehsan Yarshater, which contains commendable chapters on various genres—epic, lyric, romance—and essays on individual major figures—Niẓâmî, Sa'dî, Ḥâfiẓ—does not discuss the genre of allegory per se.[6]

Although the present scope of our knowledge renders any attempt at a comprehensive survey premature, it is nonetheless possible to identify prominent landmarks around which future research should be organized. One such landmark is *The Book of Kalîla and Dimna* by Ibn al-Muqaffa' (d. 139/756). This is a narrative of seminal significance, for it introduces into Islamic literature a genre of beast fable that has already attained a high degree of self-consciousness and sophisticated self-reflection. The book begins with three introductions that narrate the history of the work and of its transmission from the time of its supposed composition by the Indian sage Bidpai until its translation from Pahlavi into Arabic by Ibn al-Muqaffa'. Significant from the perspective of the history of Islamic allegory is that these introductions are replete with directives about how the book was formulated by a philosopher for the benefit of intellectuals (*'uqalâ'*) who should seek in it the secrets of wisdom (*al-ḥikma*). Although *Kalîla and Dimna* largely falls into the genre of political and moralistic allegory, a rationalist tradition of "double meaning" is obviously well-represented here.[7]

Another landmark of allegory is *The Treatises of the Brethren of Sin-*

cerity (*Rasâ'il Ikhwân aṣ-Ṣafâ'*), a philosophical encyclopedia composed by an anonymous group of intellectuals of Ismâ'îlî tendency who wrote in Baṣra in the latter part of the 4th/10th century.[8] In their fifty-one *Treatises*, the Brethren cover with the veneer of Islam the philosophical syncretism of late Hellenistic times, with Pythagoreanism receiving strong emphasis. The result is a concatenation of allegories and allegoreses in miniature. Deserving of literary study in themselves, the *Treatises* are also one product of a lively intellectual tradition in which currents of hermeticism, gnosticism, the occult, and extremist (*ghulât*) Shi'ism intertwined in the 3rd/9th and 4th/10th centuries. Difficult as they are to explore and unravel, these currents almost certainly made important contributions to the formation of allegorical thinking and writing in the Islamic world.[9]

The contributions of Avicenna constitute the third major landmark in the early history of Islamic allegory.

After Avicenna the history of Islamic allegory becomes more complex, with different subgenres evolving in various languages (Arabic is increasingly superseded by Persian and Turkish). In general, three thematic trends can be identified. The first, intellectual in tenor, continues to focus on philosophy and theology. Prominent here are the works of Ibn Ṭufail (d. 581/1185–86) and Shihâb ad-Dîn as-Suhrawardî al-Maqtûl (d. 587/1191), both of whom were heavily influenced by Avicenna; Ibn an-Nafîs (d. 687/1228), himself influenced by Ibn Ṭufail, represents a theological perspective.[10] The second trend highlights practical morality by exploring the broad ethical concerns of romance, a genre devoted to examining the process of personal maturation. This strain is typified by such romance writers as Niẓâmî (d. 600/1203) and Amîr Khusrau (d. 725/1325).[11] The third trend, whose influence becomes increasingly pervasive, is mystical (*ṣûfî*) in intent. Here the *mathnavî*s (narrative poetry) of the great triad of Persian mystical poets, al-Ḥakîm Sanâ'î (d. 525/1130–31), Farîd ad-Dîn 'Aṭṭâr (d. between 617-27/1220–29), and Jalâl ad-Dîn Rûmî, come to mind, although they represent only the beginning stages of this literary current.[12] Of course, these three themes are often intermixed as well. Al-Ghazâlî (d. 505/1111) and Ibn 'Arabî stand out as examples of *ṣûfî*s whose allegories or allegorizations contain heavy doses of philosophy and theology, while 'Abd ar-Raḥmân Jâmî (d. 898/1492) is a poet who wove the anagogic concerns of mysticism into the ethical considerations of romance. After the 7th/13th century, the history of Islamic allegory becomes so incorporated into the mainstream of Islamic literary history that concise description becomes difficult. Worthy of note, however, are the later allegories in Persian of 'Ârifî (d. approximately 853/1449) and Fattâḥî (d. 852/1448–49), and in Ottoman Turkish of Lâmi'î (d. 938/1531–32) and, of course, of Shaikh Ghâlib (d. 1213/1799).[13]

In addition to presenting an overview of major thematic trends, the study of Islamic allegory also demands that we establish an analytical structure that demarcates clearly the different approaches to, and degrees of, allegorical composition and interpretation. Such an enterprise must necessarily take into consideration the generic frames adopted (fictional narrative, exegesis, paraphrase, gloss), the literary techniques employed, and the variations of hermeneutical intent implied. At this point in time, little such analysis exists. Critical examination of specific techniques or individual examples are rare, and such studies that do touch upon the subject have generally been undertaken by specialists of Islamic philosophy, theology, or mysticism who have displayed more interest in doctrinal content and historical background than in aspects of literary approach or with the question of how doctrine and aesthetics interact. A.-M. Goichon or Dimitri Gutas's investigations of Avicenna, J. T. P. de Bruijn's study of Sanâ'î, even Helmut Ritter's magnum opus on 'Aṭṭâr, all excellent in themselves, treat only incidentally the allegorical dimensions of the texts with which they deal. For such scholars, allegory is a literary device that is duly noted and then passed over as they concentrate on the historical parameters or intellectual doctrines of the texts with which they work.[14] For their part, although literary historians have occasionally listed, summarized, or decoded allegories, they generally provide little analytical insight into the literary dimensions of the technique. As already noted, few literary critics have directly addressed the subject.[15]

Given this situation, it is not surprising that basic questions of analytical structure or critical terminology still need investigation. What is "Islamic allegory?" Is it justifiable or useful to employ western critical categories such as allegory, which bear such loaded historical and cultural connotations, in connection with Islamic literatures? If there is "Islamic allegory," what are its essential techniques, methods, or themes? How do they relate or correlate with those found in the history of "western" allegory? What are the respective histories and interrelationships of such terms as *tafsîr* (commentary), *ta'wîl* (interpretation), *ramz* (symbol), *ma'nâ* (meaning), *bayân* (clear exposition), or *ishâra* (allusion) in the genres of literature in which they occur? What different types of hermeneutical approach exist in the Islamic allegorical tradition?[16]

The theoretical question of the extent to which it is proper or useful to employ western critical terms for works of Islamic literatures is a general problem that can be resolved only by a comparative use of such terms in ways that are sensitive to the limits of conceptual analogy.[17] I use the term *allegory* here in reference to the Islamic tradition because I believe that the concept and, more important, its praxis have their own indigenous histories. My aim is not to distort our understanding of this historical tradition by indiscreetly applying concepts borrowed from western literature but rather to employ them carefully in order to explore literary techniques and historical permutations that developed in the Islamic world.[18]

Philosophy and Allegory

The use of allegory by philosophers has a distinguished history stretching from Plato to Sartre. *Allegoresis*, the interpretation of already existing texts according to extrinsic philosophical or dogmatic criteria, has an equally illustrious history, as any consideration of the writings of the Stoics, Philo, Augustine, and others reveals.[19] Yet whenever a philosopher produces allegories, the question arises as to how these "fictional" writings should be understood in relation to the author's "more technical" analytical discourses. In the case of Avicenna, this problem is complicated by the entanglement of several issues that have served to cloud scholars' understanding of the basic questions involved.[20] The first is the famous *al-ḥikma l-mashriqiyya* (Eastern Wisdom) controversy. Avicenna in several places states that his Peripatetic tracts represent only his exoteric views of philosophical truth. He then promises to explain his "real" ideas, which he terms *Eastern Wisdom*, in other works that, if ever written, either have been lost or have survived only as fragments. Discovering the exact nature of this Eastern Wisdom preoccupied even such a prominent later philosopher as Ibn Ṭufail, and it has been a topic of controversy among modern scholars since C. A. Nallino's well-known article appeared early in this century.[21]

The second complicating issue is the relationship of rationalism and mysticism in Avicenna's thought. The question of the nature and extent of the philosopher's mysticism has been a subject of discussion since A. F. Mehren published a group of Avicenna's texts under the unifying title *Traités mystiques d'Abou ʿAli Hosain b. Abdallah b. Sînâ ou d'Avicenne*. Later scholars have used these texts, which include the philosopher's allegories, to contend that Avicenna either had or developed a mystical—*ṣûfî*—strain in his thought.[22]

However intertwined or analogous the conceptual dichotomies of exoteric-esoteric and rational-mystical might be with that of philosophical-literary in regard to attaining an ultimate understanding of Avicenna's thought, there is no reason to believe *a priori* that they are connected. Indeed, much confusion can be avoided if these issues are at least temporarily held separate. From the perspective of this study, the exoteric-esoteric question is a matter of rhetoric, the rationalism-mysticism dichotomy belongs to the realm of doctrine, and the relationship between philosophical and literary modes of discourse is a problem of narrative expression. While it is impossible to avoid reference to the first two issues, our goal is to focus on the nature of the last dichotomy until we reach a point at which it may be used to clarify the previous two.

Logos and Muthos

In order to refer to what we above called the philosophical versus literary dichotomy, it is useful to borrow two terms from Platonic studies, *logos* and *muthos*.[23] Logos pertains to the operational narrative principles that underlie the structure of technical philosophical tracts and promote their claims to validity: apodictic proofs based upon discursive reasoning (*al-falsafa,* more specifically for Avicenna, *al-ʿilm al-fikrî*) leading to rational demonstration (*burhân*), a type of analytic discourse characteristic of Peripatetic philosophy since the time of Aristotle. The term muthos is used to denote the multilayered referential textures characteristic of aesthetic discourse organized to portray "the combination of incidents of the story" so as to produce an "imitation . . . of action and life" (to use Aristotle's phrase from Book Six of the *Poetics*), in other words, artistic narrative based on a particular conception of mimetic plot structure.[24] The best Arabic equivalent for muthos, because historically it has come to connote both the narrative causality and the mimetic simulation of muthos, is *ḥikâya* (imitation, tale, story).[25] Within the context of Avicenna's corpus, his philosophical works, with their technical terminology and rationalist style of argumentation, generally follow the literary form of logos, while his allegories are examples of a certain strain of muthos, Plato's "likely story," narrative representations of aspects of the cosmos and the place of humans in it.[26]

Since the time of Plato philosophers have questioned and indeed deprecated the value of muthos. To the extent that muthoi are obvious poetic fictions, Plato himself banishes them and their creators, the poets, from the Republic of the Philosopher King. The only muthoi he allows are stories carefully formulated and vigilantly regulated by philosophers for the common folk's moral benefit and civil guidance.[27] While degrees of emphasis vary among later philosophers, it may be generally said that the Platonic conception of the value and function of muthos remains a prominent strain in the history of philosophy until Kant. It is certainly evident in the writings of such Islamic philosophers as al-Fârâbî (d. 339/950), Avicenna, and Ibn Rushd (Averroes, d. 595/1198).[28] In light of this apparently inherent distrust of muthos, the fact that certain philosophers resort to its use to construct "likely representations" of philosophical truths can appear paradoxical. And later philosophers have frequently either politely ignored such narratives as temporary lapses from disciplinary decorum or, alternatively, strenuously sought to interpret them in order to restore their rightful logos-style form. However low the stock of philosophical muthos may be among some philosophers, it can become a source of unending speculation for those devoted to the genre of philosophical commentary.[29]

From the perspective of the sociology of knowledge, the commitment of philosophers to logos as their preferred form of narrative discourse constitutes a fundamental element in what Ibn Khaldûn (d. 808/1406) would call their *ʿaṣabiyya*, or "feeling of group solidarity." It comes to represent an allegiance that identifies them to each other and to outsiders as members of their profession. Not surprisingly, this philosophical *ʿaṣabiyya* has tended to make experts in other fields nervous and defensive.[30] Less noticed by literary historians, however, is that this disciplinary loyalty toward logos is also prevalent among historians of philosophy—a fact that is not surprising since most are scholars trained as philosophers. The displacement of muthos by logos has thus become a central motif in the modern study of Classical Greek philosophy, constituting a fundamental theme in Werner Jaeger's *Paideia*, while the decline of logos becomes for Gilbert Murray a prominent symptom of Hellenistic culture's "failure of nerve." Obversely, E. R. Dodds's *The Greeks and the Irrational* is considered exceptional as a work of philosophical history largely because it expands the traditional purview of philosophical historiography to incorporate some (otherwise fairly normal) aspects of life labeled, significantly, "irrational."[31]

From the point of view of general cultural history, there is no reason automatically to accept this disciplinary allegiance of philosophers. In fact, three possibilities logically govern the relationship of logos and muthos in regard to the representational truth-value that each may claim. Logos may be more truthful than muthos, equally true, or less true. From a schematic viewpoint classical philosophers from Plato to Descartes (including Avicenna) have espoused the first position; Kantians and phenomenologists, with caveats, the second; and Romantic writers and artists (including Nietzsche), the third.[32] The "general public" has traditionally maintained an apathetic neutrality on the matter, while the more sophisticated adherents of revealed religions would discount the truth-value of both logos and muthos, relegating them to a position below divine revelation. Generalized as it may be, this scheme is useful to bear in mind when one addresses the question of how logos and muthos relate in the writings of a philosopher who engages in both literary forms. First of all, it helps clarify hermeneutical presumptions. A philosopher or historian of philosophy with an "analytic" turn of mind naturally tends to deprecate or ignore the value of muthos; one who esteems what Kant terms "aesthetic judgment" will indulge and perhaps even emphasize it. Furthermore, it is important to be aware that differences can exist between the announced theoretical stances of philosophers concerning the relationship between logos and muthos and their actual literary practices. A philosopher such as Plato criticizes muthos in the hands of the poets but employs it in his own writings, although to what purpose is—characteristically—still a matter of debate.[33] Such, we shall see, is also the case for Avicenna. But before proceeding to examine in detail how Avicenna's logos and muthos writings interrelate, let us introduce the man himself.

Notes

1. For an analysis of the historical cohesion of this period, see Marshall G. S. Hodgson, "The Unity of Late Islamic History," *Journal of World History* 5 (1960) 878–914. A wonderful example of the cultural unity of this period is the career of Ibn Baṭûṭa (d. 770/1368–69), who traveled and worked throughout the Islamic world and beyond; see Ross E. Dunn, *The Adventures of Ibn Batuta: A Muslim Traveler of the 14th Century* (Berkeley and Los Angeles: University of California Press, 1986).

2. To cite but a few of the many possible examples, note the influence of Avicenna on Sanâ'î (d. 525/1130–31), the influence of both on Jalâl ad-Dîn Rûmî, and then the influence of these three on the much later Ottoman allegorist Shaikh Ghâlib (d. 1213/1799).

3. For the Arabic texts and French paraphrases of *Ḥayy ibn Yaqẓân* and *aṭ-Ṭair*, see A. F. Mehren, *Traités mystiques d'Abou 'Ali Hosain b. 'Abdullah b. Sînâ*, 4 fasc. (Leiden: E. J. Brill, 1889–99). Other Arabic editions of one or more of the treatises are Aḥmad Amîn, ed., *Ḥayy ibn Yaqẓân, li-bn Sînâ wa-bn Ṭufail wa-s-*

Suhrawardî, Dhakhâ'ir al-'Arab 8 (Cairo: Dâr al-ma'ârif, 1959) and Ḥasan 'Âṣî, *at-Tafsîr al-qur'ânî wa-l-lugha ṣ-ṣûfiyya fî falsafat Ibn Sînâ* (Cairo: al-Mu'assasa al-jâmi'iyya li-d-dirâsa wa-n-nashr wa-t-tauzî', 1983); 'Âṣî provides a useful collection of texts for the study of Avicenna as allegorist, but must be used with caution: the treatise, *al-'Ilm al-ladunî*, pp. 184–202, that 'Âṣî attributes to Avicenna, for example, is *ar-Risâla l-laduniyya*, usually attributed to al-Ghazâlî (although this attribution is disputed), while *Fî kalimât aṣ-ṣûfiyya* is *Kalimat at-taṣsawwuf*, usually attributed to Shihâb ad-Din Suhrawardî. The original text of *Salâmân and Absâl* is apparently lost, but Naṣîr ad-Dîn aṭ-Ṭûsî paraphrased the story as part of his commentary on Avicenna's *al-Ishârât wa-t-tanbîhât*, see S. Dunyâ's edition, 4 vols., Dhakhâ'ir al-'Arab 22 (Cairo: Dâr al-ma'ârif, 1960) 4:49–56; see also *Tis' rasâ'il fi-l-ḥikma wa-ṭ-ṭabî'ât* (Istanbul: Maṭba'at al-jawâ'ib, 1298/1881) 119–25, which also provides Hunain ibn Isḥaq's Arabic translation of the Greek version of the story, pp. 112–19. For English translations and "Corbinian" analyses of these three allegories, see Henry Corbin, *Avicenna and the Visionary Recital*, Bollingen Series 96 (New York: Pantheon Books, 1960, repr. Princeton, N.J.: Princeton University Press, 1988). Another analysis is T. Sabrî, "Avicenne, philosophe et mystique dans le miroir de trois récits: Ḥayy B. Yaqẓân, l'Oiseau, Salâmân et Absâl," *Arabica* 28,3 (1980) 257–74. For a translation and analysis of *aṭ-Ṭair*, see P. Heath, "Disorientation and Reorientation in Ibn Sînâ's *Epistle of the Bird*: A Reading," in M. M. Mazzoui and V. B. Moreen, eds., *Intellectual Studies on Islam: Essays Written in Honor of Martin B. Dickson* (Salt Lake City: University of Utah Press, 1990) 163–83. Editions of Avicenna's "Ode on the Soul" are in Carra de Vaux, "La kaçîdah d'Avicenne sur l'âme," *Journal Asiatique*, 9th ser. 14 (1899) 157–73; and Fathalla Kholeif, *Avicenna on Psychology: A Study of His Poem on the Soul (al-Qaṣîda al-'ainiyyah)* (Beirut: Beirut Arab University, 1974), in Arabic. For English translations, see E. G. Browne, *A Literary History of Persia*, 4 vols. (London: T. Fisher Unwin, 1902–24, repr. Cambridge: Cambridge University Press, 1969) 2:110–11, and A. J. Arberry, *Avicenna on Theology* London: John Murray, 1951) 77–78.

4. For editions of the *Mi'râj Nâma*, see Chapter Six, note 1. 'Âṣî's *at-Tafsîr al-qur'ânî* contains texts of several of Avicenna's short Qur'ânic commentaries (*Âyat an-nûr, Thumma stawâ ila s-samâ', Sûrat al-a'lâ, Sûrat al-ikhlâṣ, Sûrat al-falaq*, and *Sûrat an-nâs*) 84–125. Ehsan Yarshater's *Panj Risâla, taṣnîf-i Shaikh Râ'is Abû 'Alî Sînâ*, Silsila-yi intishârât-i anjuman-i athâr-i millî 27 (Tehran: Âstâd-i Danishgâh, 1953), contains Persian versions of Avicenna's commentaries on *Sûra-yi tauḥîd, Sûra-yi falaq*, and *Sûra-yi nâs*, 37–63. Also relevant are Avicenna's interpretations of various Qur'ânic verses in the second part of Avicenna's *Fî ithbât an-nubuwwât*, ed. and intro. by Michael Marmura, Philosophical Texts and Studies 2 (Beirut: Dâr an-Nahâr, 1968) 48–61, and Avicenna's exegesis of *Âyat an-nûr* in *al-Ishârât wa-t-tanbîhât*, 2:388–94.

5. Avicenna's student al-Ḥusain ibn Ṭâhir ibn Zailâ (d. 440/1048) composed a commentary on *Ḥayy ibn Yaqẓân*; see Brockelmann, *GAL* 1:593 and *GAL S.* 1:817; Mehren, *Traités mystiques*, fasc. 1; and A.-M. Goichon, *Le récit de Ḥayy Ibn Yaqẓân commenté par des textes d'Avicenne*, (Paris: Desclée de Brouwer, 1959). Corbin published another commentary, in Persian, which he attributes to Avicenna's disciple and companion, Abû 'Ubaid 'Abd al-Wâḥid al-Jûzjânî, in his *Avicenne et*

le récit visionnaire, 3 vols. (Tehran and Paris: Institut Franco-Iranien, A. Maisonneuve, 1952–54); see vol. 2 for the Persian text and vol. 3 for the French translation (= English translation, pp. 279–380). *Ḥayy ibn Yaqẓân* also strongly influenced such allegorists as Shihâb ad-Dîn as-Suhrawardî and Ibn Ṭufail, and through the latter, Ibn an-Nafîs; see below pp. 5–6. 'Umar ibn Sahlân as-Sâwajî (fl. 540/1145) composed a commentary in Persian on *aṭ-Ṭair*, which Otto Spies and S. K. Khatak have published in *Three Treatises on Mysticism, by Shihâbuddîn Suhrawardî Maqtûl*, Bonner Orientalistische Studien 12 (Stuttgart: Verlag W. Kohlhammer, 1935) 45–89 (see also Brockelmann, *GAL* 1:595, and Mehren, *Traités mystiques*, fasc. 3), while as-Suhrawardî himself translated the treatise into Persian, see as-Suhrawardî, *Opera metaphysica et mystica III*, ed., S. H. Nasr (Tehran: Institut Franco-Iranien, 1970); see also Wheeler M. Thackston, Jr.'s translation, *The Mystical and Visionary Treatises of Shihabuddin Yahya Suhrawardi* (London: The Octagon Press, 1982); for Louis Cheikho's edition of al-Ghazâlî's version of the tale, see *al-Mashriq* 20 (1901) 918–24. Aṭ-Ṭûsî's account and commentary on *Salâmân and Absâl* have been referred to above, note 3. The "Ode on the Soul" has been commented upon many times, see Brockelmann, *GAL* 1:594, *GAL S.* 1:818, and Kholeif, *Avicenna on Psychology*. The precise nature of the immense influence that Avicenna exerted on later thinkers in the Islamic world has only begun to be charted.

6. Browne, *A Literary History of Persia*; Jan Rypka, *History of Iranian Literature* (Dordrecht: D. Reidel, 1968); E. J. W. Gibb, *A History of Ottoman Poetry*, 6 vols. (London: Luzac & Co., 1900–1909, repr. 1958–63); Ehsan Yarshater, ed., *Persian Literature*, Columbia Lectures on Iranian Studies 3 (n.p.: Bibliotheca Persica, 1988).

7. For Ibn al-Muqaffa', see *EI*², 3:883–85; for a survey of the various printed editions and the many later translations and reworkings of *Kalîla and Dimna*, see *EI*², 4:503–506.

8. See *EI*², 3:1071–76; Ian R. Netton, *Muslim Neoplatonists: An Introduction to the Thought of the Brethren of Purity (Ikhwân aṣ-Ṣafâ')* (London: George Allen & Unwin, 1980); and Seyyed Hossein Nasr, *An Introduction to Islamic Cosmological Doctrines* (Boulder:Shambhala, 1978) 25–104; disappointing, considering the interest of the topic, is 'Ârif Tâmir, *Ibn Sînâ fî marâbi' Ikhwân aṣ-Ṣafâ'* (Beirut: 'Izz ad-Dîn, 1983).

9. A good preliminary overview of this tradition is Francis E. Peters, "Hermes and Harran: The Roots of Arabic-Islamic Occultism," in Mazzoui and Moreen, eds., *Intellectual Studies on Islam*, 185–215. This field deserves more detailed examination from a literary as well as doctrinal perspective. Some starting points are the alchemical treatises of Ibn Umayl (fl. first half of 4th/10th century), on which see *EI*², 3:961–62, and Manfred Ullmann, *Die Natur- und Geheimwissenschaften im Islam*, Handbuch der Orientalistik, vol. 6, part 2 (Leiden and Cologne: E. J. Brill, 1972) 218–20; and such Ismâ'îlî treatises as *Kitâb al-'Âlim wa-l-ghulâm*, concerning which see W. Ivanow, *Studies in Early Persian Ismailism*, 2nd rev. ed. (Bombay: Ismaili Society, 1955) 61–86, and H. Corbin, "Un roman initiatique Ismaélien," *Cahiers de Civilization Médiévale* 15 (1972) 1–25, 121–42, and *idem*, "L'initiation Ismaélienne ou l'ésotérisme et le verbe," *Eranos Jahrbuch* 39 (1970) 41–142.

10. Ibn Ṭufail, *Ḥayy ibn Yaqẓân*, in Aḥmad Amîn, ed., *Ḥayy ibn Yaqẓân li-bn Sînâ wa-bn Ṭufail wa-s-Suhrawardî*, trans. in Lenn Evan Goodman, *Ibn Ṭufayl's Ḥayy ibn Yaqẓân: A Philosophical Tale* (New York: Twayne Publishers, 1972; 2nd ed., Los Angeles: Gee Tee Bee Press, 1983); as-Suhrawardî's allegories are published in *Opera Metaphysica et Mystica II*, ed. Henry Corbin (Tehran: Institut Franco-Iranien, 1952) and *Opera Metaphysica et Mystica III*, ed. S. H. Nasr (see also note 5 above); for Ibn an-Nafîs, see M. Meyerhoff and J. Schacht, eds. and trans., *The Theologus Autodidactus of Ibn al-Nafîs* (Oxford: Clarendon Press, 1968).

11. A recent treatment of this theme in Persian may be found in Julie Scott Meisami, *Medieval Persian Court Poetry* (Princeton, N.J.: Princeton University Press, 1987), esp. pp. 131–79.

12. See J. T. P. de Bruijn, *Of Piety and Poetry: The Interaction of Religion and Literature in the Life and Works of Ḥakîm Sanâ'î of Ghazna*, De Goeje Fund 25 (Leiden: E. J. Brill, 1983); Helmut Ritter, *Das Meer der Seele: Mensch, Welt, und Gott in den Geschichten des Farîduddîn ʿAṭṭâr* (Leiden: E. J. Brill, 1955); a good study of Rûmî as allegorist is still a desideratum.

13. See Rypka, *History of Iranian Literature*, 284–85; and Gibb, *History of Ottoman Poetry*, vols. 3 and 4 respectively. Further information about each of these writers may be found under their respective entries in *The Encyclopedia of Islam* and the literary histories and studies mentioned above in note 6. See also the introductory section in Chapter Six below.

14. Dimitri Gutas, *Avicenna and the Aristotelian Tradition: Introduction to Reading Avicenna's Philosophical Works*, Islamic Philosophy and Theology, Texts and Studies 4 (Leiden, New York, Copenhagen, and Cologne: E. J. Brill, 1988), esp. pp. 299–307; Goichon, *Le récit de Ḥayy ibn Yaqẓân*; see also note 12 above. These are only a few typical examples; a complete bibliography of such secondary studies is, for reasons of space, impractical.

15. Thought-provoking as points of departure are Meisami, *Medieval Persian Court Poetry*, and J. Christoph Bürgel, *The Feather of Simurgh: The "Licit Magic" of the Arts in Medieval Islam* (New York and London: New York University Press, 1988).

16. For an attempt to begin to address this last question, see Peter Heath, "Creative Hermeneutics: An Analysis of Three Islamic Approaches," *Arabica* 36 (1989) 173–210; Naṣr Ḥâmid Abû Zaid, *Falsafat at-ta'wîl: Dirâsa fî ta'wîl al-Qur'ân ʿind Muḥyi d-Dîn ibn ʿArabî* (Beirut: Dâr al-waḥda, 1983), is excellent, while provocative is Jaroslav Stetkevych, "Arabic Hermeneutical Terminology: Paradox and the Production of Meaning," *Journal of Near Eastern Studies* 48,2 (1989) 81–96. The translations proffered here for these terms are general; it is precisely their specific history of use among different authors, genres, and periods that requires investigation; an initial model in this regard is Louis Massignon's *Essai sur les origines du lexique technique de la mystique musulmane*, 2nd ed. (Paris: Vrin, 1954) and, of course, his monumental study of al-Ḥallâj, *The Passion of al-Ḥallâj: Mystic and Martyr of Islam*, trans. H. Mason, 4 vols., Bollingen Series 98 (Princeton, N.J.: Princeton University Press, 1982). Also useful as tools are such concordances as A.-M. Goichon, *Lexique de la langue philosophique d'Ibn Sînâ (Avicenne)* (Paris: Des-

clée de Brouwer, 1938), and Su'âd al-Ḥakîm's impressive lexicon of Ibn 'Arabî's technical terminology, *al-Mu'jam aṣ-ṣûfî: al-Ḥikma fî ḥudûd al-kalima* (Beirut: Dandara, 1981). Another useful point of departure is the genre of Qur'ânic exegesis (both *tafsîr* and *ta'wîl*). Long neglected, the study of *tafsîr* has received renewed attention in recent years; useful studies include Ignaz Goldziher's classic, *Die Richtungen der islamischen Koranauslegung*, De Goeje-Stiftung 6 (Leiden: E. J. Brill, 1970 [repr. of the 1920 ed.]); Paul Nywia, *Exégèse coranique et langage mystique: Nouvel essai sur le lexique technique des mystiques musulmans* (Beirut: Dar el-Machreq, 1970); Helmut Gätje, *The Qur'ân and Its Exegesis: Selected Texts with Classical and Modern Muslim Interpretations* (Berkeley and Los Angeles: University of California Press, 1976); Gerhard Böwering, *The Mystical Vision of Existence in Classical Islam: The Qur'ânic Hermeneutics of the Ṣûfî Sahl At-Tustarî (d. 283/896)* (Berlin and New York: Walter de Gruyter, 1980); Andrew Rippen, ed., *Approaches to the History of the Interpretation of the Qur'ân* (Oxford: Clarendon Press, 1988); and Y. Goldfeld, "The Development of Theory on Qur'ânic Exegesis in Islamic Scholarship," *Studia Islamica* 67 (1988) 5–27.

17. For brief discussions of this problem in regard to other critical terms, see on "romance," Peter Heath, "Romance as Genre in The Thousand and One Nights," two parts, *JAL* 18 (1987) 1–21; *JAL* 19 (1988) 1–16, esp. 1:8–10; and on "courtly love," Meisami, *Medieval Persian Court Poetry*, ix–x.

18. But for a brief theoretical overview of allegory, see Appendix A below.

19. Cf. Jon Whitman, *Allegory: The Dynamics of an Ancient and Medieval Technique* (Cambridge, Mass.: Harvard University Press, 1987) 14–57; Philip Rollinson, *Classical Theories of Allegory and Christian Culture* (Pittsburgh: Duquesne University Press, 1981) 3–86; and Tzvetan Todorov, *Symbolism and Interpretation*, trans. Catherine Porter (Ithaca, N.Y.: Cornell University Press, 1982) 97–130.

20. A brief overview of Avicenna's life and thought may be found in M. Mahdi, D. Gutas, et al., "Avicenna," *Encyclopedia Iranica*, 3,1:66–111; see also *EI*², 3:941–47 and Chapter Two below. Essential are Avicenna's autobiography and the biography written by his student and close companion, Abû 'Ubaid 'Abd al-Wâḥid al-Jûzjânî, edited and translated in William E. Gohlman, *The Life of Ibn Sina: A Critical Edition and Annotated Translation*, Studies in Islamic Philosophy and Science (Albany: State University of New York Press, 1974). An excellent recent exposition of Avicenna's life and philosophical method is Gutas's *Avicenna and the Aristotelian Tradition*; also important are Jean Michot, *La destinée de l'homme selon Avicenne: Le retour à Dieu (ma'âd) et l'imagination* (Louvain: Peeters, 1987), which includes a useful annotated bibliography; and Louis Gardet, *La pensée religieuse d'Avicenne (Ibn Sînâ)*, Études de philosophie médiévale (Paris: Librairie Philosophique J. Vrin, 1951). Dated, but still helpful, are Soheil M. Afnan, *Avicenna: His Life and Works* (London: George Allen & Unwin, 1958), and Arberry, *Avicenna on Theology*. For a discussion concerning the question of the date of Avicenna's birth, see Dimitri Gutas, "Avicenna's *Madhhab*, with an Appendix on the Question of His Date of Birth," *Quaderni di Studi Arabi* 5–6 (1987–88) 323–36.

21. Gutas provides basic bibliography for this controversy as well as a synopsis of his own interpretation of it, in "Avicenna," *Encyclopedia Iranica*, 3,1:80–83; he also translates Avicenna's own statements regarding this subject in *Avicenna and*

the Aristotelian Tradition, 43–72. For Ibn Ṭufail's interpretation, see Amîn, ed., *Ḥayy ibn Yaqẓân*, 57–66; see also C. A. Nallino, "Filosophia 'Orientale' od 'Illuminativa' d'Avicenna?" *Revista degli Studi Orientali* 10 (1923–25) 433–67; Gardet, *La pensée religieuse d'Avicenne*, 23–29; Ian R. Netton, *Allâh Transcendent: Studies in the Structure and Semiotics of Islamic Philosophy, Theology, and Cosmology* (London and New York: Routledge, 1989) 174–78; and Chapter Seven below.

22. Mehren, *Traités mystiques*. See also Parviz Morewedge, "The Logic of Emanationism and Ṣûfism in the Philosophy of Ibn Sînâ," in two parts, *JAOS* 91,4 (1971) 467–76 and 92,1 (1972) 1–18; Part 1 surveys the opinions of previous scholars concerning Avicenna's mysticism. Also, Gutas, "Avicenna," *Encyclopedia Iranica*, 3,1:79–80, with bibliography supplied on p. 83; an overview of Avicenna's role in the development of *'irfân* (philosophical mysticism) may be found in Toshihiko Izutsu's article "*Ishrâqîyah*," *Encyclopedia of Religion*, 7:296–98.

23. The usage is standard; we shall, however, be using these terms within the particular context of Avicenna's thought rather than Plato's. A survey of how the term *muthos* is used in Plato as well as modern interpretations of the role it plays in Plato's writings may be found in Kent F. Moors, *Platonic Myth: An Introductory Study* (Washington: University Press of America, 1982), esp. pp. 1–25; see also Anne Freire Ashbaugh, *Plato's Theory of Explanation: A Study of the Cosmological Account of the Timaeus*, SUNY Series in Philosophy (Albany: State University of New York Press, 1988).

24. Aristotle, *Poetics*, 1450a.1, in Jonathan Barnes, ed., *The Complete Works of Aristotle: The Revised Oxford Translation*, 2 vols., Bollingen Series 71:2 (Princeton, N.J.: Princeton University Press, 1984) 2320–21. All citations from Aristotle come from this edition.

25. *EI*[2], "Ḥikâya," 3:367–78. For the philosophical use of a term derived from the same root (*muḥâkât*), see Avicenna's *Fi sh-Shi'r*, trans. in Ismail M. Dahiyat, *Avicenna's Commentary on the* Poetics *of Aristotle: A Critical Study with an Annotated Translation of the Text* (Leiden: E. J. Brill, 1974), esp. the Introduction. Also see al-Fârâbî's *Poetics*, in A. J. Arberry, "Fârâbî's Canons of Poetry," *Revista degli studi orientali* 17 (1938) 257–38; al-Fârâbî, *al-Fârâbî's The Political Regime (al-Siyâsa al-Madaniyya also known as the Treatise on the Principles of Being)*, ed. Fauzi M. Najjar (Beirut: Imprimerie Catholique, 1964) 85–87; and the corresponding passage in Richard Walzer, *al-Fârâbî on the Perfect State: Abû Naṣr al-Fârâbî's Mabâdi' ârâ' ahl al-madîna al-fâḍila* (Oxford: Clarendon Press, 1985) 210–227, 276–85; see also Chapter Seven below.

26. Plato, *Timaeus*, 29b–d, trans. by F. M. Cornford, *Plato's Cosmology: The Timaeus of Plato Translated with a Running Commentary* (London: Routledge & Kegan Paul, 1937) 23. The translation by Benjamin Jowett contained in E. Hamilton and H. Cairns, eds., Plato, *The Collected Dialogues* (Princeton, N.J.: Princeton University Press, 1961) uses the word "tale," while Ashbaugh prefers "versimilar account" in her *Plato's Theory of Explanation*, 139–40, note 1.

27. Plato, *Republic*, Book Ten, 595a–607a.

28. See, for example, the *Poetics* of each, translated excerpts of which are gathered and commented upon in Vicente Cantarino, *Arabic Poetics in the Golden Age: Selection of Texts Accompanied by a Preliminary Study* (Leiden: E. J. Brill, 1975),

and Mansour Ajami, *The Alchemy of Glory: The Dialectic of Truthfulness and Untruthfulness in Medieval Arabic Literary Criticism* (Washington, D.C.: Three Continents Press, 1988) 53–67.

29. Cf. the historical comments of Ernst Cassirer:

> But philosophy could never admit such a bifurcation [between myth and logic]. It was convinced that the creations of the myth-making function must have a philosophical, an understandable "meaning." If myth hides this meaning under all sorts of images and symbols, it became the task of philosophy to unmask it. Since the time of the Stoics philosophy has developed a special, very elaborate technique of allegorical interpretation. For many centuries this technique was regarded as the only possible access to the mythical world. It prevailed throughout the Middle Ages, and was still in full vigor at the beginning of our modern era.

An Essay on Man: An Introduction to a Philosophy of Human Culture (New Haven, Conn. and London: Yale University Press, 1944) 73–74. Cassirer uses the term *myth* here in the specific technical sense that he outlines in his "Philosophy of Symbolic Forms"; from our viewpoint, however, his description is also relevant as a portrayal of the relationship of logos and muthos.

30. Hence the "defenses" of poetry in English literature by Philip Sidney and Percy Shelley; a premodern Arabic example is the debate on the relative merits of grammar and philosophy between the grammarian Abû Sa'îd as-Sîrâfî and the logician Abû Bishr Mattâ as recorded by Abû Ḥayyân at-Tauḥîdî in his *Kitâb al-'Imtâ' wa-l-mu'ânasa*, ed. Aḥmad Amîn and Aḥmad az-Zain, 3 vols. (Beirut: Dâr maktaba l-ḥayât, n.d.) 1:107–29; trans. D. S. Margoliouth, "The Discussion between Abû Bishr Mattâ and Abû Sa'îd al-Sîrâfî," *Journal of the Royal Asiatic Society* (1905) 79–129; see also Muhsin Mahdi, "Language and Logic in Classical Islam," in G. E. von Grunebaum, ed., *Logic in Classical Islamic Culture* (Wiesbaden: Otto Harrassowitz, 1970) 51–83.

31. Werner Jaeger, *Paideia: The Ideals of Greek Culture*, trans. Gilbert Highet, 3 vols. (New York and Oxford: Oxford University Press, 1943–45); Gilbert Murray, *Five Stages of Greek Religion*, 3rd ed. (Garden City, N.Y.: Doubleday Anchor Books, 1955) 119–65; E. R. Dodds, *The Greeks and the Irrational* (Berkeley and Los Angeles: University of California Press, 1951).

32. A useful analysis of the tensions among these positions, particularly in the realm of literary criticism, is Murry Krieger, "'A Waking Dream': The Symbolic Alternative to Allegory," in Morton W. Bloomfield, ed., *Allegory, Myth, and Symbol*, Harvard English Studies 9 (Cambridge, Mass.: Harvard University Press, 1981) 1–22.

33. For the Neoplatonists' interpretation of this question, see James A. Coulter, *The Literary Microcosm: Theories of Interpretation of Late Neoplatonists*, Columbia Studies in the Classsical Tradition 2 (Leiden: E. J. Brill, 1976); for the situation in western medieval Platonism, see Peter Dronke, *Fabula: Explorations into the Uses of Myth in Medieval Platonism*, Mittellateinische Studien und Texte 9 (Leiden and

Cologne: E. J. Brill, 1974), esp. pp. 13–67; see as well the sources cited in note 23 above; more generally, note Jonathan Rée's discussion of Descartes's contradictory remarks concerning fables or the topos of "metaphysical fictions" in modern philosophy in *Philosophical Tales: An Essay on Philosophy and Literature* (London and New York: Methuen, 1987) pp. 12 and 45–55 respectively.

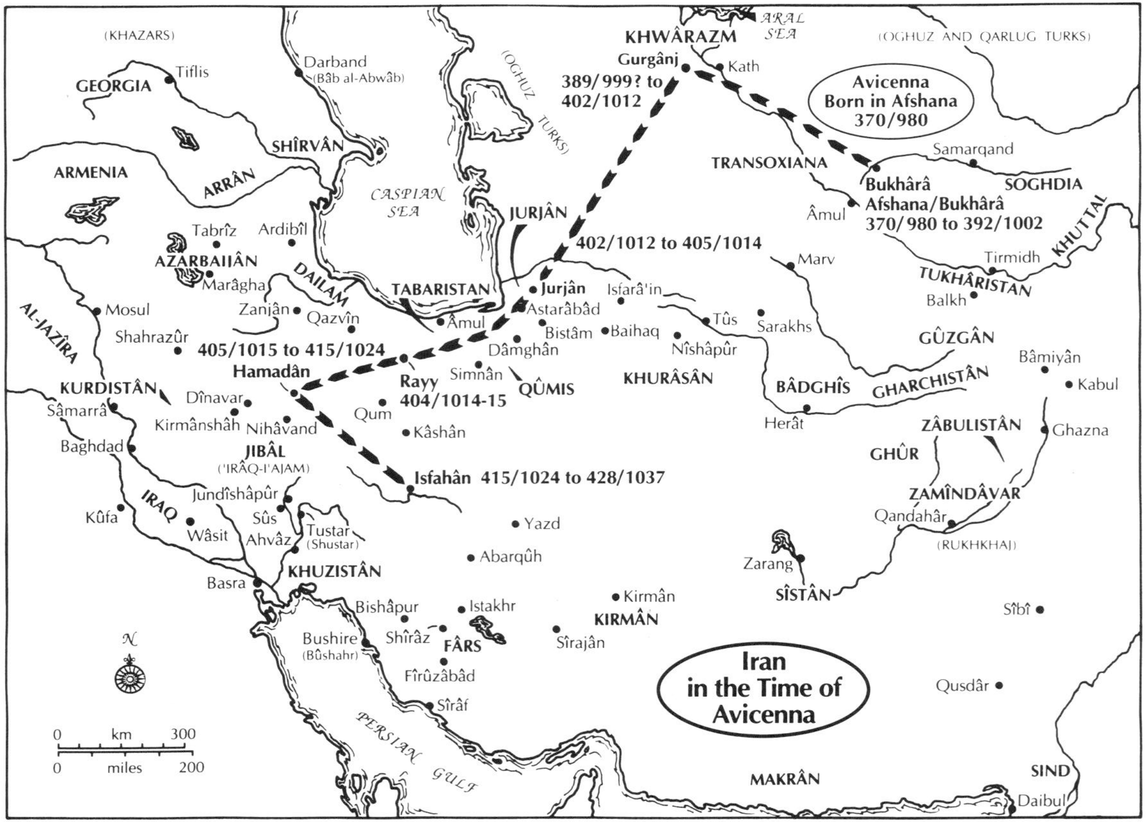
Iran
in the Time of
Avicenna
Avicenna
Born in Afshana
370/980
(KHAZARS)
(OGHUZ AND QARLUG TURKS)
(OGHUZ TURKS)
ARAL SEA
CASPIAN SEA
PERSIAN GULF
KHWÂRAZM
Gurgânj
389/999? to
402/1012
Kath
TRANSOXIANA
Samarqand
SOGHDIA
Bukhârâ
Afshana/Bukhârâ
370/980 to 392/1002
Âmul
KHUTTAL
Tirmidh
TUKHÂRISTAN
Balkh
Marv
402/1012 to 405/1014
GEORGIA
Tiflis
Darband
(Bâb al-Abwâb)
SHÎRVÂN
ARMENIA
ARRÂN
Tabrîz
Ardibîl
AZARBAIJÂN
Marâgha
DAILAM
TABARISTAN
JURJÂN
Jurjân
Isfarâ'in
Astarâbâd
Âmul
Bistâm
Baihaq
Tûs
Sarakhs
Nîshâpûr
Dâmghân
Simnân
QÛMIS
KHURÂSÂN
Mosul
AL-JAZÎRA
Zanjân
Qazvîn
Shahrazûr
405/1015 to 415/1024
Hamadân
Rayy
404/1014-15
Qum
Kâshân
KURDISTÂN
Dînavar
Sâmarrâ
Kirmânshâh
Nihâvand
Baghdad
JIBÂL
('IRÂQ-I'AJAM)
Isfahân 415/1024 to 428/1037
Jundîshâpûr
Sûs
Kûfa
IRAQ
Wâsit
Ahvâz
Tustar
(Shustar)
KHUZISTÂN
Basra
Yazd
Abarqûh
Bishâpur
Istakhr
Kirmân
KIRMÂN
Bushire
(Bûshahr)
Shîrâz
FÂRS
Sîrajân
Fîrûzâbâd
Sîrâf
GÛZGÂN
BÂDGHÎS
GHARCHISTÂN
Herât
Bâmiyân
Kabul
ZÂBULISTÂN
Ghazna
GHÛR
ZAMÎNDÂVAR
Qandahâr
(RUKHKHAJ)
Zarang
SÎSTÂN
Sîbî
Qusdâr
MAKRÂN
SIND
Daibul
N
0 km 300
0 miles 200

2. Avicenna: Courtier, Physician, Philosopher

Avicenna lived in a world rich in opportunity. After enjoying a brief era of strong central authority and cultural florescence in the first part of the 3rd/9th century, the 'Abbâsid empire had begun to experience political decentralization. Given the enormous expanse of the empire, central control from Baghdad was unwieldy at best, and it was not long before it became politically unfeasible as well. The governing families of provinces far from the capital (Aghlabids in Ifrîqiya, Ṭûlûnids in Egypt, Ṭâhirids in Khurâsân) naturally wished to achieve the greatest possible freedom of action, and they strove toward a state in which they loyally acknowledged the theoretical authority of the Caliph but kept real military and economic power in their own hands. From here it was a short step for autonomous dynasties to emerge and begin to compete both with the central authorities in Baghdad and with one another. By the time of Avicenna's birth in Afshana, near Bukhârâ, in 370/980, the Caliphs had openly acquiesced to the new political realities. Although they assiduously guarded the power that remained to them and sought to increase it whenever possible, their practical authority was restricted to the area around Baghdad itself. Meanwhile, the great powers of the day—the Ṣaffârids, Sâmânids, Bûyids, Ghaznavids, centered in various parts of Iran, Afghanistan, and Transoxiana, and the Fâṭimids in Egypt—rose and fell. Previously extraneous regions became seats of empire.[1]

Although political decentralization took its toll in periodic economic destabilization and military devastation, it actually did much to foster the blossoming of culture. Local monarchs sought to emulate the cultural patterns of 'Abbâsid court life. Such rulers were perfectly aware that the attendance of eminent poets, noted scholars, and learned theologians at their courts added an aura of cultural glory that reinforced their shaky claims to political legitimacy. Hence, they were more than willing to promote the life of the mind, even if they themselves devoted their main energies to ventures of the sword. Some monarchs, or their ministers, were genuinely interested in religion, science, or the arts, and they assembled courts whose brilliance emulated, or surpassed, the glory of the 'Abbâsid Caliphate at its height. Moreover, even minor rulers required bureaucrats able to collect their taxes, keep their books, and handle their correspondence. In such an environment Avicenna did not have to worry about finding a receptive patron, although he did expend many years searching for a sympathetic one.[2]

Avicenna's era was marked by a religious heterogeneity that matched its political diversity. Long established rivalries among schools of theology or jurisprudence continued even as once minor intellectual and religious trends ripened to fruition. While Mu'tazilî, Ash'arî, or Ḥanbalî theologians debated, or Ḥanafî and Shâfi'î law students came to blows over the respective merits or faults of their systems, new movements arose that were to exert enduring influences of enormous proportions. After centuries of relentless ferment, Shî'ism finally witnessed a major political victory in the rise of the Fâṭimid dynasty, while a series of gifted theoreticians and proselytizers developed its theology and promoted its popular appeal. On less overtly political levels, mysticism and philosophy emerged as spiritual and intellectual forces of immense potential. Disparate versions of reality and competing visions of human perfection abounded, each vying for exponents and adherents. In short, the age was replete with possibilities for the militarily ambitious, the politically canny, the artistically talented, and the intellectually astute.[3] This was the atmosphere into which Avicenna brought his own personal magnetism, extraordinary energy, and brilliant mind.

We shall never know as much as we would like about the details of Avicenna's life, but the material that exists offers lively, if fleeting, glimpses of his character and intellect. There is the biography composed by his student and companion of twenty-five years, Abû 'Ubaid 'Abd al-Wâḥid al-Jûzjânî. More exceptional (for autobiography was as rarely practiced in the premodern Islamic world as it was in the medieval West) is Avicenna's own account of his early career, also preserved by al-Jûzjânî. Whatever their factual reliability—and there is little doubt that they require careful interpretation—these two accounts provide more information and insight into the philosopher's life and personality than is customarily the case. One has only to compare the scanty primary information concerning the lives of other major Islamic philosophers, such as al-Kindî (d. cir. 258/870), al-Fârâbî (d. 339/950), or Ibn Bâjja (d. 533/1139), to feel grateful for the material regarding Avicenna that has survived.[4]

Equally important as a source for tracing the philosopher's intellectual development are his writings.[5] Several major and minor works were lost due to the intermittent vicissitudes of his personal life, in which the vagaries of war, political reversal, and personal patronage played a constant role. Nevertheless, a sufficient amount of Avicenna's corpus has been preserved to reveal a clear picture of his philosophical views and habits of thought.[6]

Avicenna's life may usefully be divided into three chronological periods. The first, consisting of his childhood and youth (from 370/980 to 392/1002), includes his education and training, his initial entry into court life in Bukhârâ as a young adult, and his first major compositions. The second period, between 392/1002 and 405/1015, is one of constant movement. During this time Avicenna traveled from Bukhârâ to Gurgânj (389/999[?]–402/1012), then to Jurjân (402/1012–405/1014), and on to Rayy (404/1014–15) in his continuous search for a patron who would provide financial and physical security and a comfortable working environment. Although this quest for a propitious court position was unsuccessful, Avicenna's writings and professional activities established his reputation as a physician and philosopher. Finally, he found more agreeable positions of longer duration at the Bûyid court in Hamadhân (405/1015–415/1024) and the Kâkûyid capital of Iṣfahân (415/1024–428/1037).[7]

One must go, however, beyond this succinct chronological scheme, and seek to understand Avicenna by examining the multifarious activities of his career, or more exactly, careers, for Avicenna engaged in many activities other than quiet philosophical contemplation. Judged by almost any standards, Avicenna's life was one of exceptional achievement, as eventful and exciting as the times in which he lived and as diverse in its varied undertakings.[8] Both his autobiography and his philosophical writings reveal that he was well aware of his own genius and displayed a sense of self-worth that in anyone of lesser intellectual qualities would be considered arrogance; he was a man who obviously had little patience for fools.[9] Even to begin to appreciate the philosopher requires that we examine his undertakings in each of his several careers of courtier, physician, and philosopher.

Courtier

Avicenna passed the greater part of his life in the world of royal courts, an environment permeated with competition and intrigue in which careers of dazzling splendor not infrequently suffered sudden, disastrous reversals. He himself experienced sufficiently drastic changes of fortune, including a few very near escapes from death, that his intellectual brashness was no doubt tempered early on by a keen awareness of his own mortality. Survival among the rulers of his time demanded the tact, sensitivity, and decorum of the professional courtier, and Avicenna was trained in these skills from birth.

Born into a family of minor functionaries, Avicenna was clearly raised for a career at court. By the end of his life he had served several of the petty princes who then held sway over different parts of western and central Iran, supporting himself either through the system of court patronage or by assuming various bureaucratic positions.[10] Like many an itinerant scholar or poet of his time, Avicenna searched throughout his life for a magnanimous, lenient, and reliable patron, so, judging from this perspective, it is not surprising that he experienced a burst of creative energy in the last fifteen years of his life when he finally found such a benefactor in the person of the Kâkûyid ruler of Iṣfahân, 'Alâ' ad-Daula Abû Ja'far Muḥammad (d. 433/1041–42), by whom the philosopher was obviously favored and to whom he dedicated several works.[11]

Despite his reputation as a physician and scholar, for most of his adulthood Avicenna earned his living chiefly as an administrator. During the last twenty years of his life he crowned his official career by serving as vezier to two rulers, the Bûyid prince Shams ad-Daula (d. 412/1021) of Hamadhân and the afore-mentioned 'Alâ' ad-Daula.[12] This latter was a position of some consequence. One source states that up to two thousand men used to attend Avicenna at his arrival to court, and that 'Alâ' ad-Daula "favoured him greatly, and had entrusted into his hands all the affairs of the kingdom and left all matters to his judgement and discretion," so that "in all matters of state importance there was no third person between him and the King."[13]

While Avicenna sometimes shirked the dangers of court employment, with its ancillary intrigues (as when he refused the ministry that Shams ad-Daula's son, 'Alî, offered to him), he also took some pride in his accomplishments as a courtier. This is probably one cause for his irritation when a philologist in Iṣfahân called into question his mastery of literary Arabic. Like any court savant, Avicenna prided himself on being a polymath, and as a well-rounded courtier he could hardly allow his literary skills in the standard language of correspondence and court administration to be impugned.[14]

Avicenna's fame as a philosopher may have played some role in securing employment at court, but only in a general fashion. "Sage as chief counsellor" is a prominent theme in Sassanian and, thereafter, Islamic theories of kingship, in which it is expected that every ideal ruler would have a wise chief minister at his elbow to provide guidance and advice. And, indeed, engaging philosophers as ministers was not unheard of in the Islamic context; in the 6th/12th century, both Ibn Bâjja and Ibn Ṭufail served as ministers to rulers of the North African Muwaḥḥidûn (Almohad) dynasty. Living in an age that witnessed the resurgence of the use of the Persian language and of Sassanian court customs (many of which were Islamic by this time anyway), this political ideal was no doubt alive in the minds of Avicenna and his contemporaries. And it was later applied to the philosopher himself; as Niẓâmî-yi 'Arûḍî remarked, "since Alexander the Great, whose minister was Aristotle, no King had had such a minister as Abû 'Alî [Ibn Sînâ]."[15]

Avicenna's royal employers were, however, induced to appoint him minister more for reasons of pragmatism than due to any deep concern for imitating past monarchs or complying with the finer shades of political theory. Judged by any standards, the philosopher was a highly trained, intelligent, and capable person whom a ruler could reasonably expect to manage affairs of state knowledgeably and successfully. Moreover, as someone brought in from outside, Avicenna was totally dependent upon royal favor and thus could be counted on to be relatively trustworthy. That troops once rebelled against him suggests that he was also valued for his abilities in the essential—if perennially unpopular—art of fiscal administration.[16]

Physician

If Avicenna ended his career as a minister, he began it as a physician. Not finding medicine "one of the difficult sciences," he claimed to have mastered it by the age of sixteen.[17] A year later he won recognition at the Sâmânid court at Bukhârâ by treating its ailing ruler, Nûḥ ibn Manṣûr (d. 387/997); some fifteen years thereafter his medical fame gained him similar employment at the Bûyid court at Rayy. Avicenna was more than a renowned practitioner, however; throughout his life he engaged in medical experiments, wrote essays on specific topics, and composed a voluminous medical encyclopedia, *al-Qânûn fi ṭ-ṭibb* (The Canon of Medicine), that became a standard advanced textbook in the Islamic world and, later, in the West for the next half millennium.[18]

Philosopher

Although Avicenna became a proficient courtier and renowned physician, his first love and chief passion remained philosophy. His political appointments resulted more from professional necessity than from any deeply seated personal ambition (or so perhaps he would like us to believe), while his medical activities were only part of his overall studies in natural philosophy (to use the term current in the West until the 19th century).[19] However deep other interests may have been, the intensity of the emotional fervor and intellectual commitment that Avicenna brought to philosophy is indisputable.

Engaged in what Dimitri Gutas has aptly termed his "undergraduate education," the young Avicenna "did not sleep completely through a single night nor devote [him]self to anything else by day" for a year and a half as he pursued his philosophical studies.[20] A similar period of intense "graduate" study occurred at Bukhârâ, in the famed library of the Sâmânid monarch Nûḥ ibn Manṣûr.[21] In the same vein, al-Jûzjânî records Avicenna's subsequent habit of engaging in philosophical writing and instruction after a full day of court business, followed by a few hours of evening relaxation. He also recalls an occasion on which his master devoted an entire night to answering a set of philosophical inquiries that had arrived by courier that very day from a group of scholars in Shîrâz so that his responses could be sent off the next morning.[22]

Avicenna's obsession with philosophy was such that neither bad times nor good deterred him from writing. He composed the outline of the whole of the *ash-Shifâ'* (The Healing) and completed its "Metaphysics" and most of its "Physics" at the pace of fifty pages a day while living in hiding from his former royal patron, 'Alî ibn Shams ad-Daula. Finally apprehended and imprisoned in the castle of Fardajân, Avicenna feared the worst.[23] Nevertheless, he continued to write during the four months he spent in prison, where he composed a summary of his philosophical system, *al-Hidâya* (The Guidance), dedicated to his brother; the allegory *Ḥayy ibn Yaqẓân*; and a short medical treatise on colic, *al-Qûlanj*.[24] This period of intense writing coupled with personal difficulties (412/1021–415/1024) holds great interest for us, for it is here that Avicenna completed the most important sections of his masterpiece, *ash-Shifâ'*, and composed at least one, perhaps more, of his allegories.[25]

Avicenna's physical worries ended with his release from prison, and when he finally moved to Iṣfahân he found in 'Alâ' ad-Daula a patron after his own heart. As al-Jûzjânî states, 'Alâ' ad-Daula warmly welcomed the philosopher to Iṣfahân:

> And from his court [*majlis*] he received the respect and esteem which someone like him deserved. Amîr 'Alâ' al-Daula designated Friday nights for learned discussions [*majlis an-naẓar*] in his presence, which all of the different classes of learned men attended, the Master among them, and he was not outclassed in any of the sciences.

The ease and comforts of this final portion of his life did nothing to blunt his penchant for philosophy. On the contrary, he entered an extremely prolific period in which he composed several major, mature philosophical treatises, as well as pursuing varied astronomical investigations at the behest of 'Alâ' ad-Daula.[26]

The enormity of Avicenna's philosophical achievement and the magnitude of his historical influence cannot be overstressed. It is not surprising that later generations called him the Chief Master (*ash-Shaikh ar-Ra'îs*), for he revived and restructured philosophy in ways that shaped its pursuit for centuries thereafter. Avicenna encountered his received tradition, the Hellenistic synthesis of Neoplatonism and Aristotelianism as reworked in the Islamic world, at a crucial moment, when its analytic rigor (notwithstanding the magnificent efforts of al-Fârâbî) was vitiated and popularized by his immediate predecessors and his contemporaries, and when its intellectual validity was easily questioned by those working outside of it (theologians, mystics, and philologists).[27] Avicenna has justly been called "the first Scholastic," for he forged what F. E. Peters and Dimitri Gutas have termed "the Aristotelian tradition" into a unified system of unprecedented cohesion and brilliance, in fullest detail in his masterpiece *ash-Shifâ'*, but also in numerous other major and minor treatises, compendia, and essays. For the next nine hundred years in the Islamic East and almost half this period in the West, philosophy was seen through the prism of the philosophical curriculum that Avicenna created.[28] As the 6th/12th century Niẓâmî-yi 'Arûḍî observed:

> For four thousand years the wise men of antiquity travailed in spirit and melted their very souls in order to reduce the Science of Philosophy to some

> fixed order, yet they could not effect this, until, after the lapse of this period, that incomparable philosopher and most powerful thinker Aristotle weighed this coin in the balance of Logic, assayed it with the touchstone of definitions, and measured it by the scale of analogy, so that all doubt and ambiguity departed from it, and it became established on a sure and critical basis. And during these fifteen centuries which have elapsed since his time, no philosopher hath won to the inmost essence of his doctrine, nor travelled the high road of his method, save that most excellent of the moderns, the Philosopher of the East, the Proof of God unto His creatures, Abû 'Alî al-Ḥusayn ibn 'Abdallâh ibn Sînâ (Avicenna). He who finds fault with these two great men will have cut himself off from the company of the wise, placed himself in the category of madmen, and exhibited himself in the ranks of the feeble-minded.[29]

But if Avicenna's passionate love of philosophy is beyond doubt and his accomplishments in it can only provoke admiration—if not awe, given the many distractions of his life—it still remains to be explained why he found the discipline so bewitching. Gutas has pointed out the philosopher's intellectual independence, and it is true that Avicenna was very much an audodidact who held a very high opinion of his own philosophical instincts and abilities. The activities of his life underscore the degree to which his pursuit of knowledge was self-motivated. He quickly surpassed his teachers in philosophical perspicuity and knowledge, and he wrote continuously throughout his career, constantly producing works great and small. Moreover, with the exception of al-Fârâbî, Avicenna held his fellow philosophers in low esteem, especially "the simple-minded Christians of Baghdad." Al-Jûzjânî remarks how when Avicenna encountered a new book he rarely read it all the way through:

> Rather, he would go directly to its difficult passages and intricate problems and look at what its author had to say about them. Thus would he seek to ascertain the level of his knowledge and the degree of his understanding.[30]

In other words, Avicenna was concerned less about what new ideas he could learn from colleagues than where he should place and evaluate their insights within the spectrum of his own philosophical program.

But to the passion, constancy, and intellectual independence that mark Avicenna's preoccupation with philosophy must be added the basic doctrinal stability of his own system, which underwent little essential change during the course of his life. In a celebrated passage in his autobiography, the philosopher states:

> So when I had reached the age of eighteen I was finished with all of these [philosophical] sciences; at that time I had a better memory for learning, but

today my knowledge is more mature; otherwise it is the same; nothing new has come to me since.[31]

However exaggerated this statement may be and whatever its rhetorical intent, scrutiny of Avicenna's works largely substantiates it. Gutas is doubtlessly correct in asserting that it applies more to the general structure or "fundamental points" (*uṣûl*) of Avicenna's philosophical system rather than to particular points or "corollaries" (*furûʿ*); nevertheless, by the time the philosopher reached the age of eighteen, or at least attained intellectual maturity, the parameters of his philosophical system were firmly in place.[32] This explains the philosopher's great productivity as a writer. Throughout his life Avicenna continually produced different refractions of this single systematic vision of reality, scrutinized in encyclopedic detail in the monumental *ash-Shifâ'*, summarized in handbooks and compendia such as *an-Najât, ʿUyûn al-ḥikma*, or *al-Hidâya*, and investigated as individual topics in monographs or treatises—the afterlife, for example, in *al-Aḍḥawiyya*, prophecy in *Fî ithbât an-nubuwwât*, dreams in *Fî taʿbîr ar-ru'yâ*, or the soul in *Fi l-quwa l-insâniyya wa-idrâkâtihâ* or *Fî kalâm ʿala n-nafs an-nâṭiqa*.[33]

The philosophical framework that resulted is characterized by structural features—comprehensive inclusiveness, hierarchical system, and mimetic verisimilitude—which upheld and guaranteed its integrity as an all-encompassing system. Yet any intellectual system that aspires to comprehensiveness does so at certain costs, for it must gloss over structural tensions fundamental to its cohesion as a system. From such tensions arise the criticisms and revisions of later philosophers. But they can also lead to processes of self-revision or recalibration on the part of the system's creator. We shall see that in Avicenna's case one such revision was the creation of allegory.

Notes

1. For a political survey of this period, see the later chapters of Hugh Kennedy, *The Prophet and the Age of the Caliphates: The Islamic Near East from the Sixth to the Eleventh Century* (London and New York: Longman, 1986). For political and cultural overviews, see Marshall G. S. Hodgson, *The Venture of Islam: Conscience and History in a World Civilization*, vol. 2: *The Expansion of Islam in the Middle Periods* (Chicago and London: University of Chicago Press, 1974), as well as the relevant chapters of R. N. Frye, ed., *The Cambridge History of Iran*, vol. 4: *From the Arab Invasion to the Saljuqs* (Cambridge: Cambridge University Press, 1975), and P. M. Holt, Ann K. S. Lambton, and Bernard Lewis, eds., *The Cambridge*

History of Islam, 2 vols. (Cambridge: Cambridge University Press, 1970). Quite useful both for its historical overview and collection of materials is Sa'îd Nafîsî, *Zindagî va-kâr va-andîshah va-rûzgâr-i Pûr-i Sînâ* (Tehran: Kitâbkhâna-yi Dânish, 1953–54).

2. Sultan Maḥmûd (d. 421/1030) of Ghazna is an example of a ruler who "collected" scholars and artists less because of any personal interest in their endeavors than because of his desire that they adorn his court. The monarchs of the Sâmânid dynasty and several Bûyid ministers of a generation earlier than Avicenna, such as Ibn al-'Amîd (d. 360/970) and aṣ-Ṣâḥib ibn 'Abbâd (d. 385/995), are examples of patrons who displayed real knowledge and even expertise in literature and the sciences. Recent scholars have begun to consider the hypothesis that court patronage actually flourished more in periods of decentralization, since one part of a ruler's aura of political legitimacy rested on his liberality in regard to cultural patronage; see, for example, Maria Eva Subtelny, "Socioeconomic Bases of Cultural Patronage under the Later Timurids," *International Journal of Middle East Studies* 20 (1988) 479–505.

3. See Hodgson, *Venture of Islam*, 2:153–200, although the whole of this second volume of Hodgson's work is pertinent to this subject.

4. For sources on Avicenna's life, see Chapter One, note 20.

5. A recent example of an acute reading of Avicenna's intellectual development based on careful examination of his texts is Gutas, *Avicenna and the Aristotelian Tradition*, esp. pp. 148–98.

6. Gohlman, *Life*, 143–52, offers the lists of Avicenna's works as found in his various biographies. The modern bibliographical studies of Georges Anawati, Yaḥyâ Mahdavî, and Osman Ergin (see Bibliography) still have their uses, but they are much outdated and in serious need of revision. Avicenna's early opus, the twenty-volume *al-Ḥâṣil wa l-maḥṣûl* (The Sum and the Substance), appears to have been lost because he made only a single copy for a friend; other texts were destroyed when troops ransacked his household in Hamadhân, while all but a few fragments of the *al-Inṣâf* (The Judgment) were destroyed when Sultan Mas'ûd of Ghazna (d. 433/1041) sacked Iṣfahân (cf. Gohlman, *Life*, 38–41, 52–53, 80–81).

7. Gutas, in Mahdi, Gutas, et al., "Avicenna," *Encyclopedia Iranica*, 3,1: 69–70. Useful chronologies of the dates of Avicenna's major works are in Gohlman, *Life*, 153–54; Gutas, *Avicenna and the Aristotelian Tradition*, 145; and Michot, *La destinée de l'homme selon Avicenne*, 6–7.

8. The following discussion of Avicenna's career is based on his autobiography and Abû 'Ubaid al-Jûzjânî's biography; see Gohlman, *Life*.

9. Gohlman, *Life*, 18–19, where Avicenna states that by the age of ten he was so accomplished that "people were greatly amazed by me." The theme recurs throughout the autobiography (17–45). One may venture to guess that Avicenna countenanced the long companionship of al-Jûzjânî precisely because the latter remained in constant awe of his master. The autobiography is a mature work and Avicenna may not always have been so self-assured in regard to his philosophical achievements; see Gutas's discussion, "The Evolution of Avicenna's Attitude toward Aristotle, the Aristotelian Tradition, and His Own Work," in *Avicenna and the Aristotelian Tradition*, 286–96.

10. As we shall notice, Avicenna engaged in medicine, administration, and philosophy during his career. In Gurgânj, however, he apparently also received a stipend as a theologian (Gohlman, *Life*, 40–41).

11. As the later historian Ibn al-Athîr (d. 630/1233) somewhat caustically remarks, "There is no doubt that Abû Ja'far ['Alâ' ad-Daula] was corrupt in his religious belief, for while in his lands Ibn Sînâ dared to undertake his heretical compositions that rejected religious dogma," 'Izz ad-Dîn Abû Ḥasan 'Alî ibn al-Athîr, *al-Kâmil fi t-ta'rîkh*, 9 vols (Beirut: Dâr al-fikr, 1978) 8:15. On the Kâkûyid dynasty in general, see C. E. Bosworth, "Dailamîs in Central Iran: The Kâkûyids of Jibîl and Yazd," *Iran* 8 (1970) 73–95, repr. in Bosworth, *The Medieval History of Iran, Afghanistan, and Central Asia* (London: Variorum Reprints, 1977) 73–95.

12. Gohlman, *Life*, 35–89; Gohlman's notes provide brief background information concerning Avicenna's other patrons.

13. This according to the report of the Bûyid prince Fakhr ad-Daula Abû Kâlîjâr, as related by Aḥmad ibn 'Umar ibn 'Alî Niẓâmî-yi 'Arûḍî (fl. mid-6th/12th century) in *Chahâr Maqâla*, ed. Mîrzâ Muḥammad ibn 'Abd al-Wahhâb al-Qazvînî (London: Luzac & Co., 1927) 92–93; trans. E. G. Browne, *Revised Translation of the Chahâr Maqâla ("Four Discourses") of Niẓâmî-i-'Arûḍî of Samarqand*, E. J. W. Gibb Memorial Series 11 (Cambridge: Cambridge University Press; London: Luzac & Co., 1921) 92. Not noted for its accuracy or reliability, this work does provide a very good idea of the anecdotes that came to surround Avicenna in the century following his death.

14. Gohlman, *Life*, 68–73.

15. Niẓâmî-yi 'Arûḍî, *Chahâr Maqâla*, 92, Browne trans., 92.

16. Gohlman, *Life*, 52–53, also 51–52, where al-Jûzjânî remarks that at one time Avicenna was responsible for the business affairs of one of his patrons.

17. Gohlman, *Life*, 24–27.

18. Again, Niẓâmî-yi 'Arûḍî provides various anecdotes concerning Avicenna's talents as a physician, skills that required, in addition to medical expertise, perspicuous insight into human nature; see *Chahâr Maqâla*, 81–82, 88–94, Browne trans., 82 and 88–93 respectively. For a description of Avicenna's medical writings and his later influence in Europe, see Goichon's article in *EI*², 942–45; Basim Musallam's contribution to Mahdi, Gutas, et al., "Avicenna," *Encyclopedia Iranica*, 3,1:94–99; and Nancy G. Siraisi, *Avicenna in Renaissance Italy: The* Canon *and Medical Training in Italian Universities After 1500* (Princeton, N.J.: Princeton University Press, 1987).

19. Al-Jûzjânî complains about the "afflictions" of Avicenna's bureaucratic services and his master's consequent lack of time for philosophy, but it is unclear whether Avicenna himself shared these sentiments; see *ash-Shifâ': al-Madkhal*, 1–2, trans. Gutas, *Avicenna and the Aristotelian Tradition*, 40–41.

20. Gohlman, *Life*, 26–27.

21. Gohlman, *Life*, 36–37. Gutas's account of Avicenna's autodidactic methods of education is perceptive and convincing; see his *Avicenna and the Aristotelian Tradition*, 149–98.

22. Gohlman, *Life*, 54–55, 76–77. In a report transmitted by Niẓâmî-yi 'Arûḍî, Fakhr ad-Daula Abû Kâlîjâr al-Bûyî remarks that Avicenna would conduct

classes with his students early in the morning before beginning his court activities, *Chahâr Maqâla*, 92, Browne trans., 92.

23. Gohlman, *Life*, 60–61; see also Chapter Seven, p. 155 below.

24. Gohlman, *Life*, 58–61; al-Jûzjânî's introduction to *ash-Shifâ': al-Madkhal*, 3–4, trans. Gutas, *Avicenna and the Aristotelian Tradition*, 41–42.

25. See below, Chapter Seven. Corbin, *Avicenna*, 184, suggests that it is "possible or probable" that Avicenna also wrote *Risâlat aṭ-ṭair* while in prison; it seems likely to me that he composed it sometime within the period of his fall from grace in Hamadhân and his move to the more relaxing circumstances of Iṣfahân.

26. Gohlman, *Life*, 56–63, 154; Gutas, *Avicenna and the Aristotelian Tradition*, 145.

27. A good analytic account of the interaction between philosophy and *adab* (belles-lettres) at this period still remains to be written; for the general outlines, see Majid Fakhry, *A History of Islamic Philosophy*, 2nd ed., Studies in Oriental Culture 5 (New York: Columbia University Press, 1983) 163–202; and Joel Kraemer's two books, *Philosophy in the Renaissance of Islam: Abû Sulaymân al-Sijîstânî and His Circle* (Leiden: E. J. Brill, 1986) and *Humanism in the Renaissance of Islam: The Cultural Revival During the Bûyid Age* (Leiden: E. J. Brill, 1986). For a careful analysis of the contemporaneous uses of the terms *failasûf* and *adîb*, see Everett K. Rowson, "The Philosopher as Littérateur: al-Tawḥîdî and His Predecessors," *Zeitschrift für Geschichte der arabisch-islamishchen Wissenschaften* 6 (1990) 50–92.

28. It was Goichon who referred to Avicenna as the first Scholastic. Detailed investigations of the extent of Avicenna's influence in the East have yet to be undertaken; for a partial summary see Francis E. Peters, *Aristotle and the Arabs: The Aristotelian Tradition in Islam*, New York University Studies In Near Eastern Civilization 1 (New York: New York University Press; London: University of London Press, 1968) 172–74, 188–200; the situation in regard to his influence on western medieval philosophy is hardly better, but for a brief overview, see A.-M. Goichon, *The Philosophy of Avicenna and Its Influence on Medieval Europe*, trans. M. S. Khan (Delhi, Patna, and Varanasi: Motilal Banarsidass, 1969), esp. chapter 3, pp. 73–105.

29. Niẓâmî-yi 'Arûḍî, *Chahâr Maqâla*, 79, Browne trans., 79–80; compare this statement with the modern evaluation of Seyyed Hossain Nasr in "Philosophy and Cosmology," in Frye, ed., *The Cambridge History of Iran*, 4:431:

> Few men have left as profound an effect upon their civilization and its subsequent history as Ibn Sînâ has left upon Islamic civilization, especially in its Persian zone. An extraordinary genius gifted at the same time with the power of synthesis and analysis, and possessing unusual physical and mental powers, he was able to achieve a lasting synthesis in the domains of both philosophy and medicine. No intellectual figure in the subsequent history of Islam can be said to have been totally free of his influence, whether that figure be a physician or a logician. Even the theologians and other authorities in the religious sciences adopted some of the basic tenets of his metaphysical doctrines.

See also Everett K. Rowson, *A Muslim Philosopher on the Soul and Its Fate: Al-'Amirî's* Kitâb al-Amad 'alâ l-abad, American Oriental Series 70 (New Haven,

Conn.: American Oriental Society, 1988) 28–29; and Gardet, *La pensée religieuse d'Avicenne (Ibn Sînâ)*, 17–18, 199–206.

30. Gohlman, *Life*, 68–69 (Gohlman's trans.); see also Gutas's trans. of the "Letter to Kiyâ" and "Memoirs of a Disciple from Rayy," in *Avicenna and the Aristotelian Tradition*, 60–64, 66–72.

31. Gohlman, *Life*, 37–39 (Gohlman's trans.).

32. Gutas, *Avicenna and the Aristotelian Tradition*, 220–21, also 199–218.

33. Compare, for example, the account of the soul in Avicenna's earliest extant work, *Mabḥath 'an al-quwa n-nafsâniyya*, with versions of the psychology written decades later in *ash-Shifâ': an-Nafs* and in *al-Ishârât wa-t-tanbîhât*. In fact, in *Fî kalâm 'ala n-nafs an-nâṭiqa*, which according to Gutas is Avicenna's last work, the philosopher urges his readers to consult the *Mabḥath*, which he had written some forty years before, for a fuller exposition of his psychology.

Part II

Allegory and Philosophy

3. The Structure and Representation of the Cosmos

Avicenna possessed an extraordinarily systematic vision of the structure of the cosmos—and of how it should be studied. Appreciating this fact is crucial if we are to understand his intellectual accomplishments; but it must also be kept in perspective. His passion for cohesiveness and completion led to the preoccupation with detail and demonstration that characterizes his logos writings: everything must fit, everything must hang together logically.[1] This being the case, it is not surprising that many later students of Avicenna, attracted by these very attributes of system, detail, and logical coherence, tend to view his philosophy through the prism of his logos texts and become equally obsessed with matters of demonstration and detail. This mind-set, understandable as it may be, can distort our apprehension of the general direction and purpose of Avicenna's thought. It is possible to become so concerned with the ways in which specific arguments are rationally demonstrated, or so preoccupied with the study of the historical origins of ideas adopted from previous thinkers, that one loses sight of the fact that such details are intended to support, not displace, Avicenna's comprehensive vision of the nature of the cosmos. This kind of logos-oriented perspective also often fails to take into account the more universal existential forces behind the creation of new philosophical systems, forces that stem from a desire to organize or reorganize our understanding of the cosmos and give meaning to our place within it. It can also obscure the inventive nature of system-building, losing sight of the fact that it is a creative act of synthesis that combines old pieces of philosophical puzzles with new in order to produce fresh, seminal intellectual configurations. In such an enterprise, it is the overall scheme, the matrix of interwoven plots, that is essential for the system-building philosopher, while the particular details drawn in to support and substantiate this scheme remain subsidiary. Close attention to particulars is merely part of the process of working out the internal bursts of intuitive philosophical revelation that inspire the development of the system as a whole. Indeed, the distinguishing mark of a superior philosopher is the ability to balance close attention to detail with a panoramic vision of a large-scale intellectual system.[2]

In studying Avicenna's system, therefore, one must not become so involved in matters of logical minutiae as to forget the relation of the part to the whole. On the contrary, one must first delineate the general intellectual concerns, motives, and intuitions that underlie Avicenna's pursuit of philosophy to show how they are typically organized. Only this path leads to a clear understanding of the relationship among the various logos and muthos formulations to which the philosopher resorts in order to represent his system.

The central plot of Avicenna's allegories is the human soul's achievement of perfection, as represented in terms of heavenly ascent. But this is only one part of a grander vision that shapes Avicenna's overarching intellectual system. This vision has two main parts: the cosmogonic unfolding of the universe from the single source of creation according to a Neoplatonic emanational scheme, and the return, or reincorporation, of the fulfilled and perfected individual human soul to its intellectual and ontological point of origin. This episteme represents the comprehensive architectonics of Avicenna's vision of the structure and operations of the cosmos. In order to participate fully in it, we will first trace the movement of cosmogonic unfolding that constitutes its first part and then investigate various representations of its second movement, the theme of spiritual return, of which the allegories constitute separate renditions.

The Structure of the Cosmos

Avicenna divides the cosmos into three connected yet essentially disparate parts. At the fount of existence stands the "Necessary Existent" (*wâjib al-wujûd*), which in many ways constitutes a synthesis of Plato's "The Good," Aristotle's "Prime Mover" and Plotinus's "The One." The Necessary Existent derives its name from the fact that, according to Avicenna, existence is an essential component of its essence. Only the Necessary Existent "exists" unconditionally. It is the "First Principle," One and Eternal, admitting neither multiplicity (*kathra*) nor change (*taghayyur*). It is also "Pure Intellect," simultaneously Intellecter, Intellect, and Intelligible (*'âqil, 'aql, ma'qûl*), Lover and Beloved (*'âshiq, ma'shûq*), Enjoyer and Enjoyed (*mul-*

tadhdh, ladhîdh), and as such All-Knowing, Wise, Good, Benevolent, and All-Powerful. As the only cosmic entity that has "real" existence, it is the primary and, ultimately, the only, Cause of all things.[3]

For Avicenna the Necessary Existent assumes some of the characteristics of a *deus absconditus*—removed from creation, Alone, Immobile, Knowing. Simultaneously, it is the source of the full expanses of the contingent universe. The Necessary Existent is pure, actual Intellect, whose knowledge includes the potential existence of a cosmic "virtuous system" (*niẓâm li-l-khair*) that the very act of intellecting brings into existence. Thus are generated the second and third divisions of the universe: the abstract immaterial substances of the celestial spheres and the material bodies of the sublunary world.[4]

The first of the celestial Beings to emerge from the Necessary Existent are the ten Intelligences (*ʿaql*, pl. *ʿuqûl*). The First, or Universal, Intelligence emanates directly from the Necessary Existent itself and then gives rise to three other existents. "In that it intellects the First [i.e. the Necessary Existent], the existence of an Intelligence below it is made necessary."[5] In such fashion the Second and other, lower Intelligences continue to be generated until the final emergence of the Tenth Intelligence, also known as the Active Intelligence (*al-ʿaql al-faʿʿâl*) or the Giver of Forms (*wâhib aṣ-ṣuwar*).[6] In addition, each Intelligence generates a Soul and a heavenly body as a result of self-reflection. When the Intelligence "intellects its essence, the sphere [*falak*] with its Soul [*nafs*] and its body [*jirm*] and the body of the sphere existing because of it [whether stars or a planet] are made necessary."[7] According to Avicenna, celestial Souls and bodies are homologous to the human soul and body.[8] Just as the human soul is the principle that animates our bodies, Souls are the principles that move the heavenly spheres.[9] The cause of this motion is the love and adoration that the Souls feel for the Necessary Existent. This love generates within each Soul a desire for self-perfection that, in turn, sets each heavenly body into eternal motion.[10] In the philosopher's own words:

> When [an Intelligence or Soul] attains the feeling of pleasure by intellecting the First Principle [i.e., the Necessary Existent], because of what it intellects or apprehends of it, whether in an intellectual or psychic manner, it becomes distracted from every other thing or consideration. Nevertheless, there emerges from this process something lesser in rank, namely, a yearning to emulate [the Necessary Existent] to the extent possible. The impetus for movement thus becomes necessary, not as being movement per se, but rather according to what we have said [i.e., as the entelechy of the Soul]. This is yearning,

> which is a consequence of the love and feeling of pleasure arising from it and the urge for perfection [which results in motion] arising from such yearning. It is in this way that the First Principle moves a heavenly body.[11]

This tri-partite system of emanation (Intelligence-Soul-Sphere) continues in this way through nine levels. By the time it reaches the level of the Tenth Intelligence, however, the energies of cosmic emanation are so dissipated that it is unable to produce another complete Soul and sphere, and its emanational force splinters into multiplicity. In place of another sphere, matter emerges, first in the simple forms of the Four Elements (Earth, Water, Air, Fire) and then in the compound forms that constitute the earth as we know it. At this point terrestrial life comes into being—plants, animals, and humans—each ultimately deriving its animation and powers of activity from the World Soul emanating from the Active Intelligence. It is only humans who retain the fragmented forces of Intelligence in themselves; only human beings rely on rational thought rather than blind instinct to determine their course in life.[12] The hierarchy described above can be schematized as shown:

Necessary Existent

First or Universal Intelligence—Universal Soul—Heaven of Heavens
Second Intelligence—Second Soul—Heaven of the Zodiac
Third Intelligence—Third Soul—Sphere of Saturn
Fourth Intelligence—Fourth Soul—Sphere of Jupiter
Fifth Intelligence—Fifth Soul—Sphere of Mars
Sixth Intelligence—Sixth Soul—Sphere of the Sun
Seventh Intelligence—Seventh Soul—Sphere of Venus
Eighth Intelligence—Eighth Soul—Sphere of Mercury
Ninth Intelligence—Ninth Soul—Sphere of the Moon
Tenth, Active, Intelligence—The World of Generation and Corruption
The Four Elements
Minerals
Plants
Animals
Humankind

This framework constitutes the mise-en-scène for Avicenna's cosmology. Cosmology, however, is founded upon cosmogony, a dramaturgy of creation and fruition, with at least the potential of final fulfillment. In Avicenna's case the conceptual impetus that motivates his cosmogony is the Aristotelian principle of entelechy, which is based on the dichotomy of potentiality and actuality. Entelechic instincts motivate the unfolding of the universe. Each Intelligence actualizes its inherent creative potential by emanating a lesser Intelligence, a celestial Soul, and a heavenly body. And because each Intelligence is a perfect essence in regard to its innate capacity for fulfillment, this process of actualization occurs necessarily. Celestial Souls generate heavenly spheres and bodies for similar reasons, just as the potential of heavenly bodies is actualized by their external revolutions. Each stage of emanation, starting with the Necessary Existent and ending with the sublunary realm, results from the internal need of its agent, which Avicenna calls love or passion (*ʿishq*), to fulfill its innate potential.[13]

The generation of Intelligences, Souls, and spheres is therefore the result of a process of cosmic teleology, in which each level of the hierarchy achieves perfection by engendering the next. Humans, in turn, complete this cosmic circle by initiating a process of fulfilling their own teleological potential for perfection. If the universe is conceived as a static structure of downward devolution from the ultimate perfection represented by the Necessary Existent, humans perfect themselves by undertaking a process that Avicenna terms "The Return" (*al-maʿâd*).[14] This undertaking has three stages: recognizing one's true purpose in life, learning how to fulfill this purpose, and finally actually fulfilling it.[15]

The scope of this system is breathtaking, and it is not surprising that Avicenna's attempt to justify it resulted in a plethora of detailed argument and syllogistic demonstration. For our purposes, however, we need only be familiar with its general outlines. In essence, what we have here is a highly organized and carefully considered version of the Neoplatonic descent from divine perfection, self-sufficiency, and permanence to terrestrial imperfection, privation, and transience. This descent is not irreversible for humans, however, and it is the potential for rectifying it through the ascent of the individual human soul that constitutes the core of the plot of "The Return."[16]

Avicenna's cosmology rests upon several fundamental assumptions. The philosopher postulates that the cosmos is a unified whole (a comprehensive inclusiveness or unity) that is arranged in a highly orderly and seamless system (a hierarchical multiplicity) that is real, true, and eternal.[17] Although only this system's lower realm of generation and corruption can be perceived empirically, its overall configuration and most of its particulars can be apprehended—if usually imperfectly—by a human intellect possessing, innately or through training, the skills of philosophical reasoning. The knowledge of the cosmos thus obtained can then be cast into language and communicated to others. It is important to remember, however, that these portrayals can either take the form of strictly logos or muthos modes of discourse, as individually developed by each philosopher or philosophical tradition, or be cast in some combination of the two, such as the allegoresis of the *Mi'râj Nâma*.

Two points require emphasis in this regard. First, each mode of depiction or explanation—logos, muthos, or some combination of the two—is by necessity partial and secondary, since no linguistic rendition can claim parity with an immediate intellectual apprehension of the true nature of the universe.[18] And second, because each representation serves specific didactic purposes, supplementing one with the other can provide a more complete picture of the structure of the universe. Since the adumbration of the cosmos offered above is derived from Avicenna's logos versions, it will be useful to examine its particular structure and purpose more fully.

The Logos Study of the Cosmos

The purpose of philosophy, according to Avicenna, is to "ascertain the true nature [*ḥaqâ'iq*] of *all things*, inasmuch as it is possible for human beings to ascertain it."[19] A precise correlation thus holds between fields of knowledge and categories of "things," the latter being either particular existents or universal essences. Indeed, the first requirement of philosophy is to delineate a typology of being so that the "true nature of things" can be recognized, its fundamentals comprehensively represented, and finally, its details and corollaries systematically investigated.[20] "Things" exist either as a result of our wills and actions or regardless of them. That is, either they stem from individual or societal choice, desire, action, or production, or they are part and parcel of the external cosmos, with an existence independent of our own.[21] The study of the first category, the results of human endeavor and activity, is the realm of practical philosophy, while the scientific study of the world at large is the domain of theoretical philosophy.

Anthropological in focus and pragmatic in nature, the aim of practical philosophy is to "perfect the soul, not only so that it knows but also so that it knows what should be done—and then does it!"[22] It has three main branches: ethics, whose goal is to perfect the social virtues of humans as individuals; household management, which investigates how best to organize and govern *particular* groups, such as the family or household unit; and politics and legislation, whether civil or religious, whose subject is the perfection of *general* groups, of society as a whole.[23] The study of external reality, the cosmos as a whole, is the task of theoretical philosophy. Its goal is "perfecting the soul so that it knows, only."[24] As Avicenna says, "While the purpose of practical philosophy is knowledge of the good, the purpose of theoretical philosophy is knowledge of the true."[25]

Theoretical philosophy has three fundamental (*aṣliyya*) parts, the natural sciences, mathematics, and metaphysics, each of which corresponds to the specific class of objects examined. Natural science investigates the empirical, material world: "existents subject to motion, conceptually and constitutionally [*taṣawwuran wa-qiwâman*] and connected with the materials of particular species."[26] Its major branches include the study of (1) motion, that is, physics, (2) the four elements, which are the basic constituents of the sublunary world, (3) generation and corruption, (4) meteorology, (5) minerals, (6) plants, (7) animals, and finally (8) the soul and sense and sensibilia.[27]

Mathematics analyzes existents separated from motion and matter "conceptually, but not constitutionally," that is, numerical or geometric entities and relationships, such as oneness and multiplicity, largeness and smallness, squareness and roundness. These are initially apprehended as joined to material existents but can be abstracted by the imagination because, "by definition, they are not necessarily connected to a body of sensible matter nor to what is in motion."[28] Its four parts are arithmetic, geometry, astronomy, and music.[29]

Metaphysics explores the nature of the immaterial, intelligible world: existents separated from motion and matter "both conceptually and constitutionally."[30] It consists of the study of (1) definitions of terms, (2) the first principles of sciences, (3) the Necessary Existent and its attributes, (4) the spiritual substances (celestial Intelligences and Souls), and (5) the subordination (*taskhîr*) of material and spiritual substances to the celestial substances (in other words, the subordination of the physical universe and both the material and spiritual dimensions of animate creatures, including human beings, to the celestial Souls and Intelligences).[31]

In addition, Avicenna enumerates the subsidiary (*far'iyya*) sciences that are corollary to these fundamental branches of theoretical philosophy. Related to the natural sciences are medicine, astrology, physiognomy, the interpretation of dreams or visions, talismans, geomancy, and alchemy. In regard to mathematics, the subsidiary divisions of arithmetic are addition, subtraction, and algebra; those of geometry are surveying, mechanics, leverage, weights and measures, instrumentation, and mirrors; those of astronomy are astronomical tables and calendars; and those of music are strange or unusual instruments. The lesser sciences of metaphysics are eschatology, prophetic revelation, and saintly inspiration and miracle-working.[32]

As a work that examines the nature of prophetic revelation, the *Mi'râj Nâma* belongs to the lesser sciences of metaphysics, which entail, as we can see from Avicenna's description, such things as:

> Knowledge of the manner of prophetic revelation and the spiritual substances that effect revelation. And how revelation is effected so that it becomes visible and audible after having been spiritual. . . . and what the Faithful Spirit [*ar-rûḥ al-amîn*] and the Holy Spirit [*rûḥ al-qudus*] are, and that the Faithful Spirit comes from the ranks of the Fixed Spiritual Substances [the celestial Souls] while the Holy Spirit comes from the ranks of the Cherubim [the Intelligences].[33]

Finally, Avicenna brings up logic, which he considers to be both a part of philosophy and its instrument. His divisions of logic are (1) the introduction or *Isogoge*, (2) categories, (3) interpretation, (4) syllogisms, or prior analytics, (5) demonstration, or posterior analytics, (6) topics, (7) sophistical refutation, (8) rhetoric, and (9) poetics.[34]

For Avicenna, this scheme embodies a full course of philosophical study that attempts to mirror the structure of the cosmos itself. A homology thus pertains between this cosmological scheme and Avicenna's philosophical curriculum. Physics is the study of the sublunary sphere of material existence. Mathematics abstracts concepts from matter, a process that enables humans to begin to think rationally and thus gain admittance to the intellectual realm of the Ten Intelligences. Finally, metaphysics concerns itself with the upper spheres of the cosmos, the celestial Intelligences, Souls, and spheres which exist as abstract, immaterial entities, leading ultimately to consideration of the nature of the Necessary Existent itself. Naturally, in order even to undertake the study of the cosmos, one must be prepared intellectually; hence the utility—indeed, the necessity—of studying logic.

The number and detail of the individual fields of study mentioned, as well as the cohesiveness of their interrelationships, all demonstrate Avicenna's intense conviction as to the validity of this epistemological scheme. Like the cosmos, philosophy is deemed inclusive on an *a priori* basis;

therefore, all types of knowledge, even those (such as astrology) whose validity Avicenna himself rejects, fall within its purview. As he says, the aim of theoretical philosophy is to prove

> the connection of the earthly to the heavenly [the planets and heavenly spheres], and the heavenly to the Active Angels [*al-malâ'ika l-'âmila*, i.e., the celestial Souls], and the Active Angels to the Representative Informing Angels [*al-malâ'ika l-mubligha l-mumaththila*, or the Intelligences], and the connection of the whole to the [divine] Command [*al-amr*], which is One, like the glance of an eye.[35]

Avicenna's intellectual independence and self-confidence were based on his conviction that knowledge is inherently comprehensive and systematic. He believed that he had grasped the basic principles of the workings of the cosmos and that, theoretically, all he had to do was to fill in the details and then report his findings to others.[36] In fact, matters were not so simple. For in order to comprehend his discoveries, others must first share the intellectual framework within which he worked, and Avicenna displays little confidence in their abilities in this regard.[37] In other words, before Avicenna could relay his findings to his audience, he first had to introduce them to the methodological principles that underlay his investigations; he had to teach them philosophy. This point is evident enough in Avicenna's own writings, but it can be initially highlighted by a broad comparison of the philosopher's didactic approach with that of his distinguished predecessor, al-Fârâbî.[38]

Al-Fârâbî adopts a position very similar to Avicenna's concerning the unified and systematic nature of the structure of the universe and, consequently, of its study. Indeed, although they differ on specific points of doctrine and have different centers of interest—al-Fârâbî being as fascinated with practical philosophy as Avicenna is with metaphysics—the two philosophers share the same fundamental epistemological, essentially Neoplatonic, postulates. Where contrasts strikingly appear is in their pedagogic principles and their literary methods of imparting knowledge.

In such major late works as *as-Siyâsa l-madaniyya* (The Political Regime) and *Mabâdi' ârâ' ahl al-madîna l-fâḍila* (The Principles of the Views of the Citizens of the Virtuous State), al-Fârâbî adopts an expository style to present a schematic survey of the structure of reality. Beginning with the source, he describes the First Cause, then the celestial Intelligences and bodies, the materials and forms of the sublunary world, and the nature of humankind. Thereafter he moves to his favorite topic, political theory, and adumbrates the nature of different political regimes, including the Virtuous City.[39]

Al-Fârâbî's method of composition suggests that he was optimistic about the ability of his readers to follow and build upon his ideas, for throughout his exposition he assumes a sophisticated level of philosophical knowledge as well as tacit agreement regarding ontological postulates and details. Indeed, Muhsin Mahdi has noted that the compositional method of these two works

> bear as much resemblance to legal codes as to philosophic treatises. They consist mainly of positive statements about the attributes of God, the order of the world, the place of man within it, and how a good society is to be organized and led. . . . They are works whose form and intention could be readily understood by a Muslim reader committed to the acceptance of a true view of the world at large and obedience to laws that promote virtue and lead to ultimate happiness.[40]

In contrast, Avicenna's compositional approach indicates that he entertained a generally pessimistic opinion of his audience's intellectual levels and capabilities, even in regard to those who claimed some degree of philosophical expertise.[41] As a result, he structured most of his philosophical treatises didactically, leading the reader through the essential components of the philosophical curriculum, beginning with logic, continuing through physics, and concluding with metaphysics. Avicenna chose this format because it forced his readers to undergo a comprehensive course of study. To understand the world correctly, they had to learn to see it, and to do this they had to work their way through his refraction of the Aristotelian-Neoplatonic philosophical tradition. This didactic intent explains Avicenna's readiness to compose handbooks that could serve as primers for the uninitiated.[42]

Simultaneously, however, Avicenna entertained a critical appreciation of the epistemological limitations of this didactic format. Although it was the best tool at hand for instructing readers on how to reflect philosophically, he did not view it as the sole—or perhaps even the best—method of imparting philosophical knowledge. An alternative, if correlative, approach was muthos, of which *Ḥayy ibn Yaqẓân* is a prime example.

The Muthos Representation of the Cosmos

Ḥayy ibn Yaqẓân presents in allegorical form the cosmic structure that is described in such detail in Avicenna's logos writings. The work begins with the philosopher stating that he is finally acquiescing to the requests of his "brothers" to help them by explaining to them the story of Ḥayy ibn Yaqẓân. A summary of this story, which is related in the first person, is as follows.[43]

One day the narrator leaves his city with three companions to visit a pleasure garden. There he encounters an attractive, vivacious, and sagacious-looking old man. Feeling drawn to the old man, the narrator engages him in conversation and asks him to divulge his name and origins. The old man declares himself to be Ḥayy ibn Yaqẓân (Alive, Son of Awake), a native of the City of the Sanctified Abode (*bait al-muqaddas*), and says that while his profession is that of perennial traveler, his father has revealed to him all types of knowledge. The narrator and Ḥayy then discuss the various branches of the sciences until they come to the subject of physiognomy (*al-firâsa*), the science that discloses the inner qualities of individuals. Ḥayy reveals himself to be a master of this science and informs the narrator that although he has a fine natural character, he is in danger of ruining it due to the pernicious influences of his three companions, one of whom is mendacious, the second violent, and the third licentious. The narrator remarks that since hearing Ḥayy's advice he has been engaged in a constant struggle to check the pernicious influences that these companions exert on him.

The narrator then eagerly asks about the road on which Ḥayy has been traveling. The old man responds that he is not yet ready to undertake such a journey, but the narrator nevertheless insists on hearing about each of the climes through which Ḥayy has traveled. Ḥayy's description of these climes constitutes the remainder of the narrative.

According to Ḥayy, the cosmos encompasses three realms. The first realm, which lies between the East and West, is well-known, for much information about it has been gathered. On either side, however, lie the regions of the Occident and the Orient, knowledge of which is barred to all but a select few (*al-khawâṣṣ*). And even these few cannot attain such knowledge through their innate nature (*al-fiṭra*) alone; they must also bathe themselves in the spring that lies near the motionless Water of Life. It is the water of this spring the gives the travelers the vigor they need to penetrate the barriers that normally restrict their entrance to the Orient and the Occident.

When the narrator requests a description of the Occident, Ḥayy explains that its far reaches consist of a large hot sea, toward which the sun sets. This area is a barren waste in which whatever is built or sown comes to naught. It is completely dark except for an occasional flash of light from the setting sun, and its only inhabitants are a few exiles who wage continual battle with one another. It is a desolate land filled with discord, tumult, and enmity, with no trace of innate beauty.

Between this far western realm and the middle region first mentioned there is another occidental domain. While the far western is the site of the foundations of the earth, the second region contains the foundations of the heavens. Although it resembles the first in some ways, this domain is more luminous, although with borrowed light, and consists of a number of kingdoms arranged in sequential order. The inhabitants of these kingdoms are also exiles, but they have a more peaceful and sedentary nature, with each group residing in a specific location and not interfering in the affairs of the others.

The inhabitants of the first kingdom, that nearest to us, are small and quick and reside in eight cities. Then comes a smaller, slower group, who live in nine cities and who love writing, the occult sciences, and subtle crafts. Next is a land of eight cities full of gay, beautiful, and fun-loving people, ruled by a beautiful queen, and then a kingdom of five cities inhabited by a tall and handsome people whose influence is propitious from a distance but harmful at close range. Thereafter comes a warlike and bloodthirsty people who inhabit seven cities and are ruled by a rapacious red monarch; that is followed by a great kingdom of wise, just, fair, and magnanimous people, who live in seven cities. Next comes a land of dark and evil-minded people who conquer through stealth and patience; they have seven cities. Thereafter is a large kingdom whose inhabitants do not live in cities but reside individually in a large desert divided into twelve parts, through which the inhabitants of cities mentioned above periodically travel or briefly pause. Finally comes an area without borders or cities, which is populated by Spiritual Angels, and from whence the divine Command (*al-amr*) and Destiny (*al-qadar*) descend to those below.

The eastern side of the cosmos is divided as follows. Closest to the middle region is a completely uninhabited region filled with a vast desert, an overflowing sea, gusting winds, and a blazing fire. Then comes a realm of mountains, rivers, wind, and rain, filled with mineral riches but without vegetation. This is followed by a similar realm which includes plants, then another which includes animals, and finally the world in which the narrator resides, which encompasses humans as well.

Moving further to the East, one finds the sun rising between the two horns, or groups, of Satan; one of these groups flies, the other walks. The latter group consists of two tribes—the first are like beasts of prey, the other resembles beasts of the fields—who live on the left side of the Orient and do constant battle. Each member of the flying group displays a different fantastic form and resides on the right side of the Orient. The one who has seized control over this area has laid out five roads for communications that are watched over by armed guards who arrest and search all who enter. The guards then report their information to their chief, who, without examining it, relays it to the Treasurer, who then presents it to the King. The Treasurer also takes charge of the prisoners, entrusting their goods to yet another Treasurer.

At times some of the members of these two groups of demons enter the narrator's realm and insinuate themselves into the hearts of its inhabitants. The members of the rapacious tribe provoke all kinds of violent and savage behavior, while the members of the bestial tribe foment lascivious and lustful deeds. The flying group celebrates the life of the senses and belittles the spiritual dimension of life. A few members of these groups, however, separate themselves from their companions and approach the realm of the terrestrial angels; at this point they become good jinn who exert a benevolent influence on those they guide and assist.

Those who go beyond this region enter the climes of the angels. Connected with the earth is the domain of the two groups of terrestrial angels: those on the right side who know and command and those on the left who obey and act. Some members of these groups descend to the world of jinn and men, while others ascend to the heavens.

Whoever is allowed to pass through this clime emerges on the other side of the heavens and catches sight of the progeny of the First Existent, the Sole, Obeyed Monarch. In this realm one first encounters industrious and pious servants of the King, whose task it is to maintain the glorious and dazzling edifices of their ruler's domain. Next comes yet another group of servants who are in direct and intimate contact with their ruler, each occupying a fixed place and rank in his service. Highest in rank among these is one they regard as their father.

Finally, there is the King himself, whose beauty and bounty are beyond description. The glory of this monarch is manifest to all, but most cannot see him because of the weakness of their faculties. Those fortunate souls who do catch a glimpse of him stand transfixed in contemplation. He amply rewards those few who emigrate toward him, so that they feel wretched when they must depart.

Ḥayy concludes his account by stating that it is only because he serves his Ruler by speaking of him that he has consented to be distracted from uninterrupted contemplation of him.

Such, in summarized form, is the story of *Ḥayy ibn Yaqẓân*. The first point to be made concerning this treatise is that it does not represent doctrines, esoteric or otherwise, substantially disparate from those embodied in Avicenna's philosophical system. Despite differences in structure, tone, and aesthetic effect, *Ḥayy ibn Yaqẓân* correlates, or can be made to correlate, with Avicenna's explication of his logos theories. The commentaries of Ibn Zailâ (d. 440/1048) or al-Jûzjânî, as well Goichon's modern study of the text based on these commentaries and her own extensive knowledge of Avicenna's system, amply demonstrate that the details of *Ḥayy ibn Yaqẓân* concur with Avicenna's philosophical ideas point by point. Goichon's assertion that "all the ideas of the text, confronted phrase by phrase, often word by word, can be found in Avicenna's philosophical works, works printed and well known" can hardly be disputed by anyone who has closely studied the text from this perspective.[44]

Thus the narrator of *Ḥayy ibn Yaqẓân* symbolizes the rational soul, his three companions represent lower elements of human personality, while Ḥayy himself stands for the Active Intelligence. The Occident refers to the realm of matter, ranging from the variegated classes of terrestrial existence to the more subtle echelons of the heavenly spheres and orbs. The Orient, conversely, represents the hierarchical structure of the realm of pure Form, ranging from the forms of the Four Elements, through the human rational soul and the celestial Souls and Intelligences, and culminating in the Necessary Existent. The middle arena, where Ḥayy meets the narrator of the story, symbolizes the domain of abstract rational thought (in Avicenna's curriculum, this is the point of contact between the final part of the *Psychology* which consummates his *Physics* and the beginning of his *Metaphysics*), where the rational soul and the Active Intelligence first encounter one another directly. To comprehend the nature of this encounter more intimately, however, as well as how it is symbolized in *Ḥayy ibn Yaqẓân*, we must first gain a more detailed understanding of Avicenna's theory of the soul.[45]

Notes

1. Cf. Edward Booth, *Aristotelian Aporetic Ontology in Islamic and Christian Thinkers*, Cambridge Studies in Medieval Life and Thought (Cambridge, London, and New York: Cambridge University Press, 1983) 111:

> [In *ash-Shifâ'*] we have here a foretaste of the systematic exposition of philosophical and theological themes in lengthy works which characterizes Western 'scholasticism'. The motivation was the same: a diffuse and even a good literary style could not encompass the material. It was necessary to take into account divergent opinions on problematic questions, and adjudicate between them, as the subject matter was expounded in ordered sequence; and all consistently with a sustained theme. Though it was not his only literary genre, Ibn Sînâ's virtual creation of this style in *ash-Shifâ'* was of even greater importance for the Christian scholastics than it was for Islam.

Despite this passion for system, there are certain key places where Avicenna's language suffers from ambiguity; Fazlur Rahman notes that "we must take notice of the fact that Avicenna's terminology is always shifting," Razlur Rahman, *Prophecy in Islam: Philosophy and Orthodoxy*, Midway Reprint (Chicago and London: University of Chicago Press, 1979) 19.

2. Here we concur with Henry Corbin, who states in regard to Avicenna that the "unity of a human personality, and of a philosopher's personality, cannot be that of a monotony or an invariability; it is the unity of a central intuition that subordinates to itself and orders all the successive data and experiences of life." (*Avicenna*, 278). Commentators, on the other hand, have different aims; compare, for example, Booth's comments (in *Aristotelian Aporetic Ontology*, 29) on the relationship between Aristotle and Alexander of Aphrodisias:

> From Aristotle to Alexander there is a change in style from that of the intense reflection of an original thinker who makes the best use of language's inadequacies, even at the cost of some inconsistency, to that of a commentator wishing (for the sake of a readership) to reduce the thoughts of his subjects to a manageable order, and to expound them with impeccable clarity.

3. Avicenna devotes all of Book Eight of *ash-Shifâ': al-Ilâhiyyât*, 327–70, to the subject of the Necessary Existent. See also *an-Najât*, 261–88; *'Uyûn al-ḥikma*, 40–53; *al-Ishârât wa-t-tanbîhât*, 3:28–55; *al-Hidâya*, 260–73; *Dânish-nâma-yi 'Alâ'î: Ilâhiyyât*, trans., 47–71. Cf. Herbert A. Davidson, "Alfarabi and Avicenna on the Active Intellect," *Viator: Medieval and Renaissance Studies* 3 (1972) 155–56.

4. *ash-Shifâ': al-Ilâhiyyât*, 403; *an-Najât*, 320; *Sharḥ kitâb* Athûlûjiyâ *al-mansûb ilâ Arisṭû*, 59–66.

5. *ash-Shifâ': al-Ilâhiyyât*, 406; *an-Najât*, 314.

6. For this latter term, see *ash-Shifâ': al-Ilâhiyyât*, 411, 413.

7. *ash-Shifâ': al-Ilâhiyyât*, 406; *an-Najât*, 314.

8. *ash-Shifâ': al-Ilâhiyyât*, 387; Davidson, "Alfarabi and Avicenna," 158; Michot, *La destinée de l'homme selon Avicenne*, 172, note 112.

9. *ash-Shifâ': al-Ilâhiyyât* 386–87, 406–7; Avicenna considered the nature of the celestial Soul's relation to the separate Intelligence and the sphere "mysterious," see Michot, *La destinée de l'homme selon Avicenne*, 110–18, esp. p. 115, note 45.

10. *ash-Shifâ': al-Ilâhiyyât* 387–93; *an-Najât*, 295–302; *Fi l-'ishq*, 2–5, 21–22; trans. Emil L. Fackenheim, "A Treatise on Love by Ibn Sînâ," *Medieval Studies* 7 (1945), 212–13, 224–25.

11. *ash-Shifâ': al-Ilâhiyyât*, 391–92; *an-Najât*, 302. I translate *shauq* as "yearning," *'ishq* as "love," and *iltidhâdh* as "feeling of pleasure."

12. *ash-Shifâ': al-Ilâhiyyât*, 410–14, 435–36. The full account of Avicenna's cosmogony and cosmology is contained in *ash-Shifâ': al-Ilâhiyyât*, 373–432 (Book Nine); for epitomes of the schema of emanation, see *ash-Shifâ': al-Ilâhiyyât*, 401; *an-Najât*, 309–10, 334–37; *al-Hidâya*, 274–79; *Fi l-'ishq*, 23–26, Emil L. Fackenheim, trans., "A Treatise on Love," 225–28; and *an-Nairûziyya*, 93–94. Useful summaries are Corbin, *Avicenna*, 93–101, 366–71; Pseudo-Avicenna, *Risâla dar ḥaqîqat wa-kaifiyyat-i silsila-yi maujûdât wa-tasalsul-i asbâb wa-musabbabât*, Intishârât-i anjuman-i âthâr-i millî 18 (Tehran: Âstân-i dânishgâh, 1952); and Nasr, *An Introduction to Islamic Cosmological Doctrines*, 202–14, which also surveys the generally contemporaneous cosmological systems of the Ikhwân aṣ-Ṣafâ' and al-Birûnî; also Gardet, *La pensée religieuse d'Avicenne*, 38–68; Michael Marmura, "Some Aspects of Avicenna's Theory of God's Knowledge of Particulars," *JAOS* 82 (1962) 305–6; Netton, *Allâh Transcendent*, 162–74; and Davidson, "Alfarabi and Avicenna," 156–58.

13. *Fi l-'ishq*, 22–27, trans. Fackenheim, "A Treatise on Love," 225–28.

14. This concept is Plotinian, of course; see A. H. Armstrong on Plotinus in Armstrong, ed., *The Cambridge History of Later Greek and Early Medieval Philosophy*, rev. ed. (Cambridge, London, and New York: Cambridge University Press, 1970) esp. 258–63, where relevant passages from the *Enneads* are cited. The term itself (*al-ma'âd*) is Qur'ânic in origin, see *EI*², 5:892–94.

15. As Avicenna argues in *al-Ishârât wa-t-tanbîhât*, 4:20–25, human beings have many urges, as each psychological faculty attempts to fulfill its innate desire; but the species' defining purpose is rational.

16. Indeed, the final chapter of Book Nine of *ash-Shifâ': al-Ilâhiyyât*, 2:423–32, is called "The Return" (*al-ma'âd*); for other renditions of this "plot," see Chapters Four, Five and Seven below.

17. The interplay between unity and multiplicity is, of course, a leitmotif of philosophy from Hellenic and Hellenistic times, see P. Merlan's "Greek Philosophy from Plato to Plotinus, in Armstrong, ed., *The Cambridge History of Later Greek and Early Medieval Philosophy*, 21–23, but also throughout his chapter, including references to "One" and "Dyad" in the index.

18. For more on this point, see Chapter Seven below.

19. *ash-Shifâ': al-Madkhal*, 12 (my emphasis); *Fî aqsâm al-'ulûm al-'aqliyya*, 71.

20. Cf. Gutas, *Avicenna and the Aristotelian Tradition*, 220–21.

21. *ash-Shifâ': al-Madkhal*, 12; *Dânish-nâma-yi 'Alâ'î: Ilâhiyyât*, trans., 11.

22. *ash-Shifâ': al-Madkhal*, 12; cf. *ash-Shifâ': an-Nafs*, 184–85, and *ash-Shifâ': al-Ilâhiyyât*, 4.

23. *ash-Shifâ': al-Madkhal*, 14; *Fî aqsâm al-'ulûm al-'aqliyya*, 72–74; *Dânish-nâma-yi 'Alâ'î: Ilâhiyyât*, trans., 11–12.

24. *ash-Shifâ': al-Madkhal*, 12; *Fî aqsâm al-'ulûm al-'aqliyya*, 72.

25. *ash-Shifâ': al-Madkhal*, 14.

26. *ash-Shifâ': al-Madkhal*, 14; *Fî aqsâm al-'ulûm al-'aqliyya*, 72; *Dânish-nâma-yi 'Alâ'î: Ilâhiyyât*, trans., 12.

27. *Fî aqsâm al-ʿulûm al-ʿaqliyya*, 74–75; *Dânish-nâma-yi ʿAlâʾî: Ilâhiyyât*, trans., 13.

28. *Dânish-nâma-yi ʿAlâʾî: Ilâhiyyât*, trans., 12; *ash-Shifâʾ: al-Madkhal*, 14; cf. *Fî aqsâm al-ʿulûm al-ʿaqliyya*, 72.

29. *Fî aqsâm al-ʿulûm al-ʿaqliyya*, 76.

30. *ash-Shifâʾ: al-Madkhal*, 14; *Fî aqsâm al-ʿulûm al-ʿaqliyya*, 72–73.

31. *Fî aqsâm al-ʿulûm al-ʿaqliyya*, 76–77. For a succinct description of this tripartite division of philosophy, as well as a more detailed examination of the nature and purpose of metaphysics, see *ash-Shifâʾ: al-Ilâhiyyât*, 1:3–28. This division of philosophy into three parts had become more or less standard by the time of Aristotle, cf. his *Metaphysics* 1026a, p. 1620; see also Merlan, "Greek Philosophy from Plato to Plotinus," in Armstrong, ed., *The Cambridge History of Later Greek and Early Medieval Philosophy*, esp. pp. 15–19, but also throughout Merlan's article. For an excursus on possible sources for Avicenna's division, see Parviz Morewedge's commentary in his translation of *Dânish-nâma-yi ʿAlâʾî: Ilâhiyyât*, 148–56.

32. *Fî aqsâm al-ʿulûm al-ʿaqliyya*, 75–79.

33. *Fî aqsâm al-ʿulûm al-ʿaqliyya*, 78. Cf. Qur'ân 26.193 for Faithful Spirit and Qur'ân 2.87 and 2.253 for the Holy Spirit; see also the text of the *Miʿrâj Nâma* in Chapter Six below.

34. *Fî aqsâm al-ʿulûm al-ʿaqliyya*, 79–80. Avicenna considers the controversy over whether logic should properly be regarded as an integral part of philosophy or merely its introduction to be "vain and foolish" (*ash-Shifâʾ: al-Madkhal*, 16). On the place of logic in Avicenna's system see also Gutas, *Avicenna and the Aristotelian Tradition*, 265–85; Avicenna, *Remarks and Admonitions, Part One: Logic*, trans. Shams C. Inati (Toronto: Pontifical Institute of Mediaeval Studies, 1984) 9–11; and Chapter Seven below.

35. *Fî aqsâm al-ʿulûm al-ʿaqliyya*, 77; *ash-Shifâʾ: al-Ilâhiyyât*, vol. 1, "Introduction," 21–23. For Avicenna's position on astrology, see Ülken, ed., *Ibn Sînâ Risâleleri* 2, *Risâla fî ibṭâl aḥkâm an-nujûm*, 49–67.

36. Gutas, *Avicenna and the Aristotelian Tradition*, 187–94.

37. Gutas, in his *Avicenna and the Aristotelian Tradition*, has assembled and translated a number of base texts in which Avicenna expresses his opinions of his fellow philosophers; see pp. 34–35, 47–49, 55–56, 60, 64, 67–72.

38. On al-Fârâbî, see *EI*², 2:778–82; Fakhry, *A History of Islamic Philosophy*, 107–28; and Miriam Galston, *Politics and Excellence: The Political Philosophy of Alfarabi* (Princeton, N.J.: Princeton University Press, 1990).

39. See Thérèse-Anne Druart's typology of al-Fârâbî's works, "Alfarabi and Emanationism," in J. F. Wippel, ed., *Studies in Medieval Philosophy*, Studies in Philosophy and the History of Philosophy 17 (Washington, D.C.: Catholic University of America Press, 1987) 23–43.

40. Muhsin Mahdi, "Alfarabi," in Leo Strauss and Joseph Copley, eds., *History of Political Philosophy* (Chicago: Rand McNally, 1963) 161–62. See also Davidson, "Alfarabi and Avicenna," 178: "Not only is Avicenna's position wider and more consistent, it is also more carefully supported with philosophic argumentation than Alfarabi's, which generally is simply asserted." For a discussion of the various

interpretations that scholars have entertained concerning al-Fârâbî's styles of writing, see Galston, *Politics and Excellence*, 35–54, 180–221.

41. See, for example, Avicenna's introduction to the Sophistics (*as-Safsaṭa*) in *ash-Shifâ'*, 4–5, trans. Gutas, *Avicenna and the Aristotelian Tradition*, 34.

42. Such as *al-Mabda' wa-l-ma'âd, 'Uyûn al-ḥikma, al-Hidâya*, *an-Najât*, and *Dânish-nâma-yi 'Alâ'î*.

43. This summary is based on Mehren's edition of *Ḥayy ibn Yaqẓân* in *Traités mystiques*, fasc. 1, 1–22; English trans. (from the French) in Corbin, *Avicenna*, 137–50, and, with al-Jûzjânî's commentary, 281–381.

44. Goichon, *Le récit de Ḥayy ibn Yaqẓân*, 9; see also her *The Philosophy of Avicenna and Its Influence on Medieval Europe*, 8. The former work contains a French translation and a full analysis of sources. Mehren's edition cites selections from the commentary by Ibn Zailâ; I have also relied on the full text of Ibn Zailâ's commentary in the British Library manuscript Add. 16659. Corbin has printed the Persian text of the commentary, which he attributes to al-Jûzjânî, as the third volume of his *Avicenne et le récit visionnaire*.

45. For further decoding of the allegorical structure of *Ḥayy ibn Yaqẓân*, see Chapters Five, Seven, and Eight below; also Goichon's *Le récit de Ḥayy ibn Yaqẓân*, or Corbin, *Avicenna*, 281–378; and Netton, *Allâh Transcendent*, who analyzes the allegory from the viewpoint of Roland Barthes's semiology.

4. Avicenna's Theory of the Soul

Psychology, the study of the soul, held a particular fascination for Avicenna. That the subject clearly lies near the heart of his concern for philosophy is indicated by the fact that he devoted numerous major and minor tracts to the subject and returned repeatedly to its elaboration throughout his life.[1] Avicenna's psychological doctrines are stable in their general parameters, but his individual presentations of them differ according to considerations of philosophical intent, generic format, and audience of address.[2] Like any psychology aspiring to comprehensiveness, Avicenna's theory addresses four considerations:

1. The nature of the soul
2. The faculties of the soul
3. The origin of the soul
4. The final end of the soul

The Nature of the Soul

At the beginning of his "Explanation of the Condition of Prophethood and Apostleship" in the *Miʿrâj Nâma*, Avicenna posits an essential bifurcation in human beings. Humans, he says, consist of body and soul. The body is a "gathering" of humors and a "combination" of elements, "adorned" with parts, each with a specific function: the foot walks, the hand grasps, and so on.[3] More detailed description of the elements, humors, and parts may be found in Avicenna's medical encyclopedia, *al-Qânûn fi ṭ-ṭibb* (The Canon of Medicine), where he explains that the material elements (*arkân*) are "simple bodies which are the primary components of human and other bodies."[4] They are four in number: earth (heavy, cold, and dry), water (heavy, cold, and wet), fire (light, hot, and dry), and air (light, hot, and wet). In their diverse combinations, or temperaments (*mizâj*), these elements constitute all the world's material bodies. The more symmetrical their mixture the more perfect the result. The human body, according to Avicenna, is the most symmetrical, and thus the most perfect, material composition.[5]

The humors (*akhlâṭ*) are bodily fluids generated from the intake of nutrients. The principal humors are also four in number: blood (hot and moist), phlegm (cold and moist), choler, or yellow bile (hot and dry), and melancholy, or black bile (cold and dry). The appropriate amount of each humor in the body and the harmony of their proportionate relationships determine a person's physical health and well-being.[6]

Finally, there are the parts or members (*a'ḍâ'*) of the body. They consist of: (1) basic components (such as flesh, skin, or bones); (2) limbs (head, hand, leg, arm, etc.); and (3) organs (liver, heart, brain, and so on). The relationship among the elements, humors, and parts of the body is hierarchically contingent. The elements, in certain combinations, produce nutrients appropriate for humans, which, when consumed, generate and sustain the body's fluids, or humors. The humors, in turn, generate and sustain the body's solid members. As Avicenna says, the bodily parts are "generated from the first mixture of the salubrious humors, just as the humors are the first mixture of the elements."[7]

Soul, for Avicenna, is an equivocal term. His generic definition is that the soul is "the first entelechy of a natural body possessing organs that potentially has life."[8] Beyond this, Avicenna offers relational descriptions. In regard to the otherwise inert body, the soul is the vital or activating principle. In relation to the body's material constituents, soul is form. In regard to entelechy (final end or perfection), the soul is a particular life form's specifying differentia, separating species from genus.[9]

According to Avicenna, the human soul is a union of three subsidiary parts, each of which is also usually termed *soul* (*nafs*). Each of these subsidiary souls is distinguished by its own specific functions and entelechy. As he states in *an-Najât*, soul is

> like a single genus divided somehow into three parts. One of them is the vegetable (soul), the first entelechy of a natural body possessing organs in regard to reproduction, growth, and nourishment. The second is the animal soul, the first entelechy of a natural body possessing organs in regard to perceiving particulars and moving through will. And the third is the human soul, the first entelechy of a natural body possessing organs in regard to what is related to its performing actions stemming from rational choiceand deduction through opinion and in regard to its perceiving universal matters.[10]

This tripartite division of the human soul into vegetable, animal, and rational parts is Avicenna's standard philosophical position.[11] The relationship of these parts to the whole is *like* (i.e., analogous, not homologous) the relationship between species and genus.[12] Each subsidiary soul resides in a particular organ of the body: the vegetable soul in the liver, the animal in the heart, and the rational in the brain.[13] Each is the active principle (*mabda'*) that governs certain types (*ajnâs*) of actions or operations.[14] In *ash-Shifâ'*, Avicenna points out that the various actions that stem from each individual soul may be more or less perfect, depending on individual choice, the capability of the organ, or factors external to the body.[15] The relationship among the three souls is hierarchical. The animal soul subsumes the faculties of the vegetable soul but has its own independent operations. Similarly, the rational soul helps coordinate the activities of the animal and vegetable souls but has certain faculties which they do not possess.[16]

Physical Soul Versus Spiritual Soul

Underlying this division of the soul, however, is a more basic conceptual dichotomy, that of physical and spiritual souls (the terms are mine, not Avicenna's). On the one hand, Avicenna, following Aristotle and the Stoics, regards the soul as the vital principle of all life forms, a "particular," material, terrestrial principle which originates and dies with the body. On the other hand, influenced by Platonic and Neoplatonic idealism, he believes the soul to be essentially angelic in nature, "universal," spiritual, celestial, immortal. In accordance with this dichotomous doctrine, the physical soul encompasses the vegetable and animal souls which pass away upon the death of the body, while the spiritual soul is the rational soul, an independent, immaterial, immortal substance.[17]

Avicenna deduces the existence of the physical soul through empirical observation. There is a vital principle which generates the movements, sensations, and actions of the otherwise lifeless, inert material body. This principle is the physical soul.[18] He also adduces numerous proofs for the existence of the rational soul as an immaterial substance, imprinted upon but essentially separate from the body. Avicenna's most famous demonstration for this doctrine is that of the "suspended person."

Imagine, he says, a person created instantaneously, perfect except for the fact that he or she cannot perceive the external world, suspended in the air, which he or she cannot even feel, and cut off from any bodily sensation or perception. Since this person can neither perceive his or her body nor use it to sense the external world, the only evidence he or she has of existence would be his or her own self-consciousness. This awareness of self proves the existence of an "I-ness" (*aniyya*), an ego, independent of physical perception, and therefore immaterial, self-sufficient, and hence a substance. This "I-ness" is the rational soul.[19]

Although this conceptual dichotomy between the physical and spiritual senses of the term soul recurs throughout Avicenna's psychology, he consistently downplays its contradictory nature. Indeed, he actively denies its existence, contending that the soul is an intrinsic unity, the substratum of all psychic faculties. After all, he argues, faculties interact and affect one another and therefore must be grounded in a single substratum. Moreover, the activities of each faculty are perceived by a single ego ("*I* hurt my hand," "*I* am angry," "*I* think"), proving that the soul is a unified entity.[20]

This, however, does not resolve the tension between the dichotomy's elements. In fact, it is not too much to say that the contradiction between the physical and spiritual souls lies near the heart of Avicenna's fascination with psychology. It certainly forms the emotive core of his allegories, each of which, as Corbin has argued, entails *ta'wîl* in the literal sense of the word, a "coming home," a flash of awakening, a shimmering revelation of self-recognition, an instant when the spiritual soul is called upon to recognize that it is more than—indeed, *essentially* other than—the physical soul.[21]

This tension is noticeable even in Avicenna's logos texts. When defining the soul in *Kitâb al-ḥudûd* (The Book of Definitions), for instance, Avicenna offers two separate definitions. In regard to natural life forms—plants, animals, and humans—he gives the above-cited definition of the physical soul as "the first entelechy of a natural body possessing organs that potentially has life."[22] He then offers a second definition, which pertains only to humans and angels, stating that the soul is

> an incorporeal substance, the entelechy of the body, moving it through choice, actually or potentially, on the basis of a rational—that is, intellectual—principle. Potentiality is the differentia [*faṣl*] of the human soul; actuality is the differentia or property of the angelic soul.[23]

In other words, he provides independent definitions for the two basic meanings of "soul." Similarly, at the beginning of *Risâla fi n-nafs*, Avicenna wrestles with the problem of formulating a general definition for the soul that can incorporate the activities and essential nature of more than two of its parts. Although in this tract he generally uses the terms vegetable, animal, and rational souls, here he divides the human soul into vegetable, animal, and angelic souls (*an-nafs al-malakiyya*), for at this point the dichotomy between his two concepts of "soul" forces explicit acknowledgment of their essential incongruence. On the one hand, he states, defining the soul as "the principle of intentional actions" encompasses the animal and angelic parts of the soul but excludes the vegetable soul. On the other hand, defining it as "an agent of oppositional [*mutaqâbila*] activities" includes the vegetable and animal souls but leaves out the angelic soul.[24] This dilemma, he explains, stems from the equivocality of the term. Soul, in its absolute sense, is the vital principle, and as such inextricably connected to corporeal bodies. Applying the term *soul* to human beings' immaterial substantial nature, therefore, is appropriate only metaphorically or by association. More properly, the correct determination for this latter entity is *intellect*.[25] In spite of this admission, Avicenna continues to use the term soul, partly to maintain the integrity of his doctrine of the soul's intrinsic unity, partly, perhaps, because for Avicenna *intellect* is itself an equivocal term with more applications than the term *soul*.[26]

This dichotomy in Avicenna's thought between physical and spiritual souls explains why his terminology shifts according to which of the two aspects of the term is being emphasized. In *al-Qânûn fi ṭ-ṭibb* or *Fî ta'bîr ar-ru'yâ*, for example, Avicenna discusses the soul from a physiological perspective and therefore emphasizes the physical soul, which he divides into "faculties" (*quwâ*) rather than "parts," employing nonphilosophical terminology. From this perspective, the first "faculty" of the soul is the natural faculty (*al-quwwa ṭ-ṭabî'î*), whose functions correspond to those of the vegetable soul. However, the animal faculty that follows does not correspond to the philosophical conception of the animal soul but is limited to the meaning of vital spirit or life principle (*ar-rûḥ*), the subtle substance generated in the heart by the gases of the humors. The third "faculty" is the psychic one (*al-quwwa n-nafsâniyya*), which encompasses all the motive and perceptive (but not the intellectual) faculties of both the animal and rational souls.[27]

Presumably, Avicenna employs the term *faculty* here because his discussion pertains to the physical constitution of human beings from the perspective of medicine, and a more profound delineation of either the concept "soul" or individual "parts" of the soul would be irrelevant in this context. In other words, he uses the term *natural faculty* simply because *vegetable soul* might cause physicians unnecessary confusion. For similar reasons, Avicenna divides the characteristics of the philosophical animal soul into two, continuing to use the term *animal faculty* in the radically truncated sense of "vital principle," while allocating the animal soul's motive and perceptive faculties to the "psychic faculty." At the close of his discussion, he mentions that rationality (*nuṭq*) is among the "psychic" faculties but adds that detailed knowledge of human rationality falls beyond the purview of physicians.[28]

At the other end of the spectrum, Avicenna often concentrates so much on the rational soul in his philosophical works that the lowly physical soul is virtually forgotten. Indeed, by the end of his description of the "angelic" or "sanctified" prophetic soul, even the lesser "potential" faculties of the rational soul assume marginal importance.[29]

Avicenna's insistence that humans partake of both physical and spiritual souls is central to his vision of humankind, which, for him, represents the point of conjunction between the terrestrial and celestial worlds. As he says in the *Miʿrâj Nâma*:

> For if (their) bases were the animal and natural [vegetable] souls, humans would not be differentiated from other animals. They would be an (equal) partner of all animals. But if He [i.e., the Necessary Existent] only put the psychic (soul in humans), they would have nothing in common with other animals. Hence He gave humans all three (souls), so that they share the animal and natural (souls) with all but in regard to their psychic (soul) are nobler than all.[30]

This anthropology determines the dualistic nature of Avicenna's psychology and tremendously influences the structure of his ethics, politics, and metaphysics. It also reveals the intellectual underpinnings of his allegories and sheds light on his otherwise confusing use of psychological terminology in such works as the *Fî taʿbîr ar-ru'yâ* and the *Miʿrâj Nâma*. It is therefore essential to understand Avicenna's equivocal conception of the term *soul*, and his flexible use of terminology in regard to it, if one wishes to comprehend those treatises in which he uses the term *soul* in three senses. In the *Miʿrâj Nâma*, for example, Avicenna initially discusses soul in the context of the dichotomy between soul and body, employing the Persian word *jân* to signify "spirit," or "animate-soul," the vital principle which animates the otherwise lifeless, material body (*tan*). Later, he refers to the human soul in the general sense of the term, physical and spiritual souls unified in the human body, using the terms *nafs* or *rûḥ* interchangeably. Thereafter, he employs either of the same two words, *nafs* or *rûḥ*, to signify any of the human soul's three parts, the vegetable, animal, or rational souls.

Instead of using the philosophical terms vegetable, animal, and rational for the parts of the soul, however, Avicenna first employs terms from *al-Qânûn*, that is, natural (*ṭabîʿî*), animal (*ḥayavânî*), and psychic (*nafsânî*). Nevertheless, his description of the faculties that each subsidiary soul governs makes it clear that although his terminology is medical, his conceptual framework is philosophical. Indeed, he quickly reverts to the use of the philosophical term rational, instead of psychic, soul. Avicenna's reason for adopting medical terminology in the early part of the *Miʿrâj Nâma* is thus a matter of rhetorical presentation.[31]

Metaphors for the Soul

In the *Miʿrâj Nâma* Avicenna does not offer a philosophical description of the relationship between the body and the soul, or of the latter's parts or faculties. However, the absence here of precise philosophical definitions for the soul or proofs of its substantiality is not surprising, since Avicenna composed the treatise for a general educated audience of the intellectual and religious elite who did not question the existence and value of the soul. Once he posits the general distinction between soul and body, Avicenna relies on two metaphors to subsume, albeit imprecisely, the main characteristics of his philosophical doctrines.

The first metaphor is that of steed and rider, the former referring to the body, the latter to the soul. The second metaphor is that of "instrument" and "splendor" or "honor." Although neither metaphor comprehensively explains Avicenna's philosophical doctrines concerning the nature of the soul (nor are they intended to do so), because they do express essential aspects of these doctrines' intent they serve Avicenna's general purposes within the context of the *Miʿrâj Nâma*.

In one sense, the rider is the mount's enlivening principle, for it is through the rider that the dichotomy, rider-mount, even comes into existence. The rider is the mount's specific defining criterion, differentiating the concept "mount" from the category of animals that are suited to serve as mounts—horses, donkeys, camels, and so on—but whose essential generic property is "animal," not "mount." Moreover, as the principle which transforms the raw material, animal, into the concept of mount, the rider may also be viewed as the latter's "form." Finally, since the rider is the mount's source of direction, and thus of movement and choice, the rider provides a second entelechy, or final end, for the mount. Without a rider, the mount is inadequate, purposeless, and thus imperfect (as a mount, that is).[32]

In regard to the second metaphor, an agent may be viewed as the "splendor" or "honor" of an instrument because it is only through active use that the instrument's full potential, its first and second entelechies, can be realized.[33] Avicenna, however, has a more pressing reason to mix his metaphors in regard to the human soul. As stated above, the human soul is the "splendor" or "honor" of the body because it possesses rationality, a heavenly quality shared solely with the angels.[34]

In general, it is important to be aware that although Avicenna's concept of the soul is both uniform and comprehensive, his texts emphasize different aspects of it according to determinants of context, format, and intent. As we have seen, in *al-Qânûn* Avicenna adumbrates the parts and functions of the soul but tends to concentrate on its aspect of "life principle." More abstruse investigations into its nature, he states there, are best left to philosophers. His mainstream philosophical texts, *ash-Shifâ'*, its summary, *an-Najât*, and his shorter handbooks, such as *'Uyûn al-ḥikma, al-Hidâya*, or *Dânish-nâma-yi 'Alâ'î*, concentrate on providing an overall portrait of the soul, emphasizing the holistic unity of the concept rather than its internal contradictions. Allusions to the tensions between the concepts of physical and spiritual souls, when they do occur, are oblique, cloaked in religious terminology, as in the final part of *al-Ishârât wa-t-tanbîhât*, or by the symbolic indirectness of allegory, as in *Ḥayy ibn Yaqẓân, Risâlat aṭ-ṭair*, or the *Mi'râj Nâma*.

The Faculties of the Soul

The human soul, we have seen, has three parts: the natural or vegetable soul, the animal soul, and the psychic or rational soul. Each part has its own purpose or entelechy, and each governs faculties that perform specific functions.

The Natural or Vegetable Soul

The natural or vegetable soul is "the first entelechy of a natural body possessing organs in regard to reproduction, growth, and nourishment." Therefore, it naturally governs the body's activities as regards these functions.[35] Subsidiary to the nutritive faculty are the "serving" faculties of expulsion or elimination, digestion, attraction or absorption, and retention.[36]

The Animal Soul

The animal soul is "the first entelechy of a natural body possessing organs in regard to perceiving particulars and moving through will."[37] In other words, life forms possessing the animal soul differ from those that only have the natural or vegetable soul in their ability to move freely as well as their capacity for sensual perception. The motive faculty of the animal soul governs two kinds of movement: active (*fâʿil*) and impulsive (*bâʿitha*). Active movement, what one might call instinctive movement, is

> distributed through the nerves and muscles, and its function is to contract the muscles and pull the tendons and ligaments towards the starting point of the movement, or to relax them and stretch them so that they move away from the starting point.[38]

Impulsive, that is, voluntary, movement is of two types: that based on desire or concupiscence (*shahwâniyya* or *shawqiyya*) and that stemming from anger or irascibility (*ghaḍabiyya*). The concupiscent faculty "impels movement that draws one near to things imagined necessary or useful, seeking pleasure." The irascible faculty "impels movement through which one repels things imagined harmful or destructive, seeking mastery (over them)."[39] These two faculties cause bodily movement as a result of the provocations of the physical senses, hunger or pain, or inner perception, whether sensual—attraction toward something beautiful, repulsion from something ugly—or conceptual—love for even an ugly baby, or fear of even a beautiful lion.

The perceptive faculty is also divided into two subsections: external senses and internal senses. The external senses are the five senses: sight, hearing, smell, taste, and touch.[40] The internal senses consist of a hierarchy of five faculties which do not immediately perceive the external world, but instead apprehend *sensibles*, forms abstracted from material entities perceived by the five external senses. Some internal senses

> perceive the forms of sensibles, some perceive the meanings of sensibles. Some . . . perceive and act together, some perceive and do not act. Some have primary perception, some have secondary perception.[41]

In regard to the first dichotomy, Avicenna gives the example of a sheep who uses certain internal faculties to perceive the form of an approaching wolf, but uses others to apprehend the significance of the wolf's approach, that is, that it presents a danger from which the sheep should flee. Some faculties both "perceive and act," in that they receive information and then process it, while other faculties "perceive and do not act" because they simply store the information they receive. Finally, a faculty has "primary perception" when it directly apprehends a sensible, and "secondary perception" when it receives information through the agency of another internal faculty.[42]

Closest to the external senses among the internal senses is the faculty of *common sense* (*al-ḥiss al-mushtarak* or *banṭâsiyâ*, i.e., fantasy). As the *Mi'râj Nâma* puts it, common sense is "the form-recipient of all things." It receives, orders, and coordinates the forms of all the empirical *sensibilia* perceived by the five external senses. This faculty organizes (i.e., both perceives and acts upon) this information so that it represents correctly the physical entities of the external world. Without these operations, one would perceive the forms provided by each external sense individually, that is, whiteness, roundness, hardness, smoothness, in regard to a wooden ball, without any idea of how they combined in existents. Common sense resides in the first part of the front ventricle of the brain.[43]

Although common sense apprehends and organizes sensible forms, it cannot retain them. This is the task of the *retentive imagination* (*khayâl*), also called *representation* (*muṣawwira*). Situated in the back part of the first ventricle of the brain, it preserves information received by common sense for distribution later to other faculties. Avicenna explains the distinction among the external senses, the common sense, and the retentive imagination by citing an example. Consider, he says, a drop of rain. Since the drop falls vertically, one can see it as straight; but since it is simultaneously turning in a circular motion, one can also see it as round. In order to perceive the drop from these different perspectives, one must view it several times. The external senses cannot do this, for they only see an entity as it is. Common sense perceives the raindrop immediately, as the senses do, but also sequentially, from the various perspectives of the drop's inherent forms: extension, straightness, or roundness. The retentive imagination, finally, apprehends the raindrop as perceived by both the external senses and common sense. It then performs the additional act of preserving these apprehensions, thus allowing one to recall images of the raindrop to mind even when it is no longer immediately present.[44]

Next in the hierarchy of the internal senses comes a faculty termed the *compositive imagination* (*mutakhayyila* or *mukhayyila*) in regard to animals, and the *cogitative* (*mufakkira*) faculty in regard to humans. This faculty, which resides in the middle ventricle of the brain, acts upon the sensible images stored in the retentive imagination. Its task is to separate and recombine these images in various ways. Hence, one is able to imagine such nonexistent entities as a man who flies or a mountain made of emerald.[45]

The *estimative faculty* (*wahm*) is the fourth internal sense. Estimation, which is located in the back part of the brain's middle ventricle, perceives "meanings" or "intentions" inherent in sensibles rather than merely their forms. It apprehends, to cite Avicenna's example, that a wolf should be fled from but that a young child should be treated gently and affectionately. Estimation is the chief governing faculty of the animal soul. It coordinates the activities of the other internal senses and thus guides animals in their actions. In humans, it performs the additional task of evaluating the empirical reality of the forms separated and recombined by the compositive imagination, permitting us to judge which are believable and which are fantastic.[46]

Finally, there is *memory*, the preservative (*ḥâfiẓa*) or recollective (*dhâkira, mutadhakkira*) faculty, situated in the rear ventricle of the brain. Memory is the storehouse of perceptions of the estimative faculty. Its function of preserving "meanings" or "intentions" for estimation is analogous to the retentive imagination's preservation of the "images" and "forms" of common sense. Memory is also termed *recollection* (*tadhakkur*) because in addition to storing information, it retrieves it for the estimative faculty in animals, and for both estimation and the intellect in humans.[47]

The Rational Soul

Human beings share the vegetable and animal souls with all other animals. They exceed them in perfection and nobility through possession of the rational soul.[48] The rational soul has two aspects: the *practical* faculty (or intellect) and the *theoretical* faculty (or intellect).

The practical faculty coordinates the relationship between the body and the vegetable and animal souls, on the one hand, and the theoretical faculty, on the other. It is "the principle that motivates the human body toward specific, particular actions, through deliberation, in accordance with opinions that it has derived from general usage (convention)."[49] This faculty is analogous to the appetitive part of the animal soul in that it produces swift emotional acts or responses, such as weeping or laughing. It is analogous to the imaginative and estimative faculties in that it devotes its attention to inferring the nature of transient activities and arts. The practical faculty, however, transcends those of the animal soul in that, in collaboration with the theoretical faculty, it can induce rational premises that are useful from practical ethical or political perspectives (that lying and oppression are evil, for example, but veracity and justice are good). The practical intellect's most important function, therefore, is to employ its inductions to guide, govern, and control the faculties and appetites of the lower souls. To the extent that it succeeds, the practical intellect promotes good ethical behavior. If the animal and vegetable souls gain mastery of the practical intellect, however, the natural order of the souls is perverted, and bad morals result.[50]

The second aspect of the rational soul is the theoretical faculty. This faculty deals only with universals, that is, rational concepts totally abstracted from matter. The theoretical faculty can, as we shall see in more detail in the next chapter, in some fashion intuit universals from the particulars derived from the animal soul's apprehensions and the practical intellect's interaction with external social conventions and opinions. It does so by stripping these particulars of most of their material attributes until it recognizes them as reflections of universals—the concept "humanity" as opposed to humans, for instance, or "justice" as opposed to good acts. The true sources of universal concepts, however, are the translunar Higher Principles (*al-mabâdi' al-'âliya*), that is, the celestial Intelligences, beginning with the Active Intelligence, ascending through the other celestial Intelligences, and culminating with the Necessary Existent.[51]

According to Avicenna, therefore, the rational soul has two aspects. The practical intellect looks downward, deriving particulars from the faculties of the lower soul, which is its window to the external material world. When it functions appropriately, the practical intellect governs the lower souls and thus produces virtuous action. The theoretical intellect, on the other hand, gazes upward. It receives universals from the celestial Intelligences, and employs them to learn about the cosmos and the place of human beings in it. As Avicenna says, the practical faculty produces "ethics" (*akhlâq*), while the theoretical faculty produces "knowledge" (*'ulûm*).[52]

The Divisions of the Theoretical Intellect

The theoretical intellect is either absolutely potential, relatively potential, or active. When it is absolutely potential, it has the capacity, although never used, to apprehend universals. Avicenna terms this epistemological condition the *material intellect* (*'aql hayûlânî*). He chooses the word "material" since this state is analogous to that of absolute matter before it receives any imprint of form. After the material intellect apprehends first intelligibles, that is, the *a priori* abstract logical premises that constitute the basic building blocks of rational thought (such as the law of contradiction, or that the whole is necessarily greater than the part), it becomes relatively potential and thus attains a state that Avicenna calls the *habitual intellect* (*ʿaql bi-l-malaka*). At this point, the intellect becomes capable of deducing second intelligibles through the use of syllogism. When it undertakes this operation, thus engaging in independent reasoning using both primary and secondary intelligibles, it attains a state that Avicenna calls the *actual intellect* (*ʿaql bi-l-fiʿl*). When the intellect is capable of doing this but does not actually do so, or does so unreflectively, in an automatic fashion, it is in a state of relative potentiality. However, when the theoretical intellect is actively engaged in rational inquiry, and is aware that it is so engaged, it attains the state of the *acquired intellect* (*ʿaql mustafâd*).

Avicenna compares these four states to a child learning to write. The child who has the innate capacity to write but does not yet know anything about writing is in a state of absolute potentiality. He or she then learns the principles of writing and the shapes of the letters but does not actually begin to write; at this point the child is in a state of relative potentiality. When he or she has learned to write, but is not doing so or is doing so without thinking about it, the child has achieved a state of relative actuality. Finally, when fully engaged in writing in an active, cognizant, and committed fashion, the child's activity is analogous to that of the acquired intellect.[53] According to Avicenna, attaining the stage of the acquired intellect "perfects the genus, animal, and the species, human being. Here human potential becomes comparable to the First Principles of all existence."[54]

The Origin of the Soul

Avicenna denies the preexistence of the human soul, asserting that it comes into being with the body. His proof for this rests on his presumption that the relation between soul and body is one of form and matter. If the soul existed before the body, it would be either a single soul or a multiplicity of souls. The latter is impossible because abstract forms are simple quiddities, not subject to internal divisions or individualities. Hence, the soul is material reception into individual bodies, each of which has its own unique arrangement of basic material constituents and dispositions that differentiates one soul from the next. Nor can souls preexist as a single soul, for this would mean that everyone participates in the same soul, which is obviously false. Therefore, concludes Avicenna, the individual soul comes into existence only when it joins the body. Every result has a cause; the cause of the soul is the Active Intelligence. Hence, when Avicenna states in the *Mi'râj Nâma* that Absolute Truth (*Ḥaqq*), or God, brought body and soul "each from a different world," he means that the body is brought from the world of Matter, while the soul comes from the world of Form inhabited by the celestial Intelligences.[55]

In spite of this doctrine, there are occasions when Avicenna implies that there is some kind of preexistent individual psychic identity for the soul. Both his "Ode on the Soul" and *Risâlat aṭ-ṭair*, for instance, seem to portray the soul more as a precorporeal sentient entity than as an unindividuated abstract form. Such personification may reflect the influence of the Neoplatonic, and even Gnostic, modes of thought that were part and parcel of the general intellectual milieu in which Avicenna lived. Plotinus's chapter "The Soul's Descent into Body," which begins the Arabic *Theology of Aristotle*, and corresponding parts of Avicenna's commentary on it, emote a cosmic dramaturgy that is closer to Gnostic myth than Neoplatonic doctrine. And although Neoplatonists (among whom Avicenna may justly be counted) struggled intellectually to resist Gnosticism's inherent dualism and its implacable enmity toward matter, nevertheless, at times they were sympathetic to the idea that although matter may not be evil, as Gnostics hold, it is intrinsically privative, less than good. References in Avicenna's writings to the individual preexistence of the soul may also be due to the inherent difficulty of referring to abstract concepts in narrative contexts without some measure of personification creeping in, an example of the fact that the use of concrete images for abstract premises can evoke presumably undesired connotations. The very use of the term *descent*, for example, denotes individual agency and some kind of negative consequence for the "one who descends." Very few spiritual beings of world mythology, one suspects, have ever had "descent" as their ideal final goal.[56]

In his commentary on the *Theology of Aristotle*, Avicenna also explains the reason for the soul's conjunction with matter. The soul "desires" material existence because in this way it attains its first entelechy; it "realizes" its innate "potential" for material existence. Subsequent possession and proper governance of material faculties thereafter pave the way for attainment of the soul's second and final entelechy, return to the spiritual world in a more actualized form.[57]

The Final End of the Soul[58]

Avicenna considers the question of the soul's final end from the perspective of entelechy. According to him, the ultimate purpose of human life is to fulfill the second entelechy of the rational soul. When individuals completely actualize the potential of the theoretical intellect, they perfect their rational souls, attain absolute happiness, and realize their purely angelic natures.[59] How this specifically comes about will be pursued in the next chapter, where I discuss Avicenna's epistemology. There is, however, another, more prosaic dimension to the concept of final end. This is the question of terminal destination, of where the soul finally ends up—in other words, the problem of the afterlife.

According to Avicenna, because the rational soul is immortal, there must be an afterlife. Although immortality is a concomitant of the rational soul rather than its ultimate purpose, its existence intensifies the urgency of achieving as great as possible perfection in this life, since Avicenna holds that whatever degree of perfection individuals achieve in this life largely determines their quota of suffering or bliss in the next.

Avicenna's proof for the immortality of the soul has two parts.[60] He first demonstrates that the soul does not perish with the body and then that it is immortal. The philosopher has already proven that the soul is an immaterial substance, independent of the body. This being the case, it cannot be considered an accident of the body, because substances are not accidents; one cannot therefore hold that the soul passes away with the body due to any accidental relationship with it. Moreover, the body is not an essential cause of the soul, neither a prior cause nor one of the four Aristotelian prime causes. It may be considered at most to be an accidental cause. Since the relationship between the two therefore entails neither substantial contingency nor essential causality, there is no basis for believing that the death of the body requires the destruction of the soul.[61]

Although this line of reasoning proves the independence of body and soul, it does not demonstrate the latter's immortality. For this, Avicenna turns to the conceptual dichotomies of potentiality-actuality and matter-form. Briefly, humans are a composite of matter and form, body and soul.

According to Avicenna (following Aristotle), matter is innately potential and form is innately active. Since the soul is humankind's simple, formal principle, it is essentially active. Therefore,

> it is clear that everything which is simple and not composite, or which is an origin and base (i.e., the substance) of a composite thing, cannot in itself have the actuality of persistence and the potentiality of corruption. If it has the potentiality of corruption, it cannot possibly have the actuality of persistence, and if it has the actuality of persistence and existence, it cannot have the potentiality of corruption. Obviously, then, the substance of the soul does not have the potentiality of corruption. . . . It is then obvious that the soul is absolutely incorruptible [i.e., immortal].[62]

In asserting the soul's immortality, Avicenna follows Plotinus rather than Aristotle.[63] He may have been influenced by Islamic beliefs in the hereafter, although since he apparently rejects the idea of bodily resurrection, such influence was obviously limited.[64] More probably, his thought was determined by philosophical premises: that entelechy is a founding principle of nature, that souls are individualized in terms of not only bodily disposition but also intellectual progress, and that there exists an essential affiliation and interaction between the rational soul and the celestial Intelligences.[65]

Avicenna's vision of the afterlife is founded upon the conception of entelechy.[66] Each bodily appetite and psychic faculty has a particular goal; attainment of this goal causes pleasure, failure to attain it induces pain. Psychic faculties are not equal in the pleasures they bring. Lust and gluttony have their satisfactions, but these are incomparable in quantity or quality to those which higher faculties prompt. Since the rational soul is the specific essence of humans, in perfecting it they perfect themselves and thus achieve the greatest possible pleasure. Deficiency in this endeavor, in turn, provokes the pain or frustration caused by yearning after an unattained, or even unattainable, goal. Which state an immortal soul finds itself in after death, therefore, depends on the degree to which it has recognized, strived for, and achieved perfection in life.[67]

Souls in the hereafter fall into four categories. A select few achieve perfection and enjoy absolute bliss. Avicenna terms these *the sanctified souls* (*al-anfus al-qudsiyya*).[68] Other souls are aware of their true purpose in life and work to attain it, but only meet partial success. In the hereafter these dwell in an intermediate state (*barzakh*), happy to the extent that they have approached their goal, suffering to the degree that they have not yet attained it. This state is not a permanent one, however, as these souls eventually perfect themselves and achieve absolute happiness.[69]

Some individuals know their purpose in life but willfully refuse to work toward it. These are the unhappiest of souls in the hereafter, for they must endure eternal pain: "they reap only loss and harm. . . . They never gain respite from it."[70]

Finally, there are souls that for one reason or another are unaware of life's purpose, either because no philosopher or prophet has expounded it to them and they were unable to figure it out by themselves, or because they were mentally deficient or very young when they died. Since they know nothing of life's true purpose, they feel neither happiness for having attained some portion of perfection nor sadness for failing to attain it at all. If they are at least aware of logical first principles, states Avicenna, they may enjoy a slight measure of happiness in the hereafter. But if they indulge themselves only in lowly bodily sensations and know no other purpose in life, they will suffer great torment and eternal frustration when they die and lose their bodies, for corporeal sensation is the only way they know of satisfying their desires.[71]

Avicenna also mentions the possibility of an "imagined" (*mutakhayyal*) version of a Qur'ânic heaven and hell in the case of souls who have so imprinted in their imaginations similitudes (*amthâl*) of the delights of heaven or the torments of hell as described in the Qur'ân that they they are unable to conceive of an afterlife assuming any other form. Since Avicenna believes in the demise of the animal soul, he himself does not espouse this view, attributing it to "a certain scholar" (*ba'ḍ al-'ulamâ'*).[72]

Remarks

Several leitmotifs of Avicenna's psychology deserve attention. One is the tension between unity and diversity, homogeneity and heterogeneity, harmony foregrounded by polyphony. Avicenna insists on the soul's inherent unity. However, his psychology, the result of an ancient and highly developed philosophical tradition, is an area of intellectual investigation in which he had a deeply serious and intensely creative personal interest. As a result, his system combines a facade of uniformity with elaborate specialization, a pretense of homogeneity with intense compartmentalization, and an interwoven unity characterized by the striking diversity of its individual elements.

Avicenna's psychology is, in fact, a highly developed bureaucracy of the soul. The soul is divided into three parts, each with its own entelechy, function, and individual faculties, whose numerous activities it must constantly supervise. Moreover, each new theoretical refinement demands still further specialization. The theory's combination of teleological functionalism, descriptive comprehensiveness, and analytic precision is, of course, its major intellectual justification. It validates itself through empirical plausibility, representational coherence, and a fine-tuned attention to detail. Everything has its place, everything can be explained.

This psychology's immense descriptive power thus makes it an ideal tool for the twin tasks of allegorical interpretation and composition. Love and hate, sin and virtue, intelligence and imbecility, every human trait, goal, or desire is subsumed into its analytic structure. Every human aspiration falls within its comprehensive embrace, every human action can be depicted by the interplay of its individual units; limitless opportunities for psychological analysis produce endless possibilities for allegorical personification. Avicenna's psychology can be used not only to describe our inner world but also to portray its personal dynamics.

Adopting the theory for such a portrayal, however, has its consequences, for this psychology implies its own value system. Body and soul are not equal, nor are all souls, nor even are the faculties within individual souls. The soul is superior to the body because it is the latter's perfecting principle, its entelechy; it brings life to the body's otherwise inert, lifeless, and passive materials; it moves the body from potentiality to realization, from passivity to activity, from imperfection to perfection. Descriptive statement, however, quickly becomes value judgment. Ontological hierarchy gives way to teleological differentiation. The soul is thus somehow "higher," superior, more valuable, than the body. Moreover, to the extent that it evinces a rational capability unshared by any other material creature, it demonstrates a "splendor" to which no purely material creature can aspire.

Hierarchy also reigns among the soul's three main parts. The movement from vegetable soul to animal to rational comes to represent ontological ascent, progression from lesser toward greater perfection. Teleology, however, is but one criterion for ontological evaluation. Psychic hierarchy is founded equally on the dichotomy of transience and permanence. The rational soul's immortality heightens its status, somehow making it *the* essential component of the soul. Despite their intrinsic activities in comparison with the body's inert material passivity, the physical constituents of the soul are mortal, perishing with the body. The rational soul, however, enduring forever, has the potential for attaining angelic parity with the Holy Substances.[73]

Hence, just as the body is hierarchically inferior to all parts of the soul, the lower souls, in their transience, are less perfectly active, and thus inferior to the rational soul. Once again, higher hierarchical status is translated into ontological, and thus ethical, superiority. The body is only the lowly instrument of the soul, the lower souls only servants of the rational soul. Hierarchy exists even within the rational soul. The intellect is "commander and superior" of the rational soul. And even the intellect has different internal gradations of activity, and hence perfection. The habitual intellect is higher than the material, and the acquired intellect loftier than them both. The prophetic intellect supersedes them all. Throughout, Avicenna assumes a homology among the ratio of activity, duration of vitality, ontological status, and ethical value. Once this equation is considered homological, rather than analogical, it is possible to combine or reverse its components. This strategy, in turn, allows Avicenna to formulate a psychological explanation of human nature, and, from this, an ethical theory of human action.

Since human actions originate from psychological impulses, a correlation may be presumed between the two. A person predominantly concerned with natural functions, such as eating and drinking, is viewed as responding mainly to the demands of the natural or vegetable soul. A person of passionate character, easily moved to extremes of anger or love, is dominated by the animal soul. One who acts moderately and reasonably, however, and favors abstract intellectual endeavors, is guided by the rational soul. Since the rational soul is the "highest" human dimension, those whom it governs are most completely fulfilling their potential for perfection, are most fully human. Correspondingly, they are the only ones who are truly virtuous. The scheme is Platonic, and Avicenna fully espouses it.

What emerges is an internal psychic world permeated with intellectual elitism and filled with the imagery of servants and masters, inferiors and superiors, baseness and nobility.[74] Implicit in these dichotomies are the alternatives of obedience and revolt, order and chaos, stability and anarchy. At this point, the concerns of personal ethics, the politics of civil society, and the Neoplatonic geography of the cosmos meet. Only the ground plan is drawn, of course; correspondences remain to be charted; but it is only a short step before each level becomes a reflection of the other.

Notes

1. Avicenna's major treatises on the soul may be usefully divided into early, middle, and late writings. In chronological order (following Gohlman, Gutas, and Michot), early works are: *Mabḥath ʿan al-quwa n-nafsâniyya* (*Aḥwâl an-nafs*), 147–78); *al-Mabdaʾ wa-l-maʿâd*, esp. pp. 75–126; *Aḥwâl an-nafs*: *Risâla fi n-nafs wa-baqâʾihâ wa-maʿâdihâ* (*Aḥwâl an-nafs*, 48–142; considered by Michot as being posterior to *ash-Shifâʾ*, cf. *La destinée de l'homme selon Avicenne*, 6, note 29); *al-Aḍḥawiyya*. Middle works include *al-Qânûn fi ṭ-ṭibb*; *ash-Shifâʾ*: *aṭ-Ṭabîʿât*. [Fann] 6: *an-Nafs*; and the various summaries or handbooks that closely resemble each other and are largely based on *ash-Shifâʾ*, such as *al-Hidâya*, 204–30; *an-Najât*, 196–231, Eng. trans. Fazlur Rahman, *Avicenna's Psychology: An English Translation of* Kitâb al-Najât, *Book II, Chapter VII with Historico-Philosophical Notes and Textual Improvements on the Cairo Edition* (Westport, Conn.: Hyperion Press, 1981 [repr. of 1952 ed., Oxford: Oxford University Press, 1952]), 25–69; *ʿUyûn al-ḥikma*, 30–40; and *Dânish-nâma-yi ʿAlâʾî*, 78–145. Late works are *al-Ishârât wa-t-tanbîhât*, 2:343–450; *al-Mubâḥathât*; and Avicenna's commentaries, *Sharḥ kitâb* Athûlûjiyâ *al-mansûb ilâ Arisṭû* and *at-Taʿlîqât ʿalâ ḥawâshî kitâb an-nafs li-Arisṭû*. Significant minor published treatises are the late *Fi l-quwa l-insâniyya wa-idrâkâtihâ* (*Tisʿ rasâʾil*, 42–48) and *Fî kalâm ʿala n-nafs an-nâṭiqa* (*Aḥwâl an-anfs*, 195–99). The authenticity of two other treatises attributed to Avicenna, *Fî maʿrifat an-nafs an-nâṭiqa wa-aḥwâlihâ* (*Aḥwâl an-nafs*, 181–92) and *Masâʾil ʿan aḥwâl an-nafs* is doubted by Jean Michot (cf. *La destinée de l'homme selon Avicenne*, pp. xxix-xxx). Compare also Anawati, *Essai de bibliographie Avicennienne* (Cairo: al-Maaref, 1950), nos. 77–109; Mahdavî, *Bibliographie d'Ibn Sina* (Tehran: Dânishgâh-i Tehran, 1954), nos. 4b., 4j., 4h., 30, 36, 38, 43, 47, 52, 59, 76, 99, 120, 121–24; and Brockelmann, *GAL* 1:591–96, and *GAL S.* 1:813–22.

2. Concerning aspects of rhetoric and philosophical intent, see Chapter Seven below. The analysis here concentrates on presenting the details of Avicenna's own exposition of psychology with no attempt to provide background concerning the question of the influence he received from Aristotelian, Neoplatonic, and previous Islamic theories of the soul. On this subject, see the introduction and notes in Rahman, *Avicenna's Psychology*; Davidson, "Alfarabi and Avicenna," 110–78; Harry A. Wolfson, "The Internal Senses in Latin, Arabic, and Hebrew Philosophic Texts," *Harvard Theological Review* 28 (1935) 69–133; Rowson, *A Muslim Philosopher on the Soul and Its Fate*; Helmut Gätje, *Studien zu Überlieferung der Aristotelischen Psychologie im Islam*, Annales Universitatis Saraviensis 2 (Heidelberg: Carl Winter Universitätsverlag, 1971); A. Altmann and S. M. Stern, *Isaac Israeli: A Neoplatonic Philosopher of the Early Tenth Century, His Works translated with Comments and an Outline of His Philosophy*, Scripta Judaica 1 (Oxford: Oxford University Press, 1958);

Phillip Merlan, *Monopsychism, Mysticism, Metaconsciousness: Problems of the Soul in the Neoaristotelian and Neoplatonic Tradition*, International Archives of the History of Ideas 2 (The Hague: Martinus Nijhoff, 1969); and Armstrong, ed., *The Cambridge History of Later Greek and Early Medieval Philosophy*.

3. *Miʿrâj Nâma*, 81; trans., 112; he repeats his assertion at the beginning of *Fî taʿbîr ar-ruʾyâ*, 274–75.

4. *al-Qânûn fi ṭ-ṭibb*, 1:5. For an English translation of the first part of *al-Qânûn*, see O. Cameron Gruner, *A Treatise on the Canon of Medicine of Avicenna, Incorporating a Translation of the First Book* (London: Luzac & Co., 1930). This translation should be checked against the original.

5. *al-Qânûn*, 1:5–10. Cf. p. 10: "Know that the Creator . . . gave to human beings the most symmetrical constitution [*âʿdal mizâj*] possible in this world"; cf. *al-Hidâya*, 204, 206, 216, and *Dânish-nâma-yi ʿAlâʾî: Ṭabîʿiyyât*, 78, 80, 101.

6. *al-Qânûn*, 1:13–19.

7. *al-Qânûn*, 19, and 19–24.

8. *Aḥwâl an-nafs*, 50–56, which provides the rationale for the definition; also *al-Ḥudûd*, 14; *Mabḥath*, 152–53.

9. *ash-Shifâʾ: an-Nafs*, 5–7, esp. 7; *Aḥwâl an-nafs*, 51; *Mabḥath*, 152–53. The concept of entelechy is of course Aristotelian.

10. *an-Najât*, 197; Rahman, *Avicenna's Psychology*, 25; and Afnan, *Avicenna*, 136; *Aḥwâl an-nafs*, 48–49; *ash-Shifâʾ: an-Nafs*, 32.

11. *ash-Shifâʾ: an-Nafs, an-Najât, Aḥwâl an-nafs, Mabḥath, ʿUyûn al-ḥikma, al-Hidâya, Dânish-nâma-yi ʿAlâʾî, al-Ishârât wa-t-tanbîhât*. Because this is so, it is often illuminating to notice when this terminology is not used.

12. Avicenna, in general, considers the relationship among the general soul and the subsidiary souls as *similar* to that of genus and species. To equate them explicitly as such, however, would mitigate the soul's intrinsic unity, something he does not wish to do. Hence, in his version of the quotation cited above in *ash-Shifâʾ: an-Nafs*, for instance, the phrase "like a genus [*jins*]," is significantly absent. On the other hand, in *al-Qânûn*, a non-philosophical work, he uses the term *genus* (*jins*) more freely, but in the general sense of "kind" rather than the technical term, *genus*, cf. *al-Qânûn*, 1:66ff. Regarding the distinction between homologous and analogous, *homologous* means "corresponding in structure or origin, as an organ or part of one animal to a similar organ or part of another"; *analogous* means "having a similar function but differing in origin and structure, as the wings of birds and insects" (*Funk & Wagnells College Dictionary*, s.v.).

13. *Miʿrâj Nâma*, 81; trans., 112–13; and *al-Qânûn*, 1:67, where Avicenna states that he follows Galen rather than Aristotle here. He also says that the nutritive faculty of the natural soul resides in the liver, and its reproductive faculty rests in the genitals.

14. *al-Qânûn*, 1:66; for elaboration of the soul's faculties, see below in this chapter, pp. 60–65.

15. *ash-Shifâʾ: an-Nafs*, 27; compare Avicenna's emphasis on physiognomy in *Ḥayy ibn Yaqẓân*, 3–4; Corbin, *Avicenna*, 138, 295–96.

16. *ash-Shifâʾ: an-Nafs*, 30.

17. See later in this chapter in the section on the rational soul. For back-

ground, see Rahman, *Avicenna's Psychology*, 3–12; Davidson, "Alfarabi and Avicenna," esp. 171–72; and the studies cited above in note 2.

18. *ash-Shifâ': an-Nafs*, 5, 22, 174–75, 178; *Aḥwâl an-nafs*, 38–39.

19. *ash-Shifâ': an-Nafs*, 13, also 8–12; and *al-Ishârât wa-t-tanbîhât*, 2:343–58; *Fî ma'rifat an-nafs an-nâṭiqa wa-aḥwâlihâ*, 183–85; *al-Aḍḥawiyya*, 94–97. For useful discussions of Avicenna's argument here, see Rahman, *Avicenna's Psychology*, 8–9; and Michael Marmura, "Avicenna's 'Flying Man' in Context," *The Monist* 69,3 (1986) 383–95. For other proofs of the immaterial existence of the rational soul, see *ash-Shifâ': an-Nafs*, 187–97; *an-Najât*, 213–20; Rahman, *Avicenna's Psychology*, 46–54; *Aḥwâl an-nafs*, 74–95; *Mabḥath*, 172–75; *Dânish-nâma-yi 'Alâ'î*, 110–13; *al-Hidâya*, 217–23; *al-Aḍḥawiyya*, 98–108; *Fi s-sa'âda wa-ḥujaj al-'ashara 'an an-nafs al-insâniyya jauhar*, 5–12.

20. *Mi'râj Nâma*, 85; trans., 116; *ash-Shifâ': an-Nafs*, 22–26; *an-Najât*, 228–30; Rahman, *Avicenna's Psychology*, 64–68, 109–15; *Mabḥath*, 167; *al-Mabda' wa-l-ma'âd*, 95–96; *Aḥwâl an-nafs*, 108–10; *al-Ishârât wa-t-tanbîhât*, 2:356–58.

21. Corbin, *Avicenna*, 16–35.

22. *al-Ḥudûd*, 14. Cf. Goichon's trans., p. 20, and note 3, which refers to Aristotle, *De Anima*, 412a, lines 27–28. For a step-by-step working out of this definition, see *Mabḥath*, 152–53, and the discussion in *Aḥwâl an-nafs*, 51–56.

23. *al-Ḥudûd*, 14. Cf. Goichon's trans., p. 20 and note 5, where she suggests that the human soul is defined as potentially rational because the intervention of the Active Intelligence is required for it to perceive intelligibles, while angelic souls by nature perceive intelligibles actually.

24. *Aḥwâl an-nafs*, 49–50. The vegetable and animal souls encompass "oppositional activities" in terms of their potential for either physical movement or repose, cf. Goichon, *Lexique*, 295. Since the angelic, rational soul is not a physical substance, it does not suffer from such corporeal oppositions.

25. *Aḥwâl an-nafs*, 53.

26. Cf. *al-Ḥudûd*, 11–13. For Avicenna on the unity of the soul, see below, pp. 82, 101 note 11.

27. *al-Qânûn*, 1:67–69; *al-Mabda' wa-l-ma'âd*, 95; *Fî ta'bîr ar-ru'yâ*, 274–77.

28. *al-Qânûn*, 1:70–73; for Avicenna's comment about *nuṭq*, see 1:72, also 1:67 on the lack of necessity for physicians to understand philosophy. Very interesting is a passage in *Fî ta'bîr ar-ru'yâ*, p. 275, where Avicenna makes an attempt to coordinate his terminology. After positing the existence of three spirits (*arwâḥ*), the vegetable, animal, and psychic (*nafsânî*), located respectively in the liver, heart, and brain, he then posits the existence of three correlative souls (*nufûs*). "The spirits in relationship to the souls," he proceeds to say, "are in the place of matter to form" (*inna r-rûḥ li-n-nafs bi-manzilati l-hayûlâ li-ṣûra*). For example, "the natural soul [*nafs*] is the form of the vegetable, natural spirit [*rûḥ*], its nature is its own [i.e. the soul's], its principle [or place of action, *mabda'*] is the liver, and its faculty [*quwwa*] proceeds through the mediation [*bi-tawassuṭ*] of the natural spirit." There is obviously an effort being made toward conceptual and terminological harmonization here, but given the lack of any clear final statement on the issue in other treatises, I believe it represents more an attempt to clarify an ongoing issue than any ultimate settlement of it. And even here the intellect is deemphasized.

29. Examination of Avicenna's psychological treatises reveals that their greater part is concerned with the rational, that is, "spiritual," soul; compare *ash-Shifâ': an-Nafs*, 181–220; *an-Najât*, 202–31; Rahman, *Avicenna's Psychology*, 32–69; *Fî ithbât an-nubuwwât* (all); *Aḥwâl an-nafs*, 65–140; *al-Mubâḥathât*; *Sharḥ kitâb* Athûlûjiyâ *al-mansûb ilâ Arisṭû*; *Fî kalâm 'ala n-nafs an-nâṭiqa*; and so on.

30. *Mi'râj Nâma*, 82; trans., 113; compare *aṭ-Ṭair*, 43: "The wonder is human beings when they rebel against sensual desires even though their forms have been fashioned to prefer them completely, or when they render total obedience to them, even though their characters have been enlightened by reason," (my trans., cf. Corbin, *Avicenna*, 187–88).

31. See *Mi'râj Nâma*, 81–85; trans. 113–16. Philosophers usually place the *nafs* above the *rûḥ*, *ṣûfî*s put it below. For general discussions of the concepts *nafs* and *rûḥ*, see *EI*[1], 3:433–36; Duncan B. Macdonald, "The Development of the Idea of Spirit in Islam," *Muslim World* 22 (1932) 25–42, 153–68; and A. S. Tritton, "Man, *Nafs*, *Rûḥ*, *'Aql*," *BSOAS* 34 (1971) 491–95; and works cited in note 2 above.

32. *Mi'râj Nâma*, 81; trans., 113. This metaphor echoes Plato's and Aristotle's references to the relation of the soul to the body being that of pilot to vessel, cf. Plato, *Phaedrus*, 495 (247c) and Aristotle, *De Anima*, 1:413a, lines 8–9). See also *Fî ta'bîr ar-ru'yâ*, 280, where Avicenna compares the soul's use of the parts of the body to "a rider [*fâris*] on a mount [*faras*]. When the rider sees that his mount has weakened and is weary from travelling, he stops using it so that it can stop, rest, and regain its strength. Then he remounts and uses it." In a more negative sense, see *Dânish-nâma-yi 'Alâ'î: Ṭabî'iyyât*, 125–26, where Avicenna describes how attachment to the body can prevent the soul from fulfilling its intellectual potential for perfection and likens the situation to that of "a rider who sits on a horse [*asb*] in order to reach a place toward which he is headed. If he cannot leave the horse, having become fond of him, and stays on its back, in the end the horse prevents him from the intention that he initially wished to attain."

33. Avicenna gives the example of a sword to distinguish between first and second entelechy. The form of a sword is its first entelechy, while appropriate "swordlike" movement and activity are its second entelechy; see *ash-Shifâ: an-Nafs*, 10.

34. References of the body's being the instrument (*âla*) of the soul are common enough in Avicenna's writings; see *ash-Shifâ': an-Nafs*, 199, 202–206, corresponding to *an-Najât*, 223, 223–27; Rahman, *Avicenna's Psychology*, 57, 58–63; *Aḥwâl an-nafs*, 99–107; *al-Aḍḥawiyya*, 108–10; and *al-Hidâya*, 222–27; *Dânish-nâma-yi 'Alâ'î: Ṭabî'iyyât*, 100. In *al-Ishârât wa-t-tanbîhât*, 2:380–86, Avicenna refers to the physical location of the internal faculties in the brain as their respective "instruments." See also Goichon, *Lexique*, 13, note 31. The closest I have been able to find in regard to references to the soul being the splendor (*raunaq*) of the body is a passage in *Sharḥ kitâb* Athûlûjiyâ *al-mansûb ilâ Arisṭû*, where he refers to the soul as the adornment (*az-zîna*) of the body. The image of the soul being the splendor (*al-bahâ'*) or light (*aḍ-ḍiyâ'*) of the body is not uncommon in Islamic Neoplatonism, see, for example, S. M. Stern, "Ibn Ḥasdây's Neoplatonist: A Neoplatonic Treatise and Its Influence on Isaac Israeli and the Longer Version of the Theology of Aristotle," *Oriens* 13–14 (1960–61) 58–120, esp. pp. 67–69, 84 (line

3), 86 (line 18). Avicenna frequently refers to the rational soul as being the more honorable or noble part of human beings; cf., for example, *Fî ta'bîr ar-ru'yâ*, 277–78.

35. *ash-Shifâ': an-Nafs*, 32; *an-Najât*, 197; Rahman, *Avicenna's Psychology*, 25; *Mabḥath*, 156–57; *al-Mabda' wa-l-ma'âd*, 92; *Aḥwâl an-nafs*, 57–58; *al-Hidâya*, 204–205; *Dânish-nâma-yi 'Alâ'î: Ṭabî'iyyât*, 78–80; *'Uyûn al-ḥikma*, 30; *Fî ta'bîr ar-ru'yâ*, 274–75; Afnan, *Avicenna*, 136.

36. *al-Qânûn*, 1:67–69; *Mi'râj Nâma*, 81; trans., 113.

37. *ash-Shifâ': an-Nafs*, 32; *an-Najât*, 197; Rahman, *Avicenna's Psychology*, 25; *al-Mabda' wa-l-ma'âd*, 93; Afnan, *Avicenna*, 136.

38. Trans. Rahman, *Avicenna's Psychology*, 26. Corresponding to *ash-Shifâ': an-Nafs*, 33, and *an-Najât*, 197–98; *Aḥwâl an-nafs*, 58–59.

39. *ash-Shifâ': an-Nafs*, 33, 172–73; *an-Najât* 198; Rahman, *Avicenna's Psychology*, 26; *Mi'râj Nâma*, 81; trans., 113; *al-Qânûn* omits discussion of these faculties; *Mabḥath*, 159; *al-Mabda' wa-l-ma'âd*, 93; *Aḥwâl an-nafs*, 58; *al-Hidâya*, 206; *Dânish-nâma-yi 'Alâ'î: Ṭabî'iyyât*, 81; *'Uyûn al-ḥikma*, 34; Afnan, *Avicenna*, 136.

40. *ash-Shifâ': an-Nafs*, 33–34, 50–141; *an-Najât*, 198–200, Rahman, *Avicenna's Psychology*, 26–29; *al-Qânûn*, 1:71–73. Avicenna also states that the sense of touch may be considered four senses, which distinguish hot from cold, wet from dry, hard from soft, and rough from smooth. According to this viewpoint, the external senses are eight in number rather than five. See also *Mabḥath*, 158–59, 161–64; *al-Mabda' wa-l-ma'âd*, 93; *Aḥwâl an-nafs*, 59–60; *al-Hidâya*, 206–211; *Dânish-nâma-yi 'Alâ'î: Ṭabî'iyyât*, 83–94; *'Uyûn al-ḥikma*, 30–32; Afnan, *Avicenna*, 136–37.

41. *ash-Shifâ': an-Nafs*, 35; *an-Najât*, 200–201; Rahman, *Avicenna's Psychology*, 30; *Aḥwâl an-nafs*, 60–61; Afnan, *Avicenna*, 137.

42. *Ibid.*

43. *Mi'râj Nâma*, 83; trans., 114; *ash-Shifâ': an-Nafs*, 35–36, 145–48; *an-Najât*, 201; Rahman, *Avicenna's Psychology*, 31; *al-Qânûn*, 1:71; *Mabḥath*, 160, 166; *Aḥwâl an-nafs*, 61; *al-Hidâya*, 211–13; *Dânish-nâma-yi 'Alâ'î: Ṭabî'iyyât*, 96–100; *'Uyûn al-ḥikma*, 32–33; *al-Ishârât wa-t-tanbîhât*, 2:380–81.

44. *ash-Shifâ': an-Nafs*, 36, 148; *an-Najât*, 201; Rahman, *Avicenna's Psychology*, 31; *al-Qânûn*, 1:71; *Mabḥath*, 160, 166; *al-Mabda' wa-l-ma'âd* 93; *Aḥwâl an-nafs*, 62; *al-Hidâya*, 213; *Dânish-nâma-yi 'Alâ'î: Ṭabî'iyyât*, 96–100; *'Uyûn al-ḥikma*, 33; *al-Ishârât wa-t-tanbîhât*, 2:374–81.

45. *Mi'râj Nâma*, 83; trans., 114; *ash-Shifâ': an-Nafs*, 36, 148, 151–61; *an-Najât*, 201; Rahman, *Avicenna's Psychology*, 31; *al-Qânûn*, 1:71–72, where the examples of the flying man and emerald mountain are cited; *Mabḥath*, 161, 166; *al-Mabda' wa-l-ma'âd*, 93–94; *Aḥwâl an-nafs*, 62; *al-Hidâya*, 214; *Dânish-nâma-yi 'Alâ'î: Ṭabî'iyyât*, 97–100; *'Uyûn al-ḥikma*, 33; *al-Ishârât wa-t-tanbîhât*, 2:382; *Fî ta'bîr ar-ru'yâ*, 277; *al-Mubâḥathât*, 231–32.

46. *Mi'râj Nâma*, 83; trans., 114; *ash-Shifâ': an-Nafs*, 36–37, 147–48; *an-Najât*, 201–2; Rahman, *Avicenna's Psychology*, 31; *al-Qânûn*, 1:72; *Mabḥath*, 161, 166–67; *al-Mabda' wa-l-ma'âd*, 94; *Aḥwâl an-nafs*, 62; *al-Hidâya*, 213–14; *Dânish-nâma-yi 'Alâ'î: Ṭabî'iyyât*, 97–100; *'Uyûn al-ḥikma*, 33; *al-Ishârât wa-t-tanbîhât*, 381–82.

47. *Mi'râj Nâma* 83; trans., 114; *ash-Shifâ': an-Nafs*, 37, 148–50; *an-Najât*, 203; Rahman, *Avicenna's Psychology*, 31; *al-Qânûn*, 1:72; *Mabḥath*, 161, 167; *al-Mabda' wa-l-ma'âd*, 94; *Aḥwâl an-nafs*, 62; *al-Hidâya*, 214; *Dânish-nâma-yi 'Alâ'î: Ṭabî'iyyât*, 97–100; *'Uyûn al-ḥikma*, 33; *al-Ishârât wa-t-tanbîhât*, 2:383–84.

48. *Mi'râj Nâma*, 82, 85; trans., 114, 116; *ash-Shifâ': an-Nafs*, 181–86; *al-Mabda' wa-l-ma'âd*, 96; *al-Hidâya*, 216; *Dânish-nâma-yi 'Alâ'î: Ṭabî'iyyât*, 101; *'Uyûn al-ḥikma*, 35; *Fî ta'bîr ar-ru'yâ*, 277.

49. *ash-Shifâ': an-Nafs*, 37, 185; *an-Najât*, 202; Rahman, *Avicenna's Psychology*, 32; *Mabḥath*, 170–71; *al-Mabda' wa-l-ma'âd*, 96; *Aḥwâl an-nafs*, 63; *al-Hidâya*, 217; *Dânish-nâma-yi 'Alâ'î: Ṭabî'iyyât*, 101–02; *'Uyûn al-ḥikma*, 37; Afnan, *Avicenna*, 138.

50. *ash-Shifâ': an-Nafs*, 37–38, also 184–86; *an-Najât*, 202–203; Rahman, *Avicenna's Psychology*, 32–33; *Mabḥath*, 170–71; *al-Mabda' wa-l-ma'âd*, 96–97; *Aḥwâl an-nafs*, 63–64; *al-Hidâya*, 218; *Dânish-nâma-yi 'Alâ'î: Ṭabî'iyyât*, 101–102; *'Uyûn al-ḥikma*, 35; *al-Ishârât wa-t-tanbîhât*, 2:387–88.

51. *ash-Shifâ': an-Nafs*, 38–39; *an-Najât*, 203–4; Rahman, *Avicenna's Psychology*, 33; *Mi'râj Nâma*, 87–88; trans., 118; *al-Mabda' wa-l-ma'âd*, 97–98; *Aḥwâl an-nafs*, 64; *al-Hidâya*, 216–17; *Dânish-nâma-yi 'Alâ'î: Ṭabî'iyyât*, 102–08; *'Uyûn al-ḥikma*, 35–36.

52. *ash-Shifâ': an-Nafs*, 38–39; *an-Najât*, 203; Rahman, *Avicenna's Psychology*, 33; *Mi'râj Nâma*, 84–85; trans., 116; *al-Mabda' wa-l-ma'âd*, 96; *Aḥwâl an-nafs*, 64; *al-Hidâya*, 215–16; *Dânish-nâma-yi 'Alâ'î: Ṭabî'iyyât*, 102; *'Uyûn al-ḥikma*, 37; *al-Ishârât wa-t-tanbîhât*, 2:387–88; *Sharḥ kitâb* Athûlûjiyâ *al-mansûb ilâ Arisṭû*, 69. Cf. Afnan, *Avicenna*, 138; Corbin, *Avicenna*, 73–77.

53. *ash-Shifâ': an-Nafs*, 38–40; *an-Najât*, 204–5; Rahman, *Avicenna's Psychology*, 32–33; *Mabḥath*, 168–69; *Aḥwâl an-nafs*, 65–68; *al-Mabda' wa-l-ma'âd*, 97–99; *al-Hidâya*, 217; *Dânish-nâma-yi 'Alâ'î: Ṭabî'iyyât*, 108–109; *'Uyûn al-ḥikma*, 36; *al-Ishârât wa-t-tanbîhât*, 2:388–91; and *Fî ithbât an-nubuwwât*, 43–44, where Avicenna gives the example of fire: fire as potentially something cold, fire that potentially can burn, and fire actually burning. Cf. Davidson, "Alfarabi and Avicenna," 160–61.

54. *ash-Shifâ': an-Nafs*, 40; *an-Najât*, 205; Rahman, *Avicenna's Psychology*, 33; *Mabḥath*, 168–69; *al-Mabda' wa-l-ma'âd*, 154–55; *Aḥwâl an-nafs*, 68; Afnan, *Avicenna*, 139–41.

55. *Mi'râj Nâma*, 81; trans., 112. For Avicenna on the temporal origin of the soul see, *ash-Shifâ': an-Nafs*, 198–201; *an-Najât*, 222–23; Rahman, *Avicenna's Psychology*, 56–58; *Mabḥath*, 154–55; *al-Mabda' wa-l-ma'âd*, 157–58; *Aḥwâl an-nafs*, 96–98; *Sharḥ kitâb* Athûlûjiyâ *al-mansûb ilâ Arisṭû*, 35 (see this last source as well for references to the "world" of the soul, for example, 41, 43, 47); Afnan, *Avicenna*, 147–48. Avicenna explicitly states that the Active Intelligence is the cause of the human soul in *al-Mabda' wa-l-ma'âd*, 198 (see also 157); cf. Davidson, "Alfarabi and Avicenna," 158–59, 171.

56. The Arabic text of the *Theology of Aristotle* is in 'Abd ar-Raḥmân Badawî, *Aflûṭîn 'ind al-'Arab*, Dirâsât islâmiyya 20 (Cairo: Dâr an-nahḍa l-'arabiyya, 1966), 18–28; Eng. trans., Geoffrey Lewis, trans., *Plotiniana Arabica*, pp. 225–31, in vol. 2 of Paul Henry and Hans-Rudolf Schwyzer, eds., *Plotini Opera*, 2 vols. (Paris: Desclée de Brouwer; Brussels: L'Édition Universelle, 1959); Plotinus, *The Enneads*,

trans. Stephen Mackenna (London: Faber and Faber, 1962), 357–64; *Sharḥ kitâb* Athûlûjiyâ *al-mansûb ilâ Arisṭû*, 37ff.; also, *al-Aḍḥawiyya*, 36–37, and Corbin, *Avicenna*, 84.

57. *Sharḥ kitâb* Athûlûjiyâ *al-mansûb ilâ Arisṭû*, 37, 45, 66; Michot, *La destinée de l'homme selon Avicenne*, 11, note 51.

58. Termed by Avicenna as "The Return" (*al-ma'âd*); on his use of this term, see Michot, *La destinée de l'homme selon Avicenne*, 10–14.

59. *ash-Shifâ': an-Nafs*, 40; *an-Najât*, 205; Rahman, *Avicenna's Psychology*, 33; *Aḥwâl an-nafs*, 68, 130. Cf. *Mabḥath*, 168–69; *Fi l-kalâm 'ala n-nafs an-nâṭiqa*, 166–67; cf. *al-Aḍḥawiyya*, 31, 115–19. Avicenna denies the possibility of the Qur'ânic conception of bodily resurrection, a point for which al-Ghazâlî would later roundly condemn him, see Michot, *La destinée de l'homme selon Avicenne*, 14–22, and Gardet, *La pensée religieuse d'Avicenne*, 86–105.

60. Avicenna's proofs for the soul's immortality correspond almost word for word in *ash-Shifâ': an-Nafs*, 202–6; *an-Najât*, 223–27; Rahman, *Avicenna's Psychology*, 58–63; and *Aḥwâl an-nafs*, 99–107. Short versions occur in *al-Aḍḥawiyya*, 109–11; *al-Hidâya*, 222–27; and *Dânish-nâma-yi 'Alâ'î*, 122–23. The subject is ignored in *Mabḥath, al-Mabda' wa-l-ma'âd, 'Uyûn al-ḥikma*, and *al-Ishârât wa-t-tanbîhât*.

61. *ash-Shifâ': an-Nafs*, 187–97; *an-Najât*, 213–20; Rahman, *Avicenna's Psychology*, 46–54; *Aḥwâl an-nafs*, 74–95; *Mabḥath*, 172–75; *al-Aḍḥawiyya*, 98–108; *al-Mabda' wa-l-ma'âd*, 154–57; *al-Hidâya* 217–23; *Dânish-nâma-yi 'Alâ'î: Ṭabî'iyyât*, 110–13; *Fi s-sa'âda*, 5–12.

62. Trans. by Rahman, *Avicenna's Psychology*, 63, corresponding to *an-Najât*, 226–27; *ash-Shifâ': an-Nafs*, 206–207; *Aḥwâl an-nafs*, 104–5.

63. See Fazlur Rahman's notes, *Avicenna's Psychology*, 108–9.

64. *al-Aḍḥawiyya*, 42–43, 51–54, 109–11, 118–22. Compare, however, *Aḥwâl an-nafs*, 127–28, *al-Mabda' wa-l-ma'âd*, 114–15, or *Fî aqsâm al-'ulûm al-'aqliyya*, 78, where Avicenna adopts a more restrained stance. He does not reject the idea of bodily resurrection but confines himself to saying that spiritual reward or punishment is the more important of the two. In *Mabḥath*, 177–78, Avicenna brings up the subject but declines to address it. Obviously, this was a subject that he handled with some care. Cf. also *ash-Shifâ': al-Ilâhiyyât*, 439, 442–43, 445–46; and *an-Najât*, 326–27.

65. Cf. *ash-Shifâ': an-Nafs*, 203; *an-Najât*, 224; Rahman, *Avicenna's Psychology*, 59; and *Fi l-'ishq*, 3, where Avicenna states "there is nothing functionless [*mu'aṭṭal*, that is, purposeless] in nature." For a discussion of the questions of psychic individualization and angelic affiliation in Avicenna's thought, see Corbin, *Avicenna*, 46–100.

66. What follows is based on *al-Aḍḥawiyya*, esp. 109–25; *al-Mabda' wa-l-ma'âd*, 109–15; *Aḥwâl an-nafs*, 127–40; *ash-Shifâ': al-Ilâhiyyât*, 423–32; *an-Najât*, 327–34; *al-Hidâya*, 300–308;. See also Michot, *La destinée de l'homme selon Avicenne*; Jean Michot, "Avicenne et la destinée humaine: À propos de la résurrection des corps," *Revue philosophique de Louvain* 79 (1981) 453–83; and Gardet, *La pensée religieuse d'Avicenne*, 86–105. Relevant as well is Michael E. Marmura, "Avicenna

and the Problem of the Infinite Number of Souls," *Medieval Studies* 22 (1960) 232–39.

67. *ash-Shifâ': al-Ilâhiyyât*, 423–29; *an-Najât*, 327–30; *al-Aḍḥawiyya*, 110–20; *al-Mabda' wa-l-ma'âd*, 109–14; *Aḥwâl an-nafs*, 127–33; *al-Hidâya*, 300–303; *al-Ishârât wa-t-tanbîhât*, 4:11–28; and *Fi l-'ishq*, 3–5.

68. *al-Aḍḥawiyya*, 120; *ash-Shifâ': al-Ilâhiyyât*, 432; *an-Najât*, 333–34; *Aḥwâl an-nafs*, 139–40; *al-Mabda' wa-l-ma'âd*, 115; *al-Ishârât wa-t-tanbîhât*, 4:30–31.

69. *al-Aḍḥawiyya*, 120–21; *Aḥwâl an-nafs*, 133–34; *ash-Shifâ': al-Ilâhiyyât*, 430–31; *an-Najât*, 332; *al-Ishârât wa-t-tanbîhât*, 4:30–31; Michot, *La destinée de l'homme selon Avicenne*, 177–78.

70. *al-Aḍḥawiyya*, 121–22; *Aḥwâl an-nafs*, 134–35; *ash-Shifâ': al-Ilâhiyyât*, 431; *an-Najât*, 332; *al-Ishârât wa-t-tanbîhât*, 4:28–29, 45; *Fî ithbât an-nubuwwât*, 56–57; Michot, *La destinée de l'homme*, 178.

71. *al-Aḍḥawiyya*, 120–22; *Aḥwâl an-nafs*, 134–35; *ash-Shifâ': al-Ilâhiyyât*, 431; *an-Najât*, 333; *Fî ithbât an-nubûwât*, 56–58.

72. *al-Aḍḥawiyya*, 124–25; *Aḥwâl an-nafs*, 138–39; *ash-Shifâ': al-Ilâhiyyât*, 431–32; *an-Najât*, 332; *al-Mabda' wa-l-ma'âd*, 114–15; *al-Ishârât wa-t-tanbîhât*, 4:35–36. In *Fî ma'rifat an-nafs an-nâṭiqa wa-aḥwâlihâ*, 191, Avicenna appears to suggest that souls are drawn to specific spheres after death; although Michot has cast doubt on the authenticity of this treatise, he himself argues in *La destinée de l'homme selon Avicenne* (see esp. pp. 18–19, 23–30) that Avicenna came to accept the idea of imaginative apperceptions of heaven and hell as espoused by this "certain scholar"; given Avicenna's explicit statements that the imagination passes away with the body, I find Michot's argument unconvincing.

73. As Avicenna calls the celestial Intelligences in *al-Ishârât wa-t-tanbîhât*, 4:43.

74. Cf. *Mabḥath*, 157, 167; *ash-Shifâ': an-Nafs*, 40–41; *an-Najât*, 206; *Fî ta'bîr ar-ru'yâ*, 276–78; *al-Ishârât wa-t-tanbîhât*, 3:380–84, for example.

5. Avicenna's Theory of Knowledge

Avicenna's epistemology is based on his conception of *what* one can know (i.e., the sensible and intelligible realms surveyed in Chapter Three) and *how* one can know (i.e., the range of perceptual faculties discussed in Chapter Four). In this chapter we will investigate the dynamic psychological processes by which humans attain knowledge. As we shall see, Avicenna describes these processes in two versions: the logos and the muthos.

Levels of Knowledge: Logos Version

For the most part, Avicenna's psychology is structured according to levels of epistemological apprehension. The vegetable and animal souls manage natural, nonperceptual activities: nutrition, growth, and reproduction in the case of the former, and motion in the case of the latter. The main task of the higher faculties, the animal and rational souls, is psychological apperception, hierarchically arranged along a conceptual spectrum that starts with empirical sensation of particular, corporeal entities and concludes with full apprehension of pure, universal abstractions. As we have noted, for Avicenna ascension through this epistemological hierarchy has ontological as well as moral ramifications: the greater the level of intellectual abstraction, the more complete the knowledge a person can attain and the more perfect he or she can become.[1]

Sources of knowledge, according to Avicenna, include the external material world, the internal operations of the human soul, and the supernal spiritual world, that is, the three domains described by Ḥayy ibn Yaqẓân (from this perspective *Ḥayy* constitutes an epistemological geography). The faculties of perception correspond to these three domains and consist of, respectively, the five external senses, the five internal faculties of the animal soul, and the various levels of intellectual actualization in the rational soul. The previous chapter adumbrated the nature of these faculties in stasis; this chapter examines how they operate.[2]

External Sense Perception

Only the external senses have direct contact with the material world; each of the five senses apprehends and abstracts the forms of external existents independently, according to its own particular capacity. These disparate sense impressions are then conveyed to the common sense, whose task it is to recombine them into a unified representation of the integrated sensible being perceived.[3]

Internal Sense Perception

Common sense's apprehension of information brought to it by the five external senses is immediate, corresponding directly to that which each sense perceives. Like the eye behind the lens of a camera, it takes in only what these senses perceive; as such, its apprehension is ephemeral and constantly displaced by new data. Prior information is not lost, however, but rather stored in the retentive imagination (or representation).[4]

The retentive imagination abstracts forms to a greater level than does common sense. While common sense abstracts forms from matter, representation continues to view them even after the physical departure of the original empirical entities. The forms lodged in the retentive imagination, however, are "particular" in that they still retain all the accidents, attributes, and attachments of specific material existents. For example, the form of a particular horse seen, touched, and heard by the external senses remains in the retentive imagination as a replica of that same horse, with its specific size, shape, color, texture, and sound.[5]

Images stored in the retentive imagination are the raw material of both the compositive imagination and estimation.[6] The compositive imagination abstracts attributes and attachments from substantial forms to a greater degree than is possible for the retentive imagination and so is able to recombine them to form images that have not been empirically apprehended, or may not even exist. It is through this faculty that one creates the "imaginary" figures of fiction, myth, and fairy tale—giants, dragons, fairies. Even though such forms are independent of external material existents, they still display specific material accidents and attributes; they are still "particular" forms. As Avicenna says, "an imagined person still resembles an individual person."[7]

Estimation moves one step further along the spectrum toward pure abstraction, concerning itself less with empirical shapes or characteristics than with inherent motives, attendant ideas, or possible consequences. To cite Avicenna's standard example, while imagination concerns itself with the physical form of a wolf, estimation apprehends the wolf's notional significance and hence the potential threat the beast's presence poses to the safety of bystanders. Nevertheless, because estimation perceives the intentions of a specific wolf rather than the universal idea "wolfness," empirical attributes still pertain.[8]

The perceptions of both the compositive imagination—or cogitation, as it becomes in humans—and estimation are stored in the faculty of memory, where they await recall by cogitation or estimation, or the attention of the intellect. As the *Miʿrâj Nâma* states, "when it is of use to the intellect, (the intellect) retrieves it by means of the faculty of recollection. Recollection thus conveys from memory whatever (the intellect) may need."[9]

Communication Between the Animal and Rational Souls

As we have seen, while the faculties of the animal soul deal only with sensible "particulars" abstracted from matter in various ways, the function of the rational soul is to apprehend "universals," immaterial ideas or essences. For example, while the animal soul perceives a particular existing human being, the rational soul apprehends the abstract concept "humanity."[10] Mediation between the "sensible" perceptions of the animal soul and the "intelligible" apprehensions of the rational soul is performed by the cogitative faculty of the animal soul on the one hand, and the practical intellect of the rational soul on the other. How exactly this transpires is a problematic area in Avicenna's epistemology. Although the chasm between the mortal, material animal soul and the immortal, immaterial rational soul seems so great, when each is treated individually, as to appear insurmountable, these two foreign psychic arenas are able to interact by virtue of being discrete parts of a single entity, the embodied human soul.[11]

Avicenna regularly states that in regard to humans the compositive imagination should be termed the cogitative faculty (*al-quwwa l-mufakkira*).[12] His exposition of this faculty's sphere of activity, however, is devoted mainly to the fabulative functions that he appears to consider the "natural" propensity of the imagination, especially in relation to the subject of imaginative prophecy.[13] References to either cogitation or discernment (*tamyîz*) are restricted to a few lines in *ash-Shifâʾ*, in which he states that the soul (*nafs*) is able to divert the imagination from its specific activity (*khâṣṣ fiʿlihâ*) of fabulative invention by using "it in activities that are connected to it in regard to discernment and thought." In these situations, "the compositive imagination is unable to behave as it usually does according to its nature but rather is drawn by the administration [*taṣrîf*] of the rational soul."[14]

How the rational soul (which only deals with universal intelligibles) interacts or communicates with the cogitative faculty (which only handles particular sensibles) is described most fully in Avicenna's earliest psychological tract, *Mabḥath ʿan al-quwa n-nafsâniyya*. There the philosopher states that the theoretical faculty "may acquire intellectual forms from sensation by means of an instinctual disposition [*jibilla gharîziyya*] that it possesses." It does this by

> using the compositive imaginative and estimative faculties to present to its essence concepts that are in the representative imagination and memory. Upon examining them, it [i.e., the theoretical faculty] finds that [these sensible concepts] participate in regard to some [intelligible] concepts but are different in regard to others; it also finds that some of these [sensible] concepts are essential and some accidental. Their participation in [intelligible] concepts is like the sharing of the concepts of human being and donkey in regard to [the concept of] life, while being distinctive in regard to those of rationality and irrationality; as for essentiality, it is like life being in both of them, while as for accidentally, it is like black and white. When we consider these two [the human being and the donkey] in this manner, each one of these essential, accidental, shared, or particular concepts is made into a single, separate, universal, intellectual concept.[15]

In short, despite their inability to apprehend universals, the faculties of the animal soul do help the rational soul in its tasks by providing (1) individual particulars that aid in the apprehension of universal concepts, (2) information that clarifies the positive or negative relationships among individual concepts, (3) data from which general premises or conclusions may be induced, and (4) general secondary reports or traditions of a stable, undisputed nature.[16] Regardless of these various kinds of assistance, it must be emphasized that the animal faculties cannot in themselves supply the rational soul with universals or intelligibles. As the *Miʿrâj Nâma* states, "The intellect has nothing to do with sensibles. . . . [It] always faces aloft." Once it acquires pertinent information from the animal faculties, the rational soul returns to its own independent operations. Thereafter, contact with the animal faculties distracts rather than helps.[17]

The practical intellect serves a similar mediational function for the rational soul, and as such plays a correspondingly problematic role in Avicenna's epistemology. On the one hand, the practical intellect is portrayed as an essential part of the rational soul, governing practical deliberations and actions, controlling the lower animal faculties and appetites, and helping to integrate relations between the animal soul and the theoretical intellect. It does this by using "the major premises related to what it is deliberating and then deriving particulars."[18] It is difficult to see how it can do this without in some way perceiving particulars directly (on a psychological, not empirical level). However, direct perception of particulars would mean that this part of the rational soul is both material and mortal, since it is an oft-stated credo in Avicenna's writings that "every particular perception is made through a physical organ."[19] Indeed, the philosopher specifically states that "the practical intellect needs the body and its physical faculties in all of its activities."[20]

Avicenna's dilemma here results from his simultaneous insistence upon the radical bifurcation between the rational and animal souls and his presumption of their intrinsic unity within the soul as a whole. In arguing that the soul only perceives universals through the medium of the intellect, he answers the question of how one attains abstract knowledge; but by making knowledge of particulars and universals so essentially divergent in nature, he tremendously complicates the question of how they interrelate within the soul. As far as I know, he nowhere explicitly recognizes this issue as being problematic, assuming perhaps that his presumption of the unity of the soul's faculties would answer any objection to this espistemologic point.[21]

Intellectual Perception[22]

Although there are times when Avicenna appears to suggest that the rational soul "abstracts" universals from the particulars that the animal faculties provide, this is an imprecise formulation of his understanding of the process involved.[23] According to him, the rational soul cannot "create" universals any more than can the animal soul. Rather, the soul matures to the point at which it is able to "take the form of intelligibles, abstracted from matter, in its essence."[24]

Initially, the human intellect exists in a state of complete potentiality, on the level of what Avicenna terms (in an analogy to the relationship between matter and form) the material intellect. To move from full potentiality to any degree of actuality requires agency. Three things are thus required for intellection: the innate, if unrealized, aptitude (*isti'dâd*) for intellectual perception that the material intellect possesses; a source from which the rational soul can "take" intelligibles; and an agent that moves the passive material intellect from inchoate formlessness toward crystalline actuality. According to Avicenna, the functions of both source and agent are carried out by the tenth celestial Intelligence, the Active Intelligence, which is both the storehouse and bestower of intelligible forms and whose intellectual power is essentially and permanently active. It is through the Active Intelligence that the process of activating our own intellects proceeds.[25] On the one hand, it "allows" the rational soul to perceive both primary and secondary intelligibles, for it is the source from which they constantly radiate. On the other hand, the Active Intelligence "causes" the rational soul to apprehend intelligibles, for its agency moves the soul from passivity to actualization. As Avicenna says, the relationship of this external agent to our potential intellect is

> like the relationship of the sun to our vision. Just as the sun illuminates by its essence in actuality, and its light illuminates in actuality that which was previously not illuminated in actuality, so, too, is the state of this intellect in regard to our souls.[26]

Human souls, therefore, do not create intelligibles, they receive them from above. They cannot, as we have stressed, obtain them from below, that is, from the perceptual apparatus of the animal soul, since this latter perceives only empirically apprehended sensibles. Nevertheless, attending to the sensible abstractions of the lower faculties of the soul is useful for the rational soul as a propaedeutic exercise.

> When the intellectual faculty beholds the particulars in the compositive imagination, and the light of the Active Intelligence illuminates them in us, as we have mentioned, they become abstracted from matter and its attachments [*'alâ'iqa*], and they become imprinted on the rational soul; not in the sense that they themselves are moved from the imagination to the intellect in us, nor in the sense that the concept [lying] obscured in [material] attachments, being in itself and in regard to its essence [*dhât*] abstract, produces [another] like itself, but rather in the sense that [the intellect's] inspection of them prepares the soul for the time when the abstract [intelligibles] from the Active Intelligence emanate unto it.[27]

Moreover, it is important to note that although for Avicenna the Active Intelligence is the proximate source of intelligibles, it is not the only one:

> On the contrary, there are many other essences higher than [the Active Intelligence], each of which resembles it in being an intellectual substance, basi-

> cally separated from matter, but differs from it in that each one is a separate species. These things are as numerous as the celestial worlds and the heavenly spheres. The higher one is the cause of the existence of what is below it and of its own world, just as the Active Intelligence is the cause of our world.[28]

Hence, Avicenna appears to suggest that humans, if they are or become sufficiently perfect, have the potential of receiving intelligibles from all the celestial Intelligences, a proposition that lays the foundation for Avicenna's allegory, *Risâlat aṭ-ṭair*, and the allegoresis of the prophet Muḥammad's ascent through the spheres described in the *Miʿrâj Nâma*.[29]

The process by which the intellect moves from potentiality to actuality has been described in the previous chapter. Immediate apprehension of the Active Intelligence's emanation, or as Avicenna sometimes terms it, "divine inspiration" (*ilhâm ilâhî*), of first intelligibles moves the material intellect into the realm of actuality.[30] These first intelligibles then become a basis for further logical operations through which secondary intelligibles are apprehended. For Avicenna, the intellectual process is potentially infinite in scope. Humans are restricted only by the constitutional disposition of their innate temperaments, the constrictions of social environment, and the processes of free choice by which individual acts result in establishing personal habits and thus molding character.[31]

According to Avicenna, the intellect cognizes intelligibles in three different ways. In the first, rational thought is a process of *discursive reasoning* (*al-ʿilm al-fikrî*) by which intelligibles are apprehended (or learned) step by step, in a detailed and methodical fashion, until comprehended as interrelated parts of a unified whole. Although reaching a "conclusion" is obviously the ultimate aim of any process of intellection, discursive reasoning also emphasizes the individual, syllogistic "steps" that logically produce the desired "conclusion." Although individual ideas may be expressed by different terms, or rearranged in various ways, without a loss in their overall sense, the intellect's apprehension of them is characterized by an intimate awareness that they are sequences of individual intelligibles organized in such a way as to produce a unified, demonstrative whole.[32]

The second form of cognition involves theoretical knowledge that the soul has previously intellected but from which it has temporarily "turned away." According to Avicenna, the intellect can neither consider nor remember more than one thing at a time. While imagination and estimation are able to store images in memory and employ recollection to return them to the appropriate faculty, the intellect must apprehend each intelligible anew. On the other hand, cognition of known intelligibles is not as difficult as apprehending unknown ones, since the intellect had acquired a certain familiarity with intelligibles previously cognized. This cognitive state of easily recalling familiar knowledge is what Avicenna terms the *habitual intellect.* It is similar to the difference between knowing how to swim, even when this knowledge is for the moment not used, and the arduous process of learning how to swim for the first time.[33]

Avicenna terms his third category of cognition *intuition* (*al-ḥads*). In this case, the soul reaches logical conclusions by means of a spontaneous connection (*ittiṣâl*) with the Active Intelligence. Here, the intellect perceives secondary intelligibles in an instantaneous and comprehensive fashion rather than through the discursive process of step-by-step logical deduction. Avicenna's standard example for this process is the ability to discover intuitively the second term of a syllogism. Nevertheless, once knowledge is apprehended in this way, step-by-step explanation, either to oneself or someone else, is easily accomplished, for the proposition in question is indeed *known.* Avicenna terms this type of cognition *simple knowledge* (*al-ʿilm al-basîṭ*). Although not immediately perceived in detail, simple knowledge is absolutely certain and intuitively known to be true (just as are primary intelligibles); in fact, simple knowledge is the cognitive principle upon which all discursive knowledge is founded.[34] As Avicenna says, this principle

> belongs to an absolute intellectual faculty among souls similar to Active Intelligences. Detailed knowledge belongs to the soul in its capacity as soul; whoever lacks it lacks psychic knowledge. But the question of how the rational soul can have a principle other than the soul, which has knowledge other than the knowledge of the soul, is one that you must know from yourself.[35]

The evasiveness of this last sentence is significant, less in terms of our eventual understanding of Avicenna's epistemology—he himself proceeds to explain what he means—than for the shifting of philosophical gears that its rhetoric signals. Once again, the philosopher is initiating a conceptual distinction that—like the differentiation between the physical and spiritual souls—is basic to his psychology, obvious to anyone who reads his works carefully, but that is nevertheless continuously underplayed or purposely "mystified" in his rhetorical representation. This conceptual distinction reflects the relation that exists in the rational soul between the passivity of "soul" and the activity of "intellect."

The intellects of the celestial Intelligences are completely active. They do not engage in discursive reasoning or regard intelligibles successively, form by form. Their intellects are both active—immediately apprehending intelligibles as single units or as clusters—and creative, for they are "the principle for each form that emanates onto the soul."[36] Perfectly actualized human intellects resemble the celestial Intelligences in their capacity for attaining equivalently infallible levels of intellectual activity and creativity. At this level, they engage in immediate and comprehensive "simple" apprehension rather than the laboriously detailed process of "discursive" reasoning that, Avicenna now states, pertains to the rational soul.

> The soul of the knower, in respect to its being a soul, cognizes in an orderly, detailed manner, which is not in every way "simple." As for every intellectual perception, it is in some way related to a form separated from matter and from its material accidents in the [simple] way mentioned above. The soul is a receptive substance that is imprinted upon; the intellect is a substance that is a creative, acting principle.[37]

Once again, the dichotomy here is clearly between passivity and activity. In comparison to the active apprehension of a "pure" intellect (and according to Avicenna such intellects are rare among humans), the systematic discursive workings of the rational soul are passive. As usual, differentiations in conceptual hierarchy assume different gradations in Avicenna's implied scale of ontological evaluation. As the *Miʿrâj Nâma* states, "In the same way that the rational soul is the commander and superior of the [lower] souls, the intellect is the commander and superior of the rational soul."[38] Nevertheless, this distinction between simple and discursive knowledge, with its resultant differentiation within the rational soul between the "active" intellect and "passive" soul, is not merely an instance of cosmological floriation. On the contrary, it lies at the heart of Avicenna's theory of how one attains true knowledge.

According to Avicenna, intelligible forms subsist in the separate Intelligences, so that learning is the process by means of which one develops the soul's ability, or "aptitude" for perceiving these forms. Such perception is of two kinds: that of the intellect is actively assimilative and that of the soul is passively reflective.

> At times the [human] intellect beholds [intelligible forms in the celestial Intelligences], at other times it ignores them. When it beholds them, they are assimilated in it; when it ignores them, they are not. For the soul is like a mirror and they are like external entities. Sometimes they appear in it, sometimes they do not, depending on the relationships that exist between them and the soul. Or the Active Principle emanates form after form onto the soul,

> according to its request, and when [the soul] turns away from it, the emanation is broken off.[39]

This passage implies that the soul may perceive some intelligibles passively, either because its particular nature endows it with a special automatic receptivity for certain primary intelligibles emanating from the celestial Intelligences, or because, as we have seen, the soul has acquired an easy familiarity with specific previously learned intelligibles. Beyond this, however, it cannot itself increase its own knowledge. Only the intellect is able to engage in the active process of increasing its "aptitude" by first assimilating intelligible forms emanating from the celestial Intelligences and then transmitting them to the soul in the form of discursive knowledge. First, one's intellect attains "simple knowledge"; thereafter, the intellect "emanates detailed forms to the soul by means of rational cogitation [*fikra*, but not that pertaining to the faculty of the animal soul]."[40] When an intellect perfects its aptitude, when it "intellects in actuality, and intellects that it intellects in actuality," then it attains the state of the acquired intellect, a state that, we have seen, perfects "the genus, animal, and the species, humankind."[41]

Intellectual Prophecy[42]

Intellectual aptitudes, according to Avicenna, are of various degrees and begin and end at different levels of perfection. Intellects that were never developed or went wrong end up in some quite unpleasant places in the hereafter, while most people never advance beyond the laborious processes of discursive reasoning that lead to intermittent interchanges with the Active Intelligence. A few rare, fortunate souls, however, begin with greater potential. Just as some humans display minimal natural talent at rational perception, a few may possess absolute ability. For such an individual, the attainment of immediate "simple" knowledge would be less a process of long-term learning through continuous practice in the art of discursive reasoning than a simple intellectual reflex. Such a person would intuitively achieve a degree of knowledge unattainable for most other people.

> This [natural] aptitude might be so powerful in a person that he or she would not need to conjoin with the Active Intelligence for many things, nor [depend on] cogitation or teaching; rather, this aptitude would be so powerful that it would seem as if the person had a second aptitude; rather, as if he or knew everything from him or herself. This is the highest level of this aptitude.[43]

Since this disposition is innate, its source is not the acquired intellect but instead a form of the otherwise humble material intellect. And because this type of material intellect has attained absolute perfection to the extent that it can call up simple knowledge whenever it wishes, Avicenna considers it to be a special type of habitual intellect, which he calls the "holy" or "angelic" intellect (*'aql qudsî, 'aql malakî*). Any person who possesses a soul "so powerful in regard to purity and conjunction with intellectual principles that he or she blazes with intuition" has been blessed with the highest intellectual faculty and is called a prophet, the highest rank of human beings, and "in whom the degrees of excellence in the realm of material forms culminate . . . [who] stands above and rules all the genera above which he or she excels."[44] At this level of intellectual excellence, the force of intuitive insight can be such that it "effulges" onto the compositive imagination, which then "represents it by sensible and audible speech."[45] This representation is "particularized," because the prophet is still a particular human being, but it is also perfect. As the *Mi'râj Nâma* states: "The motion and repose of this person is pure in religious legislative function [*shar'*]. It never admits abrogation or distortion."[46]

From the perspective of society as a whole, the existence of a prophet is a political necessity, decreed by divine Providence so that humans may have the benefit of being informed of the existence of God and His ordinances.[47] In regard to any individual person, however, the "holy" prophetic faculty is an accidental rather than essential property that in some sense elevates the prophet to the level of the Active Intelligence:

> The Active Intellect [or Intelligence], although being a supernal reality to humanity, is part and parcel of the prophet as prophet: phenomenally speaking, the prophet as human being is not the Active Intellect but since in his case the barrier between the phenomenal and the ideal (real) has broken down, he is identical with the Active Intellect.[48]

Like the Active Intelligence, prophets ultimately receive their intelligibles from—or more precisely, become actualized as intelligences by means of—the First or Universal Intelligence. In Avicenna's words: "Revelation is the emanation and the angel is the received emanating power that descends on the prophets as if it were an emanation continuous with the universal intellect."[49] Or, as the *Mi'râj Nâma* portrays it, Muḥammad is seated on the Active Intelligence (*Burâq*), while the Angel of Revelation, Gabriel, leads him in his ascent through the heavenly spheres.[50]

Levels of Knowledge: Muthos Version

Avicenna's muthos portrayal of the dynamics of psychic apprehension is, like his logos version, founded on the premise that correspondences exist among ontological categories, cosmological hierarchies, and epistemological faculties. Unlike his logos exposition, however, which encompasses the full range of human perceptive faculties in regard to both the animal and the rational souls, Avicenna's muthos rendition focuses chiefly on the rational soul, which thus explicitly assumes its philosophically demarcated role as the center of psychic self-consciousness (*ego* in modern parlance). Foregrounded as an externalized unit rather than merely one member of a complex multiplicity of internal psychological faculties, the rational soul emerges as the protagonist for Avicenna's allegories. This ego/protagonist has two aspects: the corporeal and social concerns of the practical intellect and the rational and celestial orientation of the theoretical intellect. A major theme of Avicenna's muthos version consists of a warning against the deleterious consequences of a disruption in the natural balance that ideally should hold between the two.

Narrative expression of the soul's progress (or lack thereof) toward teleological actualization is also externalized, and hence transferred from the realm of epistemolgical analysis to that of cosmological movement. Rather than being depicted as shifting from one level of internal, mental apprehension to another, the rational soul is portrayed as journeying through—and inhabiting—a hierarchy of tangible cosmological echelons. This process of representational externalization leads Avicenna to shed the narrative format of abstract, philosophical analysis that characterizes logos in favor of the incarnative, symbolizing strategies of allegory.

No single one of Avicenna's allegories delineates the complete plot sequence of his muthos version of "the metaphysics of the rational soul," that is, the story of the soul's descent into material incarceration and subsequent ascent toward the perfection of spiritual release.[51] The story can be reconstructed, however, by comparing "The Ode on the Soul," *Ḥayy ibn Yaqẓân, Risâlat aṭ-ṭair, Salâmân and Absâl*, and Book Nine of *al-Ishârât wa-t-tanbîhât*. Each of these treatises emphasizes discrete parts of the cycle, adopts distinctive formulations of dramatic perspective, foregrounds particular paradigmatic or syntagmatic features, employs specific rhetorical techniques, and displays distinct variegations of tone and texture. Nevertheless, a comparison of their plot structures reveals a single narrative design underlying their apparent diversity.[52] Viewed from this perspective, Avicenna's configuration of this psychic journey encompasses six principal moments: (1) the soul's descent into corporeal amnesia, (2) its awakening to an awareness of the existence of the spiritual realm of Intellect and of its own rightful place in this realm, (3) the struggle that ensues between the material and spiritual souls for control of the psychic ego, (4) the soul's eventual deliverance from the controlling bonds of matter and its progressive return toward its final goal of intellectual realization, (5) its temporary return to participation in the world of matter, and (6) its final release, through death, from the material domain and subsequent eternal residence in the realm of Intellect.

Descent and Forgetfulness

The pathos of the soul's descent from above and subsequent immersion within matter is touchingly portrayed in both "The Ode on the Soul" (*al-qaṣîda al-ʿainiyya*) and the "Epistle of the Bird" (*aṭ-Ṭair*). In the words of the first:

> There descended upon you from that lofty realm,
> A dove, glorious and inaccessible.
> Concealed from the eye of every seeker [*ʿârif*],
> Although openly disclosed and unveiled.
> Reluctantly she came to you,
> And reluctant, in her affliction, will she depart.
> She resisted, untamed; then upon her arrival
> She grew accustomed to this desolate waste.
> She forgot, I think, promises of sanctuary and
> abodes from which she had been unwilling to leave.
> She became attached to the D of her Descent, (moving) from
> The C of her Center down to these sandy dunes,
> Until the W of Weightiness clung to her, and she fell prostrate
> among (their) signposts and deserted campsites.[53]

The dove-soul's misfortunes are manifold here. It is deprived of its natural intellectual ability (symbolized by the ability to fly) and falls captive to the instincts and passions of the lower faculties of the animal soul. Imprisoned by the physical demands of matter, it is condemned to endless exile among the desolate wastelands and meaningless signposts of earthly existence. Worse yet, it is even deprived of memories of its past freedom (i.e., of the self-consciousness of the theoretical intellect). Indeed, a gap in identity between the dove and the addressee of the poem ("*She* descended upon *you*") is explicitly assumed. Reduced to the level of a practical intellect controlled by bodily passions, the soul has lost the rational dimensions that make it uniquely human.

Similar themes of descent, resistance, despair, and amnesia are found in *aṭ-Ṭair*. The rational soul, once again symbolized as a bird, is unsuspectingly enticed by bait left by hunters, so that it and its companions fall among snares and nets.

> We tried to move, but our difficulties only increased. So we resigned ourselves to destruction, our individual sorrow precluding each of us from caring about his or her brother. We strove to discover stratagems of escape for a time, until we were made to forget the form of our predicament. We became accustomed to nets and content with cages.[54]

Here one further motif is added, that of isolation. Entrapped, the soul is separated from its companions, estranged from its point of origin, and denied the rewards of association with prior comrades.

Awakening

Under the proper circumstances, forgetfulness can give way to remembrance. In *aṭ-Ṭair* the bird sees "a company of birds . . . flying with the remnants of snares still on their legs." At the sight of those whose theoretical intellect has been activated, either intuitively or by engaging in the study of philosophy, the bird recalls its own intellectual dimension and this, in turn, clarifies the nature of its future course. By seeking assistance (learning philosophy) from other birds who have managed to escape, the bird finds deliverance.

It is at the point of resuming its identity as theoretical intellect that the soul encounters the Active Intelligence, whom, we have seen, Avicenna frequently represents by means of the figure of Ḥayy ibn Yaqẓân.[55] When Ḥayy appears to the narrator of *Ḥayy ibn Yaqẓân*, the latter has an unaccountable, yet overwhelming, desire to engage him in conversation, the immediate result of which is that the soul turns away from its three earthbound companions, the irascible, concupiscent, and imaginative faculties, and reorients itself towards the realm of Intellect. Ḥayy need only describe this realm to foster this process; for once the soul is reoriented, it is filled with a compellingly powerful yearning to reclaim its heritage. On realizing its true nature the captive bird "almost melted with remorse, and [its] soul almost slipped away with regret."[56]

PSYCHIC DISCORD

Despite the strength of its yearning, the soul's ability first to recognize (re-cognize) its real identity and then to mobilize the will-power (*irâda*) necessary to reassert its natural psychic hierarchy should not be presumed easy. As the protagonist/narrator of *Ḥayy* remarks:

> Submitting my companions [the irascible, concupiscent, and imaginative faculties] to trial and setting myself to observe them, (I found that) experience confirmed what I had been told of them. And now I am as much occupied with curing them as with submitting to them. Sometimes it is I who have the upper hand of them, sometimes they are stronger than I am.[57]

In the story *Salâmân and Absâl* Avicenna devotes a complete narrative to depicting the psychological struggle that spiritual reorientation can provoke. Although the original text is lost, a shortened version survives in the commentary on *al-Ishârât wa-t-tanbîhât* by Naṣîr ad-Dîn aṭ-Ṭûsî (d. 672/1274), a summary of which follows.[58]

Salâmân and Absâl are royal siblings. Salâmân, the elder, has raised his younger brother, Absâl, who has grown into a noble, gracious, and handsome young man. In fact, so great is his attraction that Salâmân's wife falls in love with him. When Absâl discreetly resists her advances, she persuades her husband to marry Absâl to her sister. This marriage is only a ruse, however, for on the wedding night Salâmân's wife takes her sister's place. The night is dark and cloudy, and at first Absâl is unable to see his bride. Suddenly, however, a flash of lightning illuminates the room and reveals not the face of his bride but that of his brother's wife. Distraught, Absâl flees the room.

In order to avoid further contact with his sister-in-law, Absâl persuades Salâmân to give him command of an army and sets out to conquer nations "on sea and on land, in the east and the west." After many victories, he reckons that his brother's wife has recovered from her vain infatuation and so returns home. He soon discovers, however, that her passion for him is still very much ablaze. Later, when Absâl is appointed to head Salâmân's army against an enemy, the wife vengefully bribes the army's commanders to revolt against him. Although they desert Absâl on the field of battle, where he is wounded and left for dead, a wild animal cares for him and nurses him back to health. When he returns home to find Salâmân surrounded by enemies, he defeats them and restores the kingdom to peace and equilibrium.

Salâmân's wife, who still thirsts for revenge, then pays the royal chef and the majordomo to poison Absâl. Salâmân, overwhelmed with grief over the death of his beloved brother, renounces his kingship and retreats into solitary meditation on God, who eventually reveals to him his wife's crime. Salâmân kills her, the chef, and the majordomo by forcing them to drink the same poison they used to assassinate Absâl.

This story, replete with echoes of the theme of Joseph and Potiphar's wife, is reminiscent of the "wiles of woman" tale genre. Yet its intent is more closely aligned with the strictures of Horatian *utile* than with the idle pleasures of *dulce*. According to aṭ-Ṭûsî's interpretation, Salâmân symbolizes the rational soul; his wife, the material appetites and faculties of the animal soul; and Absâl, the theoretical intellect elevated to the level of the acquired intellect. The passion Salâmân's wife feels for Absâl is understandable, given the mixture of humanity's inherent love of beauty and the extraordinary attraction that Absâl's own grace, beauty, and wisdom evoke. But the actual fulfillment of this passion, at first provocatively concupiscent, and then vengefully irascible, will necessarily cause Absâl's death. When her initial advances are rebuffed, Salâmân's wife (the animal soul) seeks to entice Absâl into marriage with her sister, who symbolizes the practical intellect, with the intention of assuming her sister's place. Desperately fleeing her embraces, Absâl (the acquired intellect) proceeds to conquer the west and east (the sensible and intelligible worlds) and bring to the rational soul (Salâmân) the fruits of his victories. His immersion in the realm of intellect, however, causes him to slacken his discipline over the faculties of the animal soul who are therefore able to rise up in revolt. Succored by the beneficial emanations of the separate Intelligences (the wild animal), Absâl recovers from this defeat, regains control of the passions and appetites of the body, and reestablishes his brother's rule. This rule is short-lived, however, and the animal soul once again manages to repress the influence of the acquired intellect. Finally, Salâmân (the rational soul) quells bodily passions and so becomes able to devote himself entirely to contemplation of the intelligible domain.

There are several striking features in this psychomachia. The first is the absence of overt religious moralism. This is not a struggle between Good and Evil or Virtue and Sin: the acquired intellect and the animal faculties are only seeking to fulfill their natural ends.[59] The goal is a state of psychic harmony in which the faculties of the soul interact in a way that directs the total psyche toward or away from its teleologically designated actualization. Also notable is the passivity of the rational soul. Although always near the center of narrative activity, it is not until the very end that Salâmân becomes aware of the struggle that rages around him. At his wife's behest, he marries Absâl to her sister; at his brother's request, he gives him an army; nominally the ruler, he in fact only reacts to the suggestions of those around him. Only when Absâl dies does Salâmân begin to take charge of his affairs and put his kingdom in order.

This passivity is not simply a matter of narrative plotting or typecasting. In fact, it accords with Avicenna's ontological postulate regarding the constant relationship between form and matter. As we have seen, underlying Avicenna's view of the cosmos is the notion that there are progressive dialectical relationships between the passivity of matter and the activity of form; indeed, the prime purpose of *Ḥayy ibn Yaqẓân* is to explicate these ascending scales of relativity. Beginning with the absolute passivity of prime matter, specific differences among levels of being—the Four Elements, minerals, plants, animals, humans, celestial bodies, Souls, Intelligences, and finally, the Necessary Existent—are each marked by ever-increasing degrees of innate activity. This dialectic, however, is relative. In relation to minerals the vegetable soul is active, in relation to the animal soul it is passive. For Avicenna this paradigm requires increasingly precise grades of differentiation. Hence, the soul is active in relation to the body, the animal soul, active in relation to the vegetable soul, and the rational soul, active in regard to the animal soul. But the process of bifurcation continues even beyond this level. Within the rational soul, intellect is active while "soul" is passive. Furthermore, when an human intellect achieves conjunction (*ittiṣâl*) with a celestial Intelligence, it assumes a soul-like passivity in relation to the latter's more elevated intellectual activity. The existential status of all entities in the cosmos, except humans, is constant and univocal since the affiliation that holds between those below and above each one is fixed. Only the existential status of human beings is relative and equivocal; this is because, of all creatures, only humans have the potential for encompassing the apprehensible limits of the cosmos. Only humans have the potential to experience ever-escalating levels of psychic actualization.

Deliverance

When the soul reawakens to its true celestial nature and becomes reacquainted with the parameters of the cosmic geography described in *Ḥayy ibn Yaqẓân*, it experiences intense joy (as the "Ode" states "it sings for joy from a lofty mountain top") and then begins its journey home. This journey, however, is completed neither swiftly nor easily.

In *al-Ishârât wa-t-tanbîhât*, Avicenna portrays this passage as resulting from a process that combines spiritual exercise and contemplation.[60] He begins by dividing spiritual devotees into three categories: the ascetic (*az-zâhid*), who turns away from the pleasures of the world; the pious worshiper (*al-ʿâbid*), dedicated to the external acts of religious devotion; and the intellectual seeker (*al-ʿârif*), who concentrates his or her thoughts on "the holiness of divine omnipotence (*qudus al-jabarût*)." The first two worship on the basis of imaginative apprehension, desiring the pleasures of heavenly reward and fearing the punishments of divine wrath. The intellectual seeker differs in that he or she desires God (*Ḥaqq*, Absolute Truth, Reality) for His own sake. The seeker obeys the commands of religion not from desire for reward or fear of punishment, but because they are God's commands and as such intrinsically deserve obedience. The devotions of the seeker are God-centered, not self-centered, and follow a set path.[61]

The first stage of seeking God is that of the novice (*murîd*), a state of spiritual desire (*irâda*) based on either intellectual certainty or deep faith.[62] Next come devotional exercises that center on three tasks: turning aside from all that does not concern God, training the faculties of the animal soul to serve the rational soul, and awakening the soul's spiritual insight through a combination of subtle thought (*al-fikr al-laṭîf*) and virtuous passion (*al-ʿishq al-ʿafîf*).[63] After mastering these two stages, the seeker begins to experience moments of conjunction (*ittiṣâl*) with God, "delightful glimpses of God's light revealed to him, like flashes of lightning."[64] With practice, this "state" (lit. "time," *waqt*) begins to occur spontaneously outside of periods of meditation. Eventually, it becomes almost continuous, subject only to brief intervals of disruption, and the seeker is "made to ascend [*taʿrîj*] to the world of God."[65]

By this time the seeker has transcended the stage of devotional exercise and reached that of attainment (*an-nail*), a state in which the soul has become a polished mirror that reflects divine effulgences. The seeker still maintains traces of psychic duality, however, for stretches of complete immersion are still interrupted by moments of self-awareness. Finally, the seeker arrives at a state of continual contemplation, in which nothing distracts him or her from union (*wuṣûl*) with the divine realm.[66]

Although the framework (stages and states) and the terminology

(*Ḥaqq*, *wuṣûl*) Avicenna adopts in this portrayal have a distinctively *ṣûfî* tenor, there is little doubt that he is still moving within the intellectual confines of his philosophical system. Nevertheless, it is clear that once he leaves the sensible realm and moves completely into the portrayal of intelligible levels of perception, he no longer has the philosophical terminology he needs to describe the details of these new types of experience. This conclusion is amply confirmed by examination of the more overtly allegorical treatment of this same process of intellectual ascent that one finds in the "Epistle of the Bird."

If *Ḥayy ibn Yaqẓân* describes Ḥayy's peregrinations in the intelligible realm, *aṭ-Ṭair* focuses on the journey of Ḥayy's interlocutor, the individual rational soul, within the same domain. Moreover, despite his familiarity with all parts of this region—he is after all a native resident—Ḥayy inhabits a fixed place within it; his natural abode is where we meet him in the narrative, in the liminal area where the sensible and intelligible worlds meet. The final place of the bird in *aṭ-Ṭair* within the hierarchy of the intelligible realm, however, has yet to be determined. Beginning at a lower level than Ḥayy, its *telos* is potentially much more elevated.

After freeing itself from the nets and snares by which it was trapped, the bird joins his companions and encounters eight lofty mountain peaks. The group traverses six of these, but briefly rest on the seventh; this is a land of

> gardens, with grassy meadows, flourishing fields, fruit-laden trees, and flowing rivers, whose delight quenched your gaze; with forms whose splendor confounded the intellect and astonished the mind, who filled our ears with rapturous melody and heartrending songs, and our nostrils with fragrances unapproached by noble musk and fresh ambergris.[67]

The birds are enraptured and refreshed by the beauties of this province (the realm of the celestial Souls); but recognizing the dangers of being enticed by its still-sensuous charms they move on. They stop again atop the eighth mountain peak where they meet some birds (the separate Intelligences) who tell them of the palace of the great King who lives beyond the mountains. The travelers continue on their journey and finally arrive at the palace of the King, who is described as follows:

> Whatever you have attained in your mind of beauty unblemished with ugliness, and perfection unmixed with fault, in this you have hit upon a complete picture of him. Every perfection, in reality, stems from him; every fault, if

> only in metaphor, is banished from him. In his beauty, he is all a Face; in his generosity, all a Hand. Whoever serves him gains the utmost happiness; whoever forsakes him forfeits the next world and this.[68]

RETURN AND RELEASE

When the birds complain to the King about the remnants of snares that still encumber their legs, he tells them that "only those who knotted the snares will be able to undo them." He then sends the birds back home with the messenger of death who will arrange for the snares' removal. The meaning of this is that no matter how great a person's intellectual attainment is, only death completely frees one from the shackles of material existence.[69] The bird thus "returns, knowing every hidden matter of the two worlds," to live in the corporeal realm until the moment of its death.[70]

Summation

This detailed examination of the both logos and muthos versions of the progress of the soul should clarify certain aspects of their relationship. For Avicenna, philosophy can describe the human condition within the confines of sublunary existence and can to some degree even transcend these boundaries. Nevertheless, the investigation and depiction of the interaction between human beings and the intelligible realm stretches conventional philosophical terminology and modes of discourse to their limits. At this point, the philosopher is compelled to abandon logical demonstration and to employ the creative "visionary" powers of metaphor, thus bringing into play the "likely stories" of muthos.

The shift from demonstration to metaphor does not imply that muthos is any less crucial than logos for understanding the thought of a philosopher like Avicenna. The epistemological postulates that underlie Avicenna's philosophy cannot be understood without slowly and painstakingly analyzing them. In the same way, we cannot comprehend the full implications of the goal toward which he is heading, that is, the final image and *telos* of human beings that motivates his philosophical activity, unless we give equally precise and careful consideration to the details of his muthos accounts.

This brings to mind Henry Corbin's observation that to understand a philosopher one must perceive the "mode of presence . . . usually concealed between the tissue of didactic demonstrations and impersonal developments." In Corbin's view this mode of presence is inextricably intertwined with the personal, subjective, motivations that must "finally account for the 'motifs' that the philosopher adopted or rejected, understood or failed to understand, carried to their maximum of meaning or, on the contrary, degraded to trivialities."[71]

The value of this insight is that it allows us to differentiate between the intellectual impetus that compels a philosopher to examine and reexamine his or her ideas, always subjecting them to the rigors of methodological analysis, and the emotional intensity that drives the committed philosopher to ponder ideas for hours, days, or years. It also shows how these two things are not necessarily mutually contradictory. However distinct in style, tone, and process logos and muthos may be, they are modes of discourse that stem from the same wellsprings of motivation and that aim for the same goals. They are each tools that the philosopher may utilize to work toward a chosen end.

Either form, of course, may be misused. The symbols, metaphors, and emotive evocativeness of muthos can easily become just as sophistical or manipulative as the false logic or rhetorical dissemblances of pseudo-logos. Thus, equally rigorous criteria must be used in judging the respective success or effectiveness of each in achieving humanistic goals. Poetry that combines emotive affect with intellectual passion must be just as sound in method and accurate in detail as any philosophical tract. Although the modes of discourse differ in obvious ways, the labor and care that each demands are perhaps more similar than commonly supposed. To ask whether Avicenna's allegorical journey of the soul underlies and drives his philosophizing or whether the conclusions of his philosophical analysis led him logically to the use of allegory oversimplifies the issue. The point, at any rate, is moot. A more fruitful method of inquiry is one that holds both forms of discourse fully in view even when only one of them is being examined; in this way the insights derived from the investigation of one can only complement and elucidate our understanding of the processes and rewards of the other.

The muthos portrayal of Avicenna's journey of the soul that we have just examined concentrates on the progress of the individual human soul. As such it deals with a philosophical "everyman." This ignores an important part of the philosopher's intellectual epistemology: the unique place Avicenna awards to the intellectual prophet; a subject that is the main concern of the *Mi'râj Nâma*.

Notes

1. See later in this chapter, where the subject of the fulfillment of the rational soul is discussed.

2. The following is based mainly on *ash-Shifâ': an-Nafs*, 32–41; *an-Najât*, 200–210; Rahman, *Avicenna's Psychology*, 30–40; *Aḥwâl an-nafs*, 57–73; *Mabḥath*, 161–78; *Fi l-quwa l-insâniyya* (all); *al-Hidâya*, 206–30; *Dânish-nâma-yi 'Alâ'î: Ṭabî'iyyât*, 102–29; as well as the preceding chapter.

3. *ash-Shifâ': an-Nafs*, 33–35; *an-Najât*, 198, 208–10; Rahman, *Avicenna's Psychology*, 38–40; *Aḥwâl an-nafs*, 59; *Fi l-quwa l-insâniyya*, 43; *al-Hidâya*, 211–12; *Dânish-nâma-yi 'Alâ'î: Ṭabî'iyyât*, 102–3.

4. *ash-Shifâ': an-Nafs*, 35–36; *an-Najât*, 201; Rahman, *Avicenna's Psychology*, 31; *Aḥwâl an-nafs*, 62; *Fi l-quwa l-insâniyya*, 44.

5. *ash-Shifâ': an-Nafs*, 36; *an-Najât*, 208–9; Rahman, *Avicenna's Psychology*, 39; *Aḥwâl an-nafs*, 71; *Fi l-quwa l-insâniyya*, 44; *Dânish-nâma-yi 'Alâ'î: Ṭabî'iyyât*, 104–5.

6. *Mi'râj Nâma*, 83; trans., 114; *ash-Shifâ': an-Nafs*, 35; *an-Najât*, 208; Rahman, *Avicenna's Psychology*, 37; *Aḥwâl an-nafs*, 60–61; *Fi l-quwa l-insâniyya*, 44.

7. *an-Najât*, 209. I differ here from Rahman who translates *al-mutakhayyil* as pertaining to the retentive imagination or representation rather the compositive imagination or cogitative faculty; cf. Rahman, *Avicenna's Psychology*, 39; *Aḥwâl an-nafs*, 71; see also *ash-Shifâ': an-Nafs*, 35; Michot, *La destinée de l'homme selon Avicenne*, 147–48.

8. *ash-Shifâ': an-Nafs*, 36–37; *an-Najât*, 209; Rahman, *Avicenna's Psychology*, 39–40; *Aḥwâl an-nafs*, 62, 71–72; *Fi l-quwa l-insâniyya*, 44; Michot, *La destinée de l'homme selon Avicenne*, 148–50.

9. *Mi'râj Nâma*, 83; trans., 114; *ash-Shifâ': an-Nafs*, 37, 148–50; *an-Najât*, 203; Rahman, *Avicenna's Psychology*, 31; *Aḥwâl an-nafs*, 62; *al-Hidâya*, 213–14.

10. *ash-Shifâ': an-Nafs*, 38–39; *an-Najât*, 203–4, 209–10; Rahman, *Avicenna's Psychology*, 33, 40; *Mabḥath*, 168–69; *Aḥwâl an-nafs*, 63–64, 72–73; *Fi l-quwa l-insâniyya*, 44; *al-Hidâya*, 216–17; *Dânish-nâma-yi 'Alâ'î: Ṭabî'iyyât*, 106–7; *al-Mubâḥathât*, 230–31. For Avicenna's demonstrations that universals and the rational soul are both immaterial, see *ash-Shifâ': an-Nafs*, 187–96; *an-Najât*, 210–20; Rahman, *Avicenna's Psychology*, 41–54; *Aḥwâl an-nafs*, 74–86; *al-Hidâya*, 217–22; *Mabḥath*, 172–75.

11. Avicenna repeatedly points out the basic disparity that exists between the functions of the material animal soul and the incorporeal rational soul (cf., for example, *Fi l-quwa l-insâniyya*, 46), but he does this within a context that assumes the intrinsic unity of the soul; as he says in *al-Mubâḥathât*, 230 (#466), "It has been affirmed that corporeal forms and concepts are only perceived by a corporeal instrument and universal abstracts are not perceived by a corporeal instrument; both matters are together ascribed [*yunsab*] to the single soul"; or as he says in *ash-Shifâ': an-Nafs*, 152, "All of these faculties belong to the single soul; we assume that as a postulate." Cf. the previous chapter on the unity that underlies the soul's various activities; on the relationship of the rational soul to the body, see also *Fî kalâm 'ala n-nafs an-nâṭiqa*, 196.

12. See Chapter Four, p. 63.

13. This fascinating part of Avicenna's epistemology is not immediately relevant to our discussion; a good exposition is in Rahman, *Prophecy in Islam*, 36–52.

14. *ash-Shifâ': an-Nafs*, 153. Notice how Avicenna shifts perspective here in this passage, making the move from the compositive imagination to the cogitative faculty by way of the soul in general, and then specifying the agency of the rational soul in the end. In Avicenna's numerous tracts on psychology, fuzzy wording usually signals that he is still puzzling something out.

15. *Mabḥath*, 169. It is telling that Avicenna's fullest statement on this subject comes in his earliest treatise, while later references are more elliptical. It appears to me that awareness of the intrinsic gap that exists between the animal and rational souls became more obvious to Avicenna as he came more fully to realize the importance of the latter. It would be worthwhile to look at his writings in more detail to see exactly how his thinking evolved (or perhaps devolved in clarity) in regard to this subject, cf. for example, *al-Mubâḥathât*, 204–5 (#368) and Michot, *La destinée de l'homme selon Avicenne*, 105. For another analysis of cogitation in Avicenna's thought, cf. Davidson, "Alfarabi and Avicenna," 165–67. Davidson, however, confuses the thought processes (*al-fikr*) of the cogitative faculty with the discursive reasoning (*al-ʿilm al-fikrî*) of the theoretical faculty; see *al-Mubâḥathât*, 232 (#468), where Avicenna refers to *al-quwwa l-mufakkira* as *al-quwwa l-ʿaqliyya*, and *al-Ishârât wa-t-tanbîhât*, 2:392–95, where he discusses the difference between *al-fikra* and *al-ḥads*.

16. *ash-Shifâ': an-Nafs*, 197; *an-Najât*, 220–21; Rahman, *Avicenna's Psychology*, 54–55; *Aḥwâl an-nafs*, 87–88; *at-Taʿlîqât*, 83.

17. *Miʿrâj Nnâma*, 84; trans., 115. Cf. *ash-Shifâ': an-Nafs*, 197–98; *an-Najât*, 221–22; Rahman, *Avicenna's Psychology*, 55–56; *Aḥwâl an-nafs*, 88–89; *Fi l-quwa l-insâniyya*, 44–45.

18. *ash-Shifâ': an-Nafs*, 185; see also Chapter Four, p. 65.

19. *an-Najât*, 210ff.; Rahman, *Avicenna's Psychology*, 41ff.; *ash-Shifâ': an-Nafs*, 166–67; *Aḥwâl an-nafs*, 74–79, 117, 121; *al-Mubâḥathât*, 230; Michot, *La destinée de l'homme selon Avicenne*, 123, note 83, 125–33.

20. *ash-Shifâ': an-Nafs*, 185.

21. See note 11 above (from *al-Mubâḥathât*, 230). As is clear from *al-Mubâḥathât*, 234–36, the distinction between theoretical wisdom, the inquiry into first principles in physics, mathematics, and metaphysics, and practical wisdom, the study of first principles in ethics, household management, and politics, is not a problem. But this relationship is not the same as that which holds between the theoretical and practical intellects. The question is basic: How do abstract and empirical knowledge interrelate? The Peripatetic position, shared by al-Fârâbî and Ibn Rushd among Islamic philosophers, holds that whatever impulses or aid humans receive from celestial beings "above," their basic source of information is empirical knowledge from the material world "below," apprehended by the external senses and then abstracted by the intellect to the necessary degree. The Platonic tradition, to which Avicenna adheres, does not dispute the existence of empirical perception, but argues that "real," abstract knowledge is known from "above,"

either "remembered," as Plato suggests, or received through constant "emanation," as Plotinus and Avicenna hold. Correlative to the conundrum of the relationship between particular and universal knowledge in the human soul is that of the same relationship in regard to the Necessary Existent, the separate Intelligences, and the heavenly Souls, as al-Ghazâlî pointed out in the sixteenth chapter of his *Tahâfut al-falâsifa*; for a careful account of this issue see Marmura, "Some Aspects of Avicenna's Theory of God's Knowledge of Particulars," 299–312, esp. pp. 304–9; for Michot's analysis of this question, see *La destinée de l'homme selon Avicenne*, 110–18, 123–25; also relevant is Gardet, *La pensée religieuse d'Avicenne*, 71–85.

22. See also Rahman, *Prophecy in Islam*, 14–20; Davidson, "Alfarabi and Avicenna," throughout, but esp. pp. 154–78; Afnan, *Avicenna*, 138–43.

23. Cf. *an-Najât*, 203; trans. Rahman, *Avicenna's Psychology*, 33 (compare also *ash-Shifâ': an-Nafs*, 39, 212; and *Aḥwâl an-nafs*, 65):

> The function of the theoretical faculty is to receive the impressions of the universal forms abstracted from matter. If these forms are already abstract in themselves, it simply receives them; if not, it makes them immaterial by abstraction, so that no trace whatever of material attachments remains in them.

24. *ash-Shifâ': an-Nafs*, 212. On the same page Avicenna states that "the soul cognizes [*tataṣawwaru*] its essence, and its cognition of its essence makes it intellect, intellecter, and intelligible [*'aql, 'âqil, ma'qûl*]." But he rejects Aristotle's idea that the intellect becomes one with the intelligible forms it is intellecting. See Rahman, *Avicenna's Psychology*, 117–18, for further discussion.

25. *ash-Shifâ': an-Nafs*, 208–11; *an-Najât*, 231; Rahman, *Avicenna's Psychology*, 68–69; *Mabḥath*, 176–78; *Aḥwâl an-nafs*, 110; *al-Hidâya*, 229–30; *Dânish-nâma-yi 'Alâ'î: Ṭabî'iyyât*, 123–25. For a full discussion of the history of the doctrine of the Active Intelligence prior to and including Avicenna, see Davidson, "Alfarabi and Avicenna, esp., for Avicenna, pp. 154–78.

26. *ash-Shifâ': an-Nafs*, 208; also compare the sources cited in the above note (on Active Intelligence); the light analogy, of course, stems from Aristotle, *De Anima*, 1:684, 430a, 15–17; cf. Davidson, "Alfarabi and Avicenna," 118, 164–65.

27. *ash-Shifâ': an-Nafs*, 208, 209. See also *Aḥwâl an-nafs*, 111–13; *an-Najât*, 231; Rahman, *Avicenna's Psychology*, 68–69, with Rahman's helpful remarks, 116–20; and Gardet, *La pensée religieuse d'Avicenne*, 150–52.

28. *Aḥwâl an-nafs*, 113; cf. *Fî kalâm 'ala n-nafs an-nâṭiqa*, 196.

29. Avicenna emphasizes here that each level of Intelligence up to and including the "First Cause" knows what transpires below, a state of affairs, as we shall presently see, that is similar to that of a human intellect whose perfection allows it to move upward. As Gardet (*La pensée religieuse d'Avicenne*, 115) observes, "Moreover, the human intellect that has become sanctified (*qudsî*) . . . enters into contact not only with the sublunary Active Intellect, which is its immediate principle of perfection, but with the superior separate Intellects as well and, at the apex, the First Caused (*al-ma'lûl al-awwal*) which is the First Intellect or the Universal Intellect (*'aql al-kull*)."

30. As examples of *a priori* (*badîhî*) intelligibles, Avicenna gives the examples of the principle that the whole is greater than the part and the law of contradiction, *Mabḥath*, 168.

31. Hence the importance given early in *Ḥayy ibn Yaqẓân* to the science of physiognomy (*al-firâsa*) and in *Mi'râj Nâma* in regard to understanding the role in character formation of limbs and humors; a person's basic character is configured by a combination of elemental and temperamental ingredients, tempered thereafter by environmental influences; compare *Fî kalâm 'ala n-nafs an-nâṭiqa*, 197–98.

32. *ash-Shifâ': an-Nafs*, 213–14; *Fî kalâm 'ala n-nafs an-nâṭiqa*, 196, and note 15 above.

33. *ash-Shifâ': an-Nafs*, 214, 216–19; see also Rahman, *Avicenna's Psychology*, 118–20; idem, *Prophecy in Islam*, 17; and the preceding chapter on the types of the intellect.

34. *ash-Shifâ': an-Nafs*, 214–15; *al-Mubâḥathât*, 231–32; Rahman, *Prophecy in Islam*, 18–19; for a full discussion of the concept of intuition in Avicenna's thought that includes translation of the pertinent passages from the philosopher's works, see Gutas, *Avicenna and the Aristotelian Tradition*, 159–76; also Michot, *La destinée de l'homme selon Avicenne*, 83; and Sari Nuseibeh, "Al-'Aql al-Qudsî: Avicenna's Subjective Theory of Knowledge," *Studia Islamica* 69 (1989) 39–54.

35. *ash-Shifâ': an-Nafs*, 215.

36. *ash-Shifâ': an-Nafs*, 215.

37. *ash-Shifâ': an-Nafs*, 215–16.

38. *Mi'râj Nâma*, 84; trans., 114.

39. *ash-Shifâ': an-Nafs*, 217; cf., *Fi l-quwa l-insâniyya*, 44: "The [human] soul is like a mirror and the theoretical intellect is like its luster, and these intelligibles appear in it through divine emanation, just as figures appear in a polished mirror."

40. *ash-Shifâ'*: an-Nafs, 218; on the different uses of *fikra*, see note 15 above.

41. *an-Najât*, 205; Rahman, *Avicenna's Psychology*, 33; *ash-Shifâ': an-Nafs*, 40, 219; Rahman, *Prophecy in Islam*, 19–20.

42. For imaginative prophecy, inspiration (*ilhâm*), dreams, and miracles in Avicenna, see *ash-Shifâ': an-Nafs*, 154–78; *al-Hidâya*, 295–97; *al-Ishârât wa-t-tanbîhât*, 119–49; *Fî ta'bîr ar-ru'yâ*, 278–307; *Fi l-fi'l wa-l-infi'âl wa-aqsâmihâ* (all); Rahman, *Prophecy in Islam*, 36–52; Michot, *La destinée de l'homme selon Avicenne*, 108–10; S. Pines, "The Arabic Recension of *Parva Naturalia* and the Philosophical Doctrine Concerning Veridical Dreams according to *al-Risâla an-Manâmiyya* and Other Sources," *Israel Oriental Studies* 4 (Tel Aviv: Tel Aviv University, 1974) 104–53; and H. Gätje, "Philosophische Traumlehren im Islam," *ZDMG* 109 (1959) 258–85.

43. *ash-Shifâ': an-Nafs*, 219.

44. Quotes from *ash-Shifâ': an-Nafs*, 220; *Fî ithbât an-nubuwwât*, 46–47, trans. Marmura, in Mahdi and Lerner, *Medieval Political Philosophy*, 155.

45. *ash-Shifâ': an-Nafs*, 219–20; *Mi'râj Nâma*, 87–99; trans., 119–20; *an-Najât*, 205–7; Rahman, *Avicenna's Psychology*, 35–37; *Aḥwâl an-nafs*, 122–26; *Mabḥath*, 168–71; *Fî ithbât an-nubuwwât*, 44–47; *Dânish-nâma-yi 'Alâ'î: Ṭabî'iyyât*, 145–46; *Fi l-quwa l-insâniyya*, 44–45; see also Michael Marmura, "Avicenna's Psy-

chological Proof of Prophecy," *Journal of Near Eastern Studies* 22 (1963) 49–56; Rahman, *Prophecy in Islam*, 30–36; and Gardet, *La pensée religieuse d'Avicenne*, 114–18.

46. *Miʿrâj Nâma*, 88; trans., 118; *Fî ithbât an-nubuwwât*, 47.

47. *ash-Shifâ': al-Ilâhiyyât*, 441–42; *an-Najât*, 339–40; *al-Hidâya*, 298–99.

48. Rahman, *Prophecy in Islam*, 35.

49. *Fî ithbât an-nubuwwât*, 47; trans. Marmura, in Mahdi and Lerner, *Medieval Political Philosophy*, 115.

50. *Miʿrâj Nâma*, 89–90, 103–4; trans., 125ff., 117–18.

51. Gutas has coined this felicitous term; see *Avicenna and the Aristotelian Tradition*, 254–61. Corbin, *Avicenna*, 5, and throughout the book, believes that *Ḥayy ibn Yaqẓân, aṭ-Ṭair*, and *Salâmân and Absâl* constitute a sequential narrative cycle, an interpretation followed by Sabri, "Avicenne, philosophe et mystique dans le mirroir de trois récits." However prescient this formulation initially appears to be, I do not believe that it holds up under scrutiny.

52. Comparing this cumulative design with other composite reconstructions of greater magnitude—Joseph Campbell's *The Hero with a Thousand Faces*, 2nd rev. ed., Bollingen Series 17 (Princeton, N.J.: Princeton University Press, 1968), reformulations of the basics of Gnostic mythology such as one finds in Hans Jonas, *The Gnostic Religion: The Message of the Alien God and the Beginnings of Christianity*, 2nd rev. ed. (Boston: Beacon Press, 1963), or Kurt Rudolph, *Gnosis: The Nature and History of Gnosticism* (San Francisco: Harper and Row, 1987), or even Vladimir Propp's *Morphology of the Folktale*, 2nd rev. ed. (Austin: University of Texas Press, 1968)—lies beyond the scope of this study. The methodological influence of such compilations on this particular part of my investigation should, however, be obvious.

53. I use the text in Kholeif, *Avicenna on Psychology* 129–31; for other English translations, see Browne, *A Literary History of Persia*, 2:10–11, and Arberry's translation in *Avicenna on Theology*, 77–78.

54. *aṭ-Ṭair*, 44; cf. Corbin, *Avicenna*, 188; Michot, *La destinée de l'homme selon Avicenne*, 49–54.

55. See Chapter Three above; Avicenna also draws in the figure of Ḥayy ibn Yaqẓân in *Risâlat al-qadar*, in Mehren, *Traités mystiques*.

56. *aṭ-Ṭair*, 44; Corbin, *Avicenna*, 188.

57. *Ḥayy ibn Yaqẓân*, 6; trans. Corbin, *Avicenna*, 140, 305–6.

58. *al-Ishârât wa-t-tanbîhât*, 4:54–56; Corbin, *Avicenna*, 224–26.

59. Cf. *al-Ishârât wa-t-tanbîhât*, 4:46; *Fi s-saʿâda*, 19.

60. Book Nine of *al-Ishârât wa-t-tanbîhât*, 4:48–110; see also Gardet, *La pensée religieuse d'Avicenne*, 175–83.

61. *al-Ishârât wa-t-tanbîhât*, 4:48–76; *al-Ḥaqq* literally means truth or reality. The *Ṣûfîs* consistently use the term to refer to God, and since Avicenna is adopting *ṣûfî* terminology and frames of reference here, I have so translated it here; cf. *EI*², 3:82–83, and L. Gardet, *Études de philosophie et de mystique comparées*, Bibliothèque d'Histoire de la Philosophie (Paris: Librairie Philosophique J. Vrin, 1972) 71–79.

62. *al-Ishârât wa-t-tanbîhât*, 4:76–78.

63. *al-Ishârât wa-t-tanbîhât*, 4:78–85; *Fi s-sa'âda*, 19–20.

64. *al-Ishârât wa-t-tanbîhât*, 4:86.

65. *al-Ishârât wa-t-tanbîhât*, 4:87–90.

66. *al-Ishârât wa-t-tanbîhât*, 4:91–95. Whether Avicenna considers this "union" to be ontological or epistemological is open to debate, although I agree with Gardet's conclusion that for Avicenna "union is a vision—not a transformation," *La pensée religieuse d'Avicenne*, 161, also 153–57.

67. *aṭ-Ṭair*, 45; Corbin, *Avicenna*, 190.

68. *aṭ-Ṭair*, 45–47; Corbin, *Avicenna*, 190–91; regarding the King's description, compare *Ḥayy ibn Yaqẓân*, 20–21 (Corbin, *Avicenna*, 149–50), and *al-Ishârât wa-t-tanbîhât*, 3:124.

69. *aṭ-Ṭair*, 47; Corbin identifies this messenger as the Active Intelligence (*Avicenna*, 194); Avicenna himself identified him as the Angel of Death, *al-Mubâḥathât*, 172 (#259); Michot, *La destinée de l'homme selon Avicenne*, 14–18; and as-Sâwajî's commentary in Spies and Khatak, eds. and trans., *Three Treatises*, 89.

70. "Ode," line 18, Kholeif, *Avicenna on Psychology*, 131.

71. Corbin, *Avicenna*, 4.

Part III

The *Mi'râj Nâma*

6. Translation of the *Miʿrâj Nâma*

Introduction

The *Miʿrâj Nâma* is a short treatise in Persian traditionally attributed to Avicenna.[1] My reason for including a translation of it here requires a brief introductory note. When I first contemplated studying Islamic allegory, I planned to analyze a series of allegories or allegoreses dealing with the single theme of the *miʿrâj*, heavenly ascent or journey. The most prominent example of this theme in Islamic literature is the prophet Muḥammad's own *miʿrâj*, with the accompanying tradition of his Night Journey (*isrâ*) from the sacred Mosque (in Mecca) to the Further Mosque (in Jerusalem).[2] This story exists primarily in the form of clusters of prophetic traditions (*ḥadîth*) that were combined in diverse formulations over the centuries. In addition to this central narrative, however, there are several works that present nonprophetic visions of heavenly ascent or spiritual journey. Such accounts include, among others, the *miʿrâj* narrative attributed to Abû Yazîd al-Bisṭâmî, Avicenna's two allegories (*Risâlat aṭ-ṭair* and *Ḥayy ibn Yaqẓân*), Sanâ'î's *Sair al-ʿibâd ila l-maʿâd*, Ibn Ṭufail's *Ḥayy ibn Yaqẓân*, al-Ghazâlî's *Risâlat aṭ-ṭair*, several allegories by Shihâb ad-Dîn as-Suhrawardî, Shams ad-Dîn Muḥammad Bardsîrî Kirmânî's (d. before 618/1221) *Miṣbâḥ al-arvâḥ*, and Ibn 'Arabî's *Kitâb al-isrâ ilâ maqâm al-asrâ*, as well as several treatments of the *miʿrâj* in his *Futûḥât al-Makkiyya*. Finally, the well-known mystic Abu l-Qâsim 'Abd al-Karîm al-Qushairî (d. 465/1073) composed a *Kitâb al-miʿrâj* in which he discusses the status of the prophet-centered tradition in his time.[3] It appeared to me that a series of essays on some or all of these treatises would contribute much to illuminate theoretical and historical issues of Islamic allegory and provide a cornerstone for the larger project of investigating the genre as a whole.

In the course of my research, I encountered references to a *Miʿrâj Nâma* attributed to Avicenna in which the philosopher gives his "rationalist" interpretation of the story of the prophet Muḥammad's ascent to heaven. Having just completed an analysis of the same author's *Risâlat aṭ-ṭair*, I set out to examine this tract to see if it was appropriate for inclusion in my projected book.[4] In order to understand the *Mi'râj Nâma* fully, I needed to consult Avicenna's philosophical texts, and it was at this point that my study began to assume its present form of focusing on the more general and significant problem of the interplay between allegory and philosophy in Avicenna's thought as a whole.

The *Mi'râj Nâma* falls into two main parts. In the first, Avicenna establishes the conceptual framework within which he intends to interpret the story of the *mi'râj* by furnishing a summary of his psychology and epistemology. In the second part, the philosopher provides his allegorical interpretation of the ascension story itself, adopting an exegetical format in which he quotes several lines of the story and then interprets them from the perspective of his previously outlined philosophical system. Through much of the tract Avicenna also expostulates upon the relation of philosophy to allegory, remarking on how and why one should compose and understand texts from an allegorical point of view.[5]

This treatise has not received marked attention from modern or premodern students of Avicenna primarily because critical examination of Avicenna's works is still in its early stages, despite the dedicated efforts of a few specialists. Many minor works remain unedited, while some major ones require reediting; many aspects of his thought require further investigation. Equally important as a reason for the treatise's neglect by scholars has been the doubts raised concerning authenticity of the work's attribution to Avicenna. This issue is fully discussed in Appendix B, but in short I believe that the evidence supporting the authenticity of the treatise is sufficiently strong that the burden of proof falls upon those who would dispute this claim. Even those who continue to deny the tract's authenticity must admit that its doctrines accord with Avicenna's philosophical system. Despite my belief in the treatise's authenticity, I must state quite clearly that *this issue does not substantially affect my analysis of the interplay between allegory and philosophy in Avicenna's thought*, which is based on those of the philosopher's writings concerning whose authenticity there exists no doubt whatsoever. The *Mi'râj Nâma* serves only as an additional sample text. In order to make the tract more widely available and facilitate discussion of it, I decided to include a full English translation here based on a critical reading of manuscript and printed sources.[6]

The Translation of the *Mi'râj Nâma* (The Book of the Prophet Muḥammad's Ascent to Heaven)[7]

Introduction

[iv., 79] In the Name of God, the Merciful and the Compassionate. This is the treatise on the (prophet Muḥammad's) Ascension that the First Master, Abû 'Alî ibn Sînâ, may God's mercy be upon him, wrote:[8]

Thanks to the Lord of heaven and earth, praise to the Bestower of spirit [*jân*] and body [*tan*]. And greetings to His selected prophet, Muḥammad the Chosen [*muṣṭafâ*], may God bless him and his family, and to the members of his house [his descendants], and his pure companions.[9]

Now then: A friend of ours has continually inquired about the meaning [*ma'nâ*] of the Ascension, desiring it explained in a rational way [*bar ṭarîq-i ma'qûl*].[10] I was constrained (from doing this) because of the danger involved until now, when I have entered the service of the Exalted Court of 'Alâ' [ad-Daula].[11] I submitted this matter [*ma'nâ*] to his opinion. He consented and gave me permission to delve into it [2r.] and of his own will assisted, so that the bond of indolence was opened, and my diligence and effort in this (topic) could become apparent. For although many subtle truths and symbols [*ma'ânî-yi laṭîf va-rumûz*] come to mind, when there is no virtuous recipient or perfect intellectual ['*âqil*] (to receive them), they cannot be made manifest. It is a fault to divulge secrets to a stranger; the teller then becomes culpable. As they have said: "Secrets, protect them from others!"[12] But when you speak to someone capable and worthy, it is appropriate to convey the truth to one who is deserving.[13] Just as lodging secrets with someone ignorant is a mistake, withholding [80] truths [*ma'ânî*] from an intelligent person is inappropriate. And in this age of ours, no one recalls seeing a great person more perfect than the Exalted Court. Indeed, in truth it is known that the sphere [*falak*] has [2v.] not brought forth into the desert of Existence and Appearance anyone more sublime, generous, intelligent, or wise than the noble person of 'Alâ' ad-Daula.[14]

Since he is the point of conjunction of all that is praiseworthy, lofty, and sublime, whenever a truth [*ma'nâ*] comes to mind, the faculty of intellect strives to convey it to the informed ear of that great man, so (that it) becomes enobled (by being) a "part" in the shadow of that "whole." For all truths in minds incline toward him. Indeed, you would say that his pure intellect has become the center for all the intellects of the generous, since all things revolve around their center. Each word someone utters, however noble, bears no refinement and taste if the Exalted Court does not accept it. [3r.] Because his acceptance is like soul [*rûḥ*] for the words, and body without soul is worthless.

Not everyone who speaks is accepted at that Exalted Court. On the contrary, words must be free of defect and impurity in utterance and meaning for his ear to accept (them).[15] Since his ear is the Lote Tree of the Far Boundary, and nothing unrefined can reach there, (words) must be subtle and spiritual to find (their) way. But each person bears a gift in order to be accepted.[16]

We too, bravely and with good intentions toward that august man, presented these words to that Court. We delved into the symbols of the story of the Ascension as far as intellect can help, relying on the magnanimity of (this) great man. [3v.] Whatever fault he sees, may he regard it with the eye of pardon so that it may seem proper. I seek help from Life-Giving God. Only God grants success.[17] [81]

Chapter
In Explanation of the Condition of Prophethood and Apostleship

Know that Absolute Truth [*Ḥaqq*], may He be exalted, created human beings from two different things.[18] One is called body [*tan*], the other, spirit [*jân*]. He brought each from a different world [*'âlam*]. He brought together the body by gathering the humors [*akhlâṭ*] and combining the elements [*arkân*], and He united with it the spirit, through the influence of the Active Intelligence.[19] He adorned the body with parts, such as the hand, foot, head, face, belly, frame, sensation, and other things, and gave each one, such as the heart, liver, [4r.] and brain, a suitable function. Thus the hand is for taking, the foot for going. This does not do the work of that, nor that the work of this. The body is the mount [*markab*], the spirit the rider. The instrument of the spirit is the body, (while) the splendor [*raunaq*] of the body rests in the spirit. When He created the body, He chose three noble members of it, and into each He put a soul [*rûḥ*]. He put the animal (soul) [*ḥayavânî*] in the heart, the natural [*ṭabî'î*] in the liver, and the psychic [*nafsânî*] in the brain. He adorned each one of these with special faculties: the animal with concupiscence [*shahvat*] and irascibility [*ghaḍab*], external sensation [*ḥiss*], the imagination [*khayâl*], and estimation [*vahm*]; the natural with expulsion [*daf'*], digestion [*haḍm*], absorption [*jazb*], and retention [*imsâk*]; and the psychic with the faculties of cogitation [*tafakkur*], recollection [*tazakkur*], discernment [*tamayyuz*], memory [*ḥafẓ*], and other things. These (first) two souls [4v.] are subordinate. The basis [*aṣl*] of [82] this soul is the psychic (soul). Both of these (former) two are its servants. It is more perfect and nobler, because the animal and natural (souls) are exposed to transitoriness, in the bonds of mortality [*fanâ'*], but the psychic (soul) is not susceptible to mortality; it remains forever after the passing of the body. Hence when the Absolute Truth (may He be praised and exalted) brought forth the body, He made (it) the mount of the spirit [*rûḥ*]. The intent of this was that the nobility of humankind become clear and distinct, and that it be distinguished from the other animals. For if (their) bases were the animal and natural (souls), humans would not be differentiated from other animals. They would be an (equal) partner [*sharîk*] of all animals. But if He only put the psychic (soul in humans), they would have nothing in common with other animals. Hence He gave (humans) all three (souls), so that they share the animal and natural (souls) with all [5r.] but in regard to their psychic (souls) are nobler than all.

The basis of humankind is the psychic (soul). Rationality [*nuṭq*], wisdom [*khirad*], knowledge [*dânish*], and discernment are of it. The rational [*nâṭiqat*] and psychic souls are not called spirit, they are called soul [*ravân*].[20] Because the spirit is a subtle body, while the soul is not a body but rather a faculty that through the perfection of its subtle nature [*laṭâfat*] is the helper and activator of the spirit and body. It is the locus of speech [*sukhan*] and the source of knowledge [*'ilm*] and wisdom. When the spirit and body are set free, the body decays, (but) the soul does not decay.[21]

Since humanity's nobility lies in the rational soul, and the body is its mount and instrument, there must be guardians for the mount so it does not fall into harm and destruction, for then it would not function. For this reason [*ma'nâ*], [5v.] the natural soul is placed in the liver and given faculties that always seek aid from nourishment. In this way it conveys power to the body [83] and thus regulates the mount. That which is excessive, it expels by means of another faculty, partly through the pores by means of perspiration and partly by excretion. If there were no faculty for food consumption, the mount would collapse; if there were no faculty for expulsion, a person would not (be able) to burn up all the food.

The animal faculty is also given so that, by means of the irascible faculty, it holds what is not naturally compatible at a distance; while the concupiscent faculty brings near to one whatever is naturally compatible. The faculties of the (five) senses have been provided as attendants to the rational soul; hence, they take whatever sensibles [*maḥṣûṣât*] reach them and [6r.] convey (them) to the common sense [*ḥiss-i mushtarak*], which is the form-recipient of all things. Then (common sense) gives to the compositive imagination whatever is suitable, and to estimation whatever is suitable. Whatever is appropriate for the intellect, it separates, with the help of cogitation and discernment, and deposits in the storehouse of memory, so that, when it is of use to the intellect, (the intellect) retrieves it by means of the faculty of recollection. Recollection thus conveys from memory whatever (the intellect) may need.

When it is known that these three souls are put in human beings, it becomes clear that human differences and faculties originate from differences in faculties and the (varying) domination of these souls. Someone for whom the natural (soul) is dominant is concerned with whatever is connected with morsels, gluttony, and food. Someone for whom the animal (soul) is dominant prefers [6v.] concupiscence, irascibility, and other lowly attributes. Those for whom the psychic (soul) is dominant make the natural and animal (souls) their servants, so that whatever relates to learning, wisdom, cogitation, and discernment appears in them. They give way to the animal (soul) to such an extent that they are not given the name of "lifeless" and "passionless." [84] They operate the natural (soul) to the extent that the mount requires it. When the rational soul is dominant and powerful in someone, it defeats and conquers the animal and natural (souls), because the intellect restrains humans from excess and negligence [*ifrâṭ wa-tafrîṭ*] and encourages moderation [*i'tidâl*] in all actions.[22]

In the same way that the rational soul is the commander and superior of the souls, the intellect is the commander [7r.] and superior of the rational soul. It is provided as an advisor of human beings for the rational soul, which is (also) called the Holy Spirit [*rûḥ-i qudsî*] and pure soul [*ravân-i pâk*]. The senses are its servants, and memory, discernment, recollection, and cogitation are begotten through it. It also has a nourisher and director [the Active Intelligence] upon whom its eyes are fixed and at the door of whose palace of greatness it continually stands, seeking benefit. It is the intellect that perceives everything and receives all the forms, without corruption finding a way to it. Every kind of knowledge that reaches the soul and every happiness that appears in it are all the fruit of the management of the intellect. The purpose of the intellect is to promote happiness in the soul by means of knowledge [7v.]. And the purpose of the (rational) soul [*nafs*] is that, with (the intellect's) help, it separates intelligibles [*ma'qûlât*] from among sensibles [*maḥsûsât*] and conveys them to the intellect. The intellect has nothing to do with sensibles, because whatever is sensible is not on (its) rank of nobility and perfection. On the contrary, perfection, nobility, and greatness lie in intelligibles. The intellect always faces aloft. It does not look down, nor would it go from being noble to being base. However, it has provided the soul with some help, [85] for it manages the best interests of the lower world and sensible states. This (aspect of it) is called the practical intellect [*'aql-i muktasab*].[23]

The nobility of human beings thus lies in two things: the rational soul and the intellect. Neither of these two are from the world of corporeal bodies [*ajsâm*]; rather, they are from the higher world. They are the governors [*mutaṣarrif*] of the body, [8r.] not its resident [*sâkin*]. For abstract [*mujarrad*], simple [*basîṭ*] faculties, there is no extension [*ḥayyiz*] or place [*makân*]; but their effect holds the body in order.

When we say that the soul [*nafs*] and the intellect are two things, we do not mean that they are contained by way of number in a corporeal entity [*ḥaqîqat-i jismiyyat*]. Rather, the intention is verbal distinction in (regard to) that faculty's own management [*tarbiyat*] of identifying conditions, effecting benefits, and bringing forth ideas [*ma'ânî*]. It is something that provides a different benefit everywhere and assumes a different name accordingly. Similarly, the animal soul, which is in the heart, is not more than one entity [*ḥaqîqat*]; but whenever its effect becomes visible in a specific (bodily) member, it assumes a different name. The intent here is that it be easy to specify in regard to apprehending verbal expressions. Therefore, when the animal faculty [8v.] apprehends form, it is called sight [lit. light]; when it becomes a listening instrument, it is called hearing; when scent perception occurs in the locus of the nose, it is called smell; and when it perceives flavor, it is called taste. However, the aspect [*ḥaqîqat*] that occurs in the faculty of discernment is not specific to the eye, ear, place of smell, or taste. Rather, the faculty of discernment occurs in all limbs and members. Thus it is known that faculties are named according to difference(s) in effect, but are, in reality, one thing.[24]

The states of the rational soul are the same. The difference between knowledge and intellect is only in name. In reality it is one [86] faculty that perceives and knows. That which knows, perceives; and that which perceives, knows. When [9r.] it perceives truths [*ḥaqâʾiq*] as abstract forms, it does not do so in place, nor in matter, and certainly not through an instrument. Since this is the case, the forms of things are not taking each others' places, because there is no multiplicity of quantity or corporeal differentiation there. Abstract forms are received, and also (simultaneously) known and intellected. But each time that the rational faculty appears in faculties and effects a fresh benefit, it assumes a different name.

The rational soul is a substance [*jauhar*] existing through itself. It is of such subtlety that it does not accept a substratum [*mauḍûʿ*]. It exists through itself. Whatever it knows, it knows through itself. It is the knower of its own essence. It perceives its own knowledge through itself, and accepts it through itself. That aspect [*ḥaqîqat*] which perceives is called intellect and that which is perceived [9v.] is called knowledge.

When it knows through itself, and perceives and accepts, and true seeing occurs, it is called insight [*baṣîrat*]. When it perceives and seeks perception's end, it is called cogitation. When it separates bad from good, it is called discernment.[25] When it stores that which it has discerned, it is called memory. When it divulges (it again), it is called thought [*khâṭir*]. When it is close to appearance, it is called recollection. When only the wish for divulging (thoughts) is involved, it is called determination [*ʿazm*] and intention [*niyyat*]. When it is united with language, it is called discourse [*kalâm*]. When it is expressed, it is called speech [*qaul*]. From this point, it has assumed sensible accidents [*aʿrâḍ-i ḥissî*] and taken on corporeal forms [*jismâniyyât*]. [10r.] The basis [*sar*] of all these steps [*muqaddamât*] is called rationality, and the source [*manbaʿ*] of these faculties is called the rational soul.

The nobility of humanity thus stems from the (process) beginning with perception [lit. insight] and ending with speech. The nobility [87] of the bodily senses stems from that which produces speech [i.e., the rational soul]. Expression [*ʿibârat*], speech, script [*ḥarf*], and whatever is related to these, do not exist for the purpose of manifesting the nobility of human beings, but rather because of the dullness and extreme ignorance of bodily form, which only finds a way (for expression) by means of specific sensibles.

That which the rational soul affirms with the pen of knowledge [*qalam-i ʿilm*] on the tablet of intellect [*lauḥ-i ʿaql*] concerning aspects of truth [*ḥaqâʾiq-i maʿânî*] and abstract form, which is rationality, is shared with the angels.[26] It ennobles and cultivates. These others have not seen the face of majesty. For this reason it is necessary that in the lowly body and senses themselves, etched forms [10v.] be embodied. The pure original (truth) arranges itself this way so that the benefit of rational thought occur and become manifest in speech.

When this is known, know that just as the senses face the intellect, and stand in attendance for whatever it conveys and explains to them—for in this way it helps its own body to maintain the order of sensibles—the intellect also faces its own world, waiting for the emanation [*faiḍ*] of whatever its Betters [*mahtarân*] convey to it. Through their mediation it keeps straight the best interests [*maṣâliḥ*] of exoteric and esoteric (matters).

The attendance of the intellect, which is the result of the emanation of knowledge, is called aspiration [*himmat*]; while its seeking is called desire [*irâdat*].[27] Compulsion and coercion are not suitable for (the intellect). [11r.] It is the appraiser of sciences. The eye of its insight is open; by choice [*ikhtiyâr*] it constantly seeks.[28] This constancy is called yearning [*shauq*].[29] That which is revealed to its insight is concealed from sensual sight. This concealed (dimension) is called the invisible world [*ghaib*]. Thus the intellect always has the eye of knowledge opened by means of the pupil of insight; for guidance, it seeks aid from the celestial reaches.[30]

For most of humankind perfection is not perceived. Unless they transcend the eighth stage, they always receive help from the Active Intelligence [*'aql-i fa''âl*]. One who becomes guided by the First (Intelligence) [88] is united with purity and subtlety.[31] One who becomes guided by the Second has a quick wit that easily understands fields of knowledge [11v.] related to the science of calculation [*ḥisâb*] and the like. One who becomes guided by the Third loves mirth [*ṭarab*] and activity. One who becomes guided by the Fourth becomes distinguished by types of greatness and nobility. One who becomes guided by the Fifth (has an intellect) veiled by the animal faculties. One who becomes guided by the Sixth becomes endowed with asceticism, knowledge, piety, and fidelity. One who becomes guided by the Seventh becomes true in purpose and steadfast in belief [*ra'î*]. Everything toward which this person inclines is perfect; whatever he or she wants to do, he or she can do.

(But) if perfection befriends a person, and so that he or she passes through all the (levels of) guidance, and he or she is aided by all the Supernals [*'ulwiyyât*], and passes through everything, and becomes united with the First Guardian [*muhaimin-i avval*], which is the Universal Intelligence [*'aql-i kull*], (then) this person comprehends.[32] [12r.]

Unless a human being understands these preliminaries, he or she is not of a high station, and when a sensible approaches a primary intelligible that which it would have been comes to naught. That person upon whom the First Intelligence gazes, so that he or she becomes refined, cultivated, subtle, beautiful, brave, and perfect in intellect, becomes a prophet. The First Intelligence becomes for this person as our intellect (is for us). And intellect for him or her is on the level of our soul [*nafs*]. Just as the soul that grasps a truth [*maʿnâ*] from the intellect is learned, the intellect that grasps from the First Intelligence is a prophet.

But this state varies. Either it occurs in sleep, since in wakefulness the preoccupations of the senses and the multitude of activities become a hindrance; or it occurs in wakefulness, since in sleep the imaginative faculty predominates; or in each [12v.] it is full and true.[33] The motion and repose of this person is pure in legislative function [*sharʿ*]. It never admits abrogation or distortion [*faskh va-maskh*]. This person is free of worldly distractions and secular controls and is devoted to the affairs of the Necessary Existent. [89] The First Intelligence nourishes his or her soul from itself. This nourishing is called sanctification [*taqdîs*]. As the Qur'ân states, "We have supported him with the Holy Spirit."[34] (The First Intelligence] reveals itself to this person so that through (its) good auspices he or she comprehends. When he or she fully understands the universal, he or she attains knowledge of the included particulars, since this person does not need time or delay (to understand matters).[35] Thus (Muḥammad) said "My Lord instructed me; and how well was my instruction; and I instructed ʿAlî, and I instructed him well."[36] Similarly (the Qur'ân) said, "And We taught him knowledge from Us."[37] And when the Holy Spirit, [13r.] who is higher than souls, Gabriel the Trustworthy, the bearer of prophetic revelation [*vaḥy*], continually regards that person, it gives that person's movement and repose a divine tincture.[38] Thus the Qur'ân says: "The dye of God, and who is better than God as a dye."[39] That which is united to the intellect from the Holy Spirit is prophethood [*nubuvvat*]. That which becomes manifest from that intellect is apostleship [*risâlat*]. That which the prophet says is the summons [*daʿvat*]. That which becomes clear from this summons is religion [*sharîʿat*]. And the law [*qânûn*] of that religion is religious creed [*millat*]. The acceptance of all this is faith [*îmân*]. The name of that which prophets receive is revelation. When it is united with a human, and the Holy Spirit opens his or her way to itself and becomes governor of that disposition, it makes (that person) lofty in aspiration, and slight in greed, [13v.] rancourless, without envy. Whatever this person does is through that Holy Power. Just as is (found) in the (prophetic) tradition. "I ask of you a faith that my heart touches."[40]

Thus the Holy Spirit is the noblest of all souls, for all (other) souls are subordinate to the Universal Intelligence. The Holy Spirit, however, is that which is the intermediary between the Necessary Existent and the First Intelligence. The faith of that Power is the prophet, who is the messenger and bearer of the Holy Emanation [*faiḍ-i qudsî*]. That Power is the fruit of proximity to the First Intelligence. The prophet has said in a tradition: "Faith is rightward, and wisdom [*ḥikma*] is rightwardness."[41] That is: Faith is the Folk of the Right. [90] And "wisdom is rightwardness" means: they are identical. Wisdom and faith are for the Folk of the Right, and not for the Folk of the Left. The first is an expression for heaven, and [14r.] the second is an expression for hell.[42]

Faith consists of two parts: real [*ḥaqîqî*] and metaphorical [*majâzî*], the husk and the core. Prophets have real faith, the core, for they bear the core and the truth [*ma'nâ*]. Ordinary people [*'avâmm*] bear the husk, the form [*ṣûrat*]. Their faith is sensible, not intelligible. With the aid of the (intellectual) faculty, (the prophet) draws down the Holy Spirit. As he said, "I feel the breath [*nafas*] of the Merciful from the Yemen."[43] This Holy Spirit is a divine faculty. It is not a body, nor a substance, nor an accident. It is the pure divine Command [*amr-i pâk-i îzidî*]; "Indeed, His is the Command and the Creation."[44] The intent of (the word Command) is not (physical) speech and expression. People who do not consider this appropriate and consider the Holy Spirit to be a result of the Command do so because they do not know the reality of Command. There is no nobility greater than a soul joined [*muḍâf*] to the divine Command. [14v.]

Thus the Qur'ân says, "Say! The Spirit is from the Command of my Lord."[45] Absolute Command thus comes only to the prophet, while that which comes to (ordinary) people [*khalq*] is qualified [*kaifiyyat*]. The prophet brings the (absolute) truths of the (divine) Command within the boundaries of religious law [*shar'*]. Divine Command is that which is called Holy Spirit [*nafs-i qudsî*] by the intellect and Gabriel by religious legislation [*shar'*]. It is equal in nobility of rank with all the Souls and Intelligences. Such that the Qur'ân says, "A day in which the Spirit and the Angels arise in a row."[46]

When these preliminaries are known, it should (also) be known that reason comprehends truth [*ma'nâ*] through itself, while prophethood comprehends truths [*ḥaqâ'iq*] through Holy Support. Just as speech is not reason, reason is not summons, and summons is not [91] prophethood. Recollection [*zikr*] [15r.] stands between speech and reason, and apostleship between prophethood and summons. Hence, whatever rational concepts that the intellect wishes to convey to the senses, it does so by means of recollection. (The latter then) formulates it in sensible sounds and unites (it) with speech, so that hearing apprehends.[47]

Similarly, when prophets wish to comprehend the truth of the divine Command and convey (it) to created beings, they permit the faculty of apostleship to bring these concepts into the imagination and make them concrete forms; then with the language of summons, they convey (it) to the community [*ummat*]. Thus summons is like speech, and prophethood like reason. There is no speech without reason, but there is reason without speech. There is also no apostleship without prophethood, but there is prophethood without apostleship. Just as (Muḥammad) said, "I was a prophet while Adam was between water and clay," or in another version, "while Adam was moving in his clay."[48] [15v.]

The Holy Spirit is like the point, prophethood is like the line, and apostleship is like the surface. Summons is like the substance and the religious creed is like the body. The splendor of the body is in the soul. Similarly, the value of the religious creed is in prophethood. The body is general, the point particular. The body is sensible, apprehended, specific; the point is nonsensible, nonapprehended, nonspecific. So that the Qur'ân says, "Sights do not apprehend him."[49] Just as the beginning of all things is the point, the beginning of all actions is the Holy Spirit. The sovereignty of the point over (concrete) existents is known, and the sovereignty of the Holy Spirit over intelligibles is manifest. So that the Qur'ân has stated, "He is Victorious over His servants."[50]

This idea is far-fetched for estimation, since imagination adds direction and shape; but it is more reasonable for intellect, [16r.] because the locus of specifying position is (the task of) thought [*khâṭir*]. Hence [92] the Qur'ân says, "And We are nearer to him than the jugular vein." And it says, "He is with you wherever you are."[51]

Although all things need Holy Emanation, it is free, unattached to souls, unpreoccupied with bodies. (Muḥammad) thus said, "I had a time with God unrivaled by an angel drawn-near or a prophet sent."[52] Since it is (now) known that prophethood is an emanation of the Holy Spirit, it should (also) be known that the reality of the Qur'ân is divine discourse; the enunciation of the Book, however, is prophetic speech, since speech without form and pronunciation [*ḥarf*] is impossible. For these two exist the throat, lip, teeth, lungs, intestines, and (other) outlets of sounds. All this is in the body. Substance is nobler than the body. [16v.] The First Reality is not (even) substance; negation of corporeality is a primary facet of it. Hence, its discourse is not (physical) speech.

Human beings, however, are composites and have (physical) instruments of speech. So their speech [*nuṭq*] is by means of pronunciation and voice. (But) it should be known that asserting (physical) speech to that (divine) quarter is impossible. Divine discourse is the unveiling of a concept by the Holy Spirit through the mediation of the Universal Intelligence to the prophet's soul. That which is the prophet's speech [*nuṭq*] is identical with divine discourse. His control over himself is nonexistent; the name Holy befalls him; his speech [*nuṭq*] is the Qur'ân. He does not say what he says on the basis of being a created being; he speaks by leave of (divine) Command, no rather, he speaks at the discretion of (divine) discourse. He therefore said, "The Merciful taught the Qur'ân and created humanity."[53] When this unveiling [17r.] overwhelms his reason [*nuṭq*], realities and concepts become the totality of the prophet. But the community [93] cannot be informed of this, for they are bound by their senses. For the best interest of people, prophets are given permission to activate imagination and estimation. In this way, they put the emanation to work and bring that faculty into operation. That which is perceived is put into estimation, so that it makes a concrete form; that which appears is a miracle. That which is rational is put into the imagination, so that recollection [*zikr*] governs it; that which is brought forth as speech becomes a book. Because it is (produced) by divine aid, (God's name) is added, so that one says "The Book of God" just like "The House of God," "The Servant of God," and "The Apostle of God."

That which prophets thus perceive from the Holy Spirit [17v.] is pure intelligible, and that which they say is sensible, with the adornment of the imagination and estimation. Hence, (Muḥammad) said, "We, the band of prophets, He commanded us to speak to people according to the capacity of their intellects." One can perceive an abstract intelligible (only) with the abstract intellect. It is something apprehended, not something spoken.[54]

It is thus the condition of prophets that they arrange every intelligible that they perceive as a sensible and put it into speech so that the community can follow that sensible. They perceive it as an intelligible, but make it sensed and concrete for the community. They thus increase (its usefulness) for threats and promises and foster good beliefs, so that its provisions become perfect, and so that the basis and code of religious law [*shar*ʿ] [18r.] and the foundation of religious devotion not be dissolved and disordered and that which is the intention of the prophet not remain concealed. When it reaches intellectuals, they perceive it with their intellect. They know that the prophet's words are all symbols, filled with intelligibles. When it reaches ignoramuses, however, they look at the external speech; their hearts are satisfied with nonintelligible concrete forms and sensibles. They are enveloped by the imagination and do not pass beyond the doorway of estimation. [94] They ask, unknowing, and listen, uncomprehending. "And praise be to God, for indeed most of them do not know."[55]

It was for this reason that the noblest of men, the dearest of prophets, and the seal of the apostles, upon whom be peace, said to the center of the circle of wisdom, the sphere of truth, and the storehouse of intellect, the Commander of the Faithful, 'Alî, upon whom be peace, "O 'Alî, when you see people approach their Creator by (different) forms of piety, approach (Him) with (different) forms of intellect, then you will precede them."[56] [18v.]

Such talk as this is only proper for such a great man as he, for among people he was like the intelligible is among sensibles. He said, "O 'Alî, since men toil in many devotions, toil you in perceiving the intelligible, then you will precede them all."[57] And necessarily so, for with the eye of intellectual insight, he perceived secrets, comprehended all truths, and understood intelligibles. He saw (only) one Ordinance [*ḥukm*], and it was for this reason that he said, "If the veil were drawn away, I would not increase in certitude."[58]

No human fortune is better than apprehending the intelligible. To apprehend that intelligible is Paradise, adorned with (all) kinds of luxuries, ginger and nectar. Hell, with punishments [19r.] and burning thirst, consists of corporeal preoccupations; for humans fall into the burning pit of passion [*havâ*] and remain in the bonds of imagination and the torment of estimation. The bonds of imagination and the torment of estimation rise away from human beings more quickly through knowledge than through action, because action is corporeal activity and corporeal activity occurs only sensibly. But knowledge is a faculty of the soul, which occurs only intelligibly. So that the prophet, upon whom be peace, said, "A little knowledge is better than much action."[59] He also stated, "The intention [95] of the believer is better than his or her action." And the Commander of the People, 'Alî, upon whom be peace, stated that "The value of every person is that which he or she does well."[60] That is, the value of humans and the nobility of humankind is only in knowledge.

Since these preliminaries have become prolonged [19v.], I will continue no longer, so that we are not detained from the intended subjects. The intention of this book is that we explain the Ascension of the prophet, may God bless him and his family and grant them salvation, according to the intellect, such as it went and it was. For rationalists know that his intention in that was not that it was a sensible journey, but rather that it was intelligible perception that he related allegorically [*ramzî*] in sensible language, so that neither class of humans be deprived.

(I do) this only with divine support and luminous aid, for thought [*khâṭir*] receives aid and the mirror of the intellect becomes luminous in order that explanation of these words will be given, in brief, and the allegorical meaning of the Ascension, in regard to secrets, will become clear.

Only [20r.] God, may He be glorified and exalted, grants success. [96 is a blank page]

Chapter
In Introduction to the Ascension of the Prophet, Upon Whom be Peace

[97] Know that the explanation of each thing (lies) in the nature of that thing, and the road to a specified destination is determined by that destination's direction. Hence, if a person wishes to set out on the road for a (certain) destination and heads toward another destination whose road is not in that direction, he or she will never reach the destination. Thus, if a person wishes to go to Baghdad and sets out on the Samarqand road, he or she will not reach Baghdad. But when a person sets out on the Baghdad road, he or she reaches the destination. In regard to equipment, it is the same; if [20v.] a person wishes to beat gold (into gold leaf) well, but tailors, or does carpentry, or some other profession whose equipment is not appropriate (to this intention), it will not turn out right. Similarly, if a person thinks that a human body reaches a place where the intellect reaches, it is impossible. Because the intellect reaches through intelligibles; it does not reach through duration or instrument, nor does it go by means of time. Because the intellect is not in place, nor does space encompass it. Hence, a place where the intellect reaches, the body does not reach. The body is a dense substance; it does not (naturally) move upward. If it travels upwards, it does so only by accident and force. If it desires to cover quickly a distance that it has only traveled slowly, [21r.] it cannot. [98]

Destinations are of two types, either intelligible or sensible. The conveyor of sensibles is the senses; the conveyor of intelligibles is the intellect. Elevation is also of two types: either intelligible or sensible. Elevation perceived by the senses, in terms of the visual perception (of moving) upward, becomes a sensible. Intelligible elevation is by way of rank and nobility, because it is not in locality. When the (sensible) destination is downward, travel toward it is downward. When the destination is upward, motion toward it is upward.

Ascent is also of two types: upward, sensible, for the body; or by levels of intelligibles, for the soul. The body's motion to a lofty destination occurs only by movement, transversing space, and temporal motion. But when it is on the level of intelligibles, motion is spiritual, by means of the intellect, not corporeal by means of the foot.

When the body [21v.] is stationary, the faculty of perception (can still) move toward its goal on the mount of the intellect. Its travel is rapid because it moves to its center, and everything tends toward its center. Perceiving intelligibles is the task of the intellect, not the work of the senses. And gazing upon intelligibles is the task of the soul, not the work of the body. When it is known that the elevation of intelligibles is not in an upward direction, (it is understood) that (such) movement is not the work of the body, since the body is slow-moving.

Ascensions, therefore, are of two types, either corporeal, by means of the power [*quvvat*] of (corporeal) upward motion, or spiritual, by means of the power of cogitation [*quvvat-i fikrî*] toward intelligibles. Since the conditions of the Ascension [*miʿrâj*] of our prophet, upon whom be peace, [22r.] are not in the sensible world, it is known that he did not go in body, because the body cannot traverse a long distance in one moment. [99] Hence, it was not a corporeal ascension, because the goal was not sensual. Rather, the ascension was spiritual, because the goal was intellectual.

If a person imagines that when (Muḥammad) said, "I went," and explained experiences [lit. states] in the form of corporeal entities [*mujassamât*], that would have all been imagination, it would be complete stupidity because confirming impossibilities is not the task of the intellect. This is not deficiency appearing on the part of the prophet, because capability has no connection with impossibilities. Rejecting inconceivable impossibilities is a state of superiority, not a deficiency. Rather, (the Ascension account) was the symbol(ic rendition) [22v.] of intelligibles given in the language of the external senses.[61]

Explanation of the states of made and created things is provided (by him) in a way that literalists would accept within their bounds, while inquiring minds understand these truths. And indeed, people of reason know that the place to which thought goes, the body does not go, and that which insight perceives, the sense of sight does not perceive.

Since the condition of the the Ascension is related to intelligibles, I long contemplated what it could be. When (my) intellect untied this knot, the thought occurred (to me) that the explanation of the symbols of the Ascension should be given so that it would be known how noble the prophet was, and what his aim was in these sayings. [23r.] Only God grants success.

I enjoin that these words be withheld from those who are unworthy, foolish, and uninitiated ignoramuses. For reticence with outsiders in (revealing) truths is one of the religious duties. The Seal of the Apostles, upon whom be blessings and peace, said, "Do not cast pearls before the feet of dogs."[62] It has also been said, "Secrets, protect them from outsiders!" And it has been said, "Keep your secret, even from your lord!"[63] [100] May that person who would reveal these words to every inferior person be unsuccessful, because he or she would be a traitor and scoundrel. "Whoever betrays us, is not of us."[64] That person would fall into perdition, and perdition and punishment would come to the writer as well. [23v.]

When a rationalist explains an intelligible, only (another) rationalist should peruse it, so that it does not disturb sensual-minded outsiders. And may God judge between us and the unrighteous! [101]

The Beginning of the Story[65]

The best of creatures, upon him be (God's) blessing and salvation, said: *I was sleeping one night in the house. It was a night with thunder and lightning. No animal made a sound, no bird chirped, no person was awake. I was not asleep, but lying between sleep and wakefulness.* That is, I had been desirous of perceiving truths by means of insight for a long time. At night humans are freer, for bodily occupations [24r.] and sensual impediments are suspended.

So it happened one night when I was between wakefulness and sleep means that I was between the senses and the intellect; I fell into the sea of knowledge. *It was a night with thunder and lightning* means that the succor of the celestial caller prevailed so that the irascible faculty died and the faculty of imagination [*khayâl*] ceased its operations.[66] Tranquility overcame preoccupation.

Then he said: *Suddenly Gabriel descended in his own form with such beauty, splendor, and majesty that the house was alit.* He means: the faculty of the Holy Spirit in the form of the (divine) Command united with me. It had so great an effect that all the faculties of the rational soul became renewed and alit.[67] [24v., 102]

Describing the beauty of Gabriel, he said: *I saw him whiter than snow, fair of face, curly of lock. On his forehead was written in light, "There is no God but God, and Muḥammad is the Apostle of God"; fairly large of eye, delicate of brow, with seventy thousand locks of red ruby dangling down, and six hundred thousand feathers of lustrous pearl opened up.* That is, in my inner eye [*baṣîrat*], by means of intellectual abstraction, I perceived such beauty and fairness that if a trace of that beauty were to appear to the senses, that sensible would look like what he described.

The meaning of "There is no God but God" being written on his forehead is that anyone whose eye beheld his beauty [25r.] would be cleansed from the darkness of skepticism and idolatry, and would attain such certitude and belief in the affirmation of the Creator that every created thing that he beheld would increase his belief in his Oneness. And (Gabriel) was so elegant that if a person had seventy thousand tresses of musk and camphor, he would not attain his beauty. And he was so quick-moving that you would say that he flew with six hundred thousand feathers and wings. (But) he did not move in time and space.

Then he said: *When he reached me, he embraced me and kissed me between my two eyes and said, "O Sleeper, arise! How long you slumber!"* That is, when this Holy Faculty reached me, [25v.] it caressed me and admitted me into its unveiling [*kashf*] and did (me) honor. Such yearning arose in my heart that it cannot be described. Then he said: *"How long you slumber!"* That is, why are you satisfied with counterfeit imaginings? There are worlds beyond this one you are in. You can only reach them in the wakefulness of knowledge. Because of compassion, [103] I shall be your guide. Arise!

Then he said: *I was afraid and leapt up from my place because of that fear.* That is, because of his majesty, I could not think.

Then he said: *He said to me, "Be still, for I am your brother Gabriel."* That is, by the grace of the unveiling [*kashf*] of wisdom, fear was stilled in me. He introduced himself, so that [26r.] he removed my distress.[68]

Then he said: *I said, "O Brother, an enemy has taken control of me (before)." He said, "I will not hand you over to the enemy." I said, "What are you going to do?" He said, "Arise! Be observant and take heart."* That is, illuminate the faculty of memory and obey me so that I may remove difficulties from you.

Then he said: *I was amazed and astonished, and I followed Gabriel.* That is, I turned away from the world of sensibles. With the help of the instinctual intellect [*'aql-i gharîzî*], I followed the Holy Emanation.

Then he said: *Behind Gabriel,* Burâq *caught my eye*. That is, the Active Intelligence, which is the most predominant of the Holy Faculties. Its help comes to the Intelligences before it reaches the world of generation [26v.] and corruption. Among the celestial Intelligences, it is it who is a ruler for the body. It is the bestower of help to souls at any time with whatever is appropriate. (Muḥammad) likened it to *Burâq* because he was traveling [*dar ravish*], and a mount is a help [104] for one who is travelling. In that journey it would be (Muḥammad's) helper, so inevitably he called it a mount.

Then he said: *It was larger than an ass and smaller than a horse*. That is, it is greater than the human intellect and lesser than the First Intelligence.

Then he said: *Its face was like a human face*. That is, it inclines towards instructing [*tarbiyat*] humans; it has the same compassion for humans that a genus has for its species. And its resemblance [27r.] to humans is by way of compassion and instruction. Then he said: *It is long of arm and long of leg*. That is, its beneficence reaches everywhere and its emanation renews everything.

Then he said: *I wanted to sit on it, (but) it shied away. Gabriel helped me until it was tamed.* That is, because I was in the physical world, I wanted to sit on it, that is, to unite with it. But it would not accept, until the Holy Faculty [*quvvat-i qudsî*] cleansed me of the preoccupations of ignorance and impediments of the body, so that I became pure [*mujarrad*] and, through it, attained the emanation and beneficence of the Active Intelligence.

Then he said: *When I had started on the road and passed the mountains of Mekka,* [27v.] *a traveler came after me and called out, "Stop!" Gabriel said, "Do not speak, go on!" So I went on*. By this he means the faculty of estimation. That is, when I was finished considering my external limbs and extremities, and was not contemplating the senses, and had gone on, the faculty of estimation called out from behind me, "Don't go!" (This is) because the faculty of estimation governs [*mutaṣarrif*], has great authority, and is active [*kârkun*] in all states. It is a tool and instrument for all animals. It stands in the place of intellect [*khirad*], accepting what is agreeable and rejecting what is [105] contrary. It is an influence on human beings, but they should not obey estimation, for then [28r.] they remain on the level of animals. A defect in their nobility thus appears. Whomever is helped by divine beneficence does not blindly follow estimation wherever he or she is.

Then he said: *A woman, alluring in (her) beauty, called from behind me,*

"Stop! So I can reach you." Again Gabriel said, "Go on, don't stop!" That is, the faculty of imagination [*khayâl*], which is alluring and ornamented. He likened it to a woman because most natures incline toward it, and most people are in its grasp. Furthermore, whatever it does is baseless and is tainted by deceit and fraud, and this is (like) the doings of women, for the wiles and stratagems of women are known. And the faculty of [28v.] imagination is also deceitful, lying, and treacherous. In this way it allures, hunting human beings with its representations then not fulfilling its promises, for show quickly becomes false. When humans go after imagination, they never attain intelligibles; they always follow (false) adornments and fall into the grip of meaningless concrete images.

Then he said: *When I went on, Gabriel said, "If you had waited for her until she reached you, you would have become a lover of the world."* That is, the conditions of the world are baseless and quickly disappear, and the vanities and preoccupations of the world, in relation to truths [*maʿânî*], are like the states and representations of imagination in relation [29r.] to the secrets of intellect. Whoever becomes occupied with (imagination) stays away from intelligibles and, through the folly of passion, becomes a prisoner in the abyss of ignorance.

Then he said: *When I went away from the mountains and left these two persons,* [106] *I traveled to the Sanctified Abode* [bait al-muqaddas], *and I entered it.*[69] *Someone came forward and gave me three goblets, one wine, one water, and one milk. I wanted to take the wine. Gabriel did not allow this. He pointed to the milk, so I took (it) and drank.* That is, when I went away from the senses and understood the condition of imagination and estimation, I gazed within myself and entered the spiritual realm. I saw three souls, one animal, one natural, and one rational. I wanted [29v.] to follow the animal (soul). He likened it to wine since its faculties, such as lust and anger, deceive, cloak, and increase ignorance, and wine intensifies these two appetites. He likened the natural (soul) to water since it sustains the body. A person survives by managing (this soul's) servants who work in the body. (Similarly), water is the cause of animal life; it promotes growth and increase. He likened the rational (soul) to milk since it is a beneficial nutriment, full of favor and usefulness.

Then he said, *I wanted to take the wine but he only allowed me to take the milk*, because most humans obey these two souls and do not transcend the natural [30r.] and animal (souls), because they are deficient. (Such) people are deficient and remain deficient; whatever they seek, they seek only the corporeal and sensual, and the pleasure and utility of these two souls is corporeal. Inevitably, that which is animal is lust-driven or power-seeking, loving worldliness, drink, wine, sexual intercourse, and such things (on the one hand), or is irascibleness [*khashm*], which consists of driving away contraries and similar activities (on the other hand). These are all corporeal preoccupations, and a deficient person always seeks out such activities.

Those obedient to the natural soul are the same. They are always involved in eating and sleeping. But when a person is perfectly tempered, his or her rational soul [107] becomes strong. It dominates the appetites of the (other) two souls. It commands the activity of the natural (soul's) faculties [30v.] so that they benefit the body and sustain and govern the person. It also has the faculties of the animal (soul) in its bonds and orders actions at necessary and beneficial times. It directs the concupiscent (appetite) only toward modesty and well-being, so that the soul [*nafs*] continues to exist through reproduction, and the name "dead soul" is lifted from it. It directs the irascible faculty toward the conditions of bravery and piety, so that the name "ardorless" not befall it. It has all the faculties under its rule according to time, opportunity, and benefit. Human beings are called "human" [*kas*] by virtue of this. The dominion of the natural faculty is bestial, the dominion of the animal faculty is devilish, and the dominion of the rational faculty is angelic. Humankind is (such) by virtue of being [31r.] closer to the angelic and further from the devilish and bestial, so that they are not unaware of their (physical) states, nor without a share of spiritual connection.

Then he said: *I arrived there and entered the mosque. The muezzin gave the call for prayer. I was in front, and I saw the group of angels and prophets standing to the right and left. One by one they greeted me and renewed the covenant.* He means by this: when I finished examining and contemplating the animal and natural (souls), I entered the mosque, that is, I reached the brain. By "muezzin" he means the faculty of recollection. By his being "in front" he means cogitation. By "prophets and angels" he means the faculties of the mental spirits [*quvvathâ-yi arvâḥ-i dimâghî*], [31v.] such as discernment, memory, recollection, and cogitation, and that which is like it.

Their greeting him is his comprehension of all the rational faculties, because Absolute Truth [*Ḥaqq*], may He be praised and exalted, when He created human beings, divided their nature [*nahâd*] into two domains: an external one and an internal one. The [108] external domain is the body. He gave it five senses so that it deals with sensibles. He also gave the internal (domain) five senses, as servants of the intellect. The external senses are the underlings of the internal senses, and the internal senses are the servants of the intellect. The common sense stands between the two (groups) as an intermediary. The external senses receive information from various sides and deposit it with the common sense. [32r.] (Common sense) then gives it to the faculty of cogitation so that it acts on it. That which does not fully meet (cogitation's) criteria, it discards; estimation and imagination then take it, plunge into it, and make use of it. That which is intelligible and perfect is given to the faculty of memory to preserve its abstract (ideas). When they become useful to the intellect, recollection takes (them) from memory by means of representation [*muṣavvirat*] and gives (them) to it. This foundation is always well-laid [*mumahhad*].

Just as two of the external senses are the most noble, hearing and sight, and are the leaders of the rest, similarly, two of the internal senses are the most noble; cogitation and memory are the leaders of the rest. [32v.] Imagination is on the level of taste. Estimation is equivalent to touch. Estimation is always active, just as touch is never constricted to a specific bodily part at any one time. The other faculties, however, are constricted to specific bodily parts.

Humans are complete [*tamâm*] when these five senses are in place and are working without fault, far from trouble. For if disruption or disturbance appears in one, they become defective [*nuqṣânî*]. Similarly, the perfection [*kamâl*] of humans lies in their internal senses also being luminous and in their comprehending everything. For if they are negligent and do not preserve these faculties, they become deprived of and unable to control truths [*ma'ânî*]. In time of need they become lost, and then humans are deprived of the nobility of discernment. When humans know all of this, [33r.] and the internal faculties become their guide, they attain [109] the ultimate goal. If this is not the case, they are deprived of it. Just as someone who wishes to go on a roof first needs a ladder and then ascends rung by rung until he or she reaches the roof, rational faculties are like ladder rungs. When someone ascends, rung by rung, he or she reaches his or her goal.

Then he said: *When I was finished, I faced aloft. I found a ladder, one rung of silver, one rung of gold.* He means: from the external senses toward the internal senses. The intention of "silver and gold" is the nobility in rank of the one over the other.

Then he said: *When I reached the first heaven, a door opened.* [33v.] *I entered and saw Ismâ'îl seated on a chair, and a group was placed, face to face, in front of his eye. I greeted (them) and went on.*[70] He means by this the sphere of the moon and by Ismâ'îl the body [*jirm*] of the moon. By this group (he means) those whose states are guided by the moon.

Then he said: *When I reached the second heaven, I entered. I saw an angel nearer than the former, with perfect beauty. He had a wondrous form, half of his body was of snow, half of fire. Neither mixed with the other, nor were they antagonistic toward one another. He greeted me and said, "Good tidings to you to whom goodness and fortune belong!"* [34r.]

He means the sphere of Mercury. The intention in this is that every heavenly body has a specific rule, either auspicious or sinister. Mercury, however, has two kinds of influence: conjoined with auspiciousness, it is auspicious; conjoined with sinisterness, it is sinister. For it is half auspicious and half sinister. The tidings of goodness and good fortune allude to the faculty of thought [*khâṭir*] and the many [110] sciences that it bestows.

Then he said: *When I reached the third heaven, I saw an angel whose like in beauty and goodness I had never seen, joyful and glad and seated on a chair of light with angels gathered around.* He means that it was the sphere of Venus. [34v.] There is no need to explain its beauty; it rules over joy and mirth.

Then he said: *When I reached the fourth heaven, I saw an angel, complete in statesmanship,*[71] *seated on a throne of light. I greeted (him), he responded properly but with complete arrogance. Due to pride and haughtiness, he (usually) spoke to no one. (But) he smiled when he answered (my) greeting and said, "O Muḥammad, I see complete goodness and felicity in your royal splendor* [farr]. *Good tidings to you!"*

By this throne he means the fourth sphere, and by this angel he means the Sun, which rules over the conditions of kings and great men. His smile indicates its influence for good fortune as an (astrological) ascendent [35r.], and his good tidings are its bounty [*faiḍ*] for the good of everyone.

Then he said: *When I reached the fifth heaven, I entered. I learned of hell. I saw a dominion full of darkness and fear. I saw the proprietor seated at its edge busy torturing and tormenting sinful people.* By this he means the fifth sphere. By the proprietor he means Mars, which rules over the conditions of the bloodthirsty and sinful. By hell he means its sinister influence on the characteristics and conditions of people who are under its rule. [111]

Then he said: *When I reached the sixth heaven, I saw an angel seated on a chair of light, engaged in praising and sanctifying (God).* [35v.] *He had wings and tresses set with pearls and rubies. I greeted him. He responded, greeted (me), and gave tidings of goodness and happiness. He said to me, "I continually sent blessings to you."*

He means the sixth sphere, and by this angel he means Jupiter, which rules over folk of rectitude, piety, and knowledge.[72] By those wings and tresses he means the effect of its light. By his blessings he means its influence for good, for it is the most auspicious (of the planets). All good things come to humankind from it; every benefit joined to a person is the result of its gaze. Because Absolute Truth, may He be exalted, through the perfection of His knowledge, has thus ordained. "He is the Manifest, True King."[73] [36r.]

Then he said, *When I reached the seventh heaven, I saw an angel sitting on a chair of red ruby. Not everyone finds a way to him, but when someone does reach him, he is cherished. I greeted him. He responded and blessed me.*

By this he means the seventh sphere, and by this angel he means Saturn, which is red and the most sinister (of the planets). Everything it does, it does perfectly. When it does something sinister, it is completely so. When it does something auspicious, it exceeds everything else. *Not everyone finds a way to him* means that it rarely happens that it is in a good and auspicious location. [36v.] But when it is, its effect is so good that it excels all else.

Then he said: *When I went on, I reached the Lote Tree of the Far Boundary.*[74] *I saw a world* [112] *full of light and brightness so brilliant that the eye was dazzled. When I looked to the right and left, I saw all the spiritual angels busy at worship. I said, "O Gabriel, who are these people?" He said, "These never do anything except worship and praise God. They have specified oratories from which they never depart. As it is said in the Qur'ân, 'Each of us has a known station.'"*[75]

By this he means the eighth sphere, the sphere of the fixed stars. The constellations [37r.] are there. By oratories and stations he means the twelve signs (of the zodiac). Each group of them resides in a specific quarter; they do not crowd one another. Thus the southern ones have nothing to do with the northern ones; each one has a place. Some of the constellations are on the ecliptic, some are in the south, and some are in the north.

Then he said: *I saw the Lote Tree, larger than all things, roots above and branches below, for its shade falls on heaven and earth.* By this he means the greatest sphere, within which are the rest of the spheres. It is larger than all, so that it is said in the Qur'ân: [37v.] "Each gliding in a sphere."[76]

Then he said: *When I passed by I saw four seas, each one a (different) color.* That is, he cognized [*taṣavvur*] through (intellectual) abstraction [*tajarrud*] the principles of substantiality, materiality, corporality, and form, which are the principles [*ḥaqâ'iq*] of all this [*în jumlat*]. He found each one (to be) a different rank, and he expresses this rank by (the word) color.[77]

Then he said: *I saw many angels busy praising God and affirming His unity, all* [113] *immersed in grace.* That is, abstract souls, free of concupiscent and irascible desire. They are pure. For each human being whose soul becomes pure and abstract in learning and knowledge, after becoming separated from the body, is held by Absolute Truth, may He be exalted, in neither place nor locality. [38r.] He makes them like angels, adorned with eternal bliss.

He makes the comparison with angels because angels are the dwelling-place [*maskin*] of sinlessness and the celebration of God's praise.[78] That is, they become free of corruption, death, the activities of the concupiscent faculties, and the preoccupations and accidents of the irascible (faculties).[79] They attain the level of angelicness, always engaged in perceiving and learning about the invisible (world). They never look toward the lower world. This is because the body in relation to the soul is base. Noble people who look toward the lower place do so either because of necessity or because of the best interests of that location. When they become separated from that (lower) habitation by (attaining) perfection and hindrances are removed, they attain their perfect nobility. [38v.] They become happy.

That is, they withdraw from sensual preoccupation toward rational perception and become so immersed in its pleasure and ease that they never recall anything base or look toward the lower world, for corporeal need has fallen away from them. At that time, they gain rank and nobility according to the measure of (their) knowledge and perception. "Some of them bow, some prostrate themselves."[80] Some are spiritual, some praise God and attest to His unity, some sanctify (Him), and some are drawn-near. On this basis, they continue forever.

Then he said: *When I went by this group, I reached a boundless sea. However much I gazed, I could not even perceive its middle.*[81] [39r.] *At the lower part of that sea, I saw a large stream, and I saw an angel who was pouring water from the sea* [114] *into the stream. From the stream, water reached everywhere.*

By this sea he means the First Intelligence. By the stream he means the First Soul. For the First Soul is subordinate to the First Intelligence. The first thing that Absolute Truth, may He be exalted, manifested through the creativity [*ibdâʿ*] of His power [*qudrat*] and knowledge, on the level of uniqueness, keeping it pure from the annoyance of mediation and bestowing upon it the highest rank, was the First Intelligence. As the prophet, upon whom be peace, said, "The first thing God created was the intelligence."[82] By this he means "first in rank," not "first in creation"; for that substance does not admit a temporal beginning. [39v.]

When the First Intelligence appeared, the First Soul became manifest. The former was on the level of Adam, the latter on the level of Eve. Then after this, two substances became separated from (the First Intelligence) as substances and bodies, like spheres and heavenly bodies and their Souls and Intelligences. After this, it continued until the elements appeared, became divided, and assumed inclinations, (each) according to its constitution, each one in its own domain, in accordance to its nature, fineness, and coarseness, such as water and earth inclining below and air and fire inclining above. After this, it worked on minerals, and then on plants and animals, and then it brought forth human beings. [40r.] They were preferred above all. They were bestowed with the faculty of soul and intellect, so that just as the First Intelligence, who was of noble rank, came in the beginning of creation, complete and beautiful, human beings also attained that rank in nobility at the end of creation. (Humans became) a point at the end so that the circle would be complete. This priority and posteriority about which I speak concerning existents is in rank, not in creation. The intent of that which he said concerning the sea and the water and the stream is what has been said (above).

Then he said: *At the bottom of that sea I saw a great valley, larger than any* [115] *I had ever seen. However much I gazed, I found neither its beginning or end; nor could I define it by anything.* [40v.] By this he means pure existence [*wujûd-i mujarrad*]. Nothing is more general than it. Only the perfect intellect can perceive pure existence.

Then he said: *In the sea's valley I saw an angel, of complete augustness, majesty, and beauty, who was gazing tranquilly at each of the two halves (of creation). He called me to himself. When I reached him, I said, "What is your name?" He said, "Michael* [Mîkâ'îl]. *I am the greatest of the angels. Whatever is difficult for you (to understand), ask of me. Whatever you desire, seek of me so that I can show to you the intended aims of everything."*

That is, when I knew all of this, I contemplated (further). I discerned the First Command [*amr-i avval*]. By that angel [41r.] he means that which is called the Holy Spirit, said to be the Angel Drawn-Near [*malak muqarrab*]. Whoever makes his or her way to it, and receives help, comes to know so much through its help that he or she becomes cognizant of all unknown things, spiritual pleasures, and eternal felicities, the like of which he or she has never before experienced.

Then he said: *When I was finished with greeting and questioning him, I said, "I have suffered much pain and trouble to reach this place where I am. My goal in coming here was that I attain knowledge and direct vision of Absolute Truth, may He be exalted. Guide me to Him so that I attain my desire and partake of the full benefit, and so return to my house."*[83] [41v.]

That is, as he had wished from the divine Command, which is the pure Word [*kalimat*], when he was finished observing existents by way of insight, the eye of his heart became opened so that whatever was, he knew. By this he meant perceiving Absolute Existence, the First Cause, and the Necessary Existent [116] and knowing its unity [*vaḥdat*], such that plurality could not be contained in it.

Then he said: *That angel took my hand, transported me through several thousand veils, and bore (me) to a world in which I saw nothing like what I had seen in this world. When he brought me to the Presence of Glory* [ḥaḍrat-i 'izzat], *the command came to me: "Draw nearer!"*[84] [42r.]

That is, that divine, holy Presence is free of body, substance, and accident, which exist in these worlds. It is above these categories. By necessity, it neither needs nor is connected to place, time, locality, how much, how, where, when, activity and passiveness, and the like. The Necessary Existent is neither body nor substance. It is pure and transcendent, beyond admitting those accidents. It is unique in purity. The associationalism [*shirkat*] of creation [*maqdûr*] is not contained in its singleness [*fardâniyyat*]. In its singleness, it is one. The multiplicity of number does not exist in its unicity [*yagânagî*]. In this regard, it is also able, knowing, and beneficent. It is thus unadulterated being. That unadulterated being is [42v.] the world of pure unity, unaffected by the multiplicity of change and multitude.

Then he said: *I did not see sensation or movement in that Presence. I only saw tranquility* [farâghat], *stillness* [sukûn], *and sufficiency* [ghanâ]. That is, I saw the abstract knowledge of its existence to an extent that no living creature can encompass by means of sensation. For bodies are perceived through sensation, (external) forms and the imagination are preserved, and substances are cognized through the vigilance of the intellect. But the Necessary Existent is beyond these stages. It cannot be apprehended through sensation and imagination. In that Presence, there is no movement [*ḥarakat*]. Movement is change in an existent, either by being acted upon in corporeal quantity and quality, [43r.] or (by moving) from place to place desiring a benefit or fleeing an opponent or through bodily movement while remaining stationary. The former is by necessity, [117] the latter by choice. All things that are moved need a mover. But movement is not admissible for it. The Necessary Existent is that which is the mover of all things.

Then he said: *From being in awe of God* [khudâvand], *I forgot everything that I had seen and known. Such unveiling, grandeur, and pleasure from proximity was produced that you would say that I was intoxicated.*

That is, when my knowledge made its way to the gnosis of unity [*vâḥdâniyyat*] [43v.] I was no longer engaged in perceiving and preserving particulars. The rational soul achieved so much pleasure from this knowledge that all the faculties of the natural and animal (souls) stopped working. I was so immersed in unity that I was no longer engaged in the world of substances and bodies.

Then he said: *So affected was I by (divine) proximity that I began to tremble. The command was coming, "Draw nearer!" When I drew nearer, He said, "Fear not, be calm!"*

That is, when I apprehended unity, I knew that the Necessary Existent was beyond these categories. I became afraid of my boldness for a journey that had become very long in affirming unity. [44r.] I thought that it would harm me. *It was said, "Draw nearer!"* That is, draw nearer, away from this thought of mine and this fear and terror. For the realm of unity entails continual immersion in spiritual pleasure [*ladhdhat-i rûḥânî*]. One is never affected by the animal (soul), and fear and hope are conditions of the animal (soul).

Then he said: *When I drew nearer, God's greeting came to me through a voice the like of which I had never heard.* That is, the reality of the discourse [118] of the Necessary Existent, may it be exalted and sanctified, was unveiled to me. For its speech is not like the speech of creatures, with pronunciation and sound. Its speech is the affirmation of knowledge through pure abstraction in the soul. (It conveys) what it wishes by way of [44v.] universality, not particularity.

Then he said: *The command came, "Praise!" I said, "'I do not enumerate Your praises, for You have praised Yourself.'*[85] *I am unable (to say) the like of what You Yourself have said."* That is, when he perceived the beauty of unity and apprehended the reality of the discourse of the Necessary Existent, and understood that its speech does not consist of pronunciation and sound, he attained pleasure the like of which he had never experienced. He understood that the Necessary Existent was deserving of all praise, but he knew he could not praise it with language that consisted of sounds and therefore fell under (the category of) language. This type of praise is only connected with particulars and universals, [45r.] but it is not appropriate for the Necessary Existent, which is neither a universal or a particular. He knew that praising it through language was not correct, for it is not for the senses to do work befitting the intellect. The intellect knows that anyone praising one who is perfectly praiseworthy must be in agreement with him. For his knowledge must be equal to the one being praised if speech is to be suitable for the intention. The Necessary Existent is Single, One, and Incomparable, so the praise of a human is not concordant with it. Therefore (Muḥammad) left it to (the Necessary Existent's) own knowledge. It utters all knowledge, and its knowledge is the exposition of praise for itself, not through pronunciation or sound, nor through speech. It is its own adornment and it is its own splendor.

Then he said: [45v.] *The command came, "Desire something!" I said, "Give permission that whatever (problem) I encounter, I (can) ask until its difficulties are solved."* That is, when it said to me, "What [119] do you want?" I said, "Give permission!" That is, knowledge. Because in this intellectual journey, only pure intellect had remained, for he had reached the Presence of the Necessary Existent and become knowing. In Unity [*vahdâniyyat*], the only thing he could have asked for that would have been suitable for him was Absolute Knowledge [*ʿilm-i muṭlaq*]. So he was given perfect knowledge [*ʿilm-i tamâm*] in accordance with his rank. Hence, when there was afterwards any problem, he would petition (God's help) and find a clear solution. He would thus lay out the principles of religious law, such as prayer, fasting, and the like, according to the judgments of that knowledge, in the best interests of creation [46r.] and never fall into error. In the reality of the Necessary Existent, he established the goal of his knowledge within the limits of his intellect, in language [*lafẓ*] harmonious with the hearing of created beings, so that meaning be clear and the curtain of (distortion due to) self-interest not be drawn up. The help of that knowledge was that the explanation of such a journey be given set in a story of an external journey, so that only one knowledgeable in the truth would be on the path of knowing and understanding the content of his speech.

Then he said: *When I did all this, I returned to the house. Because of the swiftness of the journey, the bedclothes were still warm.* That is, the journey was intellectual [*fikrî*]. He went by thought [*khâṭir*]. (His) intellect [46v.] perceived the order of existents until the Necessary Existent. Then, when cognition [*tafakkur*] was complete, he returned to himself. No time had passed. Returning in that state was quicker than (the glance of) an evil eye. Whoever knows, knows what transpired. Whoever does not know, is excused.

It is not permissible to show the inner meanings [*ramz-hâ*] of these words to one of the ignorant masses. Only a rationalist [*ʿâqil*] is permitted to enjoy the inner meaning of these words. May God, may He be exalted, grant the favor of true speech and true knowledge.[86]

Notes

1. This translation is based on the text in N. Mâyel Heravî's *Miʿrâj Nâma (The Book of Ascent), with a Revised Text by Shamsuddîn Ibrâhîm Abarqûhî*, ed. N. Mâyel Heravî (Mashhad: The Islamic Research Foundation, Âstân-i Quds-i Raḍavî, 1986) (hereafter H.). I compared this edition closely with the facsimile edition of the manuscript of the *Miʿrâj Nâma*, prepared by Mahdî Bayânî (Tehran: Anjuman-i dûstdârân-i kitâb, 1952) (hereafter B.), that was originally transcribed by Muḥammad ibn ʿUmar ar-Râzî (Appendix C, 1), and occasionally I adopt the latter's reading. Pagination for both editions is inserted between brackets; plain page numbers refer to Heravî, numbers indicating recto and verso to Bayânî. I also consulted the generally unreliable text edited by Bahman Karîmî, *Miʿrâj Nâma* (Rasht: Matbaʿat-i urwat al-wuthqâ, n.d.) (hereafter K.) and the late Indian manuscript now in the British Library Add. 16659/4 (Appendix C, 21, hereafter BM). I identify references to the Qur'ân and to those ḥadîth that appear in A. J. Wensinck, J. P. Messing, et al., *Concordance et indices de la tradition musulmane*, 8 vols. (Leiden: E. J. Brill, 1936–88); those interested should also consult Heravî's notes to the text in his *Miʿrâj Nâma*, 167–77.

2. Qur'ân, 17.1–3. Concerning the *miʿrâj* in general, see Gerhard Böwering's article, "*Miʿrâj*," in *Encyclopedia of Religion*, 9:552–56, which provides an up-to-date bibliography; see also the articles under "*Miʿrâj*" in EI^1, 5:505–508 and and "*Isrâ*" in EI^2, 3:553–54. A good general account of the *miʿrâj* and its later influences in Islamic culture, with relevant bibliographical citations, is Annemarie Schimmel, *And Muhammad Is His Messenger: The Veneration of the Prophet in Islamic Piety* (Chapel Hill: University of North Carolina Press, 1985) 159–75. N. M. Heravî, *Miʿrâj Nâma*, 62–67, provides a useful list of *miʿrâj* accounts in Persian, while for an overview of the Turkish tradition, see Metin Akar, *Türk Edebiyatinda Manzum Miʿrâj-Nameler*, Kültür ve Turizm Bakanlığı Yayınları 804 (Ankara: Kültür ve Turizm Bakanlığı, 1987).

3. R. A. Nicholson, "An Early Arabic Version of the Miʿrâj of Abû Yazîd al-Bisṭâmî," *Islamica* 2 (1926–27) 402–14; Ḥakîm Sanâ'î, *Mathnavîhâ-yi Ḥakîm*

Sanâ'î ba-inẓimâm-i sharḥ-i sair al-'ibâd ila l-ma'âd, ed. Muḥammad Taqî Mudarris-i Raẓavî, Intishârât-i Dânishgâh-i Tihrân 1226 (Tehran: Dânishgâh-i Tihran, 1969) 180–233; Ibn Ṭufail, *Ḥayy ibn Yaqẓân*, in Amîn, ed., *Ḥayy ibn Yaqẓân, li-bn Sînâ wa-bn Ṭufail wa-s-Suhrawardî*; al-Ghazâlî, *Risâlat aṭ-ṭair*, ed. L. Cheikho, *al-Mashriq* 20 (1901) 918–24; as-Suhrawardî, *Opera Metaphysica et Mystica* II, ed. Corbin, and *Opera Metaphysica et Mystica* III, ed. Nasr; Shams ad-Dîn Muḥammad ibn Îl-ṭughân Bardsîrî Kirmânî, *Miṣbâḥ al-arvâḥ*, ed. Badî' az-Zamân Furûzânfar, Intishârât-i Dânishgâh-i Tihrân 1284 (Tehran: Dânishgâh-i Tihran, 1971); Ibn 'Arabî, *Kitâb al-isrâ ilâ maqâm al-asrâ*, in *Risâ'il Ibn 'Arabî* (Hyderabad: Dâ'irat al-ma'ârif al-'uthmâniyya, 1948), vol. 1; *idem, al-Futûḥât al-Makkiyya*, 4 vols. (Beirut: Dâr ṣâdir, n.d.) 1:117–31, 2:270–354; al-Qushairî, *Kitâb al-mi'râj*, ed. 'Alî Ḥasan al-Qâdir (Cairo: Dâr al-kutub al-ḥadîtha, 1964). An example of a nonreligious use of the *mi'râj* theme is *Risâlat al-Ghufrân*, by Abû 'Alâ' al-Ma'arrî (d. 449/1057) (Beirut: Dâr ṣâdir, 1964).

4. See Heath, "Disorientation and Reorientation."

5. Some attention has been paid to the rhetorical dimension of works of Islamic philosophy, especially by Leo Strauss and his followers. Much less has been given to this aspect of theological and mystical texts. See, for example, James Morris's well-justified complaints concerning this omission in regard to the study of Ibn 'Arabî, certainly one of the most "rhetorical" of all Muslim mystics, in James W. Morris, "Ibn 'Arabî and His Interpreters, Part I: Recent French Translations," *JAOS* 106,3 (1986) 539–51, esp. notes 8, 15, and 23. See also Chapter Seven below.

6. I initially intended to produce a critical edition of the text as well. The recent publication of the edition by Heravî, *Mi'râj Nâma (The Book of Ascent), with a Revised Text by Shamsuddîn Ibrâhîm Abarqûhî*, in combination with the facsimile edition of the excellent early manuscript of the work, *Mi'râj Nâma*, ed. Mahdî Bayânî, renders this task unnecessary. The few instances where I disagree with Heravî's readings are noted in the translation.

7. Technical terms are glossed with transliterations in their first occurrence; for further references consult the index. Terms that are equivocal (*ma'ânî, ḥaqîqa*) are glossed at each occurrence. I consider *rûḥ* the standard term for *soul* in the treatise and note instances where *nafs* is used instead.

8. This introduction is from B.

9. *Jân*, spirit, here refers to the material life force (the Stoics' *pneuma*) which animates the body rather than to the purely intelligible dimensions of human beings. For the latter sense, Avicenna customarily uses the term *nafs*. This treatise, however, interchanges *rûḥ* and *nafs* as cognates (see also above, Chapter Four, note 31). Compare this introduction with that of the *Dânish-nâma-yi 'Alâ'î* and the Persian translation of *Ḥayy ibn Yaqẓân* in Corbin, *Avicenna*, 281. Subsequent references to *Ḥayy ibn Yaqẓân* cite the edition of Mehren, *Traités mystiques*, then the two English translations (the text itself and as it stands in the Persian commentary) in Corbin, *Avicenna*.

10. H. omits the word *ma'nâ* which I take from B. *Ma'nâ* has several senses in this treatise, which are indicated in the text. Compare Corbin's comments in *Avicenna*, 301, note 9.

11. On ʿAlâʾ ad-Daula Muḥammad, see Chapter Two above. For *majlis*, see *EI*², 5:1031–33, and compare the introduction of Avicenna's *Fî taʿbîr ar-ruʾyâ*, 261–62.

12. Proverb. *Aghyâr* here connotes those who are strangers in terms of spiritual kinship rather than ordinary acquaintance. Cf. *aṭ-Ṭair*, 42.

13. *Ahl*, "worthy," also perhaps "folk," a word that is used technically to refer to members of a particular theological orientation; hence mystics are *ahl at-tasawwuf* and *Muʿtazilîs* are *ahl ar-raʾy wa-n-naẓar*; see *EI*², 1:258–67, on other common uses of the term.

14. "Appearance" (*ẓuhûr*) is from B.

15. I follow B. here.

16. For *sidrat an-muntahâ*, see Qurʿân, 53.13–18.

17. *Lâ taufîq illâ bi-llâh*, a formula consistently used by Avicenna in his writings.

18. As we have seen, Avicenna uses the term *Ḥaqq* to refer to the Necessary Existent in Book Nine of *al-Ishârât wa-t-tanbîhât*; he also uses it in *Sharḥ kitâb* Athûlûjiyâ *al-mansûb ilâ Arisṭû*, 60.

19. The four humors: blood, phlegm, choler or yellow bile, and melancholy or black bile; the four elements: earth, water, fire, and air.

20. In other words, the rational soul; for *ravân*, see *Dânish-nâma-yi ʿAlâʾî: Ṭabîʿiyyât*, 80; Corbin, *Avicenna*, 284, 285, note 4.

21. Reading from B. H. has "since spirit and body do not last."

22. For *ifrâṭ wa-tafrîṭ*, see *ash-Shifâʾ: al-Ilâhiyyât*, 429–30; *an-Najât*, 331–32; and *Fi l-quwa n-insâniyya*; for *iʿtidâl, Fi n-nafs*, 137; *Fi s-saʿâda*, 19; and Chapter Five above.

23. See *al-Mubâḥathât*, 235, where the practical sciences are called "acquired" (*muktasab*); see also *al-Hidâya*, 218.

24. Cf. *ash-Shifâʾ: an-Nafs*, 152; *al-Mabdaʾ wa-l-maʿâd*, 95; Chapter Four above.

25. Cf. *ash-Shifâʾ: an-Nafs*, 153.

26. Cf. *Fi l-quwa l-insâniyya*, 47; and Michot, *La destinée de l'homme selon Avicenne*, 117.

27. For *himmat*, see *ash-Shifâʾ: an-Nafs*, 159, 177; *Fi s-saʿâda*, 2, 4; for *irâdat*, see *al-Ishârât wa-t-tanbîhât*, 4:76, 86.

28. Cf. *al-Ishârât wa-t-tanbîhât*, 4:68–73; *as-Saʿâda*, 4.

29. Cf. *Fi l-ʿishq*; *al-Ishârât wa-t-tanbîhât*, 4:41.

30. *al-Ishârât wa-t-tanbîhât*, 4:41.

31. Avicenna begins with the sphere of the moon, that closest to earth. For the charateristics of each sphere, compare *Ḥayy ibn Yaqẓân*, 10–13; Corbin, *Avicenna*, 143–45, 333–42; and *Fi l-ajrâm al-ʿulwiyya*, 39–40.

32. I read *muhaimin-i avval* from B rather than H.'s *mahîn-i avval* (First Great One]. Cf. *Ḥayy ibn Yaqẓân*, 18–20; Corbin, *Avicenna*, 148–49, 362–71.

33. See the section on prophecy in Chapter Five above.

34. Qur'ân, 2.88.

35. See Marmura, "Some Aspects of Avicenna's Theory of God's Knowledge of Particulars," 299–312.

36. Ḥadîth (not in Wensinck, *Concordance*).

37. Qur'ân, 16.65.

38. On Gabriel in general Islamic piety, see "Djabrâ'îl," *EI²*, 2:362–63. Here Avicenna equates him with the prophetic aspect of the First Intelligence; see Nasr, *An Introduction to Islamic Cosmological Doctrines*, 268 and Corbin, *Avicenna*, 288, note 15, as well as other citations in Corbin's index, 406, for numerous references.

39. Qur'ân, 2.138.

40. Ḥadîth (not in Wensinck, *Concordance*).

41. Ḥadîth, see Wensinck, *Concordance*, 1:109.

42. Cf. Qur'ân, 56.27–48; and *an-Nafs an-nâṭiqa*, 187; Michot, *La destinée de l'homme selon Avicenne*, 191, note 2.

43. Ḥadîth, see Wensinck, *Concordance*, 6:508.

44. Qur'ân, 7.54. For *amr*, see *EI²*, 1:449–50, and J. M. S. Baljon, "The 'Amr of God' in the Koran," *Acta Orientalia* 23,1–2 (1958) 7–18; see also Corbin, *Avicenna*, 339, note 8, 342, note 20; *Fi s-sa'âda*, 2; *an-Nairûziyya*, 94; and in the translation below, 134–35.

45. Qur'ân, 17.85.

46. Qur'ân, 78.38. I prefer B.'s reading of "qualified" (*kaifiyyat*) above to H.'s "revelation" (*kashf*), because the opposition between "absolute" (*muṭlaq*) and "qualified" (*kaifiyyat*) seems to be primary here.

47. Cf. *al-'Arshiyya*, 30–31:

> (The prophet's) speech is the effulgence of sciences from (God) onto the Tablet of the heart of the Prophet, upon whom be peace, by means of the Inscribing Pen which is expressed by the Active Intelligence and the Angel Drawn-Near [*al-malak al-muqarrab*]. So speech is an expression of sciences (coming to) the Prophet, upon whom be peace. Knowledge, however, admits neither plurality [*ta'addud*] nor multiplicity [*kathra*].

See also Michot, *La destinée de l'homme selon Avicenne*, 126–29.

48. Ḥadîth (not in Wensinck, *Concordance*). As Avicenna says in *al-'Arshiyya*, 32, "We see, therefore we know; the Prophet, peace be upon him, knows, then he sees."

49. Qur'ân, 6.103.

50. Qur'ân, 6.18.

51. Qur'ân, 50.16.

52. Ḥadîth (not in Wensinck, *Concordance*).

53. Qur'ân, 55.2–3. Throughout this paragraph I follow B. rather than H.

54. Ḥadîth (not in Wensinck, *Concordance*). Pertinent here is the well-known controversy between the Mu'tazilîs and the Traditionalists concerning the issue of the "createdness" of the Qur'ân. Avicenna's position as stated here is close to that of the Mu'tazilîs in that he holds the intellectual essence of prophetic messages to be divine, but their expressed verbal forms to be material; but it is not identical to a Mu'tazilî view in that he would not necessarily declare God's speech itself to be a secondary, created phenomenon. On the Mu'tazilîs, see Fakhry, *A History of Islamic Philosophy*, 44–65, on the "createdness" of the Qur'ân, esp. 61–63.

55. Qur’ân, 31.25.

56. Ḥadîth (not in Wensinck, *Concordance*).

57. Persian rendering of the above Arabic ḥadîth.

58. Ḥadîth (not in Wensinck, *Concordance*).

59. Ḥadîth (not in Wensinck, *Concordance*).

60. Saying of ‘Alî ibn Abî Ṭâlib. Avicenna seldom quotes ‘Alî and is probably only indulging his patron by doing so; for another example, however, see the equally late *Sirr al-qadar*, 28; trans. 31.

61. I follow B. throughout this paragraph.

62. Ḥadîth (not in Wensinck, *Concordance*); see Gutas, *Avicenna and the Aristotelian Tradition*, 232.

63. Proverbs.

64. Ḥadîth, see Wensinck, *Concordance*, 4:515.

65. Passages in italics comprise Avicenna’s version of the *mi‘râj* narrative; those in regular type are his commentary. For the narrative of Avicenna’s version of the *mi‘râj* uninterrupted by commentary, see Appendix D.

66. Cf. *Ḥayy ibn Yaqẓân*, 4–5, Corbin, *Avicenna*, 139, 299–300; for Avicenna’s theory of dreams, see *Fî ta‘bîr ar-ru’yâ*, 282–94; *Fi s-sa‘âda*, 20; *Fi l-ajrâm al-‘ulwiyya*, 31; Gutas, *Avicenna and the Aristotelian Tradition*, 183–84; F. Rahman, *Prophecy in Islam*, 36–39; and Chapter Four above.

67. Cf. Avicenna’s Neoplatonic light and mirror imagery discussed in Chapter Three above, as well as his interpretations of the Light Verse (“Âyat an-nûr,” Qur’ân, 24.35) in *Fî ithbât an-nubuwwât*, 49–52, and *al-Ishârât wa-t-tanbîhât*, 2:388–94, discussed in Chapter Eight below.

68. I prefer B.’s *hamm* here to H.’s *vahm*.

69. Cf. Corbin, *Avicenna*, 292–93.

70. Reading B., *âsmân-i dunyâ*, instead of H., *âsmân-i awwal*. This appears to follow a version of the *mi‘râj* found in Ibn Isḥâq (d. 150/767) and Ibn Hishâm’s (d. 218/833 or 213/828) biography of the prophet Muḥammad in which an angel named Ismâ‘îl is mentioned as the guardian of one of the gates of heaven; see *as-Sîra an-nabawiyya*, ed. Tâhâ ‘Abd ar-Ra’ûf Sa‘d, 4 vols. (Beirut: Dâr al-Jîl, n.d.) 2:37; Ibn Isḥâq, *The Life of Muhammad*, trans. A. Guillaume (Oxford: Oxford University Press, 1955) 185.

71. Following B., I omit *pâdshâhvâr*.

72. Following B., I insert *ahl*.

73. In Arabic; compare Qur’ân, 20.114.

74. See Qur’ân, 53.15.

75. Qur’ân, 37.164.

76. Qur’ân, 21.33.

77. In this last line I follow neither B. nor H., since neither makes sense. Instead I follow K. (p. 31) and BM. (p. 374v), reading their *bi-rangî* for B. and H.’s *bar yakî* and their *‘ibârat kard* for the formers’ *‘ibâdat kard* (see note 1 above for manuscript citations).

78. Reading B., *‘ismat* (sinlessness), instead of H., *‘aql* (intellect); but H., *tasbîḥ* (praise), instead of B., *tasḥîd* (?).

79. I follow B. here.

80. Not from the Qur'ân or ḥadîth; perhaps a paraphrase?

81. Reading B., *wasṭ* (middle), instead of H., *shaṭṭ* (shore).

82. This is a common—if weak—ḥadîth; it is not in Wensinck, *Concordance*, but see *EI*[2], 1:341 and al-Ghazâlî, *Iḥyâ' 'ulûm ad-dîn*, 5 vols. (Beirut: Dâr al-ma'rifa, n.d.) 1:83, that is, the beginning of Chapter 7 (on the intellect) of Book 1; see also *al-'Arshiyya*, 37 and Jean Michot, "L'épître sur la connaissance de l'âme rationelle et de ses états, attribuée à Avicenne," *Revue Philosophique de Louvain* 82 (1984) 484, note 23.

83. This paragraph as according to B.

84. I follow B. here. H. omits "to me" (*bi-man*). B. gives the Arabic as well as the Persian of "Draw nearer!"

85. A well-known ḥadîth; see Wensinck, *Concordance*, 1:304; see also Nûrud-dîn Abdurrahmân-i Isfarâyinî, *Le révélateur des mystères (Kâshif al-Asrâr)*, intro., ed., and trans. Hermann Landolt, Islam Spirituel (Paris: Verdier, 1986), 206, note 110.

86. B. continues: "This is the end of his speech, may God sanctify his soul. Muḥammad ibn 'Umar wrote it in the middle of Ṣafar, may it be concluded in goodness and success, in 584 [C.E. April 1188]. Praise be to God, Lord of the worlds, and blessings on His prophet Muḥammad, the best of all creation, and on his family and companions."

Part IV

Interpretation and Allegory

7. The Interpretation and Function of Allegory

Avicenna's theory of allegory is straightforward, easily summarized, and, obviously, highly pertinent to an understanding of the rhetorical dimension of his allegories and philosophical writings. As with any theory of literary creation or interpretation, however, Avicenna's hermeneutics must be taken with a grain of salt. Authorial theories of composition and reading are indeed relevant, but they should not be accepted so literally that they overly determine our understanding of the workings of the texts themselves. Writers often valorize rules of composition or endorse methods of interpretation that they themselves do not completely follow in practice.[1] Avicenna's theory of interpretation is based upon his logic, poetics, and theory of prophecy, and it is to these subjects that we now must turn.

Logic and Poetics

In the Aristotelian-Neoplatonic tradition of philosophy in which Avicenna participated, poetics is a branch of logic.[2] According to this tradition, the main task of logic is to study different forms of argumentation, whether demonstrative or otherwise. The eight logical texts that came to comprise Aristotle's *Organon* therefore delineate ascending and descending levels of valid disputation and elucidate the relative degrees of philosophical certainty to which each can aspire. This program is most fully illustrated in Avicenna's own writings by his organization of logic in *ash-Shifâ'*.

Avicenna begins the logical component of his philosophy with his version of Porphyry's *Isagoge* (*al-Madkhal*), which serves as a propedeutic to the Aristotelian logical corpus proper.[3] Thereafter follow three tracts of an introductory nature. The *Categories* (*al-Maqûlât*) and *On Interpretation* (*Fi l-ʿibâra*) each put forth basic definitions and concepts, while the *Prior Analytics* (*al-Qiyâs*) introduces the syllogism. These texts form the methodological preamble to the preeminent treatise of logic, central in placement and importance, *Demonstration* (*al-Burhân*, equivalent to Aristotle's *Posterior Analytics*), which analyzes the forms of syllogistic demonstration that lead to indisputable conviction based on rational assent (*taṣdîq*). Other, less conclusive, forms of persuasion also exist, however, and these become the subject of the final four books of Avicenna's logic. *Dialectic* (*Fi l-jadal*) examines arguments based on well-founded opinions and generally accepted premises (*ẓann*); *Sophistic Refutation* (*as-Safsaṭa*) investigates arguments based on false or faulty forms of disputation. *Rhetoric* (*al-Khiṭâba*) studies the art of formulating convincing appeals to intuitive impressions of right and wrong and/or subjective opinions of affirmation or condemnation. And finally, *Poetics* (*ash-Shi'r*) examines acquiescence promoted by the creation of mimetic representations and imaginative analogies. In this schema, each of these less conclusive forms of argument, whether dialectical, rhetorical, or poetic, can reflect truthful propositions, but they cannot be used to prove them beyond dispute; only rational demonstration is able to accomplish this task. As Ismail Dahiyat observes:

> The logical art of demonstration is the center of the whole augmented *Organon* according to this scheme. The first three arts (i.e., *Categories, On Interpretation* and *Prior Analytics*) [excluding, for the moment, the *Isagoge*] are "introductions" and ways into demonstration, while the other four (dialectic, sophistic, rhetoric and poetic) are appendages and tools which are more or less useful to the process of "judicative logic" which induces necessity and truth. These arts (dialectic, rhetoric and poetic) relate to the process of "discovery" in which something more or less true is achieved but without having the logical necessity of scientific truth.[4]

It is worth noting that this logical hierarchy has obvious analogues in Avicenna's epistemological theory, for these various types of logical argumentation correlate rather precisely with the linguistic modes of expression typical of the individual psychological faculties. Rational demonstration is thus the responsibility of the theoretical intellect, while dialectic, which employs arguments based on generally accepted belief, is the natural domain of cogitation. The practical intellect then mixes these two cognitive realms by deploying rational criteria to evaluate or improve upon everyday ethical or political beliefs. Similarly, one directs rhetorical arguments toward the instinctual reactions of estimation and uses poetic discourse in order to appeal to the pictorial sensuousness of the imagination.

This comparison between logical categories of argumentation and psychic faculties of perception highlights a further tension existing among the internal faculties of the soul.[5] On the one hand, the lower internal faculties, common sense and representation, are primarily preoccupied with the internal reception and the proper storage of exact replicas of external sense perceptions. Constricted in their capacity for self-expression, they synthesize or store information but are unable to create it. On the other hand, the higher faculties—imagination, estimation, and the intellect—handle more abstract ideational functions in ways that are inherently active and creative. It is they who construct our understanding of the external world and it is through them that we are able to engage in self-expression and social interaction. It is they, therefore, who create and then utilize the peculiarly human systems of abstract signs and signals whose typical, although certainly not exclusive, means of representation is language. From this perspective, Avicenna's concept of the purview of logic widens beyond a concern for methods of syllogistic proof to the overall study, and hierarchical ordering, of all the possible forms of creative linguistic self-expression.[6]

Avicenna assumes rather than explores this point, however. For him, the primary purpose of logic is to serve as a preparatory tool for serious philosophical investigation and only secondarily to engage in the comprehensive study of language. Students become philosophers by learning appropriate technical terms and understanding prerequisite categories of thought in order to master the rules of syllogistic demonstration and so to distinguish truth from falsehood. Even philosophers, however, must recognize that nonscientific language can serve the aims of philosophy; hence, logic must encompass the study of persuasive or aesthetic forms of speech as well. Such inquiry is more than academically relevant to philosophers, because beyond their primary assignment of discovering the truth they need to develop the appropriate political styles of conveying it to audiences with no training and little interest in the science of rational demonstration. Within the context of Avicenna's thought, the most noteworthy example of such a situation is the case of revelatory apostleship.[7]

Apostleship

We have seen that the task of theoretical philosophy is to ascertain truth, while the goal of practical philosophy is to promote virtue, whether individual, familial, or civil. The endeavors of each branch of philosophy presume a thorough mastery of the techniques of logic, but its relevance to each differs. If the logical treatises leading up to and including *Demonstration* ensure that philosophers will be able to discover truth, those that follow enable them to promulgate it. Scientific proofs may guide a Zarathustra up the mountain, but when he comes down again to interact with his fellow humans, he must have mastered dialectic, rhetoric, and poetics as well, or else his descent will be in vain (as Ibn Ṭufail's character, Ḥayy ibn Yaqẓân, discovered). Humans vary in their capacities to comprehend philosophical truths; each class of intellect responds to specific types of argument. For philosophers content to promote virtue on an individual level, the diversity of human nature does not present a significant barrier because they instruct only those who are willing and able to study directly with them. More ambitious reformers, however, who yearn to promote civil virtue, must be able to inspire assent in all types of humans, and they therefore face a more complex set of problems. Such reformers, whether they be philosophers or, in the case of religious proclamation, prophets, must be able to master forms of discourse that can appeal to different types of audience, regardless of whether they are guided by intellect, imagination, or bodily appetites. They must be able to comply with words of the Qur'ân, which urges prophets to "summon to the way of your Lord by wisdom and by good preaching, and debate with them in the most effective manner."[8] Or, as the ḥadîth quoted in the *Miʿrâj Nâma* puts it, "We, the band of prophets, He commanded us to speak to people according to the capacity of their intellects."[9] The *Miʿrâj Nâma*, in fact, succinctly sums up the basic problematic when it states that

> It is thus the condition of prophets that they arrange every intelligible that they perceive as a sensible and put it into speech so that the community can follow that sensible. They perceive it as an intelligible, but make it sensed and concrete for the community. They thus increase (its usefulness) for threats and promises and foster good beliefs, so that its provisions become perfect, and so that the basis and code of religious law [*sharʿ*] and the foundation of religious devotion not be dissolved and disordered and that which is the intention of the prophet not remain concealed. When it reaches intellectuals, they perceives it with their intellects. They know that the prophet's words are all symbols, filled with intelligibles. When it reaches ignoramuses, however, they look at the external speech. Their hearts are satisfied with nonintelligible concrete forms and sensibles. They are enveloped by the imagination and do not pass beyond the doorway of estimation. They ask, unknowing, and listen, uncomprehending.[10]

Avicenna makes the same point in *Fî ithbât an-nubuwwât*, this time suggesting the different obligations that the philosopher and the prophet face:

> It has been said that it is incumbent upon the prophet that his speech be symbolic [*ramz*] and his expressions be hints [*îmâ'*]. As Plato states in the *Laws*: whosoever does not understand the meaning of the apostles' symbols [*rumûz*] will not attain the Divine Kingdom. Similarly, the foremost Greek philosophers and prophets employed symbols [*marâmîz*] and signs [*ishârât*] in their books through which they hid their secrets—men like Pythogoras, Socrates, and Plato. Plato even so blamed Aristotle for divulging wisdom and making knowledge manifest that Aristotle said, "Even if I have done so, I have still left in my books many a pitfall which only the initiate among the wise and learned can comprehend." And how else could the prophet Muḥammad (may God's prayers and peace be upon him) have brought knowledge to the uncouth nomad, not to mention the whole human race, since he was sent a messenger to all of them? As for political guidance, it and the imposition of obligations on people is an easy matter for prophets.[11]

Finally, at the end of the *Metaphysics* Avicenna argues the matter from the opposite point of view. There he warns about the dangers that the prophet/apostle incurs if he attempts to explain rational truths to the masses.

> This will simply confuse the religion [*dîn*] they have and involve them in something from which deliverance is only possible for the one who receives guidance and is fortunate, whose existence is most rare. . . . The rest would inevitably come to deny the truth . . . fall into dissensions, and indulge in disputations and analogical arguments that stand in the way of their political duties. This might even lead them to adopt views contrary to the city's welfare, opposed to the imperatives of truth.[12]

His admonition continues:

> Nor is it proper for any man to reveal that he possesses knowledge he is hiding from the vulgar. Indeed, he must never permit any reference to this. Rather, he should let them know of God's majesty and greatness through symbols and similitudes [*rumûz wa-amthila*] derived from things that for them are majestic and great. . . . But there is no harm if his addresses contain symbols and signs [*rumûz wa-ishârât*] that might stimulate the naturally apt to pursue philosophic investigation.[13]

These quotations mark the boundaries of Avicenna's doctrine of allegorical interpretation. Recapitulated, this doctrine is as follows:

(1) Human beings have different intellectual aptitudes, depending on which psychological faculties dominate their everyday behavior: intellect, cogitation (understood here as a combination of intellect, estimation, and imagination), or a combination of lower faculties comprising imagination, irascibleness, and concupiscence.

(2) In order to convey truth, legislators, whether they be political leaders, philosophers, or apostles, must select types of argumentation that appeal to the specific types of minds being addressed. Even more efficient (and thus preferable) is to provide a formulation that in itself encompasses all forms of argument (demonstration, dialectical, rhetorical, or poetic) so that diverse types of mind instinctively assent to it. Because the majority of humans are ruled not by pure intellect but rather by their lower passions and the representational faculties of the animal soul, such a means of address perforce utilizes symbols, suggestive allusions, and similitudes that can simultaneously impart the husk of the message to the masses and its gist to the intellectual elite.[14]

(3) Conversely, the apostle or political leader must refrain at all costs from attempting to communicate directly the intellectual import of revelation to types of minds unfit to receive it. First of all, it is a fruitless exercise of casting pearls before swine. Second, it is a practice that prior experience has revealed to be clearly hazardous to the health and well-being of those who engage in it. Third and most important, however, reckless direct communication of philosophical truths to the unqualified can be socially destructive in that instead of increasing apprehension of the truth, it provokes intellectual confusion and social discord. Nevertheless, some "sensible," imaginatively tangible, formulation of truth must be attempted, or otherwise society will destroy itself due to a lack of imposed social consensus. For this reason, Avicenna holds that prophecy is a social necessity, for given the diversity of human temperaments no other type of legislation can guarantee civic harmony.[15]

(4) Imparting philosophical truths directly to those of prerequisite intellectual aptitude is, of course, both proper and necessary, for it is this class of individuals who will advance knowledge as well as discern, and thereafter appropriately interpret for others, the scientific truths that underlie the symbols and similitudes promulgated by past prophets and sages. In this regard, symbols and similitudes can also serve a more specialized purpose by "stimulating" the philosophical interests of the "naturally adept beginner."[16]

Understanding this theory of rhetoric does much to explain Avicenna's wariness and equivocation when he interprets religious texts or treats sensitive points of theological doctrine, such as the true nature of the afterlife, the *mi'râj*, or the secrets of destiny. Moreover, it justifies the air of caution with which he confronts such a task even when addressing a sympathetic audience, as is the case with the *Mi'râj Nâma*. Even among friends, secrets must be protected from those unqualified to receive them.[17] Conversely, however, explicitly expostulating such hermeneutical principles in texts is an integral part of the rhetoric itself. Displaying wariness about revealing "hidden" truths, or warning others against doing so, helps to mystify—and thus to elevate the significance of—the text at hand, because it signals that reading it provides access to the inner "truths" of an esoteric tradition. In this regard, such a hermeneutical stance closely resembles the posturing of love poets who celebrate their "secret love" by publicly reciting poems in which they enumerate the charms and favors of the beloved.

Coherent and time-honored as this rhetorical theory is, the question remains as to whether it suffices to explain why Avicenna composed his allegories and undertook his allegorical interpretation. It is to this issue that we now turn.

The Function of Allegory

Dimitri Gutas has argued that Avicenna's adoption of a "symbolic" method of discourse, examples of which include the "notorious *Ḥayy ibn Yaqẓân* and *The Bird*," should be understood precisely on the basis of the rhetorical theory outlined above. On the one hand, symbolic narratives convey to the masses such elements of basic philosophical and ethical knowledge as are necessary for their "social and eschatological well-being." They also aid in identifying and attracting prospective adepts at philosophy, as well as giving advanced students training in deciphering allegories. On the other hand, symbolic discourse conceals from the common people aspects of doctrine that they would be unable to understand and hence exposure to which would be detrimental to themselves and society, while also allowing philosophers to convey their ideas to one another without placing themselves in danger from the literal-minded fanaticism of the masses.[18]

Founded as it is on the philosopher's own doctrines, this explanation for Avicenna's turn to allegory certainly merits consideration. Moreover, it has much to recommend it over that proffered by A.-M. Goichon. Although Goichon makes an important contribution to our understanding of Avicenna's allegories by demonstrating the clear doctrinal equivalence that holds between logos and muthos in *Ḥayy ibn Yaqẓân*, her answer to the question of why the philosopher composed the treatise—namely that *Ḥayy ibn Yaqẓân* is the playful result of the leisure time that Avicenna enjoyed during his four-month imprisonment in the castle of Fardajân—leaves much to be desired.[19] The composition of the allegory should naturally be understood within the context of the particular place and historical circumstances in which it was written, but it is difficult to imagine how being imprisoned under threat of death is conducive to "leisurely" or "playful" allegorical renderings of philosophical ideas.[20] Furthermore, such an interpretation hardly accords with the tone, texture, and import of the narratives themselves. A careful reading of *Ḥayy ibn Yaqẓân* or *Risâlat aṭ-ṭair* yields few signs of playfulness or frivolity.

Gutas, on the other hand, rests his interpretation on firmer ground by combining his thorough grasp of Avicenna's hermeneutical theory with the fruits of Goichon's demonstration of the doctrinal parity of Avicenna's muthos and logos representations. This latter is significant because it obviates the necessity for either positing or searching for esoteric elements in the philosopher's thought, an enterprise that Gutas himself has termed a "scholarly hoax, or non-issue, of immense proportions." However harsh such a characterization may be, the point is crucial, for it means that there is no need to mourn too deeply the loss of the vast bulk of *Kitâb al-inṣâf* or any other of Avicenna's lost or never-composed works that supposedly might portray the full details of his "Eastern Wisdom." Avicenna's extant works, we must conclude, suffice to inform us fully of the framework and details of his thought.[21]

As well-founded as Gutas's interpretation is, however, it does not completely account for Avicenna's resort to allegory. A full explanation must take into consideration two additional bodies of evidence. The first is biographical. It is extremely important that we notice the precise stage in his career at which the philosopher turned to muthos as an independent form of self-expression, for this enables us to place Avicenna's composition of allegory within the context of the evolution of his overall attitude toward his philosophical enterprise. The second type of evidence emanates from careful exploration of the exact nature of the practical relationship that holds between logos and muthos in Avicenna's writings. The philosopher's own theory of allegory is certainly pertinent in this regard, but it does not in itself provide a complete explanation of the varied ways in which these two representational forms interact.

Biographical Evidence

According to al-Jûzjânî, Avicenna spent his last months in Hamadhân, before moving to Iṣfahân in 415/1024, hiding from his political enemies at the house of Abû Ghâlib the Druggist. Prodded on relentlessly by al-Jûzjânî, he worked intensively on completing vital sections of *ash-Shifâ'*. In al-Jûzjânî's words:

> The Master wrote down the main topics in approximately twenty quires of one-eighth (octavo?) size, continuing on it for two days, until he had written down the main topics without the presence of a book or source to consult, but entirely from his own memory and by heart. Then he placed these quires before him, took a sheet of paper, examined each problem and wrote a commentary on it. He would write fifty pages every day, until he had finished all of the "Physics" and "Metaphysics," with the exception of the book on Animals.[22]

At this point Avicenna was seized by his royal erstwhile employer and imprisoned in the fortress of Fardajân. His prison conditions during the next four months could hardly have been onerous because he continued to write. Nevertheless, he was obviously not living in the most relaxed of circumstances. Indeed, the verses he reportedly uttered on entering prison indicate that the philosopher was seriously concerned about his future:

> As you can see, my entering is a certainty,
> but doubt remains on the question of my emerging.[23]

At this unsettling juncture in his career, when he had just completed those parts of *ash-Shifâ'* that embody the heart of his system, and when he faced prolonged incarceration or even death, Avicenna shifted the focus of his writing in ways that were to resonate throughout the remainder of his career. In the first place, he wrote a summary of his system dedicated to his brother (*al-Hidâya*); in the second, he wrote *Ḥayy ibn Yaqẓân*. It is tempting to attribute both of these events to the dire personal straits in which Avicenna found himself. *Al-Hidâya* could thus be regarded as a final philosophical testament intended to guide his brother. And Corbin has insinuated that the personal dilemma of imprisonment did affect the philosopher during his composition of *Ḥayy ibn Yaqẓân*.[24] I believe, however, that such an interpretation seriously misreads the situation. Avicenna's discomfort concerning his future prospects is much less important for understanding his writings at this point than the fact that his enforced hiding prior to incarceration had compelled him to work through the main parts of *ash-Shifâ'*.

At this point it is necessary to recall the distinction we previously drew between the philosopher's program and his selected modes of representation. In his autobiography Avicenna contends that

> when I had reached the age of eighteen I was finished with all of these [philosophical] sciences; at that time I had a better memory for learning, but today my knowledge is more mature; otherwise it is the same; nothing new has come to me since.[25]

This statement must naturally be taken with a grain of salt, but it also deserves serious attention. Although it is clearly presumptuous to claim that Avicenna had worked out all the details of his philosophy at this early age, this statement nevertheless indicates that he later believed that he had attained at this early stage a comprehensive vision of how all the pieces of his philosophical puzzle fit together. Once this overall conception was in place, it only remained to develop the specific arguments needed to confirm it. The natural medium for such confirmation was the tradition of philosophical discourse inherited from the late Hellenistic synthesis of Aristotelianism and Neoplatonism, as worked out in Alexandria and later incorporated into Muslim culture. The completion of *ash-Shifâ'* thus represents the culmination of this process of logos expostulation. But the full actualization of this particular medium's elucidatory potential does not necessarily mean that all the dimensions of Avicenna's philosophical program had found full expression. Indeed, the more detailed and developed Avicenna's logos exposition became, the more conscious he doubtlessly became of the ways in which it failed to express the full emotive scope of his philosophical vision.

For Avicenna learning the rules of philosophy was not an end unto itself. Rather, it served as a heuristic device that enabled practitioners to move toward psychic perfection, defined as a complete as possible attainment of theoretical knowledge.[26] More significant than the issue of specific genres of discourse, therefore, is that of the particular purpose to which each generic format is put and how these purposes fulfill the overall goal of explicating Avicenna's philosophical program. If he came to feel that logos exposition was unable to represent all aspects of his program, the philosopher would naturally begin to experiment with other means of expression.

This is not to say that Avicenna came to reject his logos doctrines in favor of "esoteric" tenets of one kind or another. On the contrary, the concentrated period of intense creative activity that wrought *ash-Shifâ'* marks the culmination of Avicenna's coming-of-age as a philosopher. Gutas has carefully traced this evolution from philosophical student through mature adherent to a philosophical school to independent master.[27] A crucial part of this process, I would argue, was Avicenna's writing out the text of *ash-Shifâ'* "without the presence of a book or source to consult, but entirely from his own memory and by heart." *Ash-Shifâ'* is no secondary scholarly commentary on Aristotle; it is Avicenna's independent formulation of his chosen intellectual tradition, "synthesized into the systematic scholastic philosophy . . . which was forever to replace Aristotelianism in Islam."[28] At this moment the philosopher crossed the boundary between disciple and master.

No longer compelled to duplicate the Aristotelian corpus in either the detail or the range of subjects covered, Avicenna subsequently addressed only those subjects pertinent to his own concerns. Thereafter he confined his Peripatetic writings to brief sketches of his own system, as in *al-Hidâya*, *an-Najât*, *'Uyûn al-ḥikma*, and *Dânish-nâma-yi 'Alâ'î*. And even in these he only treated subjects central to his interests—logic, physics, and metaphysics. Sciences of peripheral importance, such as mathematics or biology, were ignored. Moreover, Avicenna's whole attitude toward Peripateticism underwent a sea-change. The nature of this change is best revealed in remarks Avicenna made in his after-the-fact introduction to *ash-Shifâ'*.

> I also wrote a [later] book . . . in which I presented philosophy as it is in itself and as required by an unbiased attitude which neither takes into account . . . the views of colleagues in the discipline, nor takes precautions here against creating schisms among them as is done elsewhere; this is my book on Eastern philosophy. But as for the present book [i.e. *ash-Shifâ'*], it is more elaborate and more accommodating to my Peripatetic colleagues. Whoever wants the truth without indirection, he should seek the former book; whoever wants the truth in a way which is somewhat conciliatory to colleagues, elabo-

> rates a lot, and alludes to things which, had they been perceived, there would have been no need for the other book, then he should read the present book.[29]

This extraordinary statement cannot be explained by Avicenna's avowed rhetorical theory, for here he is not addressing the "masses." Nor can not it be interpreted as being the philosopher's rejection of Peripateticism as so fully elaborated in *ash-Shifā'*, for as we have seen, Avicenna's logos and muthos writings do not differ in regard to points of doctrine. Rather, this statement is Avicenna's admission that he had exhausted Peripateticism's potential as a medium of exposition. Having mastered and internalized its modes of expression, he strove to transcend them.[30]

This interpretation is close to that proposed by Henry Corbin, who argues that we must differentiate between the *situative* and *situated* aspects of Avicenna's thought. Avicenna's thought is *situative* when "its premises and their applications themselves define a particular situation of human life in relation to that cosmos," whereas it is *situated* when "the task of mediation is to understand and define its situation in respect to all the spiritual universes that the human being has borne within him, has developed in the form of myths, symbols, or dogmas." Corbin continues

> Now, in the case of Avicennism as in the case of every other system of the world, the mode of presence assumed by the philosopher by reason of the system that he professes is what, in the last analysis, appears as the genuinely *situative* element in that system considered in itself. This mode of presence is usually concealed beneath the tissue of didactic demonstrations and impersonal developments. Yet it is this mode of presence that must be disclosed, for it determines, if not always the material genuineness of the *motifs* incorporated in the philosopher's work, at least the personal genuineness of his *motivations*; it is these that finally account for the "motifs" that the philosopher adopted or rejected, understood or failed to understand, carried to their maximum of meaning or, on the contrary, degraded to trivialities. But it is not very often that the philosopher attains such a consciousness of his effort that the rational constructions in which his thought was projected finally show him their connection with his inmost self, so that the secret motivations of which he himself was not yet conscious when he projected his system lie revealed. This revelation marks a rupture of plane in the course of his inner life and mediations. The doctrines that he has elaborated scientifically prove to be the setting for his most personal adventure. The lofty constructions of conscious thought become blurred in the rays not of a twilight but rather of a dawn, from which figures always foreboded, awaited, and loved rise into view.[31]

As is the case with many of Corbin's observations, brilliantly perceptive insights are intermixed with idiosyncratic hermeneutical assumptions that require their own deconstruction. What he proposes is that Avicenna's allegories are one result of the philosopher's emergence from a detailed internal formulation of his philosophical system, as a *situative* dimension of his understanding of the cosmos, to attaining a vantage-point from which he regards and evaluates his philosophy from an external perspective, as a coherent system, now complete, that needs *to be situated* within the more comprehensive realm of multitudinous spiritual possibilities, which initially motivated, and now have forged into an articulated representation, the philosopher's logos system.

Rather than speculate about or, as Corbin appears to do, presume to know the exact reasons for this "turn" to allegory, it is more fruitful to examine the evidence presented by the texts themselves. For surely the best way to understand why the philosopher became attracted to initiating innovative muthos forms of discourse is to examine closely the relative advantages and disadvantages of muthos and logos as compared to the specific purposes Avicenna wishes to fulfill.

The Advantages of Allegory

Let us begin by considering the extent to which Avicenna's own theory of allegorical interpretation serves to explain his muthos writings. In regard to the philosopher's attempts at allegoresis, it can be argued that this theory works well. Such texts as the *Mi'râj Nâma, Fî ithbât an-nubuwwât*, or his various commentaries on Qur'ânic verses do more than simply agree with the details of his hermeneutic theory; they are prominent sources of its elaboration, since Avicenna often outlines his theory before proceeding with allegorical interpretation of specific texts.[32] Any attempt to use Avicenna's hermeneutic theory to explain his allegory is, however, unconvincing. Although it helps to contextualize how we should understand these narratives, the theory hardly suffices to explain them. This becomes clear when one considers more closely the question of the identity of the works' intended audience.

Avicenna begins *Ḥayy ibn Yaqẓân* by stating that he is composing it at the "insistence" (*iṣrâr*) of a company of his "brothers." Even if, for the moment, we take this conventional epistolary formula at face value, we must still inquire as to who precisely these "brothers" are. They are certainly not members of the masses, from whom the philosopher would be at pains to conceal his true beliefs. Nor is the suggestion that he wrote the treatise to "stimulate the naturally adept to pursue philosophic investigation" convincing. For one thing, we have seen that neither *Ḥayy ibn Yaqẓân* nor *aṭ-Ṭair* can be understood without expert prior knowledge of Avicenna's system; philosophical novices would have little chance of gleaning correct knowledge from treatises so difficult and enigmatic. Moreover, Avicenna composed both elaborate (*ash-Shifâ'*) and succinct (*al-Hidâya, 'Uyûn al-ḥikma*) renditions of his philosophy precisely for audiences comprised of generally educated readers and prospective students.

On the whole, it seems more likely that if Avicenna wrote a work as complex and indirect as *Ḥayy ibn Yaqẓân* for any public audience, it would be composed solely of his most advanced students; only they would possess sufficient knowledge of his philosophical system to have any hope of benefiting from, or even deciphering, the treatise. But even this suggestion seems doubtful, since in *aṭ-Ṭair* Avicenna adopts toward his so-called brothers a vehemently disparaging tone that alternates between utter despair and biting sarcasm in regard to their being either willing or able to hearken to his message.[33] Moreover, even here the question arises of how exactly such students would profit from study of *Ḥayy ibn Yaqẓân*. What benefits would they derive beyond those already attained from perusal of the philosopher's logos writings?

More convincing, I think, is the conclusion that Avicenna composed the allegories for himself, and that he did so in order to express aspects of his philosophical program now viewed, as Corbin has suggested, as *situated* from without. In other words, having finally finished his masterful contribution to the tradition that shaped him, Avicenna compared it to his inner philosophical vision and found it in some way wanting. In an attempt to compensate for these inadequacies, he turned to new modes of expression—whether through enigmatic references to Eastern Wisdom and oblique glosses on Aristotle, or by assembling isolated teaching notes later collected in such works as *al-Mubâḥathât* and *at-Ta'lîqât*, or by experimenting with technical terms developed by the Ṣûfîs, as in *al-Ishârât wa-t-tanbîhât*, or, finally, by exploring the symbolical narrative potential of allegory.

But even here the question still remains: What particular gaps in the philosopher's logos presentation does allegory redress? For an answer, we must examine more closely where the concerns of muthos coincide in the philosopher's thought with those of logos.

Avicenna's allegories do not encompass, or even attempt to encompass, the whole range of his philosophical inquiry. On the contrary, they confine themselves to issues pertinent to the subject of the "metaphysics of the rational soul." As we have seen, this area of investigation focuses on

> the knowledge of divine governance, universal nature, primary providence, prophetic revelation, the lordly Holy Spirit, the supernal angels, arriving at the reality of the transcendence of the Creator above polytheism and anthropomorphism, and arriving at the knowledge of what rewards befall the virtuous and what chastisement befalls the sinful, and the pleasure and torment which souls undergo after they leave the body.[34]

In other words, it explores questions of cosmic beginnings and ends and the parameters within which individuals realize their place in the cosmos among the array of existential decisions and moral choices that we all face: who are we, why are we here, toward what end do we—or should we—journey? Avicenna is not a disinterested observer in regard to the answers of these questions; indeed, they form the underlying impetus that motivates his whole philosophical program. Morality, understood as an intellectual framework that directs the actions of the individual, is not an ethical but rather a metaphysical, even an anagogic, concern for Avicenna, hence his lack of interest in the area of practical philosophy and the paucity of his explicitly ethical writings. Nor is this concern relegated only to the arena of pure intellectual inquiry; instead it is a joint venture of intellect and passion, *ʿaql* and *ʿishq* combined, for as Avicenna makes quite clear in his "Epistle on Love" (*Risâla fi-l-ʿishq*), all cosmic movement is impelled by the naturally inherent desire of existents to attain their proper final ends. Philosophy's first purpose is to clarify these ends so that correct choices can be made, but its second purpose is to motivate individuals to move toward these ends, to inspire them to "polish the rust and filth of doubt from their inner hearts" in order to enable them to actualize their human potential.[35]

Achieving the first of these goals requires rational introspection. One learns how to think correctly (logic) and then intellectually internalizes the outer world to determine its categories of organization and structure (physics). Only on the basis of this abstract construct can specific final ends be discerned (metaphysics). Initiating the process of moving toward these ends, however, requires reentry into the concrete external world and reinhabitation in it as now newly ascertained. And for Avicenna the essential dimension of this now-descried realm is not sublunary but supernal, not sensible but intelligible, not material but spiritual.

Avicenna's *Physics* concludes by examining the nature of the human soul, a subject that lies at the nexus of the sensible and intelligible domains. We have seen that the vegetable and animal souls perceive only sensory apprehensions and thus dissipate at death. The rational soul, however, partakes of the intelligible world, and, as such, is intrinsically immortal and potentially divine. If the *Physics* concludes by examining the boundaries between the human and the divine, the *Metaphysics* ends by addressing the same question from the opposite perspective, that is, how does the eternal intelligible world impinge on the ephemeral sensible one in regard to human beings? Perfecting society through the medium of prophetic revelation is one such area of concern; such matters as predestination and divine providence are a second; a third is the question of the afterlife, *maʿâd*.

Explication of the interaction between the human and the divine realms is by nature problematic, because it entails surmounting the intrinsic logical contradictions that exist between such concepts as motion as opposed to stasis, the particular versus the universal, the sensible as opposed to the intelligible, and the mortal versus the immortal.[36] In regard to the afterlife, for example, the philosopher must explain the conundrum of how the *imperfect, particular* rational soul is able to *move* through diverse levels of psychic *perfection* within the *static* realm of the transcendently *universal* Godhead. Avicenna's philosophical discourse can state this problem and argue for certain solutions, but in doing so it also relegates the inquiry to the domain of academic abstraction rather than crucial moral choice. This, in turn, intensifies the contradictory tension between the particular subject requiring portrayal and the representational capabilities of the available form of discourse.

Philosophical discourse could represent, indeed was the best representational mode for, the first and greater part of Avicenna's philosophical program: logic and most of the physics and metaphysics. But it could not adequately portray the crucial climax of his program, *maʿâd*, as understood not in terms of conventional Muslim eschatology but in the specific Plotinian sense of "journey of the alone to the alone." Both the subject involved and the parameters of Avicenna's tradition of philosophical discourse rendered it impossible for him to represent *concretely* the *abstract progress* of the individual human soul in the *motionless* hereafter. And yet, as I have argued, this is not some minor academic interest involved here, but rather one of immediate urgency whose investigation is, in Avicenna's view, the very raison d'être for pursuing the study of philosophy. Although it is doubtful that any form of discourse can adequately depict such a journey, Avicenna was nevertheless impelled by his own intense vision of it to seek, or at least experiment with, more precise, more immediate, and more evocative forms of expression.

Paul de Man has observed that "the difficulty of allegory is [that its] . . . emphatic clarity of representation does not stand in the service of something that can be represented."[37] In other words, allegory has no tangible, objective correlative. Conversely, however, it is the genre's major virtue that it possesses the power to depict certain realms, belief in which is notionally or emotionally overpowering but whose adequate portrayal is inherently beyond the limits of empirical representation. Although philosophy can describe the human condition within the confines of sublunary existence and can to some degree even transcend these boundaries, there comes a point in elucidating the interaction between humans and the intelligible realm at which philosophical terminology and modes of discourse are stretched beyond their structural and semantic limits. To pursue further the insights of his philosophical intuition, the philosopher is compelled to leave off logical demonstration and to resort to the creative, suggestive powers of metaphor. As Avicenna remarks in his *Poetics*:

> Mimetic imitation [*muḥâkâ*] has an element of wonder [*taʿjîb*] that truth [*ṣidq*] lacks, because a known truth is evident and devoid of novelty while an unknown truth is neglected. When a truthful utterance is turned from the commonplace and attached onto something congenial to the soul, however, it may combine both demonstrative assent [*taṣdîq*] and imaginative appeal [*takhyîl*].[38]

In other words, poetic utterance has the potential to fashion demonstrative intelligibles and ontological realities into representational scenes and embodied entities. To this extent it can provide for a philosopher so-motivated the tools to depict concretely an abstract spiritual cosmos that is invisible to the senses but is known by him or her to be more real than the physical world that surrounds us. Indeed, poetic discourse is uniquely suited to such a task, for "if the imitation of a thing which is untrue moves the soul, then it is no surprise that the depiction of a true thing as such moves the soul, too. Indeed, the latter is even more necessary!"[39] In such fashion, "something which cannot be represented" finds portrayal.

This interpretation suggests the role that the philosopher's allegorical treatises serves in his corpus. They neither espouse esoteric or mystical knowledge as some scholars have proposed nor represent mere "symbolic" renditions of low-level philosophical truths expressed as stories, intended for either advanced students or the masses. Rather, embodying dimensions of Avicenna's philosophical program that Peripatetic discourse cannot satisfactorily express, they serve a heuristic function correlative to that of Avicenna's philosophical discourse itself. As such, they fulfill a specific function in Avicenna's communication of his thought that encompasses neither greater nor lesser truth-value than the philosopher's technical logos compositions.[40]

Careful examination of both *Ḥayy ibn Yaqẓân* and *aṭ-Ṭair* supports this hypothesis. Through their use of symbolic equivocation, these treatises evoke a measure of representational animation, emotive concentration, and experiential immediacy that Avicenna's logos renditions lack. For one thing, the level of didactic address turns inward (or upward). In his logos writings, Avicenna is positioned squarely in the sublunary realm as the teacher who introduces students to the elevated domain of the intelligible universe. In *Ḥayy ibn Yaqẓân* and *aṭ-Ṭair*, however, it is the Active Intelligence who is the instructor, and it addresses not Avicenna's students, but the philosopher's own narrative persona; speech now emanates directly from a lofty resident of the intelligible universe rather than from the depths of sensible, terrestrial existence.[41] This ascent in level of discourse is further revealed by *Ḥayy ibn Yaqẓân*'s depiction of cosmic geography. The narrator has left the corporeal "city" and moved to the level of rational abstraction that is Ḥayy's natural habitat. Ḥayy, in turn, describes the cosmos not in terms of the vertical directions of up and down, but rather in terms of the horizontal coordinates of East and West, right and left.

In regard to the subjects of instruction, the logos stage of learning has been transcended. The study of logic is at this point moot, while the innumerable arguments and proofs that fill Avicenna's *Physics* and *Metaphysics* are now assumed as postulates. The narrator is instead confronted with a compellingly vivid description of the intelligible cosmos rendered not as abstract ideas requiring demonstration but as direct encounters with individual celestial beings. Having attained the goals of logos and achieved immediate contact with the Active Intelligence, the narrator now aspires to move along the chain of heavenly ascent toward direct intercourse with the exalted inhabitants of the intelligible universe.[42]

Another advantage of allegory is that its powers of externalized mimesis permit individuation. The rational soul is extricated from the mass of other human faculties and appetites that Avicenna surveyed in his *Psychology* and becomes crystalized into a pure *daemonic agent*. Similarly, each member of the echelons of the cosmic hierarchy that the philosopher wishes to foreground is assigned an individual mien, a distinctive garb, and a specific personal identity.[43]

Inducing movement through the noetic levels of the cosmological hierarchy is intrinsic to Avicenna's concept of the purpose of philosophy. Correct "becoming" is for the individual soul a matter of fateful magnitude. But the Scholastic pronouncements of philosophy seem woefully dry and sadly inadequate as a means of portraying the soul's momentous plight as it stands poised between earth and sky, beastliness and angelicness, hell and heaven. Allegory, with its capacity for mimetic evocativeness, metaphorical resonance, and dramaturgical intensity, enables Avicenna to portray more vibrantly the kinetic progress/regress of the rational soul within the motionless realm of the intelligible world.[44]

Any shift from demonstration to metaphor implies a transfer from intellect to imagination. Contrary to Samuel Taylor Coleridge's assertion that allegory initiates a "disjunction of faculties," however, its mimetic powers actually serve to integrate intellect and imagination. Avicenna's allegories do not displace, undermine, or duplicate his philosophy; rather they portray, embody, and highlight its crucial areas of concern. In their capacity to reflect accurately the aesthetic dynamics and open-ended spiritual flux that constitutes so fundamental a motivation for Avicenna's philosophical inquiry, they enliven its expressiveness and vitalize the significance of its conclusions. In Avicenna's case allegory does not compete with philosophy but shares its basic task in depicting and justifying the path that each of us, as spiritual entities, should pursue.

Notes

1. Wimsatt and Beardsley's famous injunction against the intentional fallacy has suffered too much criticism to be considered the critical law it once was, but it is still a useful caveat to keep in mind. See W. K. Wimsatt, Jr. and Monroe C. Beardsley, "The Intentional Fallacy," in *The Verbal Icon: Studies in the Meaning of Poetry* (New York: Noonday Press, 1953) 3–18; for a critique of this position using E. D. Hirsch, Jr.'s interpretative theory, see P. D. Juhl, *Interpretation: An Essay in the Philosophy of Literary Criticism* (Princeton, N.J.: Princeton University Press, 1980) 45–65.

2. See A. C. Lloyd, "The Later Neoplatonists," in Armstrong, ed., *The Cambridge History of Later Greek and Early Medieval Philosophy*, esp. pp. 314–22; and R. Walzer, "Zur Traditionsgeschichte der aristotelischen Poetik," in *Greek into Arabic*, Oriental Studies 1 (Oxford: Oxford Univesity Press, 1962) 129–36; Deborah L. Black, "The 'Imaginative Syllogism' in Arabic Philosophy: A Medieval Contri-

bution to the Philosophical Study of Metaphor," *Medieval Studies* 51 (1989) 242–67; and *idem, Logic and Aristotle's* Rhetoric *and* Poetics *in Medieval Arabic Philosophy*, Islamic Philosophy and Theology, Texts and Studies 7 (Leiden, New York, Copenhagen, and Cologne: E. J. Brill, 1990). For the "context" approach to Aristotle's logic, see Dahiyat, *Avicenna's Commentary on the* Poetics, 12–20; and Black, *Logic and Aristotle's* Rhetoric *and* Poetics, 1–102. I have found both Dahiyat's introduction to his translation and Black's studies particularly useful and gratefully acknowledge my debt to them in composing this section of the chapter. Also relevant are Wolfhart Heinrichs, "Die antike Verknüpfung von phantasia und Dichtung bei den Arabern," *ZDMG* 128 (1978) 252–98, and G. Schoeler, "Der poetische Syllogismus: Ein Beitrag zum Verständnis der 'logischen' Poetik der Araber," *ZDMG* 133 (1983) 82–89.

3. See Peters, *Aristotle and the Arabs*, 79–87.

4. Dahiyat, *Avicenna's Commentary on the* Poetics, 18.

5. As opposed to the previously discussed tensions between the physical and spiritual souls, the external and internal senses, and the cognitive faculties of the animal and rational souls.

6. This is not to suggest that Avicenna regarded this hierarchy as reflective of the truth-value of its forms of assent, which he specifically did not; see Black, "The 'Imaginative Syllogism' in Arabic Philosophy," 246ff., and the same author's careful historical examination of this issue throughout her *Logic and Aristotle's* Rhetoric *and* Poetics. It is in fact these "higher" forms of expression that are the subject matter of the modern science of semiotics, on which see, *inter alia*, Umberto Eco, *Semiotics and the Philosophy of Language* (Bloomington: Indiana University Press, 1984), esp. pp. 14–86, and Jonathan Culler, *The Pursuit of Signs: Literature, Semiotics, Deconstruction* (Ithaca, N.Y.: Cornell University Press, 1981), esp. pp. 18–43.

7. As Avicenna makes clear in the *Mi'râj Nâma*, prophethood is the noetic state in which the intellect most fully perceives intelligibles. Apostleship, however, is less a matter of noetics than of rhetoric, for it involves the problem of how to propagate the message of revelation to those unable to apprehend it directly. In his logos works Avicenna uses the term for prophethood (*nubuwwa*) for both conditions, but it makes sense to distinguish between them in the present discussion.

8. Qur'ân, 16.125, cited by Ibn Rushd (Averroes) in his *Kitâb faṣl al-maqâl wa taqrîr mâ bain ash-sharî'a wa-l-ḥikma min al-ittiṣâl* (The Decisive Treatise, Determining What the Connection Is between Religion and Philosophy), ed. Muḥammad 'Imâra (Cairo: Dâr al-ma'ârif, 1972) 31. English translation quoted from George F. Hourani, *Averroes on the Harmony of Religion and Philosophy*, E. J. W. Gibb Memorial Series (London: Luzac & Co., 1961) 49, see also 92, note 59, for the citing of this *âya* by other philosophers or theologians.

9. *Mi'râj Nâma*, 93; trans., 121.

10. *Mi'râj Nâma*, 93–94; trans., 121–22.

11. *Fî ithbât an-nubuwwât*, 48; my trans., based partly on Marmura's trans. in Lerner and Mahdi, *Medieval Political Philosophy*, 115–16.

12. *ash-Shifâ': al-Ilâhiyyât*, 442–43; trans. Marmura, in Lerner and Mahdi, *Medieval Political Philosophy*, 100.

13. *ash-Shifâ': al-Ilâhiyyât*, 443; trans., slightly modified, from Marmura, in Lerner and Mahdi, *Medieval Political Philosophy*, 100–101; cf. *an-Najât*, 339–40; trans. in Gutas, *Avicenna and the Aristotelian Tradition*, 300–301.

14. *al-Aḍḥawiyya*, 44–51; *Mi'râj Nâma*, 86–96; trans., 115–23; *ash-Shifâ': al-Ilâhiyyât*, 442–43; cf. also *Mabḥath*, 168–69.

15. *ash-Shifâ': al-Ilâhiyyât*, 441–42; *an-Najât*, 338–40; *al-Aḍḥawiyya*, 45; *al-Hidâya*, 298–99; *Sirr al-qadar*, ed. and trans. in George F. Hourani, "Ibn Sînâ's 'Essay on the Secret of Destiny,'" *BSOAS* 29 (1966) 27 (text) and 31 (trans.), quoted in Gutas, *Avicenna and the Aristotelian Tradition*, 303.

16. In its general outlines, this hermeneutics is not peculiar to Avicenna but is in fact typical of his inherited philosophical tradition. Compare, for instance, al-Fârâbî, *as-Siyâsa l-madaniyya*, 85–86, trans. Lerner and Mahdi, *Medieval Political Philosophy*, 40–41; Rowson, *A Muslim Philosopher*, 88–89; Gutas, *Avicenna and the Aristotelian Tradition*, 225–34; and Heath, "Creative Hermeneutics," 190–200.

17. *Mi'râj Nâma*, 79, 95; trans., 111, 122–23; *Mabḥath*, 141–42; *al-Aḍḥawiyya*, 58–62.

18. Gutas, *Avicenna and the Aristotelian Tradition*, 299–307, esp. pp. 306–7.

19. Goichon bases this suggestion on Ludwig Edelstein's argument concerning Plato's mythmaking being "a pastime, an amusement, a playful game (*paidia*), a recreation from arguments concerning ideas, a means by which to while away our leisure (*schole*)." See Edelstein, "The Function of the Myth in Plato's Philosophy," *Journal of the History of Ideas* 10,4:463–81 (quote from 469–70); and Goichon, *Le récit de Ḥayy ibn Yaqẓân*, 14–15.

20. Cf. Avicenna's verses concerning his entry into prison, below, p. 155.

21. Gutas, *Avicenna and the Aristotelian Tradition*, 2–5, *idem*, "Mysticism," in Mahdi, Gutas, et al., "Avicenna," *Encyclopedia Iranica*, 3:82. Michot essentially takes the same position, see *La destinée de l'homme selon Avicenne*, 3–5, 7–9.

22. Gohlman, *Life*, 58–59 (trans. Gohlman).

23. Gohlman, *Life*, 60–61.

24. Corbin, *Avicenna*, 125.

25. Trans. Gohlman, *Life*, 37–39; see also Gutas, *Avicenna and the Aristotelian Tradition*, 29.

26. Note his distinction between *'ibâda* (ritual prayer), which is conducted for the reward of attaining Paradise in the afterlife, and *'irfân* (spiritual knowledge), which is pursued for the sake of pyschic development, *al-Ishârât wa-t-tanbîhât*, 4:59ff.

27. Gutas, *Avicenna and the Aristotelian Tradition*, 286–96.

28. Gutas, *Avicenna and the Aristotelian Tradition*, 289.

29. *Madkhal*, 9–11, trans. Gutas, *Avicenna and the Aristotelian Tradition*, 52–53; see also *Mantiq al-mashriqiyyîn*, 3; trans. Gutas, *Avicenna and the Aristotelian Tradition*, 49.

30. Michot, *La destinée de l'homme selon Avicenne*, 8.

31. Corbin, *Avicenna*, 3–4.

32. Compare Hourani's suggestion in "Ibn Sînâ's 'Essay on the Secret of Destiny,'" 42: "But, beside the more 'exoteric' works of philosophy and the more 'esoteric' mystical ones, there is a third group that appear at first sight more popu-

lar, presenting subjects in a short and simple manner, but that in fact contain deeper meanings only perceptible to thoughtful readers."

33. See the beginning and end of *aṭ-Ṭair*, and Heath, "Disorientation and Reorientation."

34. See *Mabḥath*, 169; trans. from Gutas, *Avicenna and the Aristotelian Tradition*, 19.

35. *aṭ-Ṭair*, 42; *Risâla fî l-ʿishq* is in Mehren, *Traités mystiques*, fasc. 3, pp. 1–27; see also Gardet, *La pensée religieuse d'Avicenne*, 27–28.

36. Cf., for instance, John D. Caputo, *Radical Hermeneutics: Repetition, Deconstruction and the Hermeneutic Project*, Studies in Phenomenology and Existential Philosophy (Bloomington and Indianapolis: Indiana University Press, 1987) 1–2, 11–12.

37. Paul de Man, "Pascal's Allegory of Persuasion," in Stephen J. Greenblatt, ed., *Allegory and Representation* (Baltimore, Md., and London: Johns Hopkins University Press, 1981) 1–2.

38. Avicenna, *ash-Shifâ': al-Manṭiq* [Fann 9] *ash-Shiʿr*, ed. ʿAbd ar-Raḥmân Badawî, Comité pour la Commémoration de millénaire d'Avicenna (Cairo: Dâr al-Miṣriyya li-t-taʾlîf wa-t-tarjama, 1966) 24; trans., modified, from Dahiyat, *Avicenna's Commentary on the* Poetics, 62–63.

39. Avicenna, *ash-Shifâ': al-Manṭiq* [Fann 9] *ash-Shiʿr*, 24; trans., modified, from Dahiyat, *Avicenna's Commentary on the* Poetics, 62; cf. Black, "The 'Imaginative Syllogism' in Arabic Philosophy," 253–56.

40. Of obvious interest here is the question (unanswerable, given our lack of direct source references) of how Avicenna himself evaluated the relative merits of his logos and muthos writings. That he expressed dissatisfaction with his Peripatetic writings in no sense indicates that he was more satisfied with his allegories. Indeed, that he only composed a few allegories suggests that he did not find muthos suitable as a replacement for logos but rather only, as I would hold, as a complement to them.

41. Such is also the case in *al-Qadar*, in which Ḥayy ibn Yaqẓân appears to respond to the philosopher's queries concerning destiny and divine providence.

42. Mimetic narratives customarily serve as reflections, projections, or facsimiles of human experience; but this in no way means that Avicenna's allegories stem from actual emotional or "mystical" experience. The question of whether they were written as a result of a mystical state experienced by Avicenna is compelling, but (*pace* Ibn Ṭufail) it cannot be proven one way or the other on the basis of the evidence provided by the treatises themselves. For an overview of Greek Neoplatonic approaches to this question, see Coulter, *The Literary Microcosm*, 32–60.

43. Cf. Angus Fletcher, *Allegory: The Theory of a Symbolic Mode* (Ithaca, N.Y.: Cornell University Press, 1964) 25–69.

44. In comparing the modes of thought of Shihâb ad-Dîn as-Suhrawardî (d. 587/1191) and ʿAin al-Quḍât al-Hamadânî (d. 525/1131), Hermann Landolt has drawn a useful distinction between the "preponderant dynamism of the first," a characteristic that, Landolt notes, as-Suhrawardî shares with Avicenna, and the "static quality . . . (and) predilection for balanced structures" of the second, which is also typical of such thinkers as Ibn ʿArabî. The first group base their philosophy on the

epistemological principle of Becoming, which must be thereafter portrayed in terms of movement within or among hierarchies; the second group on that of Being within a "sort of pre-established harmony." See Hermann Landolt, "Two Types of Mystical Thought in Muslim Iran: An Essay on Suhrawardî Shaykh al-Ishrâq and 'Aynulquḍât al-Hamadânî," *Muslim World* 68 (1978) 187–204, esp. pp. 201–4; see also Chapter Eight below.

8. Allegory and Allegoresis

Until now we have examined Avicenna's allegories mainly in terms of their relationship to his philosophical writings, muthos in conjunction with logos. But his formulation of allegory itself deserves attention since it constitutes only one of the many possible expressions that the genre encompasses, whether in terms of general theoretical potentiality or in regard to specific historical manifestations appearing in premodern Islamic literatures. In this chapter we will situate Avicenna's allegories and allegoreses more precisely within the realm of the praxis of allegory per se by investigating in greater detail their modes of description and metaphoric structure.

Descriptional Imagery

We have seen that Avicenna conceives of the cosmos as a graduated ontological hierarchy running between the two antithetical poles of pure Form (the Necessary Existent) and primary Matter (Non-Being), whose most important divisions demarcate the borders among the material (sensible), the spiritual (intelligible), and the supra-intelligible (purely Divine) realms. The directional coordinates of Avicenna's allegories mirror this conceptual structure, although each emphasizes different aspects of cosmic geography. *Ḥayy ibn Yaqẓân* organizes its description along a longitudinal, West-East, axis. *Risâlat aṭ-ṭair* adopts an ascending latitudinal perspective: the bird escapes from its cage and flees over the nine mountain ranges of the material spheres before it finally arrives at the palace of the Great King. *Salâmân and Absâl* concentrates on the earthly portion of the scheme in its depiction of the tempestuous struggle between the animal and rational souls for control over the human psyche. Finally, the *Miʿrâj Nâma* portrays Muḥammad's journey as combining the terrestrial, horizontal *isrâ* from Mecca to Jerusalem, during which the prophet surveys the lower psychic faculties, with the celestial, vertical *miʿrâj*, during which he is introduced to the spheres, Paradise, and the divine Presence. Despite such differences in detail and emphasis, the overall cosmological paradigm remains constant, as can be seen from the chart below, drawn primarily from *Ḥayy ibn Yaqẓân* but also with reference to *aṭ-Ṭair, Salâmân and Absâl*, and the *Mi'râj Nâma*.

The West (Matter) **The East (Form)**

The Necessary Existent
(The Great King, situated above
Form and Matter)

The Ten Intelligences
(Cherubim or Angels Drawn-Near)

The Ten Celestial Souls

The Material Celestial Spheres
Fixed Stars
The Zodiac
Saturn
Jupiter
Mars
The Sun
Venus
Mercury
The Moon

Human Beings

The Rational Soul

The Theoretical Faculty
(The Ordering Angel)

The Acquired Intellect
The Habitual Intellect
The Material Intellect

The Practical Faculty
(The Recording Angel)

The Animal Soul

The Five Internal Senses
- Memory
- Estimation
- Imagination (Cogitation in humans)
- The Retentive Imagination
- Common sense

The Five External Senses
- Sight
- Hearing
- Smell
- Touch
- Taste

The Appetites
- Irascibility
- Concupiscence

Matter for Natural Species
- Animal
- Plant
- Mineral

Forms for Natural Species
- Animal
- Plant
- Mineral

The Forms of the Four Elements
- Fire
- Air
- Water
- Earth

Primary Matter
(Privation, Non-Being)

Human beings, of course, hold a unique position in this cosmography because of their ability to journey throughout its disparate realms. Although few actually take full advantage of this opportunity, those who do precipitate a momentous personal transformation. Avicenna emphasizes the impact of this initiation by rendering it as a direct encounter with a representative of the intelligible world. The narrator of *Ḥayy ibn Yaqẓân* meets the attractive and beguiling Ḥayy; the reader in *aṭ-Ṭair* is challenged and confounded by the "herald of God"; and in the *Mi'râj Nâma* Muḥammad is accompanied on his heavenly ascent by the Archangel Gabriel, the embodiment of the sacred divine Command. Since Muḥammad holds the exalted rank of legislative Apostle, the Active Intelligence is reduced here to the figure of the heavenly mount, *Burâq*.[1]

In regard to external mimetic representation, Idea dominates Image in Avicenna's allegories.[2] Close adherence to the structure of his cosmology lends his narratives an abstract, "visionary" quality. General directional coordinates are given, but details of time and place are ignored. Instead space and time are condensed, divested of commonplace particulars and everyday events. Similarly, characters are "flat," stripped of external mimetic features and unencumbered by nuances of psychological complexity. This minimalist approach to shaping a narrative world makes Avicenna's allegories initially difficult to understand because the signposts and guides one relies on to proceed are submerged in an abstract ideational system. But such minimalism also has a positive emotive impact; it creates an atmosphere of symbolism and mystery of enormous potency. Faced with such a beguiling, enigmatic realm, captivated readers willingly follow where Avicenna leads.

Avicenna builds his description around conceptual dichotomies. Typical of this tendency is his use of the antithesis of light and dark. The realm of Form is the luminous East, the Orient, while that of Matter is the "Perpetual Darkness" of the West, the Occident. Knowledge is the "rising sun" (*ash-shâriq*); ignorance is the "Darkness around the Pole" (*al-quṭb*).[3] The general phenomenological associations of lightness-darkness and East-West are common literary and religious motifs, so it is not surprising that Avicenna adopts them. Nevertheless, he does not emphasize them; with the obvious exception of *Ḥayy ibn Yaqẓân*, Avicenna is more attracted to the vertical axis of ascent-descent than to an East-West orientation. Even his famous concept of "Eastern Wisdom" is based on mundane considerations of human geography (he resided in the East, his rivals in Baghdad in the West) rather than on numinous evocations inherent in the directional axis.[4] A century and a half later, Shihâb ad-Dîn as-Suhrawardî would greatly develop the symbolic potential of the East-West, light-dark, knowledge-ignorance metaphorical complex; but Avicenna himself is no proponent of a Suhrawardian, "Ishrâqî" illuminationism.

The most important source for the imagery that Avicenna employs is, in fact, the social environment in which he lived. The domain of the far West is more than just dark. Avicenna portrays it as a wild, desolate, uncivilized, and inhospitable region bounded by a "hot, muddy sea," with soil that is impossible to cultivate or settle. Crops fail as soon as they are planted; buildings crumble as soon as they are raised. The West is "a place of devastation, a desert of salt, filled with troubles, wars, quarrels, tumults," infested with creatures who are ferocious and horribly mutated.[5] Its human inhabitants are rapacious barbarians, among whom reigns

> perpetual quarreling or, rather, mortal battle. Any group that is strongest seizes the homes and goods of the others and forces them to emigrate. They try to settle; but in their turn they reap only loss and harm. Such is their behavior. They never cease from it.[6]

He describes the region of the distant East in quite different terms. Its inhabitants are "a most pure people, who respond to no solicitation of gluttony, lust, violence, jealousy, or sloth," who are ruled justly and wisely by a Great King to whose service and honor they devote themselves completely. (Interesting, given Avicenna's own position at court, is his description of the chief minister, who is portrayed as the closest associate of the ruler, through whom "the King's word and order emanate."[7]) The people of the East

> live in cities; they occupy lofty castles and magnificent buildings, whose material was kneaded with such care that the result is a compound that in no wise resembles the clay of your clime. Those buildings are more solid than diamond and jacinth, than all things that require the longest time to wear away. Long life has been bestowed upon that people.[8]

Avicenna's terms of description embody the social values of his age and class. From this perspective his allegories represent paeans to the virtues of civilization, in which the chaos and unending civil strife of the material world are counterpoised with the innate tranquility and social harmony of the intelligible realm. The West is filled with ecological turbulence and political turmoil to the extent that any attempt to establish sedentary prosperity is rendered impossible; its inhabitants are doomed to lives that are inexorably "nasty, brutish, and short." It is only at the pinnacle of this plane of existence, on the level of the Material Spheres, that civilization finally emerges. But it does so hand-in-hand with social stratification; each sphere contains monodimensional groups that reduplicate shared traits of appearance and temperament: swiftness of movement, love of knowledge, physical beauty, and so on. Peace exists only because each group is internally homogeneous and externally autonomous, each resides in "its own fixed domain, into which no other comes to inflict violence."[9]

In contrast, the lives of inhabitants of the spiritual world are permeated by an atmosphere of social harmony and personal piety. Citizens are well-mannered and industrious, cities are well-organized and adorned with beautiful buildings, and daily existence is peaceful and serene. While the inhabitants of the West suffer the continual strife that political anarchy breeds, those of the East are blessed with the peace and prosperity that only the wise and beneficent administration of an enlightened monarch can foster.

The same descriptive matrix recurs when Avicenna describes the human soul. On the left (i.e., the western) side of human nature dwell "troops of demons," one of which comprises two further tribes (the irascible and concupiscent appetites), who exhibit, respectively, "the ferocity of beasts of prey" and the "the bestiality of quadrupeds," and between whom "there is perpetual war." The other troop of demons is composed of the transmutable form-changers of the imagination, some of whom have "two natures, others of three, others of four," while others are "reduced to a half, or a fragment of a nature."

Adjoining this region is a city, but it is not a center of peace and prosperity. Instead it is an armed camp outfitted for war. "Men at arms" guard "fortified bulwarks" and capture all who travel the "five great roads" of the kingdom.[10] Despite such precautions, the troops of demons sometimes overrun and capture this city and enslave its inhabitants. To the right (East) of this city, however, lies the peaceful dominion of the terrestrial angels (the rational soul), and those who manage to safeguard themselves from the assaults of the western attackers discover there the gateway to the realm of pure spirit.

For Avicenna, an inhabitant of the "mid-arid region" of "the Nile to Oxus zone" (as Hodgson terms it), the competition between desert or steppe and city is an obvious source of imagery. And there is no doubt that as a city-dweller he would value the political order and social harmony of settled life over the seeming physical desolation and political chaos of desert or steppe society. But Avicenna does more than note this frame of reference in passing; he invokes it to fashion the warp and weft of his descriptive tapestry. We remarked in connection with Avicenna's logos doctrines that his psychology represents a highly developed bureaucracy of the soul; such socially derived imagery is even more forcefully articulated in the dramaturgical description of his allegories.[11]

Of comparable importance is another descriptive polarity, that of solitude versus society. Avicenna appears to harbor a natural, although perhaps unconscious, distrust of groups.[12] This sentiment is obvious in his allegorical rhetoric where he constantly warns of the ignorance of the masses, but it is just as apparent in the imagery of his narratives in which the disorderly throngs of the West, whether those that belong to the external cosmos or those that lurk hidden within human nature, are contrasted with the peaceful solitaries of the far reaches of the East.

For Avicenna isolation is a precondition for spiritual progress. The narrator of *Ḥayy ibn Yaqẓân* removes himself from the crowds of the city by visiting a pleasure garden, where he meets the solitary traveler Ḥayy, who informs him that if he wishes to obtain further happiness he must first subdue and then abandon even his three remaining companions. Salâmân ends his life by relinquishing the rule of his kingdom and the pleasures of society to devote himself completely to solitary contemplation of God. And when Muḥammad embarks on his journey in the still of a night when "no animal made a sound, no bird chirped, no person was awake," he encounters groups and individuals, but in the end he leaves them all behind, even Gabriel.[13]

This is not to say that solitude is unequivocally positive, or that association with groups completely negative. The caged bird is in a state of lonely misery until it is rescued by a passing flock of birds. And Muḥammad begins his ascent in Jerusalem by meeting an assembly of "prophets and angels." But the virtues of communal association are ultimately unreliable. The narrator of *aṭ-Ṭair* meets only ridicule from his audience. And although Muḥammad greets the prophets and angels, he does so "one by one" as a preliminary to proceeding toward intimate colloquy with his Lord.[14] The social order of sedentary life may provide an initial basis for intellectual/spiritual wayfaring, but completion of the process, it seems, requires seclusion and solitude.

Metaphoric Structure

From ancient times allegory has been defined as "an extended metaphor," so it is hardly surprising to find that Avicenna relies on metaphor to create the polysemous referential matrices of his own allegories.[15] But he does so in a particular way. To clarify this point we must recall the distinction between metaphor and simile. The first expresses direct equivalences (X *is* Y), while the second denotes indirect ones (X is *like* Y). Although rhetoricians usually differentiate between the two, classical literary theorists—from Aristotle on—commonly consider the distinction between them to be "slight" and include both figures under the general category of metaphor.[16] For Avicenna, however, the difference is not so slight. Let us consider an example.

In *Risâlat aṭ-ṭair* the "herald of God" (*munâdi llâh*) invokes the "Brothers of Truth" to

> Shed your skins as snakes do! Crawl as worms crawl! Be scorpions whose weapons are in their tails! For Satan deceives human beings only from behind. Gulp down poison and you will live! Prefer death and you will attain life! Fly! Do not take a nest to which you constantly return, for the hunting grounds of birds are their nests. And if want of wings hinders you, then become a thief, and you will snatch success. The best of the vanguard are those strong of flight.[17]

This passage, like others in which "God's herald" offers advice, creates an ambiance that combines emotive passion with semantic obscurity to a degree unusual even for Avicenna. Nevertheless, it is typical in that it begins with similes but ends with metaphors. Although initially one is instructed to "crawl *as* worms crawl," by the end of the passage one is directly told: "Fly!" This move from simile to metaphor marks a semantic transition of crucial significance for Avicenna. The simile still maintains the sensible, material world as its standard for comparison ("Shed your skins *as* snakes do!"). But Avicenna does not judge reality by the criterion of the transient material world. On the contrary, it is the eternal, intelligible realm that he considers to be truly *real*. Hence, one of his basic goals is to invert our empirically based sense of reality so that we come to regard the abstract realm of the intellect as more vivid and more genuine than that formulated by sensual apperception. To do this he relies on the metaphor. Rather than being invited into a world that is clearly derived and dependent upon the sensible realm, we enter one that has a parallel, if abstract, existence of its own, a world in which we are not urged to be *like* a bird, but to become one.

Engagement in such a world is, of course, voluntary; not everyone will accept such a reversal of priorities; indeed, many will certainly refuse. At the end of *aṭ-Ṭair*, Avicenna himself complains:

> How many a brother, when my story struck his ear, then said, "I see that your mind is touched; you have become slightly deranged. No, by God, you did not fly! Rather, your mind flew. Nor were you hunted! Rather, your heart was hunted. How does a human being fly? Or a bird speak?"[18]

But such literal-minded rejection is not a universal response. Some readers agree to accept the terms of Avicenna's metaphorical construct and, by doing so, gain admission to his semantic world.

This world is complex, both because of the intricacies of Avicenna's philosophical system and, more pertinently, because of the various ways he structures his use of metaphors. For instance, Avicenna often heightens our sense of semantic depth and emotive richness by superimposing new layers of metaphor on the first. If it does not suffice, for example, that you *are* the bird, "then become a thief!" Or once a bird, then become a specific type: "Be ostriches who gulp down hot stones" or "bats who do not emerge in the day." After all, "the best of birds are bats."[19] This technique adds to the polysemous texture of Avicenna's allegories, although it does little to increase their lucidity. But then lucidity is not one of Avicenna goals. Aristotle's statement that "metaphors imply riddles" is a principle that Avicenna frequently embraces.[20]

Much of the enigmatic quality of Avicenna's allegories stems from the nature of metaphor itself. Metaphor is a figure of speech that is founded on a contradiction. It equates subject and predicate on the syntactic level but juxtaposes disparate concepts on the semantic level. Hence, to succeed, a metaphor must forge harmony from incongruity; it must create a situation in which one continues "to identify the previous incompatibility *through* the new compatibility."[21] To coin metaphors thus requires no small talent; Aristotle calls mastery in the creation of metaphors "a sign of genius" since it "implies an intuitive perception of the similarity of dissimilars."[22]

Metaphors vary in their transparency. They can juxtapose dissimilar terms to form images that are strikingly clear or darkly enigmatic. Similarly, allegories differ in how explicitly they reveal to readers both terms of the metaphorical equations upon which they are based. Most provide some measure of help. The author of a naive allegory gives characters names such as "Hope" or "Sloth" to clarify the nature of their personalities and significances. Even a sophisticated allegorist like Dante provides well-marked signposts along the way to alert us to where we have come in our journey through the cosmos. But Avicenna supplies few such clues. He rarely names his characters, and those he does, he gives names whose meanings are oblique. In *Ḥayy ibn Yaqẓân* only Ḥayy is identified by name, and in *Ḥayy* and *aṭ-Ṭair* only titles (such as the "Great King") or succinct descriptions provide an idea of a character's position and function. Even in the family melodrama of *Salâmân and Absâl*, only the protagonists have names, and these would have symbolic significance only to the few persons who were familiar with the obscure Hermetic version of the tale that Hunain ibn Isḥâq translated from Greek.

Moreover, Avicenna obscures the meaning of his allegories in another way. Metaphors do not exist in isolation; crucial for their effect is their relationship with the semantic dimension of general referential context. Hence, Avicenna's allegories remain closed books to anyone unfamiliar with his cosmology and psychology. A good example of this is the passage of the "herald of God" quoted above. Anyone can understand its literal meaning, but only someone familiar with its referential context, that is, Avicenna's conception of the relationship between the material and rational souls, will understand what it signifies. Even the meaning of such simple statements as "the rational soul is a bird" or "Ḥayy ibn Yaqẓân symbolizes the Active Intelligence" remain a mystery without prior knowledge of what a rational soul or an Active Intelligence in fact is.

A final way that Avicenna mystifies his allegories is that he consistently omits the first term of his metaphorical constructs. *Risâlat aṭ-ṭair* is, once again, a good example of this practice. The central metaphor for this narrative is "the rational soul is a bird." But the allegory never mentions the first term of the metaphor, rational soul. Instead, it only provides an unexplained second term, bird. The same is true in *Ḥayy ibn Yaqẓân*. Readers are expected to know, either through prior knowledge or by intuitive presentiment, that, for instance, the narrator symbolizes the rational soul, that the guarded city is the animal soul, and that the "Spring of Life" refers to the study of logic. Without such knowledge, the narrative is reduced to a conundrum.

The Principle of Equivalence

We can sum up Avicenna's technique for constructing allegories as consisting of five separate steps.

1. He begins with his vision of the structure of the cosmos and the place of humans within it.
2. He selects the particular aspect of this vision that he wishes to focus on.
3. He weaves together a series of metaphorical equivalences in order to express it in allegorical form.
4. He pares from his allegories general contextual references.
5. He drops the first terms of the metaphors around which he structures his narrative.

To some degree, this is the procedure every philosophical allegorist uses. But three points are unusual in Avicenna's use of this technique. He begins with an exceptionally detailed and systematic cosmological model. He accentuates the opaqueness of his allegories through the use of metaphor discussed above; while most allegories are enigmatic to some degree, Avicenna pushes this inherent tendency to the extreme. And finally and most important, he embraces the principle of semantic equivalence with extraordinary stringency. This last point warrants further consideration.

The principle of equivalence is intrinsic to metaphor and, by extension, to allegory. But the degree to which Avicenna relies on it is, in the context of Islamic allegory, quite exceptional. For contrast, let us compare his approach to that of the Ikhwân aṣ-Ṣafâ' (the Brethren of Purity).[23]

In their Treatises (*Rasâ'il*), the Ikhwân aṣ-Ṣafâ' undertake an intellectual enterprise that on the surface resembles Avicenna's in significant ways. Like Avicenna, they claim to offer a complete and coherent theory of the universe, whose study, they believe, should be founded on philosophical inquiry. And they espouse a theory of rhetoric, based on a differentiation among the levels of understanding of which the elite and masses are capable, that is akin to that proposed by Avicenna. Finally, cosmology and psychology are central foci of concern for them, as they are for Avicenna. But once we move from superficial to close comparison of the two systems—and the ways in which they are depicted—we notice considerable differences. Disregarding for the moment tenets of philosophical doctrine, the main methodological distinction that distinguishes Avicenna from the Ikhwân aṣ-Ṣafâ' is that while he grounds his arguments on the concept of equivalence, they found theirs on the notion of correspondence. Avicenna thus employs the equations of the syllogism in his logos writings, and he emphasizes the equivalences of metaphor in his muthos works. In contrast, the Ikhwân aṣ-Ṣafâ' depend on a combination of dialectical argument (arguments based on preconceived opinions), analogy, and extended similes. A brief quote will help illustrate this point. At the beginning of their discussion of the relationship of the body and the soul, the Ikhwân aṣ-Ṣafâ' state:

> Know that the name "human being" [*insân*] refers to this body, which is *like* a constructed house, and to the soul, which lives in this body. They are both together two parts and the human being is their combination and constituted from them. But one of the two parts is nobler, and it is *like* the kernel, and as for the other part, the body, it is *like* the husk. And the human being is their combination and constituted from them. But one of the two parts, the soul, is *like* the tree and the other *like* the fruit. From another perspective, one of

them, the soul, is *like* the stirrups, and the other, the body, is *like* the mount, and the combined human being is *like* the rider. [my emphasis][24]

And this is only the beginning. The Ikhwân then proceed to compare, point by point and with great elaboration, the constitution of the body with (1) the various building materials used to construct a city, (2) the parts of a house and the accoutrements of a household, (3) the tools and utensils of a craftsman, and (4) the various parts and facets of a flourishing city.[25] Nor do they end here, for this is only the body; their discussion of the soul is equally permeated with analogy and simile. Their entire approach to philosophy, in fact, is based on a theory of correspondence whose major premise is the assertion that human beings are microcosms (*al-insân aṣ-ṣaghîr*) who in all essential features replicate the structure of the cosmic macrocosm (*al-insân al-kabîr*).[26] In pursuing the implications of this premise, the Ikhwân aṣ-Ṣafâ' reveal an intense infatuation with the powers of analogy.[27]

Quite in contrast is Avicenna's approach. In his logos writings he uses metaphor infrequently and eschews simile altogether, while in his muthos narratives he relies almost totally on metaphor. The descriptive imagery analyzed in the previous sections, for instance, is completely based on metaphorical equivalence. That Avicenna was undoubtedly well-acquainted with the ideas of the Ikhwân aṣ-Ṣafâ' and other Ismâ'îlî and Ṣûfî thinkers makes his avoidance of analogy and simile all the more notable.[28]

Once observed, Avicenna's preference for equivalence over analogy is worth considering in itself. Is it an innate mental trait? If so, it may explain why he favored philosophy over speculative theology (also dependent upon *qiyâs*, analogy), or why his "soul would not accept" the Ismâ'îlî doctrines that both his father and brother espoused.[29] At any rate, this preference also finds reflection in his incorporation of religious terminology into his logos writings. We have seen that Avicenna is fully aware that most people are unable to recognize, and hence will forever disagree about, the stratum of truth that underlies successive dispensations of divine revelation.[30] Nevertheless, he also believes in the inherent congruence of this stratum. As he states in *Fî ta'bîr ar-ru'yâ*, any "group of people who have intellect, deliberation, reflection, and the sum of investigative knowledge" will discern the same pertinent forces at work in the world, although "each group will give it a different name." Hence, the ancient Sabians call it

the Nearest Ruler (*al-mudabbir al-aqrab*), the Greek sages the Divine Emanation (*al-fayḍ al-ilâhî*) and the Divine Providence (*al-'inaya al-ilâhiyya*); the

> Syrians (*al-suryâniyyûn*) call it the Word (*al-kalima*); it is this (force) which is called in Arabic the Indwelling (*al-sakîna*) and the Holy Spirit (*rûḥ al-quds*). The Persians (*al-ʿajam*) call it the *Amesha Spentas*. The Manicheans (*al-mânawiyya*) call it the "Good Spirits" (*al-arwâḥ al-ṭayyiba*); and the Arabs call it the "angels" (*al-malâʾika*) and the "Divine Strengthening" (*al-taʾyîd al-ilâhî*). All these different names indicate one force.[31]

Avicenna's belief concerning the essential equivalence of such concepts probably explains the liberty with which he began to include religious terminology in his own mature writings. Part of the science of prophetic revelation is

> how revelation is effected so that it becomes visible and audible after having been spiritual . . . and what the Faithful Spirit [*ar-rûḥ al-amîn*] and the Holy Spirit [*rûḥ al-qudus*] are, and that the Faithful Spirit comes from the ranks of the Fixed Spiritual Substances while the Holy Spirit comes from the ranks of the Cherubim.[32]

In such passages, the philosopher does not just align religious and philosophical terms on a superficial level, or allegorize the former in terms of the latter; here religious and philosophical terminology are equivalent, interchangeable. For Avicenna the Intelligences are not *like* Cherubim; they *are* Cherubim, and one of their members *is* the Holy Spirit.

This is a moment of singular importance for the development of later Islamic religion and culture, for it marks a large step toward the terminological integration of religion and philosophy and hence the creation of what over time was to become a new religious-philosophical-mystical language. For sophisticated theologians, mystics, and poets in the centuries after Avicenna, the Necessary Existent, the First Cause, and God are synonymous terms; the Cherubim do not symbolize the Neoplatonic Separate Intelligences, they directly signify them, and Ptolemy's spheres and orbs have become the Seven Heavens of the Qur'ân.[33]

Allegoresis

It is on the basis of his conviction concerning the essential semantic equivalence of fundamental concepts that Avicenna was able, perhaps even compelled, to interpret verses from the Qur'ân and religious traditions such as the story of the *miʿrâj*. From the perspective of the five-step paradigm of allegorical creation suggested above, Avicenna's approach is quite simple: he is reversing the last step (5) of the recipe to reinstate, through allegoresis, the "dropped" first term of the metaphor. In part this process is quite straightforward, as is clear from the way that he interprets several brief chapters from the Qur'ân. "Sûrat al-Ikhlâṣ" (Sincere Religion), for example, states

In the name of God, the Merciful, the Compassionate
Say: 'He is God, One,
God, the Everlasting Refuge,
who has not begotten, and has not been begotten,
and equal to Him is not anyone.'[34]

The subject of this *sûra* is obviously God's Unicity, Eternity, and Incomparability. Avicenna responds by providing an eight-page analysis (in the printed Arabic version) of such divine attributes as understood from the perspective of his concept of the Necessary Existent.[35] In interpreting "Sûrat al-Falaq" (Daybreak), which begins: "*Say: 'I take refuge with the Lord of the Daybreak, from the evil of what he has created,'*" Avicenna discusses his theory of predestination and his explanation for the existence of evil.[36] Similarly, "Surat an-Nâs" (Humankind) states:

In the Name of God, the Merciful, the Compassionate
Say: 'I take refuge with the Lord of humankind,
the King of humankind,
the God of humankind,
from the evil of the slinking whisperer
who whispers in the breasts of humankind
of jinn and humans.'[37]

This passage provokes a brief commentary from Avicenna on the relationship that holds between God and human beings and how differences in human physical temperament and intellectual aptitude affect it. In regard to specific glosses, he identifies the "slinking whisperer" as the faculty of imagination, while he sees symbols for the external and internal senses, respectively, in the the final words "*jinn*" and "humans."[38]

Avicenna's willingness to equate philosophical concepts with Qur'ânic imagery is most apparent in his reading of the lovely "Light Verse" (*âyat an-nûr*).

God is the Light of the heavens and earth;
the likeness of His Light is as a niche
wherein is a lamp,
the lamp in a glass
the glass as it were a glittering star,
kindled from a Blessed Tree,
an Olive that is neither of the East nor of the West
whose oil wellnigh would shine, even if no fire touched it;
Light Upon Light;
God guides to His Light whom He will.[39]

Avicenna interprets this verse in accordance with his theory of intellection and prophecy. God is "light" because He is "Good" and the "Cause of Good." The "heavens and earth" are the cosmos. The "niche" is the material intellect; the "lamp" is the acquired intellect; between the two stands a "glass," in other words, the habitual intellect. The blessed olive tree is cogitation (*al-fikra*), which, although not itself part of the intellect, serves as the basis for intellectual apprehension; for this reason it is referred to as being "neither of the East nor of the West," that is, foreign to the intelligible world (East) and yet somehow beyond the sensible world (West). "Fire" is the Universal Intelligence (*al-ʿaql al-kullî*) or the Sanctified Faculty (*al-quwwa l-qudsiyya*). Cogitation would "shine" even if one was never touched by this faculty; but when the acquired intellect comes into contact with it, the result is splendid "Light Upon Light."[40]

Such an extended gloss appears to lend credence to the assertion that allegoresis is indeed simply the process of reinserting the missing "first term" of an allegorical metaphor. And yet other factors are at work here, and "Sûrat an-Nûr," of which the "Light Verse" constitutes only a few lines, is an apt example of the limitations of this way of thinking about allegory and allegoresis. Most of the sixty-four verses of "Sûrat an-Nûr" deal not with the metaphorical splendors of the "Light Verse" but rather with mundane questions of social propriety and legal code. These may be prosaic in nature, but they are also of indisputable consequence for Islamic doctrine and history. It is in "Sûrat an-Nûr," for example, that one finds the legal criteria according to which the crimes of fornication and adultery are to be judged and punished, as well as the penalties to be exacted for false accusations of such crimes. The *sûra* also provides general guidelines for proper dress inside and outside the house, including the verse that some Muslims interpret as stating that women must wear veils outside of the house. Moreover, in true Qur'ânic fashion it contains verses that warn unbelievers of the suffering they will encounter in the hereafter while enjoining believers to perform faithfully their religious duties.

Avicenna would doubtlessly argue that such verses deal with religious corollaries rather than with fundamentals and therefore would consider them to be unfit for allegorization. And yet such a view highlights the essential point that Avicenna is successful at interpreting verses only because he preselects those on which he wishes to comment. Interpretation is easy when the commentator fully controls the choice of material to be interpreted.

At this point we can begin to appreciate the naiveté of the five-step allegorical paradigm we proposed above. Although it outlines the mechanics of formulating allegories or allegoreses, it ignores the idiosyncratic impulses that underlie what is in essence a creative process. Both allegories and allegoreses are fully subject to such forms of authorial control as preselection of topics and images and the degree to which some parts of narratives or commentaries are emphasized and others ignored. Furthermore, the creation and interpretation of allegories constitute a historical occurrence. Avicenna's interpretation of the *miʿrâj*, for example, is particular to the philosopher, but it is also unique to a certain period in his career, and perhaps even to a particular personal mood within this period. Can one say with certainty that another interpretation composed a decade earlier, or later, would be exactly the same? And just as Avicenna himself could vary his choice of materials or points of emphasis, later exponents of his doctrines did the same, either by interpreting a passage differently or by choosing a different passage to interpret, or by using Avicenna's ideas or practices as a springboard from which to develop new lines of approach. Such later allegorizers as al-Ghazâlî, Ibn Ṭufail or, in a different way, as-Suhrawardî started with Avicenna but ended by moving in radically new directions.

More important than the simple principle of preselection is the creative power of metaphor itself. On one level the metaphor is a figure of speech used to enhance the expression of meaning; but on another level it is a creative act. Linking two incongruent concepts can produce forms of thought that become more than the sum of their parts and, as a result, transform the way we think. Or, to put it another way, metaphors can create new habits of thought. Encountering the Active Intelligence in the guise of an attractive and sprightly sage can alter how we, and Avicenna, visualize it thereafter. Similarly, exposure to Avicenna's interpretation of the "Light Verse" transforms the way we understand it now and also enhances the range of connotative referentiality that we bring to succeeding readings of it. Apt metaphors and artistically effective allegories transfigure how we think about previously abstract concepts, just as new concepts often alter the way we visualize the world. As such, metaphors can create new bases upon which similar transformations are enacted in the future. From this perspective, the metaphor is a linguistic figure of extraordinary potency. Once its powers have been successfully invoked, it is impossible to return to the way things were before.

Avicenna's Legacy

A full investigation of the influence that Avicenna's logos or muthos writings exerted on later generations or the permutations that they underwent in succeeding centuries is an enterprise requiring further detailed inquiry, for which this book is intended to serve as a preamble. One final point does deserve mention, however. In his study of the "licit magic" of artistic expression in the later centuries of premodern Islamic culture, J. Christoph Bürgel observes that at a certain point "Islam, its culture and its spirit, took a turn in [the] particular direction" of mysticism. Concomitant with this "turn" was a cluster of operative theories and principles. One of these was the adoption of the theory of emanation. Another was the espousal of the ideal of the "Perfect Human Being" (*al-insân al-kâmil*). A third was the pursuit, at least by some thinkers, of the overarching theory of correspondences based on analogical styles of thought that we noted above in our discussion of the Ikhwân aṣ-Ṣafâ'. Intertwined throughout all of these trends was a hermeneutic perspective based on dividing understanding into exoteric-esoteric (*ẓâhir-bâṭin*) levels of thought.[41] Bürgel himself acknowledges that this schematization of the intellectual mind-set of the later premodern era is highly generalized. But it is nonetheless useful to adopt it temporarily for the purposes of initially evaluating the contours of Avicenna's influence in later Islamic thought.

The results of such an evaluation are mixed. Although it is true that Avicenna's elaborate theory of emanation became a major source and model for all later theorists, his own reaction to the other trends Bürgel highlights would have been less than accommodating. Whatever terminology he might have borrowed from ṣûfism in his later years, Avicenna was no adherent of the concept of supernatural mysticism. Such an approach goes against the rationalism upon which he founded his whole philosophy. Similarly, his vision of human perfection was different in emphasis and generally less ambitious than the all-encompassing theory of the "Perfect Human Being" as developed in the aftermath of Ibn ʿArabî. Finally, Avicenna would have solidly opposed any theory of cosmic correspondence or any persistent reliance on the hermeneutical dichotomy of exotericism-esotericism.[42] It is one of the ironies of Avicenna's legacy that, antagonistic as he was to these trends, his thought (both logos and muthos) was nonetheless adopted, adapted, and subsumed by their later exponents. In fact, it would be possible to argue that it was only this process of assimilation and incorporation that kept the philosopher's ideas alive through the ensuing centuries.

But to put the matter so negatively is misleading. The equation can also be reversed. Any later thinker of serious intellect had, at one point, to come to terms with Avicenna's philosophical system. Avicenna's concept of the soul, for example, remained the standard psychology for centuries to follow, and as such became an essential source from which most allegorists, from Sanâ'î and Rûmî on, would draw. Moreover, his narratives continued to be read, commented upon, and translated and thus continued to exert a potent influence on later composers of allegories. Such writers might accept, modify, or reject this influence, but they could not avoid the encounter.

Notes

1. See Corbin's discussion of this phenomenon, in the section of *Avicenna* titled "The Cosmic Crypt: The Stranger and the Guide" (16–28); however, his comparative approach, despite the immense erudition he brings to his discussion, clouds as much as it elucidates Avicenna's ideas. The problem here, which is of some complexity and requires further investigation among texts that predate and postdate Avicenna, concerns the relationship that holds in Avicenna's thought among the Active Intelligence (*Burâq* here), the prophetic dimension of the First Intelligence (represented by Gabriel), and the revelatory dimension of the Necessary Existent with which, it seems, only prophets can come into contact (the Holy Spirit, *rûḥ al-qudus*). For al-Fârâbî, a human being perfects him- or herself by coming into contact with the Active Intelligence. Avicenna posits that one achieves intellectual (and thus spiritual) perfection by coming into contact with the First, or Universal, Intelligence. But the *Miʿrâj Nâma* (trans. 119, para. 2), supported by Avicenna's interpretation of the "Light Verse" in *al-Ishârât wa-t-tanbîhât* (see above, 185), suggests that there is a degree of knowledge above this that results

from direct contact with the prophetic-cosmogonic aspect of the Necessary Existent, a faculty that Avicenna appears to denote (at times, at least) when he uses the term "Holy Spirit." I suspect that in these instances Avicenna has moved away from a purely Neoplatonic understanding of the potential connection between God and human being, in which any individual of appropriate temperament, intellectual capability, and education can aspire to perfection, but certainly not to direct contact with the "One" (his standard position), toward a more prophetological-oriented strain of thought that awards a special status to legislative apostles, who alone are granted direct contact with the divine (we disregard Ṣûfî interpretations for the moment). This whole subject is admittedly controversial and requires further independent examination, which I hope to undertake in the near future.

2. Cf. Graham Hough's discussion of the poles of *Idea* and *Image* in allegory in his *A Preface to the Faerie Queen* (New York: W. W. Norton, 1962) 105–11.

3. *Ḥayy ibn Yaqẓân*, 8–9; Corbin, *Avicenna*, 142, 324, 327–28. Cf. also *Ḥayy ibn Yaqẓân*, 14; Corbin, *Avicenna*, 146, 346, for the "sun rising." Quotes from *Ḥayy ibn Yaqẓân* in this chapter are from Corbin's translation in *Avicenna*.

4. See S. Pines, "La 'Philosophie orientale' d'Avicenne et sa polémique contre les baghdadiens," *Archives d'Histoire doctrinale et Littéraire du Moyen Âge* 19 (1952) 5–37; also Gutas, *Avicenna and the Aristotelian Tradition*, 60–64, 66–72.

5. *Ḥayy ibn Yaqẓân*, 9–10; Corbin, *Avicenna*, 143, 331.

6. *Ḥayy ibn Yaqẓân*, 9; Corbin, *Avicenna*, 142, 327–28.

7. *Ḥayy ibn Yaqẓân*, 20; Corbin, *Avicenna*, 149, 364–65.

8. *Ḥayy ibn Yaqẓân*, 18–19; Corbin, *Avicenna*, 148, 363.

9. *Ḥayy ibn Yaqẓân*, 10; Corbin, *Avicenna*, 143, 334.

10. That is, the five external senses capture sensory impressions and convey them to common sense. *Ḥayy ibn Yaqẓân*, 14–16; Corbin, *Avicenna*, 146, 346–47.

11. Cf. the final section of Chapter Four above. The ultimate source of the imagery of civil society is, of course, Plato and the Platonic tradition. Among more immediate sources may be counted al-Fârâbî, in terms of philosophy, but for imagery more especially the treatises of the "Brethren of Purity," Ikhwân aṣ-Ṣafâ', whose anthropology, as we shall see below (pp. 180–82), is permeated with such similes comparing both body and soul to various facets of society.

12. See Heath, "Disorientation and Reorientation," 178–80.

13. *Ḥayy ibn Yaqẓân*, 1; Corbin, *Avicenna*, 137, 283; *Mi'râj Nâma*, 101; trans. 125.

14. *aṭ-Ṭair*, 44, 47–48; trans. 5–6, 8–9; *Mi'râj Nâma*, 107; trans. 129.

15. For a history of the term *allegory*, see Whitman, *Allegory*, 263–68; see also Richard A. Lanham, *A Handlist of Rhetorical Terms: A Guide for Students of English Literature* (Berkeley and Los Angeles: University of California Press, 1969) 3.

16. Aristotle, *Rhetoric*, 1406b-1407a; *Poetics*, 1457b-1458a; also, Lanham, *A Handlist of Rhetorical Terms*, 66–67; for an overview of the various ways modern theorists view metaphor, see Sheldon Sacks, ed. *On Metaphor* (Chicago and London: University of Chicago Press, 1978). Premodern Arabic literary theory considers metaphor to be a type of simile.

17. *aṭ-Ṭair*, 43.

18. *aṭ-Ṭair*, 47.

19. *aṭ-Ṭair*, 43; for analysis and commentary on the meaning of the imagery in *aṭ-Ṭair*, see Heath, "Disorientation and Reorientation."

20. Aristotle, *Rhetoric*, 1405b.

21. Paul Ricoeur, "The Metaphorical Process as Cognition, Imagination, and Feeling," in Sacks, ed., *On Metaphor*, 146.

22. Aristotle, *Poetics*, 1459a.

23. See Chapter One, pp. 4–5.

24. *Rasâ'il Ikhwân aṣ-Ṣafâ'*, 2:379.

25. *Rasâ'il Ikhwân aṣ-Ṣafâ'*, 2: 380–95.

26. See Nasr, *An Introduction to Islamic Cosmological Doctrines*, 66–74; also George P. Conger, *Theories of Macrocosms and Microcosms in the History of Philosophy* (New York: Columbia University Press, 1922) 46–51, who observes (50–51) that "it is in the *Encyclopædia* of the Brethren of Sincerity that the theory that man is a microcosm first becomes imposing . . . of all who have written on man as a microcosm, only Fechner has tried to point out more resemblances" (between human beings and the universe).

27. Both Julie Scott Meisami and J. Christoph Bürgel have recently pointed out the pervasiveness of this analogical mode of thought. As Meisami remarks, "By the mid-twelfth century (and perhaps even earlier), an analogical style of composition appears and becomes increasingly widespread in Persian literature of all types," *Medieval Persian Court Poetry*, 34 (see also 30–39). On Bürgel's comments in *The Feather of Simurgh*, see herein, 186–87. For an analysis of this phenomenon in western literature, see S. K. Heninger, Jr., *Touches of Sweet Harmony: Pythagorean Cosmology and Renaissance Poetics* (San Marino, Cal.: The Huntington Library, 1974).

28. The version of Avicenna's life in Baihaqî's *Tatimma* even asserts that as a youth the philosopher "pondered over [*The Epistles of Ikhwân aṣ-Ṣafâ'*] from time to time." But this is most likely an interpolation in the text; see Gohlman, *Life*, 20–21; and Gutas, *Avicenna and the Aristotelian Tradition*, 24.

29. Gohlman, *Life*, 18–19; Gutas, *Avicenna and the Aristotelian Tradition*, 24. Avicenna, recall, even considered poetics as a form of syllogism; see Dahiyat, *Avicenna's Commentary*, 31–32; and Black, "The 'Imaginative Syllogism' in Arabic Philosophy."

30. *al-Aḍhawiyya*, 44–51, and Chapter Seven above.

31. *Fî taʿbîr ar-ru'yâ*, 291–92; trans. by Pines in "The Arabic Recension of *Parva Naturalia*," 117.

32. *Fî aqsâm al-ʿulûm*, 78; also Chapter Three above.

33. The best brief introduction to this interreferential system, the philosophical dimension of which is pure Avicenna, is still Gibb, *A History of Ottoman Poetry*, 1:31–69.

34. *The Koran Interpreted*, trans. A. J. Arberry, 2 vols. (New York: Macmillan, 1955) 2:353.

35. 'Âṣî, *at-Tafsîr al-Qur'ânî*, 106–13; Persian trans. in Yarshater, ed., *Panj Risâla*, 37–50.

36. 'Âṣî, *at-Tafsîr al-Qur'ânî*, 116–20; Persian trans. in Yarshater, ed., *Panj Risâla*, 51–58.

37. *The Koran Interpreted*, 2:354 (trans. slightly modified).

38. ʿÂṣî, *at-Tafsîr al-Qur'ânî*, 123–25; Persian trans. in Yarshater, ed., *Panj Risâlah*, 59–63.

39. *The Koran Interpreted*, 2:51 (trans. slightly modified).

40. See *Fî ithbât an-nubuwwât*, 49–52; trans. Marmura, 116–18; *al-Ishârât wa-t-tanbîhât*, 2:389–92. The first refers to fire (*nâr*) as the Universal Intelligence, the second, as the Sanctified Faculty (see above, note 1). Also relevant is *al-Mabda' wa-l-maʿâd*, 117, which quotes a line of the *âya* in its discussion of prophecy.

41. Bürgel, *The Feather of Simurgh*, 16, 40ff.

42. Cf. the Persian commentator, perhaps al-Jûzjânî, of *Ḥayy ibn Yaqẓân*, who criticizes the Ismâʿîlî penchant for continually seeking esoteric interpretations of revealed texts.

> Furthermore, knowledge of the motive [of divine revelation to humans] and of the esoteric exegesis, in which there would then be a second divine communication, would constitute a formulation that in its turn would involve something esoteric, since, according to those of this school, everything that is external (lit., *ẓâhir*) also has some inner (esoteric, *bâṭin*) meaning. This divine communication supposedly dispensed for the purpose of esoteric exegesis would now in its turn have to be called a third communication. Similarly, each esoteric exegesis would in turn postulate a new divine comunication, and so on ad infinitum. . . . This is why all that is said by those of this school is only words inspired by their vain cogitations; it is in accordance neither with philosophical reason nor with the revealed Law.

Corbin, *Avicenna*, Persian text in the French ed., 2:31–32; Eng. trans., 314–16.

Appendices

Appendix A: On Allegory

Allegory, Northrop Frye has observed, is less a literary genre than a "structural principle of fiction" that establishes close referential correlation between the events of a fictional narrative and some "simultaneous structure of events or ideas, whether historical events, moral or philosophical ideas, or natural phenomena."[1] Frye purposely keeps his description broad in order to emphasize, on the one hand, that allegory utilizes various genres—epic, romance, drama—to serve its literary purposes and to indicate, on the other hand, that political and social satire represents a referential correlative that is just as "allegorical" as the religious, moral, and philosophical ideational structures traditionally associated as allegory's intellectual counterpart.

Allegory is thus by definition polysemous, designed to be both inclusive and exclusive in semantic accessibility and audience appeal. While its literal levels are intended to be comprehensible and attractive to a broad spectrum of readers, its symbolic levels direct restricted levels of meaning, whether political, moral, or anagogic, to select groups or individuals. Thus aiming to be simultaneously democratic and elitist, the genre rests on an aesthetic contradiction. But such a stance is not duplicitous, for allegory offers truth to everyone, each according to his or her capacity for apprehension. Indeed, for exponents of allegory, the enigmatic ambivalence of its polysemous nature is one of the main virtues of the genre.

Ever-present to some extent, allegory is exceptional in the degree to which it undergoes alternate periods of critical favor or rejection. It is generally a technique favored by practitioners of elite literature (creators of popular literature tend to use brief forms, such as the moralistic fable or the proverb), and its popularity alternates between periods in which almost all sophisticated literary works are saturated in the indeterminacy of its ambiguous referentiality (the Islamic world from the 5th/11th to 13th/19th centuries, Europe from the high Middle Ages through the Renaissance) and intervals of such severe critical animosity that the technique is thoroughly rejected—if mentioned at all (19th- and early 20th-century world literature). Sophisticated authors and audiences alike, it seems, embrace or forswear allegory with extraordinary totality.

The ebbs and flows of allegory as a literary fashion are important for literary and intellectual historians to notice, because they reflect the predominance of certain intellectual paradigms within a particular culture. As Edwin Honig has remarked: "At certain points in cultural development allegory is an indispensable instrument of thought and belief" that "reveals a fundamental way of thinking about man and the universe."[2] Most broadly expressed, allegory is popular in periods that are dominated by an intellectual *épistème* (to borrow Foucault's term) that combines philosophical idealism with cultural sophistication. The idealism of the age assumes the form of a monolithic world-view that aspires to dominate as many cultural spheres—religious, cosmological, and political—as possible, in both public and private realms of life. By explicitly working on interpreting and even promoting such monolithic intellectual systems, allegory can be accused of being a reactionary form of literature, in both the literal and political senses of the term.

Nevertheless, allegory cannot exist in societies in which intellectual totalitarianism has completely taken hold. The ambiguities upon which it thrives signify maturity rather than callowness, and it only flourishes in societies that have achieved a certain level of sophisticated intellectual polyphony. Hence, it begins to flourish when alternative intellectual currents emerge to compete with the dominant episteme. It is the goal of allegory to create a harmonic balance among the competing tensions of such currents. The most sophisticated examples of allegory thus arise not in an atmosphere of ideological dichotomy in which idea and symbol relate on a one-to-one basis but rather in an environment of intellectual polyphony in which competing doctrines coexist as major and minor leitmotifs. Dante's *Divine Comedy*, for example, is just as much concerned with republican politics, courtly love, and ancient philosophy as it is with Christian theology. This acceptance of ideas that run counter to the tenets of the dominant episteme has led to charges of allegory being a radical and subversive form of literature.

Writing allegory is by definition dangerous. Authors conceal secrets (the solutions to their enigmas or ambiguities) in their texts because they (ostensibly) deem their disclosure hazardous for intellectual, social, or political reasons.[3] For this reason, allegory especially flourishes in environments in which the boundaries of freedom of expression or action are explicit; indeed, the aura of peril evoked by writing—and reading—it is a major allure of the genre. Correspondingly, allegory atrophies when the borders that impinge upon free expression fade and the danger of transgression disappears. The genre's decline in critical favor in modern times may thus be attributed to the demise of a firm belief in concepts of Absolute Truth and the attendant polemics or disputes over how this one Truth should be understood. In open-ended intellectual environments, the puzzles that allegory offers lose their fascination while the effort required for their solution becomes irksome rather than rewarding, an exercise in irrelevance.[4]

When a social environment conducive to allegory exists, however, and the genre thrives, authors must cultivate an appropriate hermeneutical program. The task of this program is twofold. On the rhetorical level, it effects a sirenic call regarding the respective pleasures or dangers of entering the maze of allegory, a call that is simultaneously evocative to prospective initiates and menacing to those unfit to be exposed to the secrets of the text. On the substantive level, it must serve as an interpretative conduit that guides the wayfarer through allegory's esoteric mysteries. Allegory demands interpretation, and yet it also must offer clues as to the ways in which such interpretation should proceed. Here we refer not to the explicit guides who lead travelers through allegories—Avicenna's Ḥayy ibn Yaqẓân, 'Aṭṭâr's hoopoe bird, or Dante's Virgil—but rather to a more comprehensive interpretive framework that continuously contextualizes and explains to readers how they should appreciate the various levels of the narrative. In western literature, for example, from Origen and St. Augustine through Aquinas and Dante and into the Enlightenment, the hermeneutical paradigm for composing and interpreting allegory stemmed from the patristic model of multilayered levels of meaning. As concisely formulated in Dante's famous letter to Can Grande, allegory embraces four levels of meaning: the literal, the typological, the moral, and the anagogic.[5] This interpretive model is not historically relevant to Islamic texts (although there is no reason it cannot be used to good effect if judiciously employed by modern critics), but analogous Islamic models of hermeneutical analysis do exist.

One such model is the standard approach of traditionalist Qur'ânic commentary (*tafsîr*), which assembles materials of a historical and philological nature to help clarify and explain the meaning of the text. More radical hermeneutical approaches assume a semantic bifurcation between exoteric (*ẓâhir*) and esoteric (*bâṭin*) levels of meaning. The Qur'ân itself provides a foundation for this stance when it states that its text consists of "verses whose meaning is clear [*al-muḥkamât*], which are the heart of the book [*umm al-kitâb*], and others whose meaning is ambiguous [*al-mutash-*

âbihât]." The text goes on to say that such a distinction might allow those so inclined to create dissension among the believers and, as a result, affirms that indeed "Only God knows its true interpretation."[6] Nevertheless, an opening for esoteric interpretation of Qur'ânic "ambiguities" had been breached, and the distinction between exoteric and esoteric significances came to thrive in succeeding centuries.

At variance, of course, were the particular bases upon which such two-layered interpretation would be founded. Philosophers such as al-Fârâbî, Ibn Rushd, and Avicenna held that only those with philosophically trained intellectual capabilities could ascertain the true import of texts; Shi'îs believed that only the Imâm, or those guided by him, were qualified to interpret; while Ṣûfîs felt that those who had achieved mystical awareness would best understand the inner meanings of religious works. Each group naturally disputed the claims of the others.[7]

The modernist criticism of allegory (as opposed to the postmodernist approach, which has been more sympathetic) comes from two sides. Philosophers disdain it as "a form of literature," while exponents of imaginative fiction decry its apparent reliance on doctrine rather than imaginative creativity, or distrust its simplistic use as "a philosophical or rhetorical weapon."[8] The stance of each of these schools of thought is revealing. Contrary to Coleridge's well-known adage, allegory "presumes no disjunction of faculties" between imagination and intellect, but is in itself a form of symbolic writing that aims at uniting them.[9] Indeed, it is the main function of allegory to synthesize the operations of these otherwise happily disparate groups; while periods in which it suffers most acutely from critical disdain are those in which the separation between intellect and imagination is most severe.

Allegory avowedly represents a particular method of creating or reading narratives, significant parts of whose literary constituents—plot, character, structure, style, and meaning—correlate with one or more specific, explicitly formulated belief systems. But because these systems exist in a state of competition, the creation of allegory is less a static or "mechanical" act than, as J. Stephen Russell has noted, a dynamic process of composition and/or reading. In fact, often "the 'encoding' and 'decoding' processes are far more interesting and mysterious than the decoded messages (if any)."[10] In general, the practice of allegory runs along two complementary lines: compositional allegory, the creation of narratives intended to be read on two or more levels, and interpretive allegory, or allegoresis, the exegesis of a narrative according to a specific, explicit belief system, regardless of whether or not such interpretation was intended by the text's original author(s). The infusion of external belief systems as a driving force within the structural, semantic, and aesthetic levels of narrative is an essential feature of both aspects of allegory, and it is assumed in both that the reader is conscious that the process of decoding is a fundamental aspect of the experience of reading.[11]

Frye has observed that "all literary commentary, or the relating of the events of a narrative to conceptual terminology, is in one sense allegorical."[12] Allegory assumes generic characteristics, however, rather than being merely a structural principle, when the expectation of systematic hermeneutical decoding according to one or more belief systems becomes a continuous and controlling feature of the reader's experience of the text. Herman Melville's *Moby-Dick* and Niẓâmî's *Khusrau u Shîrîn*, in this regard, can be read allegorically because of their rich textures of symbolic connotation. But they are not allegories per se, because narrative event, character development, and detail overshadow allegorical allusion and because each lacks a readily identifiable and consistently foregrounded ideological program. Such works as Dante's *Divine Comedy* or 'Abd ar-Raḥmân Jâmî's *Yûsuf u Zulaikha*, on the other hand, belong to the genre of allegory because such an explicit program comprehensively controls semantic dimensions of the texts. Although it would be possible to experience these narratives on a purely literal level, such an approach seriously distorts each author's intent and greatly lessens the readers' enjoyment of and edification from the text.

An essential feature of texts that belong to the genre of allegory, therefore, is that they demand a specific framework of allegoresis. There are historical instances, however, when texts that *objective* readers (an ideal, of course, but at times a necessary heuristic construct) would not consider as predominantly allegorical in character are, for various historical or cultural reasons, subjected to what Rosemund Tuve has termed "imposed allegory." Examples of this phenomenon are Stoic readings of Homer, Christian exegeses of the Old Testament, or, more recently, reductionist Freudian or Marxist interpretations of literary works. In such instances, a large measure of reductionist coercion is involved in the hermeneutical process.[13]

This initial definition of the genre of allegory, therefore, assumes the following points: (1) that it must involve a narrative, that is, have a story, although whether the narratives take the form of prose or poetry, or are epic, romantic, or mythic in tone is irrelevant; (2) that the narrative is to a great extent hermeneutically prescriptive, that is, the reader is somehow explicitly "informed" that it is intended to be understood within the interpretive framework of one or more distinct belief systems; and (3) that the correlation between narrative elements and particular points of the belief systems is generally, if not totally consistently, maintained. Whether these belief systems are theological, mystical, gnostic, philosophical (rationalist), aesthetic, historical, political, or some combination of them all, is irrelevant to our definition.[14]

As stated, allegory's inherent demand for interpretation requires that the author alert readers to the fact that the narrative should be read interpretively as well as indicate the particular interpretive perspectives needed. This rhetorical dimension of allegory runs along a continuum whose two extremes are hermeticism, that is, conspiratorial invocations for concealing the "true" significance of the secrets concealed in the narrative, on the one hand, and self-confident openness in regard to the real meaning of the story, on the other. The latter alternative is mostly clearly evident in works that fall in the category Graham Hough (partially following Northrop Frye) has termed "naive" allegory, while narratives that are avowedly obscurist, so that their meaning is clear only to those already initiated, he calls "symbolic" and "emblematic."[15] Where the rhetoric of allegory in a particular text falls along this continuum says much about the social status (i.e., degree of orthodoxy) of the particular belief systems being espoused in the historical period in which the allegory is composed.

Notes

1. Northrop Frye, "Allegory," in *Princeton Encyclopedia of Poetry and Poetics*, ed. Alex Preminger (Princeton, N.J.: Princeton University Press, 1974) 12.

2. Edwin Honig, *Dark Conceit: The Making of Allegory* (Evanston, Ill.: Northwestern University Press, 1959) 6–7.

3. The classic statement on this approach to reading philosophical texts is Leo Strauss, *Persecution and the Art of Writing* (Glencoe, Ill.: Free Press, 1952). Allegories vary, however, in the degree that they adopt hermetic rhetoric for real reasons or just rhetorical effect. A truly secret doctrine would presumably never be written at all.

4. Cf. Joel Fineman, "More historically, we can note that allegory seems regularly to surface in critical or polemical atmospheres, when for political or metaphysical reasons there is something that cannot be said," "The Structure of Allegorical Desire," in Greenblatt, ed., *Allegory and Representation*, 28.

5. Dante, *Dantis Alagherii Epistolae: The Letters of Dante, Emended Text*, intro. and trans. Paget Toynbee (Oxford: Clarendon Press, 1966) 199. See Augus-

tine's *On Christian Doctrine*, trans. D. W. Robertson, Jr. (Indianapolis, Ind.: The Library of the Liberal Arts, 1951); for Aquinas, Umberto Eco, *The Aesthetics of Thomas Aquinas*, trans. Hugh Bredin (Cambridge, Mass.: Harvard University Press, 1988) 136–89. For a general analysis of the strategies of patristic interpretation, see Todorov, *Symbolism and Interpretation*, 97–130; on the four levels of meaning, see 112–24.

6. Qur'ân, 3.7.

7. For more on this, see Heath, "Creative Hermeneutics," and the works cited in Chapter 1, notes 9 and 16. An example of elaboration of this two-level method of interpretation is that outlined by the mystic Sahl at-Tustarî (d. 283/896):

> Each verse (*âyah*) of the Qur'ân has four senses (*ma'ânin*), a literal (*ẓâhir*) and a hidden sense (*bâṭin*), a limit (*ḥadd*) and a point of transcendency (*maṭla'*). The literal sense is the recitation (*tilâwah*), the hidden sense the understanding (*fahm*, of the verse). The limit (defines what is declared) lawful (*ḥalâl*) and unlawful (*ḥarâm*) by (the verse) and the point of transcendency is the command of the heart (*ishrâf al-qalb*) over the meaning intended (*murâd*) by it as understood from (the vantage point) of God (*fiqhan min Allâh*). The knowledge of the literal sense (*'ilm aẓ-ẓâhir*) is common knowledge (*'âmm*), the understanding (*fahm*) of it is hidden sense and the meaning intended (*murâd*) by it is select knowledge (*khâṣṣ*).

See Böwering, *The Mystical Vision of Existence in Classical Islam*, 135–42, quote from p. 139. Al-Ghazâlî presents other important statements on how to read texts allegorically throughout his *Mishkât al-anwâr*, ed. Abu l-'Alâ 'Afîfî (Cairo: Dâr al-qaumiyya li-ṭibâ'a wa-n-nashr, 1963).

8. Honig, *Dark Conceit*, 6.

9. *Miscellaneous Criticism*, cited by Honig, *Dark Conceit*, 46. Honig's reevaluation of the traditional Romantic prejudice against allegory (pp. 39–54) is important and has been echoed by most succeeding studies (see texts cited in note 11, below); for a more recent exposition of the problem, see Tzvetan Todorov, *Theories of the Symbol*, trans. Catherine Porter (Ithaca, N.Y.: Cornell University Press, 1982) 198–221.

10. J. Stephen Russell, ed., in his intro. to *Allegoresis: The Craft of Allegory in Medieval Literature* (New York and London: Garland Publishing, 1988) xi.

11. Whitman, *Allegory*, 3–10, is a useful recent survey of the western tradition of allegory and allegoresis. In addition to previously cited works, also pertinent for their theoretical and historical insights are Fletcher, *Allegory: The Theory of a Symbolic Mode*; Maureen Quilligan, *The Language of Allegory: Defining the Genre* (Ithaca, N.Y.: Cornell University Press, 1979); and Gay Clifford, *The Transformations of Allegory* (London and Boston: Routlege & Kegan Paul, 1974). Recent collections of articles are Bloomfield, ed., *Allegory, Myth, and Symbol*,; Russell, ed., *Allegoresis*; and Stephen A. Barney, ed., *Allegories of History, Allegories of Love* (Hamden, Conn.: Archon Books, 1979).

12. Frye, "Allegory," 12; cf. his *Anatomy of Criticism: Four Essays* (Princeton, N.J.: Princeton University Press, 1957) 89.

13. Cf. Rosemund Tuve, *Allegorical Imagery: Some Medieval Books and Their Posterity* (Princeton, N.J.: Princeton University Press, 1966) 219–331; Quilligan, *The Language of Allegory*, 30–33, 224–25; and *idem*, "Allegory, Allegoresis, and the Deallegorization of Language: The *Roman de la rose*, the *De Planctu naturae*, and the *Parlement of Foules*," in Bloomfield, ed., *Allegory, Myth, and Symbol*, 163–86, esp. 163–64 and 182.

14. This provisional definition of allegory basically accords with that proposed by Northrop Frye in "Allegory," 12–15. Allegory resembles the novel—which has largely displaced it in the West since 1800 and the Middle East since 1900—in its literary omnivorousness, that is, in its ability to manipulate and make use of various preexisting genres, such as romance or epic. In a general sense, the two forms—allegory and the novel—offer alternative approaches to the awarding of priority to meaning over narrative (allegory) or narrative over meaning (novel). Romantic poetics had thus tended to valorize the novel because it was "symbolic" while allegory was "only" allegorical, see Frye, "Allegory," 14, and C. S. Lewis, whose distinction between allegory and symbol in *The Allegory of Love* (London, Oxford, and New York: Oxford University Press, 1936) 44–48, is typical of this perspective. More profitable is a theoretical viewpoint that see the question of the explicitness of correlation between narrative and belief system as points along a continuum; a good example of this approach is Hough's circle of allegory in his *A Preface to The Faerie Queene*, 100–111. Frye himself rejects the notion that allegory is itself a genre ("Allegory," 12). I believe, however, that genres should be identified with structural and thematic elements that dominate our reaction to them; see Heath, "Romance as Genre in *The Thousand and One Nights*," 18:9–10.

15. For naive allegory, see Graham Hough, *A Preface to the Faerie Queene*, 106–11 and Frye, *Anatomy of Criticism*, 89–91.

Appendix B: On the Attribution of the Mi'râj Nâma

The *Mi'râj Nâma* is not a prominent or famous treatise, nor does it have a well-established textual tradition that proves beyond doubt that Avicenna composed it. So it is perhaps not surprising that several modern scholars have disputed the authenticity of its attribution. I will argue, however, that, although the issue of attribution may be such that it can never be settled irrefutably, there is enough external and internal evidence pointing to Avicenna actually being the tract's author that the burden of proof falls to those who would argue otherwise.

It is worthwhile here to raise the general problem of the textual history of Avicenna's writings (not to mention similar problems regarding writings attributed to such other major thinkers as al-Ghazâlî and Ibn 'Arabî). The authenticity of Avicenna's major works is not in question. One may desire critical—or revised critical—editions of such treatises as *an-Najât, al-Aḍḥawiyya*, or *Aḥwâl an-nafs*, but there is no doubt concerning the correctness of their attribution to the philosopher. The situation differs in regard to Avicenna's *opera minora*. Here we find many treatises whose authenticity modern scholars have generally accepted, such as all of the treatises in the collection known as *Tis' rasâ'il* (including *Fî ithbât an-nubuwwât*), as well as such treatises as *Fî ta'bîr ar-ru'yâ, Fi s-sa'âda*, and *al-'Arshiyya*, whose names fail to appear in the bibliographies of Avicenna's early biographers and whose textual history has yet to be studied in any detail. Obviously, much more basic philological work of a historical and analytical nature is required before a clear picture of Avicenna's writings emerges.[1]

It may be that even after such investigations have been carried out doubts will remain concerning the authenticity of certain works, even though they closely follow Avicenna's thought in doctrine and tone. One may in fact have to resort to creating a category of *Avicennian writings* that falls between those writings that are incontrovertibly authentic and those that are demonstrably pseudonymous.

The testimony of both external and internal evidence on the question of the *Miʿrâj Nâma*'s authenticity is as follows.

External Evidence

External evidence concerning the identity of the author of the *Miʿrâj Nâma* is conflicting. The treatise is not mentioned in al-Jûzjânî's short list of Avicenna's works, or in the longer lists provided by al-Baihaqî (d. 565/1169–70), Ibn al-Qifṭî (d. 646/1248), or Ibn Abî Uṣaibiʿa (d. 668/1270).[2] Ḥâjjî Khalîfa [Kâtib Chelebî] (d. 967/1557) does attribute such a work to Avicenna.[3] The lack of such citation in the case of the *Miʿrâj Nâma* is not in itself sufficient to disprove its genuineness, since many treatises (including those referred to above) whose authenticity are generally accepted also fail to appear in these lists.

Among modern bibliographers, Osman Ergin fails to mention the treatise, while Georges C. Anawati and Yaḥyâ Mahdavî doubt its authenticity.[4] Father Anawati appears to base his opinion on Charles Rieu's rejection of the genuineness of the work. In his *Catalogue of Persian Manuscripts in the British Museum*, Rieu comments that

> The author, who does not give his name, states at the beginning, that he had written this tract in answer to the repeated questions of a friend, and with the permission of a spiritual guide designated as *majlis-i ʿâlâ ʿâlâ'î* and further on as *dhât-i sharîf ʿalâ' ad-daula*. No work of this kind is mentioned among the writings of Ibn Sînâ, either by ʿAbd ul-Vâḥîd Jûzjânî, or by Ibn Abi Uṣaibiʿah. Its attribution to the celebrated philosopher rests on the doubtful authority of Haj. Khal., vol. iii. p. 443, on the heading in the present MS. *în risâla îst dar miʿrâj ki shaikh ar-ra'îs Abî ʿAlî Sînâ sâkhtah ast*, and on a similar title in another copy, Add. 16839, art. XXV. It was probably suggested by the ʿAla ud-Daulah mentioned in the preface, who, however, as a religious teacher, has nothing but the name in common with the prince to whom the Dânish Nâmah was dedicated. A celebrated saint of that name, ʿAlâ ud-Daulah Simnânî, died A. H. 736. [sic][5]

Rieu gives no reasons for distrusting Ḥâjjî Khalîfa's testimony. Moreover, comparison of his remarks with the beginning of the *Miʿrâj Nâma* itself casts doubt on his assertion that the work was written for a spiritual rather than temporal authority. The treatise specifically states, for example, that the author was asked to explain the *miʿrâj* "in a rational way" (*Miʿrâj*

Nâma, 79; trans., 111). Hence, there is no apparent reason to suppose that the mention of 'Alâ' ad-Daula in the treatise's introduction refers to a religious mentor instead of Avicenna's Kâkûyid patron 'Alâ' ad-Daula Muḥammad; the use of the term *majlis-i 'âlî 'âlâ'î* rather than *shaikh* or *pîr* hardly connotes that the work was written for a spiritual guide. Furthermore, the interpretation of the *mi'râj* that the author offers is thoroughly philosophical and hardly accords with the tenets of mainstream Islamic mystical theology. Since Rieu provides no real evidence for his judgment, Anawati's doubts concerning the treatise's authenticity also lack foundation.

Mahdavî doubts the work's authenticity because the question of authorship in the manuscript tradition is not clear-cut. One early manuscript (dated 727/1326–27, see Appendix C, no. 4) attributes the work to an anonymous *Murshid al-Kifâyah* (Guide of Sufficiency). But this title could easily refer to Avicenna; the hermetic rhetoric that the author invokes in the treatise might be one way to explain why a latter scribe would omit explicit reference to the philosopher's name.[6]

Another manuscript (dated 659/1261, see Appendix C, no. 2) attributes the treatise to Shihâb ad-Dîn as-Suhrawardî. This attribution was put to rest, however, when Mahdî Bayânî discovered the earliest known manuscript of the *Mi'râj Nâma*. The scribe of this manuscript (dated 584/1188, Appendix C, no. 1), which Bayânî published in facsimile, uses the phrase *qaddas Allâh sirrahû* (may God sanctify his secret) in the colophon when referrning to the author, signaling that the latter had already died. Bayânî deduces from this that the work could not be as-Suhrawardî's, since the latter died in 587/1191, three years after the manuscript was transcribed.[7]

This scribe, by the way, identifies himself as Muḥammad ibn 'Umar ar-Râzî, whom Bayânî assumes to be the famous Ash'arî theologian, Fakhr ad-Dîn ar-Râzî (d. 606/1209). As Bayânî says, it is unlikely that there would be two contemporaneous Muḥammad ibn 'Umars from Rayy who were sufficiently interested in philosophical texts to transcribe them in their own hands.[8] In 584/1188 ar-Râzî would have been forty-one years old, still in the midst of his travels and just beginning to make a name for himself. According to Fathalla Kholeif, ar-Râzî returned to Rayy from Transoxiana in 582/1186 and shortly afterwards set off for the court of Shihâb ad-Dîn al-Ghûrî in Ghazna. In 584/1188 he would, therefore, either have been in Rayy or on his way to or in Ghazna. In any case, one can easily imagine that, encountering a manuscript of the *Miʿrâj Nâma*, he would have wanted to make a copy for himself.[9]

A third attribution was made by M. Minovi and Ghulâmḥusain Yûsufî, who suggested that the work's author was Abu l-Muẓaffar Manṣûr ibn Ardashîr ʿAbbâdî (d. 547/1153), presumably on the basis of such an attribution in a late manuscript currently in the Faculty of Law Library at Tehran University (11th/16 century, see Appendix C, no. 16).[10] N. Mâyel Heravî disputes this claim on both textual and doctrinal grounds. Only one manuscript makes this attribution, and it seems extremely doubtful that ʿAbbâdî, who wrote on Ṣûfîsm, would write a work so patently philosophical and one that also embraces the idea that the prophet's ascension was spiritual rather than corporal. The *Miʿrâj Nâma* by Shams ad-Dîn Ibrâhîm Abarqûhî (late 7th/13th–early 8th/14th century)—published by Heravî with his edition of Avicenna's *Miʿrâj Nâma*—is, for example, a Ṣûfî recasting of the text that explicitly rejects the idea that the *miʿrâj* was only a spiritual phenomenon. Abarqûhî's work, in general, is modified to be more in tune with mystic rather than philosophical beliefs, and its existence is a good argument against the idea that the *Miʿrâj Nâma* under discussion was written by a Ṣûfî.[11]

Henry Corbin devotes a chapter to the *Miʿrâj Nâma* in his *Avicenna and the Visionary Recital* in which he refers to the problem of attribution, but he offers no conclusions concerning it. M. Achena also mentions but does not discuss the treatise in his *Encyclopedia Iranica* article on Avicenna's Persian works, stating that he did not have an opportunity to examine it.[12]

In sum, although the external and textual evidence is not sufficiently strong to be considered conclusive, the cases that have been made against attributing the treatise to Avicenna are not, once examined, based on either firm or extensive evidence. On the other hand, the large majority of manuscripts do cite Avicenna as the treatise's author. Moreover, those who have examined the work most closely, its modern editors—Ghulâmḥusain Ṣadîqî, Mahdî Bayânî, and N. Mâyel Heravî—unanimously concur that the work is by Avicenna.

Internal Evidence

Internal evidence regarding the treatise's authenticity may be divided into five categories: stylistic, terminological, expressional, structural, and doctrinal (see also the notes to the translation).

1. Achena, in the aforementioned article on the Persian works of Avicenna in *Encyclopedia Iranica*, accepts the authenticity of only two Persian works attributed to Avicenna, *Andar dânish-i rag* (On the Science of the Pulse) and the *Dânish-nâma-yi ʿAlâʾî*, without, it must be remembered, having seen the *Miʿrâj Nâma*. Achena points out that Avicenna's Persian works were not intended for specialists. They were

> manuals written for the use of an uninitiated person and possessing appropriate qualities: Clear language, near-colloquial phraseology . . . choice of themes and questions which give access to relatively elementary knowledge in each field, exclusion of subjects which could only be of interest to specialists, reduction of chapter length, and frequent use of explanatory description rather than logical definition.[13]

This, one could argue, is a fair description of the style of the *Miʿrâj Nâma*. The language is early Persian, with frequent use of such forms as *andar*, *mar*, and *hamî*. Sentences are short; their meaning is clear but their phrasing could hardly be called elegant. A comparison of this style with that of Avicenna's main philosophical work in Persian, the *Dânish-nâma-yi ʿAlâʾî*, reveals that the *Miʿrâj Nâma* lacks the terminological consistency and clarity of expresson that marks the former. It must be remembered, however, that the *Dânish-nâma-yi ʿAlâʾî* belongs to a genre that Avicenna had honed to perfection by the time he arrived at ʿAlâʾ ad-Daula's court in Iṣfahân, that of philosophical compendium, the concise handbook that summarizes the author's philosophical views. The *Dânish-nâma-yi ʿAlâʾî*, therefore, is less an independent treatise than a Persian version of such congruent Arabic works as *an-Najât*, *al-Hidâya*, and *ʿUyûn al-ḥikma*. The *Miʿrâj Nâma*, on the other hand, is an original work rather than a formulaic abridgement, and one would expect that its composition entailed a creative struggle in order to mold the still inchoate and unsophisticated philosophical language of early Modern Persian into the required form. Furthermore, the treatise belongs to a symbolic genre that occasionally values allusion and opacity over lucidity; as such, its style is not unlike that which one would expect Avicenna to use.[14]

2. The terminology of the *Miʿrâj Nâma* is throughout Avicenna's. One may register surprise that the psychological terms initially used to describe the three parts of the soul (*ṭabîʿî*, *ḥayavânî*, and *nafsânî*) are not those found in his philosophical works. On the other hand, Avicenna does employ these terms in nonphilosophical treatises, such as *Fî taʿbîr ar-ruʾyâ* and *al-Qânûn fi ṭ-ṭibb*.[15] In the latter, Avicenna expressly states that he is

not writing for a philosophical audience. If Avicenna therefore wrote the *Miʿrâj Nâma* with a sympathetic but nonspecialist court audience in mind, he might very well be less consistent in his use of terminology, especially if he composed the work when he first arrived in Iṣfahân, before he composed the *Dânish-nâma*. At any rate, all the terminology used in the *Miʿrâj Nâma* does have correlates in Avicenna's other works.

3. There are places in the *Miʿrâj Nâma* where one finds echoes or duplications of expressions or descriptions from other works by Avicenna. The portrayal of the rational soul facing both upward and downward, for example, is standard for Avicenna, appearing in *ash-Shifâʾ*, *an-Najât*, and elsewhere. The description of the spheres and their natures is very close to that found in *Ḥayy ibn Yaqẓân* and *Fi l-ajrâm al-ʿulwiyya*.

4. In general structure, that is, philosophical introduction followed by allegorical interpretation, the treatise is in accord with the form found in other works by Avicenna, such as *Fî ithbât an-nubuwwât* or *Fî taʿbîr ar-ruʾyâ*.

5. Finally, in terms of doctrine, the chapters of this book should amply demonstrate that the psychology and epistemology presented in the *Miʿrâj Nâma* and the theory of prophecy that stems from them are pure Avicenna. If prophethood is not presented in terms of an intellectual ascension through the various ranks of the intellect, as is the case in *ash-Shifâʾ* or *Fî ithbât an-nubuwwât*, it is depicted in terms of celestial ascent, as is the case with *Ḥayy ibn Yaqẓân* and *Risâlat aṭ-ṭair*. On the other hand, there are places where the doctrines expressed in the *Miʿrâj Nâma* go beyond those that Avicenna presents in other works. A major example is the depiction in the work of the *rûḥ al-qudus* as an intermediary between the First Intelligence and the Necessary Existence. Even in such places, however, the doctrines of the *Miʿrâj Nâma* do not contradict ideas Avicenna expresses elsewhere.[16]

In summation, if one cannot prove the attribution of the *Miʿrâj Nâma* to Avicenna conclusively, the bulk of the evidence suggests that the work is indeed his and that he wrote the treatise soon after his arrival at Iṣfahân.[17] The style fits, the terminology is appropriate, one finds echoes of expressions and descriptions from his other works, and the doctrines clearly accord with those of Avicenna. Finally, the topic of the treatise also rings true. Psychology and prophethood are near the core of Avicenna's philosophical interests. What better way to combine them for the purpose of instructing his new patron and his court than to compose a rational interpretation of the prophet Muḥammad's *miʿrâj*?

Notes

1. Cf. Michot, *La destinée de l'homme selon Avicenne*, 1–9.

2. See Gohlman, *Life*, 143–52.

3. "The Chief Master [*ash-shaikh ar-ra'îs*] composed a Persian treatise on it [the *mi'râj*] in which he investigated and established its possibility." Ḥâjjî Khalîfa [Kâtib Chelebî], *Kashf az-ẓunûn*, eds. Sh. Yaltkaya and R. Bilge, 2nd ed., 2 vols. (Istanbul: Devlet Kitapları, 1971) 1: 892.

4. See Osman Ergin, *Ibni Sina Bibliografyası*, Istanbul Üniversitesi Tip Fakültesi Yayınlarından 20 (Istanbul: Osman Yalçın Matbaası, 1956); G. C. Anawati, *Essai de bibliographie Avicennienne* (Cairo: al-Maaref, 1950) 321–22; and Yaḥyâ Mahdavî, *Bibliographie d'Ibn Sina* (Tehran: Dânishgâh-i Tihran, 1954) 297–98.

5. Charles Rieu, *Catalogue of Persian Manuscripts in the British Museum* 3 vols. (Oxford: Trustees of the British Museum, 1966 [repr. of the 1879–83 ed.]) 2:438–39.

6. Mahdavî, *Bibliographie d'Ibn Sina*, 297.

7. Bayânî, *Mi'râj Nâma* , intro., 7.

8. Bayânî, *Mi'râj Nâma*, intro., 7–8.

9. Fathalla Kholeif, *A Study on Fakhr ad-Dîn al-Râzî and His Controversies in Transoxiana*, Pensée arabe et musulmane 31 (Beirut: Dar el-Mashreq Éditeurs, 1966) 18–19.

10. See Heravî, *Mi'râj Nâma*, 68–71.

11 Ibid.

12. Corbin, *Avicenna*, 165–78. M. Achena, "[Avicenna's] Persian Works," in Mahdi, Gutas, et al., "Avicenna," *Encyclopedia Iranica* 3,1:99–104, esp. 104.

13. Achena, "[Avicenna's] Persian Works," in Mahdi, Gutas, et al., "Avicenna," *Encyclopedia Iranica* 3,1:99–100.

14. The styles of *Ḥayy ibn Yaqẓân* and *aṭ-Ṭair*, for example, are much more complex and opaque than that of *ash-Shifâ'* or even that of *al-Ishârât wa-t-tanbîhât*. Moreover, the style of some of Avicenna's works written in Arabic for a general, nonspecialist audience are very similar to the Persian style of the *Mi'râj Nâma*, for example, his *Risâla fî ta'bîr ar-ru'yâ*.

15. *al-Qânûn*, 1:66–73.

16. As I remarked above (Chapter Eight, note 1), the question of the place of the Holy Spirit (*rûḥ al-qudus*) in Avicenna's thought deserves individual study.

17. Note in the first chapter of the *Mi'râj Nâma*, where the author states that he had long wished to compose this work and finally, after his arrival at the court of 'Alâ' ad-Daula, felt free to do so.

Appendix C: The Manuscripts

Anawati (pp. 321–22), Mahdavî (pp. 297–98), and Aḥmad Munzavî, *A Catalogue of Persian Manuscripts*, 5 vols. (Tehran: Regional Cultural Institute, 1970–73) 2:846–48 cite a total of thirty-seven manuscripts of the *Mi'râj Nâma*. The following lists them in chronological order.

1. **Sanâ** 219 [6:481], Tehran (Munzavî 7866). Date, 15 Ṣafar 584/1188. Scribe, Muḥammad ibn 'Umar ar-Râzî. This is the text that Bayânî printed in facsimile. [Used by Heravî, *Bâ'*.]
2. **Millî** 992/5, Tehran (Mahdavî 227). Date, 659/1261. Attributed to Shihâb ad-Dîn as-Suhrawardî.
3. **Riḍavî** 1013 *Ḥikmat* [4:248], Mashhad (Munzavî 7867). Date, 6th to 7th/12th to 13th century. Attributed to Avicenna in the *fihrist*. [Used by Heravî, *Râ'*.]
4. **Fâtiḥ** 5426, Istanbul (Munzavî 7868, Mahdavî p. 297). Date, 727/1326–27. Attributed to *Murshid al-Kifâya*. [Used by Heravî, *Fâ'*.]
5. **Köprülü** 1589/67, Istanbul (Munzavî 7869). In a *daftar* dated 753-54/1352–53. There is a microfilm in Dânishgâh, no. 462 (Microfilms 1:484). [Used by Heravî, *Kaf*.]
6. **Majlis** 1226 [4:15 and 5:503], Tehran (Munzavî 7870). Date, 845/1441–42. The scribe was "reportedly Ḥusain the son of Muḥammad, known as Qavvâm-i Kâshî" (Munzavî).
7. **Dânishgâh** 4732/5 [14:3682], Tehran (Munzavî 7871). Date, 962/1554–55. Attributed to Avicenna at its beginning. Titled *Risâla-yi nubuvvat*.
8. **Malik** 4196/19, Tehran (Munzavî 7872). Date, 1016/1607–8. Written in Aḥmadabâd, Gujarat.
9. **Malik** 4694/14, Tehran (Munzavî 7873). Date, 1024/1615–16. Scribe, 'Abd al-Qâdir Ardûbâdî. Written in Shîrâz.
10. **Majlis** 2381/14 [5:163], Tehran (Munzavî 7874). In a *daftar* dated 1061/1650.
11. **Majlis** 3321/8 [10:983], Tehran (Munzavî 7875). Date, 1067/1656–57.

12. **Majlis** 5180/8, Tehran (Munzavî 7876). Date, 1069/1658–59.
13. **Yazd** 1342/5 [6 : 630] (Munzavî 7877). Date, 1070/1659–70. Scribe, Shâh Muḥammad son of Muḥammad Zamân. Written in Yazd.
14. **Dânishgâh** 253/19, Tehran (Munzavî 7878). Date, 1086/1675–76. Scribe, Ḥaidar Kurkî.
15. **Sipahsâlâr** 2911/23 [5 : 604], Tehran (Munzavî 7879). Date, 1092/1681–82. Written in Ajmîr.
16. **Ḥuqûq** 62b./2 [199], Tehran (Munzavî 7880). Date, 11th/16th century. Attributed in the *fihrist* to Abu l-Muẓaffar Manṣûr ibn Ardashîr ʻAbbâdî Marzavî (d. 547/1153).
17. **Dânishgâh** 1035/6 [3 : 387], Tehran (Munzavî 7881). Date, 1101/1689–90. Attributed to Avicenna at the text's beginning.
18. **Majlis** 1807/13 [5 : 212], Tehran (Munzavî 7882). Date, 1102/1690–91. No attribution in the text, but in a collection of Avicenna's treatises.
19. **Majlis** 1807/12 [9 : 399], Tehran (Munzavî 7883). Date, 1102-1107/1690–95.
20. **Ilâhiyyât** 209/2 Āl Aqâ [1 : 735], Tehran (Munzavî 7884). Date, 1 Shawwal, 1177/1763. Attributed to Avicenna in the *fihrist*.
21. **British Library** Add. 16659/4, London (Anawati 275, Mahdavî 227). Date, 1182/1768. Attributed to Avicenna in the work's title.
22. **Ilâhiyyât** 14j./17 [1 : 152], Tehran (Munzavî 7885). Date, 12th/18th century. Scribe, Ibn Ghiyâth ad-Dîn ʻAlî al-Khâdim Muḥammad Bâqir Sharîf for Sirâj ad-Dîn Maulânâ Qâsim. At the end, the date 9, Jumâdî al-Awwal, 751/1350 appears.
23. **Dânishgâh** 2731/1 [1 : 1603], Tehran (Munzavî 7887). Date, 12th/18th century. Scribe, Maḥmûd son of Muḥammad Taqî Shîrâzî.
24. **Dânishgâh** 2731/2 [10 : 1603], Tehran (Munzavî 7887).
25. **Majlis** 3256/5 [10 : 1387], Tehran (Munzavî 7888). Date, 12th/18th century.
26. **Majlis** 631/7 [2 : 392], Tehran (Munzavî 7889). Date, 1268/1851–52. Titled *Ithbât an-nubuvvat* in the *fihrist*.
27. **Riḍavî Ḥikmat** 1014 [4 : 248], Mashhad (Munzavî 7890). Date, 1273/1856–57.
28. **Dânishgâh** 761/11, Tehran (Munzavî 7891). Date, 1283/1866–67.
29. **Majlis** 1923/3 [424], Tehran (Munzavî 7892). Date, 1294/1877.
30. **Majlis** 4126/3 [5 : 199], Tehran (Munzavî 7893). Date, 1294/1877.
31. **Riḍavî Ḥikmat** 700 [4 : 145], Mashhad (Munzavî 7894). No date. Attributed to Avicenna at the work's beginning.

32. **Sulaimâniyya**, Meḥmed Murâd Efendî 209 (71), Istanbul (Munzavî 7895). No date. A microfilm is in Dânishgâh, no. 199.
33. **Bodlian**, Persian 1904/15, Oxford (Mahdavî 227).
34. **Asiatic Society of Bengal**, Curzon Collection 487, Calcutta (Mahdavî 227).
35. **Nûr 'Uthmâniyya** 4894/40, Istanbul (Mahdavî 227).
36. **Faiḍ Allâh** 1216, Istanbul (Anawati 275).
37. **Juliana** 1422/2 (Anawati 275).

Appendix D: The Text of Avicenna's Version of the Mi'râj *(without his attendant commentary)*

The best of creatures, upon him be (God's) blessing and salvation, said:

I was sleeping one night in the house. It was a night with thunder and lightning. No animal made a sound, no bird chirped, no person was awake. I was not asleep, but lying between sleep and wakefulness. Suddenly Gabriel descended in his own form with such beauty, splendor, and majesty that the house was alit. I saw him whiter than snow, fair of face, curly of lock. On his forehead was written in light, "There is no God but God, and Muḥammad is the Apostle of God"; fairly large of eye, delicate of brow, with seventy thousand locks of red ruby dangling down; and six hundred thousand feathers of lustrous pearl opened up. When he reached me, he embraced me and kissed me between my two eyes and said, "O Sleeper, arise! How long you slumber!

I was afraid and leapt up from my place because of that fear. He said to me, "Be still, for I am your brother Gabriel." I said, "O Brother, an enemy has taken control of me (before)." He said, "I will not hand you over to the enemy." I said, "What are you going to do?" He said, "Arise! Be observant and take heart." I was amazed, and I followed Gabriel. Behind Gabriel, *Burâq* caught my eye. It was larger than an ass and smaller than a horse. Its face was like a human face. It is long of arm and long of leg. I wanted to sit on it, (but) it shied away. Gabriel helped me until it was tamed.

When I had started on the road and passed the mountains of Mekka, a traveler came after me and called out, "Stop!" Gabriel said, "Do not speak, go on!" So I went on. A woman, alluring in (her) beauty, called from behind me, "Stop! So I can reach you." Again Gabriel said, "Go on, don't stop!" When I went on, Gabriel said, "If you had waited for her until she reached you, you would have become a lover of the world."

When I went away from the mountains and left those two persons, I traveled to the Sanctified Abode, and I entered it. Someone came forward and gave me three goblets, one wine, one water, and one milk. I wanted to take the wine. Gabriel did not allow (this). He pointed to the milk, so I took (it) and drank.

I arrived there and entered the mosque. The muezzin gave the call for prayer. I was in front, and I saw the group of angels and prophets standing to the right and left. One by one they greeted me and renewed the covenant. When I was finished, I faced aloft. I found a ladder, one rung of silver, one rung of gold.

When I reached the lowest heaven, a door opened. I entered and saw Ismâ'îl seated on a chair, and a group was placed, face to face, in front of his eye. I greeted (them) and went on. When I reached the second heaven, I entered. I saw an angel nearer than the former, with perfect beauty. He had a wondrous form, half of his body was of snow, half of fire. Neither mixed with the other, nor were they antagonistic toward one another. He greeted me and said, "Good tidings to you to whom goodness and fortune belong." When I reached the third heaven, I saw an angel whose like in beauty and goodness I had never seen, joyful and glad and seated on a chair of light with angels gathered around. When I reached the fourth heaven, I saw an angel, complete in statesmanship, seated on a throne of light. I greeted (him), he responded properly but with complete arrogance. Due to pride and haughtiness, he (usually) spoke to no one. (But) he smiled when he answered (my) greeting and said, "O Muḥammad, I see complete goodness and felicity in your royal splendor. Good tidings to you!" When I reached the fifth heaven, I entered. I learned of hell. I saw a dominion full of darkness and fear. I saw the proprietor seated at its edge busy torturing and tormenting sinful people. When I reached the sixth heaven, I saw an angel seated on a chair of light, busy with praising and sanctifying (God). He had wings and tresses set with pearls and rubies. I greeted him. He responded, greeted (me), and gave tidings of goodness and happiness. He said to me, "I continually sent blessings to you." When I reached the seventh heaven, I saw an angel sitting on a chair of red ruby. Not everyone finds a way to him, but when someone does reach him, he is cherished. I greeted him. He responded and blessed me.

When I went on, I reached the Lote Tree of the Far Boundary. It was a world full of light and brightness so brilliant that the eye was dazzled. When I looked to the right and left, I saw all the spiritual angels busy at worship. I said, "O Gabriel, who are these people?" He said, "They never do anything except worship and praise God. They have specified oratories from which they never depart. As it is said in the Qur'ân, '*Each of us has a known station.*'" I saw the Lote Tree, larger than all things, roots above and branches below, for its shade falls on heaven and earth.

When I passed by I saw four seas, each one a (different) color. I saw many angels busy praising God and affirming His unity, all immersed in grace. When I went by this group, I reached a boundless sea. However much I gazed, I could not even perceive its middle. At the lower part of that sea, I saw a large stream, and I saw an angel who was pouring water from the sea into the stream. From the stream, water reached everywhere. At the bottom of that sea I saw a great valley, larger than any I had ever seen. However much I gazed, I found neither its beginning nor its end; nor could I define it by anything. In the sea's valley I saw an angel, of complete augustness, majesty, and beauty, who was gazing tranquilly at each of the two halves (of creation). He called me to himself. When I reached him, I said, "What is your name?" He said, "Michael. I am the greatest of the angels. Whatever is difficult for you (to understand), ask of me. Whatever you desire, seek of me so that I can show to you the intended aims of everything."

When I was finished with greeting and questioning him, I said, "I have suffered much pain and trouble to reach this place where I am. My goal in coming here was that I attain knowledge and direct vision of Absolute Truth, may He be exalted. Guide me to Him so that I attain my desire and partake of the full benefit, and so return to my house." That angel took my hand, transported me through several thousand veils, bore (me) to a world in which I saw nothing like what I had seen in this world. When he brought me to the Presence of Glory, the command came to me: "Draw nearer!" I did not see sensation or movement in that Presence. I only saw tranquility, stillness, and sufficiency. From being in awe of God, I forgot everything that I had seen and known. Such unveiling, grandeur, and pleasure from proximity was produced that you would say that I was intoxicated. So affected was I by (divine) proximity that I began to tremble. The command was coming, "Draw nearer!" When I drew nearer, He said, "Fear not, be calm!"

When I drew nearer, God's greeting came to me through a voice the like of which I had never heard. The command came, "Praise!" I said, "'I do not enumerate Your praises, for You have praised Yourself.' I am unable (to say) the like of what You Yourself have said." The command came, "Desire something!" I said, "Give permission that whatever (problem) I encounter, I (can) ask until its difficulties are solved."

When I did all this, I returned to the house. Because of the swiftness of the journey, the bedclothes were still warm.

Bibliography

Abarqûhî, Shamsuddîn Ibrâhîm. *Mi'râj Nâma*. See Avicenna, *Mi'râj Nâma*, ed. N. Mâyel Heravî.

Abu l-'Alâ, Muḥammad Muṣṭafâ, ed. *al-Quṣûr al-'awâlî min rasâ'il al-Imâm al-Ghazâlî*. 4 vols. Cairo: Maktabat al-Jundî [al-Gindî], 1970. For individual treatises, see al-Ghazâlî.

Abû Zaid, Ḥâmid. *Falsafat at-ta'wîl: Dirâsa fî ta'wîl al-Qur'ân 'ind Muḥyi d-Dîn ibn 'Arabî*. Beirut: Dâr al-waḥda, 1983.

Achena, M. "[Avicenna's] Persian Works." In Mahdi, Gutas, et. al. "Avicenna." *Encyclopedia Iranica* 3,1 : 99–104.

Afnan, Soheil M. *Avicenna: His Life and Works*. London: George Allen & Unwin, 1958.

———. *A Philosophical Lexicon in Persian and Arabic*. Beirut: Dar el-Mashreq, 1969.

al-Ahwânî, Aḥmad Fû'âd, ed. *Aḥwâl an-nafs: Risâla fi n-nafs wa-baqâ'ihâ wa-ma'âdihâ li-sh-Shaikh ar-Ra'îs Ibn Sînâ*. Cairo: 'Isa l-Bâbi l-Ḥalabî, 1952.

Ajami, Mansour. *The Alchemy of Glory: The Dialectic of Truthfulness and Untruthfulness in Medieval Arabic Literary Criticism*. Washington, D.C.: Three Continents Press, 1988.

Akar, Metin. *Türk Edebiyatinda Manzum Mi'râj-Mameler*. Kültür ve Turizm Bakanlıgı 804. Ankara: Kültür ve Turizm Bakanlığı, 1987.

Altman, Alexander. *Studies in Religious Philosophy and Mysticism*. Ithaca, N.Y.: Cornell University Press, 1969.

——— and Samuel M. Stern. *Isaac Israeli: A Neoplatonic Philosopher of the Early Tenth Century, His Works Translated with Comments and an Outline of His Philosophy*. Scripta Judaica 1. Oxford: Oxford University Press, 1958.

Amîn, Aḥmad, ed. *Ḥayy ibn Yaqẓân, li-bn Sînâ wa-bn Ṭufail wa-s-Suhrawardî*. Dhakhâ'ir al-'Arab 8. Cairo: Dâr al-ma'ârif, 1959.

Anawati, Georges C. *Essai de bibliographie Avicennienne*. Cairo: al-Maaref, 1950.

———. "La destinée de l'homme dans la philosophie d'Avicenne." In *L'homme et son destin d'après les penseurs du Moyen Âge, Actes du premier congrès international de philosophie médiévale*, Louvain: Éditions Naulwelaerts; Paris: Béatrice-Naulwelaerts, 1958, 257–66.

Arberry, Arthur J. *Avicenna on Theology*. The Wisdom of the East Series. London: John Murray, 1951.

———. "Fârâbî's Canons of Poetry." *Revista degli Studi Orientali* 17 (1938) 257–78.

———, trans. *The Koran Interpreted*. 2 vols. New York: Macmillan, 1955.

Aristotle. *The Complete Works of Aristotle: The Revised Oxford Translation*. Ed. Jonathan Barnes. 2 vols. Bollingen Series 71,2. Princeton, N.J.: Princeton University Press, 1984.

———. *De Anima (On the Soul)*. Trans., intro., and notes, Hugh Lawson-Tancred. Harmondsworth, Middlesex: Penguin Books, 1986.

Arkoun, Mohammad. *Lectures du Coran*. Islam d'Hier et d'Aujourd'hui 17. Paris: Maisonnueve et Larose, 1982.

Armstrong, A. H., ed. *The Cambridge History of Later Greek and Early Medieval Philosophy*. Rev. ed. Cambridge: Cambridge University Press, 1970.

Ashbaugh, Anne Freire. *Plato's Theory of Explanation: A Study of the Cosmological Account of the Timaeus*. SUNY Series in Philosophy. Albany: State University of New York Press, 1988.

ʿÂṣî, Ḥasan. *at-Tafsîr al-Qurʾânî wa-l-lugha ṣ-ṣûfiyya fî falsafat Ibn Sînâ*. Cairo: al-Muʾassasa l-jâmiʿiyya li-d-dirâsa wa-n-nashr wa-t-tauzîʿ, 1983.

Augustine of Hippo. *On Christian Doctrine*. Trans. D. W. Robertson, Jr. Indianapolis, Ind.: The Library of the Liberal Arts, 1951.

Averroes. See Ibn Rushd.

Avicenna (Ibn Sînâ, Abû ʿAli l-Ḥusain). *al-Aḍḥawiyya (fi l-maʿâd)*. In Dunyâ, ed., *Ibn Sînâ wa-l-baʿth*, 30–125.

———. *Aḥwâl an-nafs: Risâla fi n-nafs wa-baqâʾihâ wa-maʿâdihâ*. In al-Ahwânî, ed., *Aḥwâl an-nafs*, 48–142; also in Ülken, ed., *Ibn Sina Risâleleri 2*, 109–54.

———. *al-ʿArshiyya fî ḥaqâʾiq at-tauḥîd wa-ithbât an-nubuwwa*. Ed. Ibrâhîm Hilâl. Dirâsât fi l-Islâm 2. Cairo: Dâr an-nahḍa l-ʿarabiyya, n.d.

———. *Dânish-nâma-yi ʿAlâʾî:* [Part 2] *Ṭabîʿiyyât*. Ed. Muḥammad Mishkât. Intishârât-i anjuman-i âthâr-i millî 13. Tehran: n.p., 1952.

———. *Dar ḥaqîqat va-kaifiyyat-i silsila-yi maujûdât va-tasalsul-i asbâb va-musabbbabât*. See Pseudo-Avicenna.

———. *ad-Duʿâʾ*. In ʿÂṣî, *at-Tafsîr al-Qurʾânî*, 297–99.

———. *Fi l-ʿahd*. In Avicenna, *Tisʿ rasâʾil*, 99–105.

———. *Fi l-ajrâm al-ʿulwiyya*. In Avicenna, *Tisʿ rasâʾil*, 27–40.

———. *Fî aqsâm al-ʿulûm al-ʿaqliyya*. In Avicenna, *Tisʿ rasâʾil*, 71–80.

———. *Fî dafʿ al-ghamm min al-maut*. In Mehren, *Traités mystiques*, 3:49–57, French paraphrase, 3:28–32; and in ʿÂṣî, *at-Tafsîr al-Qurʾânî*, 272–80.

———. *Fi l-fiʿl wa-l-infiʿâl wa-aqsâmihâ*. Haidarâbâd: Majlis dâʾirat al-maʿârif al-uthmâniyya, 1933–34.

———. *Fî ʿilm al-akhlâq*. In Avicenna, *Tisʿ rasâʾil*, 107–10.

———. *Fî ʿishq*. In ʿÂṣî, *at-Tafsîr al-Qurʾânî*, 243–69; and in Mehren, *Traités mystiques*, 3:1–27, French paraphrase, 3:1–15; trans. in Fackenheim. "A Treatise on Love."

———. *Fî ithbât an-nubuwwât*. Ed. and intro. Michael Marmura. Philosophical Texts and Studies 2. Beirut: Dâr an-Nahâr, 1968. Also in Avicenna, *Tisʿ rasâʾil*, 82–90; trans. in Marmura, "Avicenna's Proof of Prophecy," in Lerner and Mahdi, eds., *Medieval Political Philosophy*, 113–21.

———. *Fî kalâm ʿala n-nafs an-nâṭiqa*. In al-Ahwânî, ed., *Aḥwâl an-nafs*, 195–99.

———. *Fî lugha*. In Yarshater, ed., *Panj Risâla*, 7–18.

———. *Fî mâhiyyat al-ḥuzn*. In ʿÂṣî, *at-Tafsîr al-Qurʾânî*, 316–17.

———. *Fî mâhiyyat aṣ-ṣalât*. In ʿÂṣî, *at-Tafsîr al-Qurʾânî*, 205–22; and in Mehren, *Traités mystiques*, 3:28–43, French paraphrase, 3:16–24.

———. *Fî maʿrifat an-nafs an-nâṭiqa wa-aḥwâlihâ*. In al-Ahwânî, ed., *Aḥwâl an-*

nafs, 182–92. Trans. in Michot, "L'Épître sur la connaissance de l'âme rationelle et de ses états, attribuée à Avicenne."
———. *Fî mawâ'iẓ*. In 'Âṣî, *at-Tafsîr al-Qur'ânî*, 308–9.
———. *Fi n-nafs*. Text and trans, in Michot, "L'épître sur la disposition des formes intelligibles vaines après la mort d'Avicenne: Édition critique, traduction et index."
———. "Fi n-nufûs. al-Fann al-khâmis min al-kitâb ath-thânî min kitâb *an-Nukat wa-l-fâwa'id fi l-'ilm aṭ-ṭabî'î*." Ed. Wilhelm Kutsch. See Iran Society, Calcutta, *Avicenna*, 147–78.
———. *Fi l-quwa l-insâniyya wa-idrâkâtihâ*. In Avicenna, *Tis' rasâ'il*, 42–48.
———. *Fi s-sa'âda wa-l-ḥujaj al-'ashara 'alâ 'an an-nafs al-insâniyya jauhar*. Haidarâbâd: Majlis dâ'irat al-ma'ârif al-uthmâniyya, 1353/1933–34.
———. *Fî sirr al-qadar*. In 'Âṣî, *at-Tafsîr al-Qur'ânî*, 302–5. Trans. in Hourani, "Ibn Sînâ's 'Essay on the Secret of Destiny.' "
———. *Fî sirr aṣ-ṣalât*. See Avicenna, *Fî mâhiyyat aṣ-ṣalât*.
———. *Fî ta'bîr ar-ru'yâ*. See Avicenna, "On the Interpretation of Dreams."
———. *Fi ṭ-ṭabî'iyyât min 'Uyûn al-ḥikma*. In Avicenna, *Tis' rasâ'il*, 2–25. See also Avicenna, *'Uyûn al-ḥikma*.
———. *al-Firdaus fî mâhiyyat al-insân*. In 'Âṣî, *at-Tafsîr al-Qur'ânî*, 129–47.
———. *Ḥathth adh-dhikr*. In 'Âṣî, *at-Tafsîr al-Qur'ânî*, 312–13.
———. *Ḥayy ibn Yaqẓân*. In Mehren, *Traités mystiques*, fasc. 1 (text, intro., and French paraphrase); and in Amîn, ed., *Ḥayy ibn Yaqẓân*, 43–53; trans. in Corbin, *Avicenna*, 137–50.
———. *al-Hidâya, li-bn Sînâ: Naṣṣ 'arabî falsafî lam yasbuq nashruhû*. Ed. Muḥammad 'Abduh. Cairo: Maktabat al-Qâhira al-ḥadîtha, 1974.
———. *al-Ḥudûd*. In Avicenna, *Tis' rasâ'il*, 50–69. Trans. in Goichon, *Avicenne, livre des définitions*.
———. *al-Ishârât wa-t-tanbîhât*. Ed. Sulaimân Dunyâ. 4 vols. Dhakhâ'ir al-'Arab 22. Cairo: Dâr al-ma'ârif, 1960. Also ed. J. Forget. *Ibn Sînâ: Le livre des théorèmes et des avertissements*. Leiden: E. J. Brill, 1892. Trans. in Goichon, *Ibn Sînâ: Livre des directives et remarques*. See also Avicenna, *Remarks and Admonitions*, and aṭ-Ṭûsî, *Sharḥai l-ishârât*.
———. *al-Karâmât wa-l-mu'jizât wa-l-â'âjîb*. In 'Âṣî, *at-Tafsîr al-Qur'ânî*, 225–40. [Attributed to Avicenna.]
———. *al-Khauf min al-maut*. See, Avicenna, *Fî daf' al-ghamm min al-maut*.
———. *Kitâb ash-Shaikh Abî Sa'îd ibn Abi l-Khair (qaddasa sirrahû) ilâ ash-Shaikh ar-Ra'îs Ibn Sînâ fî ma'na z-ziyâra wa-kaifiyyat ta'thîrihâ wa-jawâb ash-Shaikh ar-Ra'îs*. In Mehren, *Traités mystiques*, 3:44–48, French paraphrase 3:25–27; and in 'Âṣî, *at-Tafsîr al-Qur'ânî*, 284–88.
———. *al-Mabda' wa-l-ma'âd*. Ed. A. Nûrânî. Wisdom of Persia Series 36. Tehran: Institute of Islamic Studies, McGill University-Tehran University, 1984. Trans. in Michot, "L'épitre sur la genèse et le retour attribuée à Avicenne: Présentation et essai de traduction critique."
———. *Mabḥath 'an al-quwa n-nafsâniyya*. In Ahwânî, ed., *Aḥwâl an-nafs*, 148–79; also in S. Landauer, "Die Psychologie des Ibn Sînâ." *ZDMG* 29 (1875) 335–418

(with German trans.); and in Edward C. Van Dyck, *Mabḥath ʿan al-quwa n-nafsâniyya, au kitâb fi n-nafs ʿalâ sunnat al-ikhtiṣâr*, Cairo: n.p., 1907.
———. *al-Majmûʿ, au al-ḥikma al-ʿarûḍiyya fî maʿânî kitâb* Riṭûriqa. Ed. Muḥammad Salîm Sâlim. Cairo: Maṭbaʿat an-nahḍa l-miṣriyya, 1950.
———. *al-Majmûʿ, au al-ḥikma al-ʿarûḍiyya fî maʿânî kitâb* ash-Shiʿr. Ed. Muḥammad Salîm Sâlim. Cairo: Maṭbaʿat dâr al-kutub, 1969.
———. *al-Malâʾika*. In ʿÂṣî, *at-Tafsîr al-Qurʾânî*, 291–94. [Attributed to Avicenna.]
———. *Manṭiq al-mashriqiyyîn*. Cairo: Maktabat as-salafiyya, 1910.
———. *Masâʾil an aḥwâl ar-rûḥ (al-jawâb li-bn Miskawaih)*. In Ülken, ed., *Ibn Sina Risâleleri 2*, 68–70. Trans. in Michot, "Les questions sur les états de l'esprit: Problèmes d'attribution et essai de traduction critique."
———. *Miʿrâj Nâma (The Book of Ascent), with a Revised Text by Shamsuddîn Ibrâhîm Abarqûhî*. Ed. N. Mâyel Heravî. Mashhad: The Islamic Research Foundation, Âstân-i Quds-i Raḍavi, 1986.
———. *Miʿrâj Nâma*. Facsimile edition prepared by Mahdî Bayânî. Tehran: Anjuman-i dûstdârân-i kitâb, 1952.
———. *Miʿrâj Nâma*. Ed. Bahman Karîmî. Rasht: Matbaʿat-i urwat al-wuthqâ, n.d.
———. *al-Mubâḥathât*. In Badawî, *Aflûṭîn ʿind al-ʿArab*, 118–239.
———. *an-Nairûziyya*. In Avicenna, *Tisʿ rasâʾil*, 92–97.
———. *an-Najât*. Ed. Mâjid Fakhrî. Beirut: Dâr al-âfâq al-jadîda, 1985.
———. *On the Interpretation of Dreams* [Arabic text]. See M. A. M. Khan, ed., "A Unique Treatise on the Interpretation of Dreams," in Iran Society, Calcutta, *Avicenna*, 255–307.
———. *al-Qadar*. In Mehren, *Traités mystiques*, 4:25, French paraphrase, 4:1–12.
———. *al-Qânûn fi ṭ-ṭibb*. 2 vols. Beirut: Dâr ṣâdir, n.d. Partial trans. in Gruner, *A Treatise on the Canon of Medicine of Avicenna*.
———. *al-Qaṣîda al-ʿainiyya*. See Kholeif, *Avicenna on Psychology*; and Carra de Vaux, "La kaçîdah d'Avicenne sur l'âme."
———. *Remarks and Admonitions, Part One: Logic*. Trans. Shams C. Inati. Toronto: Pontifical Institute of Mediaeval Studies, 1984.
———. *Risâlat baʿḍ al-âfâḍil ilâ madînat as-salâm fî maqûlât ash-Shaikh ar-Raʾîs*. In Yarshater, *Panj Risâla*, 73–90. [Attributed to Avicenna.]
———. *Risâla ilâ Abî ʿUbaid al-Jûzjânî fî amr an-nafs*. In Ülken, ed., *Ibn Sina Risâleleri 2*, 70–72.
———. *Risâla-yi nafs*. Ed. Mûsâ ʿAmîd. Intishârât-i anjuman-i âthâr-milli 14. Tehran: n.p., 1952. [Persian trans. of *Aḥwâl an-nafs*.]
———. *Sharḥ kitâb* Athûlûjiyâ *al-mansûb ilâ Arisṭû*. In Badawî, *Aflûṭîn ʿind al-ʿArab*, 35–74. Trans. in Vajda, "Les notes d'Avicenne sur la 'Théologie d'Aristote.'"
———. *ash-Shifâʾ: al-Ilâhiyyât (1) (La Métaphysique)*. Ed. G. C. Anawati and S. Zayed. Intro. Ibrahim Madkour. Cairo: Organisation Générale des Imprimeries Gouvernementales, 1960.
———. *ash-Shifâʾ: al-Ilâhiyyât (2) (La Métaphysique)*. Ed. M. Y. Moussa, S. Dunya,

and S. Zayed. Intro. Ibrahim Madkour. Cairo: Organisation Générale des Imprimeries Gouvernementales, 1960.

———. *ash-Shifâ': al-Manṭiq (La Logique).* [Fann] 1: *al-Madkhal (L'Isagoge).* Ed. Ibrahim Madkour, M. el-Khodeiri, G. Anawati, and F. al-Ahwânî. Publication du Ministre de l'Instruction Publique (Culture Générale) à l'Occasion du Millénaire d'Avicenne. Cairo: Imprimerie Nationale, 1952.

———. *ash-Shifâ': al-Manṭiq.* [Fann] 9: *ash-Shi'r.* Ed. 'Abd ar-Raḥmân Badawî. Comité pour la Commémoration de millénaire d'Avicenne. Cairo: Dâr al-miṣriyya li-t-ta'lîf wa-t-tarjama, 1966. Trans. in Ismalil M. Dahiyat, *Avicenna's Commentary on the* Poetics *of Aristotle.*

———. *ash-Shifâ': aṭ-Ṭabî'ât.* [Fann] 6: *an-Nafs.* Ed. G. C. Anawati and S. Zayed. Preface and revisions Ibrahim Madkour. Cairo: al-Hai'a l-miṣriyya l-'âma li-l-kitâb, 1975. See also Rahman, ed., *Avicenna's* De Anima *(Arabic Text), Being the Psychological Part of* Kitâb al-Shifâ'. London, New York, and Toronto: Oxford University Press, 1959.

———. *ash-Shifâ': aṭ-Ṭabî'iyyât.* [Fann] 2: *as-Samâ' wa-l-'âlam.* [Fann] 3: *al-Kaun wa-l-fasâd.* [Fann] 4: *al-Af'âl wa-l-infi'âlât.* Ed. Maḥmûd Qâsim. Intro. and rev. Ibrahim Madkour. al-Maktaba l-'arabiyya li-t-turâth. Cairo: Dâr al-kâtib al-'arabî li-ṭ-ṭibâ'a wa-n-nashr, 1969.

———. *Tafsîr "al-A'lâ"* [Qur'ân, 87]. In 'Âṣî, *at-Tafsîr al-Qur'ânî,* 96–103.

———. *Tafsîr "Âyat an-nûr"* [Qur'ân, 24.35]. In 'Âṣî, *at-Tafsîr al-Qur'ânî,* 86–88.

———. *Tafsîr "al-Falaq"* [Qur'ân, 113]. In 'Âṣî, *at-Tafsîr al-Qur'ânî,* 116–20. Persian version in Yarshater, ed., *Panj Risâla,* 51–58.

———. *Tafsîr "al-Ikhlâṣ"* [Qur'ân, 112]. In 'Âṣî, *at-Tafsîr al-Qur'ânî,* 106–13.

———. *Tafsîr "an-Nâs"* [Qur'ân, 114]. In 'Âṣî, *at-Tafsîr al-Qur'ânî,* 123–25. Persian version in Yarshater, ed., *Panj Risâla,* 59–63.

———. *Tafsîr sûra-yi tauḥid.* In Yarshater, ed., *Panj Risâla,* 37–50.

———. *Tafsîr "Thumma istawâ ila s-samâ' wa-hiya dukhân"* [Qur'ân, 41.11]. In 'Âṣî, *at-Tafsîr al-Qur'ânî,* 91–93.

———. *aṭ-Ṭair.* In Mehren, *Traités mystiques,* 2:42–48, French paraphrase, 2:25–32; also in 'Âṣî, *at-Tafsîr al-Qur'ânî,* 338–43; and Cheikho, ed., *Risâlat aṭ-ṭair, al-Mashriq* 19 (1901) 882–87. Trans. in Corbin, *Avicenna,* 186–93.

———. *at-Ta'lîqât 'alâ ḥawâshî* Kitâb an-nafs *li-Arisṭû.* In Badawî, ed., *Aflûṭîn 'ind al-'Arab,* 75–116.

———. *Tis' rasâ'il fi l-ḥikma wa-ṭ-ṭabîiyyât, ta'lîf ash-Shaikh ar-Ra'îs Abî 'Alî al-Ḥusain ibn 'Abd Allâh ibn Sînâ.* Istanbul: Maṭba'at al-jawâ'ib, 1881. Repr. Bombay, 1900, and Cairo, several times. All references are to the Istanbul ed.

———. *'Uyûn al-ḥikma.* See Ülken, ed. *Ibn Sina Risâleleri 1.*

———. *al-Wird al-a'ẓam.* In 'Âṣî, *at-Tafsîr al-Qur'ânî,* 320.

Badawî, 'Abd ar-Raḥmân, ed. *Aflûṭîn 'ind al-'Arab.* Dirâsât islâmiyya 20. Cairo: Dâr an-nahḍa l-'arabiyya, 1966.

———. *al-Aflâṭûniyya al-muḥdatha 'ind al-'Arab.* Kuwait: Wakâlat al-maṭbû'ât, 1977.

———. *Arisṭû 'ind al-'Arab.* 2nd ed. Kuwait: Wakâlat al-maṭbû'ât, 1978.

Bakhtin, M. M. *The Dialogic Imagination: Four Essays.* Ed. Michael Holquist.

Trans. Caryl Emerson and Michael Holquist. University of Texas Press Slavic Series 1. Austin: University of Texas Press, 1981.

Bal, Mieke. *Narratology: Introduction to the Theory of Narrative*. Trans. Christine van Boheemen. Toronto, Buffalo, and London: University of Toronto Press, 1985.

Baljon, J. M. S. "The 'Amr of God' in the Koran." *Acta Orientalia* 23, 1–2 (1958) 7–18.

Barney, Stephen A., ed. *Allegories of History, Allegories of Love*. Hamden, Conn.: Archon Books, 1979.

Barricelli, Jean-Pierre, and Joseph Gibaldi, eds. *Interrelations of Literature*. New York: Modern Language Association of America, 1982.

Black, Deborah L. "The 'Imaginative Syllogism' in Arabic Philosophy: A Medieval Contribution to the Philosophical Study of Metaphor." *Medieval Studies* 51 (1989) 242–67.

———. *Logic and Aristotle's* Rhetoric *and* Poetics *in Medieval Arabic Philosophy*. Islamic Philosophy and Theology, Texts and Studies 7. Leiden, New York, Copenhagen, and Cologne: E. J. Brill, 1990.

Bloomfield, Morton, W., ed. *Allegory, Myth, and Symbol*. Harvard English Studies 9. Cambridge, Mass.: Harvard University Press, 1981.

Blumenthal, H. J. "Body and Soul in Philoponus." *The Monist* 69,3 (1986) 370–82.

———. *Plotinus' Psychology: His Doctrines of the Embodied Soul*. The Hague: Martinus Nijhoff, 1971.

Booth, Edward. *Aristotelian Aporetic Ontology in Islamic and Christian Thinkers*. Cambridge Studies in Medieval Life and Thought, Third Series 20. Cambridge, London, and New York: Cambridge University Press, 1983.

Bosworth, C. E. "Dailamîs in Central Iran: The Kâkûyids of Jibîl and Yazd," *Iran* 8 (1970) 73–95. [Repr. in Bosworth, *The Medieval History of Iran, Afghanistan, and Central Asia*. London: Variorum Reprints, 1977, 73–95.]

Böwering, Gerhard. "*Mi'râj*." In *Enclyclopedia of Religion*, 9:552–56.

———. *The Mystical Vision of Existence in Classical Islam: The Qur'ânic Hermeneutics of the Ṣûfî Sahl At-Tustarî (d. 283/896)*. Studien zur Sprache, Geschichte und Kultur des islamischen Orients 9. Berlin and New York: Walter de Gruyter, 1980.

Bréhier, Émile. *The Philosophy of Plotinus*. Trans. J. Thomas. Chicago: University of Chicago Press, 1958.

Brockelmann, Carl. *Geschichte der arabischen Litteratur*. 2nd ed. 2 vols. Leiden: E. J. Brill, 1943–49. *Den Supplementbänden angepasste Auflage*. 3 vols. Leiden: E. J. Brill, 1937–42.

Browne, Edward G. *A Literary History of Persia*. 4 vols. London: T. Fisher Unwin, 1902–24; repr. Cambridge: Cambridge University Press, 1969.

———, trans. *Revised Translation of the Chahâr Maqâla ("Four Discourses") of Niẓâmî-i-'Arûḍî of Samarqand*. E. J. W. Gibb Memorial Series 11. Cambridge: Cambridge University Press; London: Luzac & Co., 1921.

de Bruijn, J. T. P. *Of Piety and Poetry: The Interaction of Religion and Literature in the Life and Works of Ḥakîm Sanâ'î of Ghazna*. De Goeje Fund 25. Leiden: E. J. Brill, 1983.

Bürgel, J. Christoph. *The Feather of Simurgh: The "Licit Magic" of the Arts in Medieval Islam.* New York and London: New York University Press, 1988.
Butterworth, Charles E. "The Study of Arabic Philosophy Today," Appendix (1983–87). In Druart, ed., *Arabic Philosophy and the West.*
Campbell, Joseph. *The Hero with a Thousand Faces.* 2nd ed. Bollingen Series 17, Princeton, N.J.: Princeton University Press, 1968.
Cantarino, Vicente. *Arabic Poetics in the Golden Age: Selection of Texts Accompanied by a Preliminary Study.* Studies in Arabic Literature 4. Leiden: E. J. Brill, 1975.
Caputo, John D. *Radical Hermeneutics: Repetition, Deconstruction and the Hermeneutic Project.* Studies in Phenomenology and Existential Philosophy. Bloomington and Indianapolis: Indiana University Press, 1987.
Carra de Vaux. "La kaçîdah d'Avicenne sur l'âme." *Journal Asiatique* 9th ser. 14 (1899) 157–73.
Cascardi, Anthony J., ed. *Literature and the Question of Philosophy.* Baltimore: Johns Hopkins University Press, 1987.
Cassirer, Ernst. *An Essay on Man: An Introduction to a Philosophy of Human Culture.* New Haven, Conn., and London: Yale University Press, 1944.
———. *Language and Myth.* Trans. Suzanne K. Langer. New York: Dover Publications, 1946.
———. *The Philosophy of Symbolic Forms.* Trans. Ralph Manheim. 3 vols. New Haven, Conn.: Yale University Press, 1953–57.
Chaix-Ruy, Jules. "Du Pythagorisme d'Avicenne au soufisme d'al-Ghazâlî." *Revue de la Méditerranée* 19,4–5 (1959) 289–327.
———. "L'homme selon Avicenne." *L'homme et son destin d'après les penseurs du Moyen Âge. Actes du premier congrès international de philosophie médiévale.* Louvain: Éditions Naulwelaerts; Paris: Béatrice-Naulwelaerts, 1958. Pp. 243–55.
Cheikho, Louis, ed. "Risâlat aṭ-ṭair li-bn Sînâ." *al-Mashriq* 19 (1901) 882–87.
———. "Risâlat aṭ-ṭair li-l-Ghazâlî." *al-Mashriq* 20 (1901) 918–24.
Clifford, Gay. *The Transformations of Allegory.* London and Boston: Routledge & Kegan Paul, 1974.
Conger, George P. *Theories of Macrocosms and Microcosms in the History of Philosophy.* New York: Columbia University Press, 1922.
Corbin, Henry. *Avicenna and the Visionary Recital.* Trans. Willard R. Trask. Bollingen Series 66. New York: Pantheon Books, 1960. Repr. Princeton, N.J.: Princeton University Press, 1988
———. *Avicenne et le récit visionnaire.* 3 vols. Tehran and Paris: Institut Franco-Iranien, A. Maisonneuve, 1952–54.
———. *Creative Imagination in the Ṣufism of Ibn 'Arabî.* Trans. Ralph Manheim. Bollingen Series 91. Princeton, N.J.: Princeton University Press, 1969.
———. "La initiation Ismaélienne, ou l'ésotérisme et le verbe." *Eranos Jahrbuch* 39 (1970) 41–142.
———. "Un roman initiatique Ismaélien." *Cahiers de Civilization Médiévale* 15 (1972) 1–25, 121–42.
———. *Temple and Contemplation.* Islamic Texts and Contexts. London and New York: KPI and Islamic Publications, 1986.
———, ed. See as-Suhrawardî. *Opera Metaphysica et Mystica* II.

Cornford, F. M. *Plato's Cosmology: The Timaeus of Plato Translated with a Running Commentary*. London: Routledge & Kegan Paul, 1937.

Coulter, James A. *The Literary Microcosm: Theories of Interpretation of Late Neoplatonists*. Columbia Studies in the Classsical Tradition 2. Leiden: E. J. Brill, 1976.

Culler, Jonathan. *The Pursuit of Signs: Literature, Semiotics, Deconstruction*. Ithaca, N.Y.: Cornell University Press, 1981.

Daftary, Farhad. *The Ismâ'îlîs: Their History and Doctrines*. Cambridge, New York and Port Chester: Cambridge University Press, 1990.

Dahiyat, Ismail M. *Avicenna's Commentary on the* Poetics *of Aristotle: A Critical Study with an Annotated Translation of the Text*. Leiden: E. J. Brill, 1974.

Dante Alighieri. *Dantis Alagherii Epistolae: The Letters of Dante, Emended Text*. Intro. and trans. Paget Toynbee. Oxford: Clarendon Press, 1966.

Davidson, Herbert A. "Alfarabi and Avicenna on the Active Intellect." *Viator: Medieval and Renaissance Studies* 3 (1972) 109–78.

Dodds, E. R. *The Greeks and the Irrational*. Berkeley and Los Angeles: University of California Press, 1951.

Dronke, Peter. *Fabula: Explorations into the Uses of Myth in Medieval Platonism*. Mittellateinische Studien und Texte 9. Leiden and Cologne: E. J. Brill, 1974.

Druart, Thérèse-Anne. "Al-Farabi and Emanationism." In John F. Wippel, ed. *Studies in Medieval Philosophy*, 23–43.

———, ed. *Arabic Philosophy and the West: Continuity and Interaction*. Washington: Center for Contemporary Arab Studies, Georgetown University, 1988.

Dunn, Ross E. *The Adventures of Ibn Batuta: A Muslim Traveler of the 14th Century*. Berkeley and Los Angeles: University of California Press, 1986.

Dunyâ, Sulaimân, ed. *Ibn Sînâ wa-l-ba'th*. Cairo: Dâr al-fikr al-'arabî, 1949.

———. *al-Ishârât wa-t-tanbîhât*. See Avicenna, *al-Ishârât wa-t-tanbîhât*.

Eco, Umberto. *The Aesthetics of Thomas Aquinas*. Trans. Hugh Bredin. Cambridge, Mass.: Harvard University Press, 1988.

———. *Semiotics and the Philosophy of Language*. Bloomington: Indiana University Press, 1984.

Edelstein, Ludwig. "The Function of the Myth in Plato's Philosophy." *Journal of the History of Ideas* 10,4:463–81.

Ergin, Osman. *Ibni Sina Bibliografyası*. Istanbul Üniversitesi Tip Fakültesi Yayınlarından 20. Istanbul: Osman Yalçın Matbaası, 1956.

Ethé, Herman. "Avicenna als persischer Lyriker." *Nachrichten von der Königliche Gesellschaft der Wissenschaften und der G. A. Universität zu Göttingen* 21 (1875) 555–67.

Fackenheim, Emil L. "The Possibility of the Universe in al-Farabi, Ibn Sina, and Maimonides," in Hyman, ed., *Essays*, 303–34.

———, trans. "A Treatise on Love by Ibn Sînâ." *Medieval Studies* 7 (1945) 211–28.

Fakhry, Majid. *A History of Islamic Philosophy*. 2nd ed. Studies in Oriental Culture 5. New York: Columbia University Press, 1983.

———. "Al-Suhrawardî's Critique of the Muslim Peripatetics (*al-Mashâ'ûn*)." In Morewedge, ed., *Philosophies of Existence*, 279–84.

al-Fârâbî, Abû Naṣr Muḥammad ibn Muḥammad. *Mabâdî ârâ' ahl al-madîna al-fâḍila*. See Walzer, *al-Fârâbî*.

———. *Qawânîn ṣinâ'at ash-sh'ir*. See Arberry, "Fârâbî's Canons."

———. *al-Siyâsa l-Madaniyya. Al-Fârâbî's The Political Regime (al-Siyâsa al-Madaniyya, also known as the Treatise on the Principles of Being)*. Ed. Fauzi M. Najjar. Beirut: Imprimerie Catholique, 1964. Partial trans. by Najjar in Lerner and Mahdi, eds., *Medieval Political Philosophy*, 31–57.

———. *Taḥṣîl as-sa'âda*. Ed. Ja'far al-Yâsîn. Beirut: Dâr al-Andalus, 1983. Trans. in Mahdi, *Alfarabi's Philosophy*, 13–50.

Fenton, Paul B. "The Arabic and Hebrew Versions of the *Theology of Aristotle*." In Kraye, Ryan, et al., eds., *Pseudo-Aristotle*, 241–64.

Fletcher, Angus. *Allegory: The Theory of a Symbolic Mode*. Ithaca, N.Y.: Cornell University Press, 1964.

Foucault, Michel. *The Archeology of Knowledge and the Discourse on Language*. Trans. A. M. Sheridan Smith. Harper Torchbooks. New York, Hagerstown, San Francisco, and London: Harper & Row, 1972.

———. *The Order of Things: An Archeology of the Human Sciences*. World of Man. New York: Vintage Books, 1973.

Frye, Northrop. "Allegory." In Alex Preminger, ed., *Princeton Encyclopedia of Poetry and Poetics*, Princeton, N.J.: Princeton University Press, 1974, 12–15.

———. *Anatomy of Criticism: Four Essays*. New York: Atheneum, 1970.

Frye, Richard N., ed. *The Cambridge History of Iran*. Vol 4.: *From the Arab Invasion to the Saljuqs*. Cambridge: Cambridge University Press, 1975.

Galston, Miriam. *Politics and Excellence: The Political Philosophy of Alfarabi*. Princeton, N.J.: Princeton University Press, 1990.

Gardet, Louis. "Avicenne commentateur de Plotin." In Gardet, *Études de philosophie et de mystique comparées*, Bibliothèque d'Histoire de la Philosophie, Paris: Librairie Philosophique J. Vrin, 1972, 135–46.

———. *La connaissance mystique chez Ibn Sînâ, et ses présupposés philosophiques*. Mémorial Avicenne 2. Cairo: Publications de l'Institut Français d'Archéologie Orientale du Caire, 1952.

———. *La pensée religieuse d'Avicenne (Ibn Sînâ)*. Études de philosophie médiévale. Paris: Librairie Philosophique J. Vrin, 1951.

Gätje, Helmut. "Philosophische Traumlehren im Islam." *ZDMG* 109 (1959) 258–85.

———. *The Qur'ân and its Exegesis: Selected Texts with Classical and Modern Muslim Interpretations*. Trans. and ed. Alford T. Welch. The Islamic World Series. Berkeley and Los Angeles: University of California Press, 1976.

———. *Studien zu Überlieferung der Aristotelischen Psychologie im Islam*. Annales Universitatis Saraviensis 2. Heidelberg: Carl Winter Universitätsverlag, 1971.

Genette, Gérard. *Narrative Discourse: An Essay in Method*. Trans. J. E. Lewin. Ithaca, N.Y.: Cornell University Press, 1980.

al-Ghazâlî, Abû Ḥâmid Muḥammad ibn Muḥammad. *al-Ajwiba l-Ghazâliyya fî l-masâ'il al-ukhrawiyya (al-Madnûn aṣ-ṣaghîr)*. In Abu l-'Alâ', ed. *al-Quṣûr al-'awâlî min rasâ'il al-Imâm al-Ghazâlî*, 4 vols., Cairo: Maktabat al-Jundî [al-Gindî], 1970, 2 : 156–86.

———. *Iḥyâ' 'ulûm ad-dîn*. 5 vols. Beirut: Dâr al-mar'rifa, n.d.

———. *Minhâj al-ʿârifîn*. In Abu l-ʿAlâ', ed., *al-Quṣûr al-ʿawâlî*, 1:81–96.
———. *Miʿrâj as-sâlikîn*. In Abu l-ʿAlâ', ed. *al-Quṣûr al-ʿawâlî*, 3:94–177.
———. *Mishkât al-anwâr*. Ed. Abu l-ʿAlâ ʿAfîfî. Cairo: Dâr al-qaumiyya li-ṭibâʿa wa-n-nashr, 1963. Also in *al-Quṣûr al-ʿawâlî*, 2:4–49.
———. *ar-Risâla l-laduniyya*. In Abu l-ʿAlâ', ed., *al-Quṣûr al-ʿawâlî*, 1:97–122. [Attributed to al-Ghazâlî.]
———. *Risâlat aṭ-ṭair*. In Abu l-ʿAlâ', ed., *al-Quṣûr al-ʿawâlî*, 2:50–54; and Cheikho, ed., *al-Mashriq* 20 (1901) 918–24.
———. *Sirr al-ʿâlamîn, wa-maʿahu d-Durra al-fâkhira fî kashf ʿulûm al-âkhira*. Ed. Muḥammad Muṣṭafâ Abu l-ʿAlâ. Cairo: Maktabat al-Jundî [al-Gindî], n.d.
———. *Tahâfut al-falâsifa*. Eng. trans. S. A. Kamali, *Al-Ghazali's Tahafut al-Falasifah [Incoherence of the Philosophers]*. Pakistan Philosophical Congress Publication 3. Lahore: The Pakistan Philosophical Congress, 1958.
Gibb, E. J. W. *A History of Ottoman Poetry*. 6 vols. London: Luzac & Company, 1900–1909; repr. 1958–63.
Gilson, Étienne. *History of Christian Philosophy in the Middle Ages*. New York: Random House, 1955.
Gohlman, William E. *The Life of Ibn Sînâ: A Critical Edition and Annotated Translation*. Studies in Islamic Philosophy and Science. Albany: State University of New York Press, 1974.
Goichon, Amélie-Marie. *Avicenne, livre des définitions: Édité, traduit, et annoté*. Mémorial Avicenne 6. Cairo: Publications de'Institut Français d'Archéologie Orientale du Caire, 1963. Pp. 1–45.
———. *La distinction de l'essence et de l'existence d'après Ibn Sînâ (Avicenne)*. Paris: Desclée de Brouwer, 1937.
———. *Lexique de la langue philosophique d'Ibn Sînâ (Avicenne)*. Paris: Desclée de Brouwer, 1938.
———. *The Philosophy of Avicenna and Its Influence on Medieval Europe* Trans. M. S. Khan. Dehli, Patna, and Varanasi: Motilal Banarsidass, 1969.
———. *Le récit de Ḥayy ibn Yaqẓân commenté par des textes d'Avicenne*. Paris: Desclée de Brouwer, 1959.
———. "Selon Avicenne, l'âme humaine est-elle créatrice de son corps?" *L'homme et son destin d'après les penseurs du Moyen Âge. Actes du premier congres international de philosophie médiévale*. Louvain: Editions Naulwelaerts; Paris: Béatrice-Naulwelaerts, 1958.
———, trans. *Ibn Sînâ: Livre des directives et remarques (Kitâb al-Ishârât wa-l-Tanbîhât)*. Beirut: Commission internationale pour la Traduction des chefs d'oeuvre, 1951.
Goldfeld, Y. "The Development of Theory on Qur'ânic Exegesis in Islamic Scholarship." *Studia Islamica* 67 (1988) 5–27.
Goldziher, Ignaz. *Die Richtungen der islamischen Koranauslegung*. De Goeje-Stiftung 6. Leiden: E. J. Brill, 1970. [Repr. of the 1920 ed.]
Goodman, Lenn Evan. *Ibn Ṭufayl's Ḥayy ibn Yaqẓân: A Philosophical Tale*. New York: Twayne Publishers, 1972; 2nd ed. Los Angeles: Gee Tee Bee Press, 1983.
Greenblatt, Stephen J., ed. *Allegory and Representation*. Baltimore and London: Johns Hopkins University Press, 1981.

Grunebaum, G. E. von, ed. *Logic in Classical Islamic Culture*. First Giorgio Levi Della Vida Biennial Conference. Wiesbaden: Otto Harrassowitz, 1970.

Gruner, Cameron O. *A Treatise on the Canon of Medicine of Avicenna, Incorporating a Translation of the First Book*. London: Luzac & Co., 1930.

Gutas, Dimitri. *Avicenna and the Aristotelian Tradition: Introduction to Reading Avicenna's Philosophical Works*. Islamic Philosophy and Theology, Texts and Studies 4. Leiden, New York, Copenhagen, and Cologne: E. J. Brill, 1988.

———, Muhsin Mahdi, et al. "Avicenna." *Encyclopedia Iranica*, 3,1 : 66–111.

———. "Avicenna's *Madhhab*, with an Appendix on the Question of His Date of Birth." *Quaderni di Studi Arabi* 5–6 (1987–88) 323–36.

Ḥâjjî Khalîfa [Kâtib Chelebî]. *Kashf aẓ-ẓunûn*. Eds. Sh. Yaltkaya and R. Bilge. 2nd ed. 2 vols. Istanbul: Devlet Kitapları, 1971.

al-Ḥakîm, Su'âd. *Al-Mu'jam aṣ-ṣûfî: al-Ḥikma fî ḥudûd al-kalima*. Beirut: Dandara, 1981.

Halperin, David J. *The Faces of the Chariot: Early Jewish Responses to Ezekiel's Vision*. Tübingen: J. C. B. Mohr (Paul Siebeck), 1988.

Hartman, Geoffrey H. "Imagination." In Arthur A. Cohen and Paul Mendes-Flohr, eds., *Contemporary Jewish Religious Thought: Original Essays on Critical Concepts, Movements, and Beliefs*, New York: Charles Schribner's Sons, 1987, 451–72.

——— and Sanford Budick, eds. *Midrash and Literature*. New Haven, Conn.: Yale University Press, 1986.

Heath, Peter. "Creative Hermeneutics: An Analysis of Three Islamic Approaches." *Arabica* 36 (1989) 173–210.

———. "Disorientation and Reorientation in Ibn Sînâ's *Epistle of the Bird*." In Mazzoui and Moreen, eds., *Intellectual Studies on Islam*, 163–83.

———. "Romance as Genre in *The Thousand and One Nights*." Two parts. *JAL* 18 (1987) 1–21; 19 (1988) 1–16.

Heinrichs, Wolfhart. "Die antike Verknüpfung von phantasia und Dichtung bei den Arabern." *ZDMG* 128 (1978) 252–98.

———. "Rose versus Narcissus: Observations on an Arabic Literary Debate." In G. J. Reinink and H. L. J. Vanstiphout, eds., *Dispute Poems and Dialogues in the Ancient and Medieval Near East*, Orientalia Lovaniensia 42, Leuven: Departement Oriëntalistiek; Peeters, 1991.

Heninger, S. K., Jr. *Touches of Sweet Harmony: Pythagorean Cosmology and Renaissance Poetics*. San Marino, Cal.: The Hungtington Library, 1974.

Henry, Paul, and Hans-Rudolf Schwyzer, eds. *Plotini Opera*. 2 vols. Paris: Desclée de Brouwer; Brussels: L'Édition Universalle, 1959.

Hernadi, Paul, ed. *The Rhetoric of Interpretation and the Interpretation of Rhetoric*. Durham, N.C. and London: Duke University Press, 1989.

Hirsch, E. D., Jr. *The Aims of Interpretation*. Chicago and London: University of Chicago Press, 1976.

———. *Validity in Interpretation*. New Haven, Conn. and London: Yale University Press, 1967.

Hodgson, G. S. "The Unity of Late Islamic History." *Journal of World History* 5 (1960) 878–914.

———. *The Venture of Islam: Conscience and History in a World Civilization.* 3 vols. Vol. 1: *The Classical Age of Islam*; vol. 2: *The Expansion of Islam in the Middle Periods*; vol. 3: *The Gunpowder Empires and Modern Times*. Chicago and London: University of Chicago Press, 1974.

Holt, P. M.; Ann K. S. Lambton; and Bernard Lewis, eds. *The Cambridge History of Islam.* 2 vols. Cambridge: Cambridge University Press, 1970.

Honig, Edwin. *Dark Conceit: The Making of Allegory*. Evanston, Ill.: Northwestern University Press, 1959.

Hough, Graham. *A Preface to the Faerie Queen*. New York: W. W. Norton, 1962.

Hourani, George F. *Averroes on the Harmony of Religion and Philosophy*. E. J. W. Gibb Memorial Series and International Commission for the Translation of Great Works. London: Luzac & Co., 1961.

———. "Ibn Sînâ's 'Essay on the Secret of Destiny.'" *BSOAS* 29 (1966) 25–48.

———. "Ibn Sînâ on Necessary and Possible Existence." *The Philosophical Forum* 4,1 (1972) 74–86.

al-Ḥulw, 'Abduh. *Ibn Sînâ: Failasûf an-nafs al-bashariyya*. Baghdad: Bait al-ḥikma, 1967.

Hyman, Arthur. "Aristotle's 'First Matter' and Avicenna's and Averroes' 'Corporeal Form.'" In Hyman, ed., *Essays*, 335–56.

———, ed. *Essays in Medieval Jewish and Islamic Philosophy: Studies from the Publications of the American Academy for Jewish Research*. New York: KTAV Publishing House, 1977.

Ibn 'Arabî, Muḥyi d-Dîn. *al-Futûḥât al-Makkiyya*. 4 vols. Beirut: Dâr ṣâdir, n.d.

———. *Kitâb al-isrâ ilâ maqâm al-asrâ*. In *Risâ'il Ibn 'Arabî*, Hyderabad: Dâ'irat al-ma'ârif al-'uthmâniyya, 1948.

Ibn al-Athîr, 'Izz ad-Dîn Abû Ḥasan 'Alî. *al-Kâmil fi t-ta'rîkh*. 9 vols. Beirut: Dâr al-fikr, 1978.

Ibn Hishâm, Abû Muḥammad 'Abd al-Malik. *as-Sîra n-nabawiyya*. Ed. Tâhâ 'Abd ar-Ra'ûf Sa'd. 4 vols. Beirut: Dâr al-Jîl, n.d. Trans. in Ibn Isḥâq, *The Life of Muhammad*, trans. A. Guillaume, Oxford: Oxford University Press, 1955.

Ibn Isḥâq. See Ibn Hishâm.

Ibn Qayyim al-Jauziyya, Shams ad-Dîn Abû 'Abd Allâh. *ar-Rûḥ: fi l-kalâm 'alâ arwâḥ al-amwât wa l-aḥyâ' bi-d-dalâ'il min al-kitâb wa-sunna wa-l-âthâr wa-aqwâl al-'ulamâ'*. Ed. Muḥammad Iskandar Yildâ (?). Beirut: Dâr al-kutub al-'ilmiyya, 1982.

Ibn Rushd, Abu l-Walîd Muḥammad ibn Aḥmad (Averroes). *Averroes on Plato's "Republic"*, see Lerner, Ralph.

———. *Fasl al-maqâl fî mâ bain al-ḥikma wa-sh-sharî'a min al-ittiṣâl*. Ed. Muḥammad 'Imara. Dhakhâ'ir al-'Arab 47. Cairo: Dâr al-ma'ârif, 1972. Trans in Hourani, *Averroes on the Harmony of Religion and Philosophy*, 44–71.

———. *Tahâfut at-tahâfut*. Ed. Sulaimân Dunyâ. 2 vols. Dhakhâ'ir al-'Arab 37. Cairo: Dâr al-ma'ârif, 1971.

Ibn Sînâ. See Avicenna.

Ibn Ṭufail, *Risâlat Ḥayy ibn Yaqẓân*. In Amîn, ed., *Ḥayy ibn Yaqẓân*; trans. in Goodman, *Ibn Ṭufayl's Ḥayy ibn Yaqẓân: A Philosophical Tale*.

Ihde, Don. *Hermeneutic Phenomenology: The Philosophy of Paul Ricoeur*. Northwestern University Studies in Phenomenology and Existential Philosophy. Evanston, Ill.: Northwestern University Press, 1971.

Inati, Shams, trans. *Remarks and Admonitions*. See Avicenna, *Remarks and Admonitions*.

Iran Society, Calcutta. *Avicenna Commemoration Volume*. Calcutta: Iran Society, 1956.

'Iraqî, Muḥammad 'Âṭif. *al-Falsafa ṭ-ṭabî'iyya 'ind Ibn Sînâ*. Cairo: Dâr al-ma'ârif, 1971.

Isfarâyinî, Nûruddîn Abdurrahmân-i. *Le révélateur des mystères* (*Kâshif al-Asrâr*). Intro., ed., and trans. Hermann Landolt. Islam Spirituel. Paris: Verdier, 1986.

Ivanow, W. W. *Studies in Early Persian Ismailism*. 2nd rev. ed. Ismaili Society Series A, no. 6. Bombay: Ismaili Society, 1955.

Izutsu, Toshihiko. "*Ishrâqîyah*." *Encyclopedia of Religion*, 7:296–98.

Jabr, Rajâ' 'Abd al-Mun'im. *Riḥlat ar-rûḥ bain Ibn Sînâ wa-Sanâ'î wa-Dantî*. Munîra: Maktabat ash-shabâb, n.d.

Jaeger, Werner. *Paideia: The Ideals of Greek Culture*. Trans. Gilbert Highet. 3 vols. New York and Oxford: Oxford University Press, 1943–45.

Jakobson, Roman. *Language in Literature*. Cambridge, Mass.: Belknap Press of Harvard University Press, 1987.

Janowitz, Naomi. *The Poetics of Ascent: Theories of Language in a Rabbinic Ascent Text*. Albany: State University of New York Press, 1989.

Jonas, Hans. *The Gnostic Religion: The Message of the Alien God and the Beginnings of Christianity*. 2nd rev. ed. Boston, Mass.: Beacon Press, 1963.

Juhl, P. D. *Interpretation: An Essay in the Philosophy of Literary Criticism*. Princeton, N.J.: Princeton University Press, 1980.

Kamali, Sabih Ahmad. See al-Ghazâlî, *Tahâfut al-falâsifa*. al-Kâshî, Yaḥyâ ibn Aḥmad. *Aperçu sur la biographe d'Avicenne*. Ed. A. F. al-Ahwany. Mémorial Avicenne 1. Cairo: Publications de l'Institut Français d'Archéologie Orientale du Caire, 1952.

Kennedy, Hugh. *The Prophet and the Age of the Caliphates: The Islamic Near East from the Sixth to the Eleventh Century*. London and New York: Longman, 1986.

Kermode, Frank. *The Genesis of Secrecy: On the Interpretation of Narrative*. The Charles Eliot Norton Lectures 1977–1978. Cambridge, Mass.: Harvard University Press, 1979.

Kholeif, Fathalla. *Avicenna on Psychology: A Study of His Poem on the Soul (al-Qaṣîda al-'ainiyyah)*. Beirut: Beirut Arab University, 1974.

———. *A Study on Fakhr ad-Dîn al-Râzî and His Controversies in Transoxiana*. Pensée arabe et musulmane 31. Beirut: Dar el-Mashreq Éditeurs, 1966.

Kirmânî, Shams ad-Dîn Muḥammad ibn Îl-ṭughân Bardsîrî. *Miṣbâḥ al-arvâḥ*. Ed. Badî' az-Zamân Furûzânfar. Intishârât-i Dânishgâh-i Tihrân 1284. Tehran: Dânishgâh-i Tihran, 1930.

The Koran Interpreted. Trans. A. J. Arberry. 2 vols. New York: Macmillan, 1955.

Kraemer, Joel L. *Humanism in the Renaissance of Islam: The Cultural Revival During the Bûyid Age*. Studies in Islamic Culture and History Series 7. Leiden: E. J. Brill, 1986.

———. *Philosophy in the Renaissance of Islam: Abû Sulaymân al-Sijistânî and His Circle*. Studies in Islamic Culture and History Series 8. Leiden: E. J. Brill, 1986.

Kraye, Jill; W. F. Ryan; and C. B. Schmitt, eds. *Pseudo-Aristotle in the Middle Ages: The* Theology *and Other Texts*. London: Warburg Institute, University of London, 1986.

Krieger, Murray. "'A Waking Dream': The Symbolic Alternative to Allegory." In Bloomfield, ed., *Allegory, Myth, and Symbol*, 1–22.

———. *Theory of Criticism: A Tradition and Its System*. Baltimore, Md., and London: Johns Hopkins University Press, 1976.

Lanham, Richard A. *A Handlist of Rhetorical Terms: A Guide for Students of English Literature*. Berkeley and Los Angeles: University of California Press, 1969.

Landolt, Hermann. "Two Types of Mystical Thought in Muslim Iran: An Essay on Suhrawardî Shaykh al-Ishrâq and 'Ainulquḍât al-Hamadânî." *Muslim World* 68 (1978) 187–204.

———, trans. See Isfarâyinî, *Le révélateur des mystères*.

Leaman, Oliver. *An Introduction to Medieval Islamic Philosophy*. Cambridge, London, and New York: Cambridge University Press, 1985.

Lerner, Ralph, trans. *Averroes on Plato's "Republic."* Agora Paperback Editions. Ithaca, N.Y. and London: Cornell University Press, 1974.

Lerner, Ralph and Muhsin Mahdi, eds. *Medieval Political Philosophy: A Sourcebook*. Agora Paperback Editions. Ithaca, N.Y.: Cornell University Press, 1963.

Lewis, C. S. *The Allegory of Love*. London, Oxford, and New York: Oxford University Press, 1936.

Lewis, Geoffrey, trans. *Plotiniana Arabica*. In vol. 2 of Paul Henry and Hans-Rudolf Schwyzer, eds., *Plotini Opera*, 2 vols., Paris: Desclée de Brouwer; Brussels: L'Édition Universalle, 1959

Le livre du millénaire d'Avicenne (Jashnâma-yi Ibn Sînâ). 4 vols. Tehran: Imprimerie de l'Université de Tehran, 1956.

al-Ma'arrî, Abû 'Alâ'. *Risâlat al-Ghufrân*. Beirut: Dâr ṣâdir, 1964.

Macdonald, Duncan B. "The Development of the Idea of Spirit in Islam." *Acta Orientalia* (1931) 307–51. Repr. in *Muslim World* 22 (1932) 25–42, 153–68.

Madkour, Ibrahim. *Fi l-falsafa l-islâmiyya: manhaj wa-taṭbîqihi*. Maktabat ad-dirâsa l-falsafiyya. 2nd rev. ed. Cairo: Dâr al-ma'ârif, 1968.

Mahdavî, Yaḥyâ. *Bibliographie d'Ibn Sina*. Tehran: Dânishgâh-i Tihran, 1954.

Mahdi, Muhsin S. "Alfarabi," in Leo Strauss and Joseph Copley, eds., *History of Political Philosophy*, Chicago: Rand McNally, 1963.

———. "Alfarabi on Religion and Philosophy." *Philosophical Forum* 4,1 (1972) 5–25.

———, trans., with intro. *Alfarabi's Philosophy of Plato and Aristotle*. Agora Paperback Editions. Ithaca, N.Y.: Cornell University Press, 1962.

———. "Language and Logic in Classical Islam." In G. E. von Grunebaum, ed., *Logic in Classical Islamic Culture*, First Giorgio Levi Della Vida Biennieal Conference, Wiesbaden: Otto Harrassowitz, 1970, 51–83.

———, ed. See Lerner, ed., *Medieval Political Philosophy*.

Mahdi, Muhsin S., Dimitri Gutas, et al. "Avicenna." *Encyclopedia Iranica*. Ed. Ehsan Yarshater. London and New York: Routledge & Kegan Paul, 1982-, 3:66–110.

Maḥmûd, ʿAbd al-Ḥalîm. *at-Taṣawwuf ʿind Ibn Sînâ: Dirâsa li-nuṣûṣ min* al-Ishârât. Cairo: Maktabat al-Angilû al-miṣriyya, n.d.

Maimonides, Moses. *The Guide for the Perplexed*. 2 vols. Trans. and intro. Shlomo Pines. Intro. essay Leo Strauss. Chicago and London: University of Chicago Press, 1963.

Margoliouth, D. S. "The Discussion between Abû Bishr Mattâ and Abû Saʿîd al-Sîrâfî." *Journal of the Royal Asiatic Society* (1905) 79–129.

Marmura, Michael E. "Avicenna and the Problem of the Infinite Number of Souls." *Medieval Studies* 22 (1960) 232–39.

———. "Avicenna's 'Flying Man' in Context." *The Monist* 69,3 (1986) 383–95.

——— , trans. "Avicenna On the Proof of Prophecy." In Lerner and Mahdi, eds., *Medieval Political Philosophy*, 113–21.

———. "Avicenna's Psychological Proof of Prophecy." *Journal of Near Eastern Studies* 22 (1963) 49–56.

———. "Some Aspects of Avicenna's Theory of God's Knowledge of Particulars." *JAOS* 82 (1962) 299–312.

———, ed. *Fî ithbât an-nubuwwât*. See Avicenna, *Fî ithbât an-nubuwwât*.

———. *Islamic Theology and Philosophy: Studies in Honor of George F. Hourani*. Albany: State University of New York Press, 1984.

Marshall, Donald G., ed. *Literature as Philosophy, Philosophy as Literature*. Iowa City: University of Iowa Press, 1987.

Massignon, Louis. *Essai sur les origines du lexique technique de la mystique musulmane*. 2nd ed. Paris: J. Vrin, 1954.

———. *The Passion of al-Ḥallâj: Mystic and Martyr of Islam*. Trans. H. Mason. 4 vols. Bollingen Series 98. Princeton, N.J.: Princeton University Press, 1982.

———. "La philosophie orientale d'Ibn Sînâ et son alphabet philosophique." Mémorial Avicenne 4: Miscellanea. Cairo: Publications de L'Institut Français d'Archéologie Orientale du Caire, 1954.

Mazzeo, Joseph Anthony. *Varieties of Interpretation*. Notre Dame and London: University of Notre Dame Press, 1978.

Mazzoui, Michel M., and Vera B. Moreen, eds. *Intellectual Studies on Islam: Essays Written in Honor of Martin B. Dickson*. Salt Lake City: University of Utah Press, 1990.

McCarthy, Richard J. *Freedom and Fulfillment: An Annotated Translation of Al-Ghazâlî's* al-Munqidh min al-Ḍalâl *and Other Relevant Works of al-Ghazâlî*. Library of Classical Arabic Literature 4. Boston: Twayne Publishers, 1980.

Megill, Allan. *Prophets of Extremity: Nietzsche, Heidegger, Foucault, Derrida*. Berkeley and Los Angeles: University of California Press, 1987.

Mehren, A. F. *Traités mystiques d'Abou ʿAli Hosain b. ʿAbdallah b. Sînâ ou d'Avicenne*. 4 fasc. Leiden: E. J. Brill, 1889–99.

Meisami, Julie Scott. *Medieval Persian Court Poetry*. Princeton, N.J.: Princeton University Press, 1987.

Merlan, Phillip. "Greek Philosophy from Plato to Plotinus." In Armstrong, ed., *The Cambridge History of Later Greek and Early Medieval Philosophy*, 14–132.

———. *Monopsychism, Mysticism, Metaconsciousness: Problems of the Soul in the Neoaristotelian and Neoplatonic Tradition*. International Archives of the History of Ideas 2. The Hague: Martinus Nijhoff, 1969.

Meyerhoff, Max, and J. Schacht, eds. and trans. *The Theologus Autodidactus of Ibn al-Nafîs*. Oxford: Clarendon Press, 1968.

Michot, Jean. "Avicenne et la destinée humaine: À propos de la résurrection des corps." *Revue philosophique de Louvain* 79 (1981) 453–83.

———. "Avicenne et le *Kitâb al-Madmûn* d'al-Ghazâlî." *Bulletin de Philosophie Médiévale* 18 (1976) 51–59.

———. "Avicenna's 'Letter on the Disappearance of the Vain Intelligible Forms after Death.'" *Bulletin de Philosophie Médiévale* 27 (1985) 94–103.

———. *La destinée de l'homme selon Avicenne: Le retour à Dieu (ma'âd) et l'imagination*. Louvain: Peeters, 1987.

———. "L'épître sur la connaissance de l'âme rationelle et de ses états, attribuée à Avicenne." *Revue Philosophique de Louvain* 82 (1984) 479–99. Trans. of Avicenna, *Fî ma'rifat an-nafs an-nâṭiqa wa-aḥwâlihâ*.

———. "L'épître sur la disposition des formes intelligibles vaines après la mort d'Avicenne: Édition critique, traduction et index." *Bulletin de Philosophie Médiévale* 29 (1987) 152–70. See also Avicenna, *Fi n-nafs*.

———. "L'épitre sur la genèse et le retour attribuée à Avicenne: Présentation et essai de traduction critique." *Bulletin de Philosophie Médiévale* 26 (1984) 104–18. See also Avicenna, *al-Mabda' wa-l-ma'âd*.

———. "Paroles d'Avicenne sur la sagesse." *Bulletin de Philosophie Médiévale* 19 (1977) 45–49.

———. "Les questions sur les états de l'esprit: Problèmes d'attribution et essai de traduction critique." *Bulletin de Philosophie Médiévale* 24 (1982) 44–53. See also Avicenna, *Masâ'il aḥwâl ar-rûḥ*.

Millénaire d'Avicenne, Congrès de Baghdad, 20–28 Mars 1952. Ligue des États Arabes, Direction Culturelle. Cairo: Imprimerie Misr SAE, 1952.

Miskawayh, Abû 'Alî Aḥmad ibn Muḥammad. *Tahdhîb al-akhlâq*. Ed. Constantine K. Zurayk. American University of Beirut Centennial Publications. Beirut: American University of Beirut, 1966. Eng. trans., Constantine K. Zurayk, *The Refinement of Character*, Beirut: American University of Beirut, 1968.

Moors, Kent F. *Platonic Myth: An Introductory Study*. Washington, D.C.: University Press of America, 1982.

Morewedge, Parviz. "Greek Sources of Some Near Eastern Philosophies of Being and Existence." In Morewedge, ed., *Philosophies of Existence, Ancient and Modern*, 285–336.

———. "Ibn Sînâ's Concept of the Self." *Philosophical Forum* 4,1 (1972) 49–73.

———. "The Logic of Emanationism and Ṣûfism in the Philosophy of Ibn Sînâ (Avicenna)." *JAOS* 91,4 (1971) 467–76; 92,1 (1972) 1–18.

———. *The* Metaphysica *of Avicenna (ibn Sînâ): A Critical Translation, Commentary, and Analysis of the Fundamental Arguments in Avicenna's* Metaphysica *in the* Dânish Nâma-i 'Alâ'î (The Book of Scientific Knowledge). Persian Heritage Series 13. London: Routledge & Kegan Paul, 1973.

———, ed. *Islamic Philosophical Theology*. Studies in Islamic Philosophy and Science. Albany: State University of New York Press, 1979.

———. *Philosophies of Existence, Ancient and Modern*. New York: Fordham University Press, 1982.

Morris, James W. "Ibn 'Arabî and His Interpreters, Part I: Recent French Translations." *JAOS* 106,3 (1986) 539–51.

Mueller-Volmer, Kurt, ed. *The Hermeneutics Reader: Texts of the German Tradition from the Enlightenment to the Present*. New York: Continuum, 1985.

al-Muḥâsibî, Abû 'Abd Allâh al-Ḥârith ibn Asad. *Kitâb at-tawahhum*. Cairo: Maktabat an-naḥḍa l-islâmiyya, 1980.

Munzavî, Aḥmad. *A Catalogue of Persian Manuscripts*. 5 vols. Tehran: Regional Cultural Institute, 1970–73.

Murray, Gilbert. *Five Stages of Greek Religion*. 3rd ed. Garden City, N. Y.: Doubleday Anchor Books, 1955.

Mûsâ, Muḥammad Yûsuf. *La sociologie et la politique dans la philosophie d'Avicenne*. Mémorial Avicenne 1. Cairo: Publications de l'Institut Français d'Archéologie Orientale du Caire, 1952.

Musallam, Basim. "[Avicenna's] Biology and Medicine." In Mahdi, Gutas, et al., "Avicenna," *Encyclopedia Iranica*, 3:94–99.

Nafîsî, Sa'îd. *Zindagî va-kâr va-andîshah va-rûzgâr-i Pûr-i Sînâ*. Tehran: Kitâbkhâna Dânish, 1953–54.

Najâtî, Muḥammad 'Uthmân. *al-Idrâk al-ḥissî 'ind Ibn Sînâ*. Cairo: Dâr al-ma'ârif, 1948.

Nallino, C. A. "Filosophia 'Orientale' od 'Illuminativa' d' Avicenna?" *Revista degli Studi Orientali* 10 (1923–25) 433–67.

Nasr, Seyyed Hossein. *An Introduction to Islamic Cosmological Doctrines*. Rev. ed. Boulder: Shambhala, 1978.

———. "Post-Avicennan Islamic Philosophy and the Study of Being." In Morewedge, *Philosophies of Existence, Ancient and Modern*, 337–44.

———. *Three Muslim Sages: Avicenna, Suhrawardî, Ibn 'Arabî*. Cambridge, Mass.: Harvard University Press, 1964.

———, ed. See as-Suhrawardî, *Opera metaphysica et mystica III*.

Netton, Ian R. *Allâh Transcendent: Studies in the Structure and Semiotics of Islamic Philosophy, Theology, and Cosmology*. London and New York: Routledge, 1989.

———. *Muslim Neoplatonists: An Introduction to the Thought of the Brethren of Purity (Ikhwân aṣ-Ṣafâ')*. London: George Allen & Unwin, 1980.

Nicholson, R. A. "An Early Arabic Version of the Mi'râj of Abû Yazîd al-Bisṭâmî." *Islamica* 2 (1926–27) 402–14.

Niẓâmî-yi 'Arûḍî, Aḥmad ibn 'Umar ibn 'Alî. *Chahâr Maqâla*. Ed. Mîrzâ Muḥammad ibn 'Abd al-Wahhâb al-Qazvînî. London: Luzac & Co., 1927. Trans. in Browne, *Revised Translation of the Chahâr Maqâla ("Four Discourses") of Niẓâmî-i-'Arûḍî of Samarqand*.

Nuseibeh, Sari. "Al-'Aql al-Qudsî: Avicenna's Subjective Theory of Knowledge." *Studia Islamica* 69 (1989) 39–54.

Nywia, Paul. *Exégèse coranique et langage mystique: Nouvel essai sur le lexique technique des mystiques musulmans*. Beirut: Dar el-Machreq, 1970.

Origen. *An Exhortation to Martyrdom, Prayer, First Principles: Book IV, Prologue to the Commentary on the Song of Songs, Homily XXVII On Numbers*. Trans. and intro. Rowan A. Greer. The Classics of Western Spirituality. New York, Ramsey, and Toronto: Paulist Press, 1979.

Özkaya, Tüten. "Yayın Haberleri: Sovyetler Birligi'nde Ibn Sînâ Üzerine Çalısmalar." *Erdem: Atatürk Külür Merkezi Dergisi* 4 (1988) 627–40.

Palmer, Richard E. *Hermeneutics*. Northwestern University Studies in Phenomenology and Existential Philosophy. Evanston, Ill.: Northwestern University Press, 1969.

Peters, Francis E. *Aristotle and the Arabs: The Aristotelian Tradition in Islam*. New York University Studies in Near Eastern Studies 1. New York: New York University Press; London: University of London Press, 1968.

———. "Hermes and Harran: The Roots of Arabic-Islamic Occultism," in Mazzoui and Moreen, eds., *Intellectual Studies on Islam*, 185–215.

———. "The Origins of Islamic Platonism: The School Tradition." In Morewedge, ed., *Islamic Philosophical Theology*, 14–45.

Pines, Shlomo. "The Arabic Recension of *Parva Naturalia* and the Philosophical Doctrine Concerning Veridical Dreams according to *al-Risâla al-Manâmiyya* and Other Sources." *Israel Oriental Studies* 4. Tel Aviv: Tel Aviv University, 1974, pp. 104–53.

———, trans. *A Guide for the Perplexed*. See Maimonides.

———. "Ibn Sina et l'auteur de la *Risalat al-Fusus fi'l-Hikma*: Quelques données du problème." *Revue des Études Islamiques* 19 (1951) 121–24.

———. "La longue recension de la théologie d'Aristote dans ses rapports avec la doctrine ismaélienne." *Revue des Études Islamiques* 22 (1954) 7–20.

———. "La 'Philosophie Orientale' d'Avicenne et sa polémique contre les baghdadiens." *Archives d'Histoire Doctrinale et Littéraire du Moyen Âge* 19 (1952) 5–37.

———. "A Tenth Century Philosophical Correspondence." In Hyman, ed., *Essays*, 357–390.

Plato. *The Collected Dialogues, Including the Letters*. Ed. Edith Hamilton and Huntington Cairns. Bollingen Series 81. Princeton, N.J.: Princeton University Press, 1961.

Plotinus. *The Enneads*. Trans. Stephen MacKenna. 3rd ed. London: Faber and Faber, 1962. See also Geoffrey Lewis, trans., *Plotiniana Arabica*; and Paul Henry and Hans-Rudolf Schwyzer, eds., *Plotini Opera*.

Propp, Vladimir. *Morphology of the Folktale*. 2nd rev. ed. Austin, Texas: University of Texas Press, 1968.

Pseudo-Avicenna. *Risâla dar ḥaqîqat wa-kaifiyyat-i silsila-yi maujûdât wa-tasalsul-i asbâb wa-musabbabât*. Intishârât-i anjuman-i âthâr-i millî 18. Tehran: Âstân-i dânishgâh, 1952.

Qiṣṣat Salâmân wa-Absâl, turjamat Ḥunain ibn Isḥâq al-ʿibâdî min al-yunânî. In Avicenna, *Tisʿ rasâʾil*, 112–26.

Quilligan, Maureen. "Allegory, Allegoresis, and the Deallegorization of Language: The *Roman de la rose*, the *De planctu naturae*, and the *Parlement of Foules*." In Bloomfield, ed., *Allegory, Myth, and Symbol*, 163–86.

———. *The Language of Allegory: Defining the Genre*. Ithaca, N.Y.: Cornell University Press, 1979.

Qumiyar, Yûḥanna. *Ibn Sînâ: Dirâsa, mukhtârât*. 2 vols. Beirut: al-Maṭba'a l-kâthûlîkiyya, 1955 (vol. 1) and 1966 (vol. 2).

Qur'ân. See *The Koran Interpreted*.

al-Qurṭubî, Shams ad-Dîn 'Abd Allâh Muḥammad ibn 'Aḥmad. *at-Tadhkira fî aḥwâl al-mautâ wa-umûr al-âkhira*. Ed. Aḥmad Hajâzî as-Saqâ. Beirut: Dâr al-kutub al-'ilmiyya, n.d.

al-Qushairî, Abu l-Qâsim 'Abd al-Karîm. *Kitâb al-mi'râj*. Ed. 'Alî Ḥasan al-Qâdir. Cairo: Dâr al-kutub al-ḥadîtha, 1964.

Rahman, Fazlur. *Avicenna's Psychology: An English Translation of* Kitâb al-Najât, *Book II, Chapter VI with Historico-Philosophical Notes and Textual Improvements on the Cairo Edition*. Westport, Conn.: Hyperion Press, 1981; repr. of 1952 ed., Oxford: Oxford University Press, 1952.

———. "Mulla Ṣadrâ's Theory of Knowledge." *The Philosophical Forum* 4,1 (1972) 141–52.

———. *Prophecy in Islam: Philosophy and Orthodoxy*. Midway Reprint. Chicago and London: University of Chicago Press, 1979.

———, ed. *Avicenna's De Anima (Arabic Text) Being the Psychological Part of* Kitâb al-Shifâ'. London, New York, and Toronto: Oxford University Press, 1959.

Ray, William. *Literary Meaning: From Phenomenology to Deconstruction*. Oxford: Basil Blackwell, 1984.

ar-Râzî, Fakhr ad-Dîn Muḥammad ibn 'Umar. *Kitâb an-nafs wa-r-rûḥ wa-sharḥ quwâhumâ*. Ed. M. Ṣ. Ḥ. Ma'ṣûmî. Islamabad: Islamic Research Institute, n.d. Trans. in M. Ṣ. Ḥ. Ma'ṣûmî, *Imâm Râzî's 'Ilm al-Akhlâq*, Islamabad: Islamic Research Center, n.d. [1969?].

———. *Sharḥ al-ishârât wa-t-tanbîhât*. See, aṭ-Ṭûsî.

Rée, Jonathan. *Philosophical Tales: An Essay on Philosophy and Literature*. Ideas. London and New York: Methuen, 1987.

Ricoeur, Paul. *The Conflict in Interpretations: Essays in Hermeneutics*. Ed. Don Ihde. Northwestern University Studies in Phenomenology and Existential Philosophy. Evanston, Ill.: Northwestern University Press, 1974.

———. *Hermeneutics and the Human Sciences: Essays on Language, Action, and Interpretation*. Ed. and trans. John. B. Thompson. Cambridge: Cambridge University Press; Paris: Éditions la Maison des Sciences de l'Homme, 1981.

———. *Time and Narrative*. Trans. K. Blamey and D. Pellauer. 3 vols. Chicago and London: University of Chicago Press, 1984–88.

Rieu, Charles. *Catalogue of Persian Manuscripts in the British Museum*. 3 vols. Oxford: Trustees of the British Museum, 1966; repr. of the 1879–83 ed.

Rippen, Andrew, ed. *Approaches to the History of the Interpretation of the Qur'ân*. Oxford: Clarendon Press, 1988.

Rist, John M. *The Mind of Aristotle: A Study in Philosophical Growth*. Toronto, Buffalo, and London: University of Toronto Press, 1989.

Ritter, Helmut. *Das Meer der Seele: Mensch, Welt und Gott in den Geschichten des Farîduddîn 'Aṭṭâr*. Leiden: E. J. Brill, 1955.

Robinson, Daniel N. *Aristotle's Psychology*. New York and Oxford: Columbia University Press, 1989.

Rollinson, Philip. *Classical Theories of Allegory and Christian Culture*. Pittsburgh: Duquesne University Press; Brighton, Sussex: Harvester Press, 1981.

Rorty, Richard. *Philosophy and the Mirror of Nature*. Princeton, N.J: Princeton University Press, 1979.

Rosenthal, Franz. *Knowledge Triumphant: The Concept of Knowledge in Medieval Islam*. Leiden: E. J. Brill, 1970.

Rowson, Everett K. *A Muslim Philosopher on the Soul and Its Fate: Al-ʿAmirî's* Kitâb al-Amad ʿalâ l-abad. American Oriental Series 70. New Haven, Conn., American Oriental Society, 1988.

———. "The Philosopher as Littérateur: al-Tawḥîdî and His Predecessors," *Zeitschrift für Geschichte der arabisch-islamischen Wissenschaften* 6 (1990) 50–92.

Rudolph, Kurt. *Gnosis: The Nature and History of Gnosticism*. San Francisco, Cal.: Harper and Row, 1987.

Russell, J. Stephen, ed. *Allegoresis: The Craft of Allegory in Medieval Literature*. With an Afterword by Julian Waserman. New York and London: Garland Publishing, 1988.

Rypka, Jan. *History of Iranian Literature*. Ed. Karl Jahn. Dordrecht, Holland: D. Reidel, 1968.

Sabânû(?), Aḥmad Ghassân. *Ibn Sînâ fî dawâʾir al-maʿârif al-ʿarabiyya wa-kutub al-ʿilâm*. N.p.: Dâr al-qutaiba, 1984.

Sabrî, T. "Avicenne, philosophe et mystique dans le miroir de trois récits: Ḥayy b. Yaqẓân, l'Oiseau, Salâmân et Absâl." *Arabica* 28,3 (1980) 257–74.

Sacks, Sheldon, ed. *On Metaphor*. Chicago and London: University of Chicago Press, 1978.

Saly, John. *Dante's* Paradisio*: The Flowering of the Self, An Interpretation of the Anagogical Meaning*. New York: Pace University Press, 1989.

Sanâʾî, Ḥakîm. *Mathnavîhâ-yi Ḥakîm Sanâʾî ba-inẓimâm-i sharḥ-i sair al-ʿibâd ila l-maʿâd*. Ed. Muḥammad Taqî Mudarris-i Raẓavî. Intishârât-i Dânishgâh-i Tihrân 1226. Tehran: Dânishgâh-i Tihran, 1969.

Schacht, J., and M. Meyerhoff, eds. and trans. *The Theologus Autodidactus of Ibn al-Nafîs*. Oxford: Clarendon Press, 1968.

Schimmel, Annemarie. *And Muhammad Is His Messenger: The Veneration of the Prophet in Islamic Piety*. Chapel Hill: University of North Carolina Press, 1985.

Schoeler, G. "Der poetische Syllogismus: Ein Beitrag zum Verständnis der 'logischen' Poetik der Araber," *ZDMG* 133 (1983) 82–89.

ash-Shahrastânî, Abu l-Fatḥ Muḥammad. *Kitâb al-milal wa-niḥal. Book of Religious and Philosophical Sects*. Ed. William Cureton. London: Society for the Publication of Oriental Texts, 1896.

Sherif, Mohammad Ahmad. *Ghazali's Theory of Virtue*. Studies in Islamic Philosophy and Science. Albany: State University of New York Press, 1975.

Siraisi, Nancy G. *Avicenna in Renaissance Italy: The* Canon *and Medical Training in Italian Universities After 1500*. Princeton, N.J.: Princeton University Press, 1987.

Spies, Otto, and S. K. Khatak, eds. and trans. *Three Treatises on Mysticism, by Shihâbuddîn Suhrawardî Maqtûl*. Bonner Orientalistische Studien 12. Stuttgart: Verlag W. Kohlhammer, 1935.

Stern, Samuel M. "Ibn Ḥasdây's Neoplatonist: A Neoplatonic Treatise and its Influence on Isaac Israeli and the Longer Version of the Theology of Aristotle." *Oriens* 13–14 (1960–61) 58–120.

Stetkevych, Jaroslav. "Arabic Hermeneutical Terminology: Paradox and the Production of Meaning." *Journal of Near Eastern Studies* 48,2 (1989) 81–96.

Strauss, Leo. "Farabi's Plato." In Hyman, ed., *Essays*, 391–427.

———. *Persecution and the Art of Writing*. Glencoe, Ill.: Free Press, 1952.

——— and Joseph Copley, eds. *History of Political Philosophy*. Chicago: Rand McNally, 1963.

Subtelny, Maria Eva. "Socioeconomic Bases of Cultural Patronage under the Later Timurids." *International Journal of Middle East Studies* 20 (1988) 479–505.

as-Suhrawardî, Shihâb ad-dîn al-Maqtûl. *Opera Metaphysica et Mystica II*. Ed. Henry Corbin. Tehran: Institut Franco-Iranien, 1952.

———. *Opera Metaphysica et Mystica III*. Ed. Seyyed Hossein Nasr. Tehran: Institut Franco-Iranien, 1970.

———. See also Spies and Khatak, eds. and trans.; and Thackston, trans.

Tâmir, 'Ârif. *Ibn Sînâ fî marâbi' Ikhwân aṣ-Ṣafâ'*. Beirut: 'Izz ad-Dîn, 1983.

at-Tauḥîdî, Abû Ḥayyân. *Kitâb al-'Imtâ' wa-l-mu'ânasa*. Ed. Aḥmad Amîn and Aḥmad az-Zain. 3 vols. Beirut: Dâr maktabat al-ḥayât, n.d.

Thackston, Wheeler M. Jr., trans. *The Mystical and Visionary Treatises of Shihabuddin Yahya Suhrawardi*. London: Octagon Press, 1982.

Todorov, Tzvetan. *Introduction to Poetics*. Trans. Richard Howard. Theory and History of Literature 1. Minneapolis: University of Minnesota Press, 1981.

———. *Symbolism and Interpretation*. Trans. Catherine Porter. Ithaca, N.Y.: Cornell University Press, 1982.

———. *Theories of the Symbol*. Trans. Catherine Porter. Ithaca, N.Y.: New York: Cornell University Press, 1982.

Tritton, A. S. "Man, *Nafs, Rûḥ, 'Aql*." *BSOAS* 34 (1971) 491–95.

Turbayne, Colin M. *The Myth of Metaphor*. Rev. ed. Columbia: University of South Carolina Press, 1970.

aṭ-Ṭûsî, Naṣîr ad-Dîn. *Sharḥai l-ishârât li-l-Khwâja Naṣîr ad-Dîn aṭ-Ṭûsî wa-li-l-Imâm Fakr ad-Dîn ar-Râzî*. Cairo: Maṭba'at al-khairiyya, 1907.

Tuve, Rosemund. *Allegorical Imagery: Some Medieval Books and Their Posterity*. Princeton, N.J.: Princeton University Press, 1966.

Ülken, Hilmi Ziya, ed. *Ibn Sina Risâleleri 1: Les opuscules d'Ibn Sina, 'Uyûn al-ḥikma et l'opuscule d'Abu'l Faraj et la réfutation d'Ibn Sina*. Ankara: Türk Tarih Kurumu Basımevi, 1953.

———. *Ibn Sina Risâleleri 2: Les opuscules d'Ibn Sina et "Le livre de la différence entre l'esprit et l'âme" par Qosta b.Luqa*. Istanbul Üniversitesi Edebiyat Facültesi Yayınlarından 552. Istanbul: Ibrahim Horoz Basımevi, 1953.

Ullmann, Manfred. *Die Natur- und Geheimwissenschaften im Islam*. Handbuch der Orientalistik, vol. 6, part 2. Leiden and Cologne: E. J. Brill, 1972.

Vajda, G. "Les notes d'Avicenne sur la 'Théologie d'Aristote.'" *Revue Thomiste* 51 (1951) 346–406.

Walzer, Richard. *Al-Fârâbî on the Perfect State: Abû Naṣr al-Fârâbî's Mabâdi' ârâ' ahl al-madîna al-fâḍila: A Revised Text with Introduction, Translation, and Commentary*. Oxford: Clarendon Press, 1985.

———. *Greek into Arabic: Essays on Islamic Philosophy*. Oriental Studies 1. Oxford: Oxford University Press, 1962.

Wensinck, A. J., J. P. Messing, et al. *Concordance et indices de la tradition musulmane*. 8 vols. Leiden: E. J. Brill, 1936–1988.

Whitman, Jon. *Allegory: The Dynamics of an Ancient and Medieval Technique*. Cambridge, Mass. and London: Harvard University Press, 1987.

Wickens, G. M., ed. *Avicenna, Scientist and Philosopher: A Millenary Symposium*. London: Luzac, 1952.

Wimsatt, W. K., Jr., and Monroe C. Beardsley. "The Intentional Fallacy." In Wimsatt and Beardsley, *The Verbal Icon: Studies in the Meaning of Poetry*. New York: Noonday Press, 1953. Pp. 3–18.

Wippel, John F., ed. *Studies in Medieval Philosophy*. Studies in Philosophy and the History of Philosophy 17. Washington, D.C.: Catholic University of America Press, 1987.

Wolfson, Harry A. "The Internal Senses in Latin, Arabic, and Hebrew Philosophic Texts." *Harvard Theological Review* 28,2 (1935) 69–133.

Yarshater, Ehsan, ed. *The Cambridge History of Iran 4: From the Arab Invasion to the Saljuqs*. Cambridge: Cambridge University Press, 1975.

———. *Panj Risâla, taṣnîf-i Shaikh Ra'îs Abû 'Alî Sînâ*. Silsila-yi intishârât-i anjuman-i athâr-i millî 27. Tehran: Âstâd-i Danishgâh, 1953.

———. *Persian Literature*. Columbia Lectures on Iranian Studies 3. N.P.: Bibliotheca Persica, 1988. Distributed by State University of New York Press.

Zedler, Beatrice H. "Saint Thomas and Avicenna." *Traditio* 6 (1948) 105–59.

Zimmerman, F. W. "The Origins of the So-called *Theology of Aristotle*." In Kraye, Ryan, and Schmitt, eds., *Pseudo-Aristotle*, 110–240.

Index

University of Pennsylvania Press
MIDDLE AGES SERIES
Edward Peters, General Editor

F. R. P. Akehurst, trans. *The* Coutumes de Beauvaisis *of Philippe de Beaumanior.* 1992

Peter Allen. *The Art of Love: Amatory Fiction from Ovid to the* Romance of the Rose. 1992

David Anderson. *Before the Knight's Tale: Imitation of Classical Epic in Boccaccio's* Teseida. 1988

Benjamin Arnold. *Count and Bishop in Medieval Germany: A Study of Regional Power, 1100–1350.* 1991

Mark C. Bartusis. *The Late Byzantine Army: Arms and Society, 1204–1453.* 1992

J. M. W. Bean. *From Lord to Patron: Lordship in Late Medieval England.* 1990

Uta-Renate Blumenthal. *The Investiture Controversy: Church and Monarchy from the Ninth to the Twelfth Century.* 1988

Daniel Bornstein, trans. *Dino Compagni's* Chronicle *of Florence.* 1986

Betsy Bowden. *Chaucer Aloud: The Varieties of Textual Interpretation.* 1987

James William Brodman. *Ransoming Captives in Crusader Spain: The Order of Merced on the Christian-Islamic Frontier.* 1986

Kevin Brownlee and Sylvia Huot, eds. *Rethinking the* Romance of the Rose*: Text, Image, Reception.* 1992

Otto Brunner (Howard Kaminsky and James Van Horn Melton, eds. and trans.). Land *and Lordship: Structures of Governance in Medieval Austria.* 1992

Robert I. Burns, S. J., ed. *Emperor of Culture: Alfonso X the Learned of Castile and His Thirteenth-Century Renaissance.* 1990

David Burr. *Olivi and Franciscan Poverty: The Origins of the* Usus Pauper *Controversy.* 1989

Thomas Cable. *The English Alliterative Tradition.* 1991

Anthony K. Cassell and Victoria Kirkham, eds. and trans. *Diana's Hunt/Caccia di Diana: Boccaccio's First Fiction.* 1991

Brigitte Cazelles. *The Lady as Saint: A Collection of French Hagiographic Romances of the Thirteenth Century.* 1991

Anne L. Clark. *Elizabeth of Schönau: A Twelfth-Century Visionary.* 1992

Willene B. Clark and Meradith T. McMunn, eds. *Beasts and Birds of the Middle Ages: The Bestiary and Its Legacy.* 1989

Richard C. Dales. *The Scientific Achievement of the Middle Ages.* 1973

Charles T. Davis. *Dante's Italy and Other Essays.* 1984

Katherine Fischer Drew, trans. *The Burgundian Code: The Book of Constitutions or Law of Gundobad and Additional Enactments.* 1972

Katherine Fischer Drew, trans. *The Laws of the Salian Franks.* 1991

Katherine Fischer Drew, trans. *The Lombard Laws.* 1973

Nancy Edwards. *The Archaeology of Early Medieval Ireland.* 1990

Margaret J. Ehrhart. *The Judgment of the Trojan Prince Paris in Medieval Literature.* 1987

Richard K. Emmerson and Ronald B. Herzman. *The Apocalyptic Imagination in Medieval Literature.* 1992

Robert D. Fulk. *A History of Old English Meter.* 1992

Patrick J. Geary. *Aristocracy in Provence: The Rhône Basin at the Dawn of the Carolingian Age.* 1985

Peter Heath. *Allegory and Philosophy in Avicenna (Ibn Sînâ), With a Translation of the Book of the Prophet Muhammad's Ascent to Heaven.* 1992

J. N. Hillgarth, ed. *Christianity and Paganism, 350-750: The Conversion of Western Europe.* 1986

Richard C. Hoffmann. *Land, Liberties, and Lordship in a Late Medieval Countryside: Agrarian Structures and Change in the Duchy of Wrocław.* 1990

Robert Hollander. *Boccaccio's Last Fiction: Il Corbaccio.* 1988

Edward B. Irving, Jr. *Rereading* Beowulf. 1989

C. Stephen Jaeger. *The Origins of Courtliness: Civilizing Trends and the Formation of Courtly Ideals, 939–1210.* 1985

William Chester Jordan. *The French Monarchy and the Jews: From Philip Augustus to the Last Capetians.* 1989

William Chester Jordan. *From Servitude to Freedom: Manumission in the Sénonais in the Thirteenth Century.* 1986

Ellen E. Kittell. *From* Ad Hoc *to Routine: A Case Study in Medieval Bureaucracy.* 1991

Alan C. Kors and Edward Peters, eds. *Witchcraft in Europe, 1100–1700: A Documentary History.* 1972

Barbara Kreutz. *Before the Normans: Southern Italy in the Ninth and Tenth Centuries.* 1992

E. Ann Matter. *The Voice of My Beloved: The Song of Songs in Western Medieval Christianity.* 1990

María Rosa Menocal. *The Arabic Role in Medieval Literary History.* 1987

A. J. Minnis. *Medieval Theory of Authorship.* 1988

Lawrence Nees. *A Tainted Mantle: Hercules and the Classical Tradition at the Carolingian Court.* 1991

Lynn H. Nelson, trans. *The Chronicle of San Juan de la Peña: A Fourteenth-Century Official History of the Crown of Aragon.* 1991

Charlotte A. Newman. *The Anglo-Norman Nobility in the Reign of Henry I: The Second Generation.* 1988

Joseph F. O'Callaghan. *The Cortes of Castile-León, 1188–1350.* 1989

William D. Paden, ed. *The Voice of the Trobairitz: Perspectives on the Women Troubadours.* 1989

Edward Peters. *The Magician, the Witch, and the Law.* 1982

Edward Peters, ed. *Christian Society and the Crusades, 1198–1229.* Sources in Translation, including The Capture of Damietta by Oliver of Paderborn. 1971

Edward Peters, ed. *The First Crusade: The* Chronicle of Fulcher of Chartres *and Other Source Materials*. 1971

Edward Peters, ed. *Heresy and Authority in Medieval Europe*. 1980

James M. Powell. *Albertanus of Brescia: The Pursuit of Happiness in the Early Thirteenth Century*. 1992

James M. Powell. *Anatomy of a Crusade, 1213–1221*. 1986

Michael Resler, trans. Erec *by Hartmann von Aue*. 1987

Pierre Riché (Michael Idomir Allen, trans.). *The Carolingians: A Family Who Forged Europe*. 1992

Pierre Riché (Jo Ann McNamara, trans.) *Daily Life in the World of Charlemagne*. 1978

Jonathan Riley-Smith. *The First Crusade and the Idea of Crusading*. 1986

Barbara H. Rosenswein. *Rhinoceros Bound: Cluny in the Tenth Century*. 1982

Joel T. Rosenthal. *Patriarchy and Families of Privilege in Fifteenth-Century England*. 1991

Steven D. Sargent, ed. and trans. *On the Threshold of Exact Science: Selected Writings of Anneliese Maier on Late Medieval Natural Philosophy*. 1982

Sarah Stanbury. *Seeing the* Gawain-*Poet: Description and the Act of Perception*. 1992

Thomas C. Stillinger. *The Song of Troilus: Lyric Authority in the Medieval Book*. 1992

Susan Mosher Stuard. *A State of Deference: Ragusa/Dubrovnik in the Medieval Centuries*. 1992

Susan Mosher Stuard, ed. *Women in Medieval History and Historiography*. 1987

Susan Mosher Stuard, ed. *Women in Medieval Society*. 1976

Jonathan Sumption. *The Hundred Years War: Trial by Battle*. 1992

Ronald E. Surtz. *The Guitar of God: Gender, Power, and Authority in the Visionary World of Mother Juana de la Cruz (1481–1534)*. 1990

Patricia Terry, trans. *Poems of the Elder Edda*. 1990

Frank Tobin. *Meister Eckhart: Thought and Language*. 1986

Ralph V. Turner. *Men Raised from the Dust: Administrative Service and Upward Mobility in Angevin England*. 1988

Harry Turtledove, trans. *The* Chronicle *of Theophanes: An English Translation of* anni mundi *6095–6305 (A.D. 602–813)*. 1982

Mary F. Wack. *Lovesickness in the Middle Ages: The* Viaticum *and Its Commentaries*. 1990

Benedicta Ward. *Miracles and the Medieval Mind: Theory, Record, and Event, 1000–1215*. 1982

Suzanne Fonay Wemple. *Women in Frankish Society: Marriage and the Cloister, 500–900*. 1981

This book has been set in Linotron Galliard. Galliard was designed for Mergenthaler in 1978 by Matthew Carter. Galliard retains many of the features of a sixteenth-century typeface cut by Robert Granjon but has some modifications that give it a more contemporary look.

Printed on acid-free paper.